Macmillan Law

Law of

C000216180

Macmillan Law Masters

Law Series Editor **Marise Cremona**

Law of the European Union

Second Edition

Jo Shaw
Professor of European Law, University of Leeds

Law series editor: Marise Cremona
Senior Fellow, Centre for Commercial Law Studies
Queen Mary and Westfield College, University of London

MACMILLAN

First published 1993 as *European Community Law*
Reprinted three times
Second edition published 1996 by
MACMILLAN PRESS LTD
Houndmills, Basingstoke, Hampshire RG21 6XS
and London.
Companies and representatives
throughout the world

ISBN 0–333–66481–7

A catalogue record for this book is available
from the British Library.

10   9   8   7   6   5   4   3   2   1
05   04   03   02   01   00   99   98   97   96

Copy-edited and typeset by Povey-Edmondson
Okehampton and Rochdale, England

Printed and bound in Great Britain by
Biddles Ltd, Guildford and King's Lynn

Contents

Part III   THE EU LEGAL ORDER AND THE NATIONAL LEGAL ORDERS

Preface and Acknowledgements

In response to the ever increasing volume of material on EC law, it was decided for this second edition to create two separate books on the law of the constitution and institutions of the EU, and on the social and economic law of the EU. As this book shows, it is not only the Court of Justice (and the Court of First Instance) which have been active in a law-making capacity since 1993 and the publication of the first edition. In addition, there are substantial bodies of institutional practice which have changed in order to absorb and respond to the novelties of the Treaty of Maastricht, and the institutions continue to be active in the legislative and 'soft-law-making' spheres. It is hoped that the approach taken here not only reflects the current 'new institutionalist' mantra that 'institutions matter' but also puts across the idea that 'institutions are interesting'. The book will have succeeded in its purpose if it continues to be used – like the first edition – across a range of disciplines and in countries with sharply differing legal systems and conceptions of the EU legal order.

This book is a greatly expanded and adjusted version of Chapters 1–10 of *European Community Law* (1993). New chapters have been added on EU constitutionalism, and by way of a conclusion. The material on the relationship between EC law and national law, and on the control of the EU institutions has been substantially expanded and updated and divided into additional chapters. As before, I have attempted to write an introductory text, which stimulates the reader and leads onto additional reading (of cases and of secondary literature), rather than to make a definitive statement of the law. The approach is in general terms 'contextual', and is influenced by the development of a larger body of work which considers EC law and EU institutions from an interdisciplinary perspective.

A number of colleagues and friends have continued to be a source of support. They are too numerous to mention individually, but I would like to thank in particular Kenneth Armstrong, Gráinne de Búrca, Tammy Hervey and Gillian More. I would like to thank Jo Hunt for diligent proofreading. As ever I owe a great debt to Sally Wheeler, never one of nature's Europhiles, but nonetheless consistently supportive of my endeavours. However, she was not on hand when Leo Shaw's school was closed by flooding after Easter. Leo showed remarkable (but not perfect) patience as I struggled with producing the final manuscript. I would also like to thank my parents for their practical assistance and support. Finally I would like to dedicate this book to the memory of Brian Wilkinson, a good friend and sadly missed.

Jo Shaw

Table of Cases

A: Cases before the European Court of Justice

1 By Case Number (in year order)

2 Alphabetical list

3   Opinions delivered pursuant to Article 228 EC

B: Cases before the Court of First Instance

1 By Case Number (in year order)

2 Alphabetical list

C: Cases before National Courts

1 English Courts

2   German Courts

3   Irish Courts

4   Belgian Courts

5   French Courts

D: Cases before the European Court of Human Rights

xl

Table of Treaties Establishing the European Communities and the European Union

Table of UK Statutes

List of Abbreviations

AC	Appeal Cases
AJCL	*American Journal of Comparative Law*
AJIL	*American Journal of International Law*
All ER	*All England Law Reports*
BEUC	Bureau Européen des Unions Consommateurs
CAP	Common Agricultural Policy
CCT	Common Customs Tariff
CE	Compulsory expenditure
CEDEFOP	European Centre for the Development of Vocational Training
CEEP	Comité Européen des Entreprises Publiques
CFSP	Common Foreign and Security Policy
CJHA	Cooperation in Justice and Home Affairs
CMLR	*Common Market Law Reports*
CMLRev.	*Common Market Law Review*
Col. LRev.	*Columbia Law Review*
Comp. Pol. Studs.	*Comparative Political Studies*
COPA	Confederation of Professional Agricultural Organizations
COREPER	Committee of Permanent Representatives
CREW	Centre for Research on European Women
DG	Directorate General
DTEU	Draft Treaty establishing a European Union
EBLR	*European Business Law Review*
EC	European Community
ECB	European Central Bank
ECHR	European Convention on Human Rights
ECLR	*European Competition Law Review*
ECOSOC	Economic and Social Committee
ECR	*European Court Reports*
ECSC	European Coal and Steel Community
EDC	European Defence Community
EEA	European Economic Area
EEC	European Economic Community
EEIG	European Economic Interest Grouping
EFTA	European Free Trade Association
EIB	European Investment Bank
EJIL	*European Journal of International Law*

ELJ	*European Law Journal*
ELRev.	*European Law Review*
EMI	European Monetary Institute
EMS	European Monetary System
EMU	Economic and Monetary Union
EPC	European Political Corporation
EPL	*European Public Law*
ERM	Exchange Rate Mechanism
ERPL	*European Review of Private Law*
ERTA	European Road Transport Agreement
ESCB	European System of Central Banks
ETUC	European Trade Union Confederation
EU	European Union
EUI	European University Institute
Euratom	European Atomic Energy Community
Eur. J. Pol. Res.	*European Journal of Political Research*
Eur. Pub. L	*European Public Law*
FAO	Food and Agriculture Organization (of UN)
FSR	*Fleet Street Reports*
FYROM	Yugoslav Republic of Macedonia
GATT	General Agreement on Tariffs and Trade
GNP	Gross National Product
ICLQ	*International and Comparative Law Quarterly*
IGC	Intergovernmental Conference
ILJ	*Industrial Law Journal*
Intl. Aff.	*International Affairs*
ILO	International Labour Organization
IO	*International Organization*
IRLR	*Industrial Relations Law Reports*
JBL	*Journal of Business Law*
JCMS	*Journal of Common Market Studies*
JEPP	*Journal of European Public Policy*
JSWFL	*Journal of Social Welfare and Family Law*
LIEI	Legal Issues of European Integration
LQR	*Law Quarterly Review*
LS	*Legal Studies*
MCAs	Monetary Compensatory Amounts
MEP	Member of the European Parliament
MJ	*Maastricht Journal of European and Comparative Law*
MLR	*Modern Law Review*
NCE	Non-compulsory expenditure
NILQ	*Northern Ireland Legal Quarterly*
OECD	Organization for Economic Cooperation and Development
OEEC	Organization for European Economic Cooperation
OJ	*Official Journal*
OJLS	*Oxford Journal of Legal Studies*

OOPEC	Office of Official Publications of the European Communities
PL	*Public Law*
QMV	Qualified Majority Voting
SEA	Single European Act
TEU	Treaty on European Union
UN	United Nations
UNICE	Union of Industries of the European Community
VAT	Value Added Tax
WEU	West European Union
W. Eur. Pols.	*West European Politics*
WTO	World Trade Organisation
YEL	*Yearbook of European Law*

Part I

Introducing the European Union

1 Studying the Law of the European Union

1.1 Beginning the Law of the European Union

The purpose of this introductory chapter is to equip you, the reader, with the basic tools you need to embark upon the study of the law of the European Union, a subject which has something of a reputation for being impenetrable. It assumes that you have some knowledge of the basic components of a legal system, but very little knowledge of what the European Community (EC) or European Union (EU) can do, what they cannot do (or indeed whether and why there is a difference between these two entities), and why it is important in a specifically legal sense to understand what they can do. It offers in 1.5 a brief overview of the EU legal system, containing basic pointers on to which more detailed study can be grafted, which highlights the pivotal role of the Court of Justice in the system of integration as set up by the Treaties of Rome and Paris in the 1950s and as evolved through the Single European Act (SEA) and the Treaty of Maastricht or Treaty on European Union (TEU) in the 1980s and 1990s.

The creation of the European Community, and latterly the European Union, has not only involved the establishment of a new type of legal order operating in the international or transnational sphere – one which can only be understood if certain basic precepts of the study of national law are set aside; it has also brought into being a legal order in which a very specific and clear purpose is dominant. This is the promotion of a process of integration, leading towards a 'union' of European states and peoples. This purpose operates at a number of different levels, including the economic (breaking down the barriers to trade between states), the monetary (the goal of creating a single currency), and the political (creating political and legal institutions outside the nation state; creating a common political identity within the EU, particularly on the global stage), but it is ever present. The Court of Justice never loses sight of the aim of integration when it is interpreting EC law, and nor should those who study it. 1.3 contains an outline sketch of this aim, and the concept of 'integration' is one of those which receives attention in 1.4, which attempts to demystify certain aspects of the language of European integration.

In comparison to most national legal systems, and certainly in comparison to the legal systems of the states which form its constituent members, the legal system of the EU is particularly unstable and in a state of constant flux and change. Changes mainly come about either because of a dynamic intervention on the part of the Court of Justice in the interpretation of EC law, or because the Member States have negotiated further amendments to the constitution of the EU – its basic Treaties (see Chapter 3). Since the reasons for these changes lie more frequently in the field of politics than law, it will be apparent that EC law can only properly be understood in its wider political and economic context, and that the successful study of EC law presupposes the acquisition of a substantial body of contextual knowledge. Some guidance on acquiring that knowledge is offered in 1.7. 1.6 offers assistance in locating the treaties, legislation and official documentation of the EU, and in making a basic selection from amongst the voluminous legal literature available. We begin, however, with some basic facts about the European Union and the European Community.

1.2   The European Union and the European Community: The Basic Facts

What we now call the European Union started out as a Community of six in the 1950s: France, the Federal Republic of Germany, Italy, Belgium, Luxembourg and the Netherlands. In 1973 Denmark, Ireland and the UK acceded; Norway signed a Treaty of Accession, but did not join when membership was rejected by popular vote in a referendum. Further expansion occurred in 1980 with the accession of Greece, and in 1986 with the accession of Spain and Portugal, creating a Community of twelve. *De facto* expansion occurred once again in 1990, with the unification of Germany having the effect of bringing the former German Democratic Republic into the Community, although not as a separate member. The most recent accession process was completed at the beginning of 1995, with Austria, Finland and Sweden becoming members. Once again the people of Norway declined through a referendum vote to take up the opportunity of membership negotiated for them by their government. Further expansion around the end of the century remains likely: since the collapse of Communism in central and eastern Europe, and with the ever closer trading links between the various European countries, membership of what is now termed the European Union has become an increasingly coveted prize. Candidates for membership at present include Poland, Hungary, the Czech Republic and Slovakia amongst the countries of Central and Eastern Europe, and Cyprus, Malta and Turkey from Southern Europe and the Mediterranean region. The next enlargement will involve Cyprus and Malta, and is likely to be followed soon thereafter by successive enlargements to incorporate many of the countries of Central and Eastern Europe. The process of enlargement now depends upon the outcome of the intergovernmental conference (IGC) on the revision of the Treaties which began in 1996.

The term 'European Community' was the designation commonly used up to the end of 1993 for a political entity, composed of a number of distinct legal entities with separate international legal personality, which came to be generally identified as a single unit. These are the three Communities, of which two are confined in their application to particular sectors of the economy: the European Coal and Steel Community (ECSC), formed by the Treaty of Paris concluded in 1951 which came into force on July 25 1952, and the European Atomic Energy Community (Euratom), formed by the Treaty of Rome concluded in 1957 which came into force on January 1 1958. Also created in 1958 by a second Treaty of Rome 1957 was the European Economic Community (EEC), the 'everything else' Community, which acquired a hegemonic position within the political and legal framework of the Community. Confusingly, Article G of the Treaty on European Union redesignates the European Economic Community as the 'European Community', leaving the other two sectoral Communities with their existing titles. The Articles of what must now be termed the 'EC Treaty' are referred to in this book as Article 1 EC, etc. Where necessary, Articles of the 'old' EEC Treaty are designated Article 2 EEC, etc. Most of the discussion in this book will be concerned with the provisions of the Treaties establishing and amending this 'general' Community and with legislation adopted under the enabling powers of those Treaties, in particular those governing the creation of the internal market. Legally, the three Communities remain distinct, although they have common institutions, formed in 1967 by the Merger Treaty. However, the powers of the institutions differ slightly between the three Communities. The ECSC Treaty also differs from the two later Treaties in that it can be described as a *traité loi*, or 'treaty-law' which itself prescribes in detail the policies to be pursued by the Community, and leaves merely issues of policy implementation to the institutions. The EEC and Euratom Treaties were developed as *traités cadre*, or 'framework treaties', which contain only the outlines of policy objectives to which the institutions must give concrete form with legislative instruments. A further important distinction is that the ECSC Treaty was concluded for 50 years, and is due to expire in 2002, whereas the Euratom and EEC Treaties were concluded for an indefinite duration.

The EEC Treaty was significantly amended in 1986 by the Single European Act, which established the so-called '1992' deadline, and sought to give the institutions the powers they needed to achieve the goal of completing the internal market by 31 December 1992. The Single European Act also introduced a form of institutionalised intergovernmental cooperation between the Member States regarding foreign policy, termed 'European Political Cooperation'.

The effect of the Treaty of Maastricht, or 'Treaty on European Union', is to link the three Communities even closer together within the common structure of a European Union, a new entity built around the framework offered by the existing Communities. The Union does not as such have legal personality, and so is not a legal body in the same way as the

Communities. The freestanding provisions of the Treaty of European Union are designated in this book Article A TEU etc. It is served by a single institutional framework, which is essentially that of the Communities themselves. The Treaty of Maastricht also introduces a 'three pillar' structure, of which the existing corpus of law based around the Communities is the central pillar. The side pillars are (1) Common Foreign and Security Policy (which has evolved out of European Political Cooperation) (the 'Second Pillar'), and (2) Cooperation in the fields of Justice and Home Affairs (the 'Third Pillar') (see Figure 1.1; the constitutional structure of the EU will be discussed in greater detail in Chapter 3). The Treaty of Maastricht was finalised in December 1991 following two intergovernmental conferences lasting one year on the subjects of economic and monetary union and political union, and was signed in February 1992. It was due to come into force on 1 January 1993, but difficulties in the ratification process involving an initial rejection in a referendum in Denmark, ratification by only a small majority in a referendum in France and considerable opposition in the UK Parliament delayed the coming into force of the Treaty until 1 November 1993. The Treaty of Maastricht itself provided for a further revision process to begin in 1996, with the convening of a conference of representatives of the Member States (an intergovernmental conference or 'IGC') (Article N TEU). This IGC, which began in March 1996, may in turn lead to significant constitutional changes in the structure of the EU, particularly in relation to the pillar structure.

This section shows that in strict legal terms the EU is a very limited body. However, just as the strictly incorrect term 'European Community' gained widespread acceptance in the 1970s and 1980s, so the term EU is being used more and more as the general overall descriptive term, and is not limited to its narrow political or geographical connotations. As 1.1 has already indicated, this book will frequently refer to the 'EU', the 'Union' or occasionally the 'EC/EU' when talking about the broad political and constitutional structures established by the Treaties, and also uses the term 'legal order of the EU' where appropriate in order to highlight the relevance of law and legal institutions right across the three pillar structure. Chapters 4 and 5 will give further details on the strict differences between the work of the institutions across the EC and the EU. However, to emphasise the greater legal relevance and powers of the Communities proper, the term 'EC law' and 'Community competence', and not 'EU law' and 'Union competence' are adopted.

As a body based on international agreements between sovereign states, the EU is in many senses a creature of international law; however the Member States have endowed its institutions with uniquely far-reaching powers for the achievement of the objectives contained in the Treaties.

The EU has a distinctive institutional structure. The main legislative role has so far been fulfilled by the Council of the European Union which is composed of representatives of the Member States at ministerial level. The Member States are also represented in the European Council, a

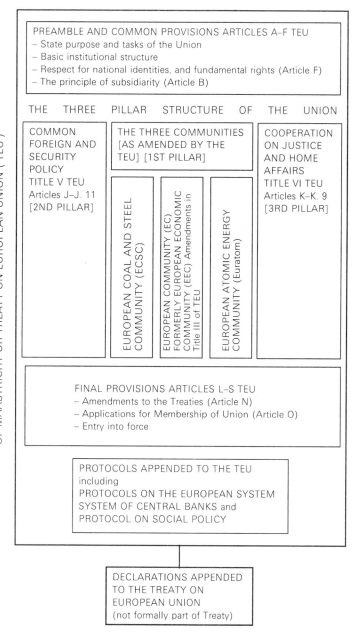

Figure 1.1   The constitutional structure of the European Union

summit conference of Heads of State and Government who meet twice yearly to give overall policy direction to the EU. The European Parliament, while it is now directly elected by universal franchise and is therefore representative of the people, has fewer powers in the legislative field than the Council, and its role ranges between that of a consultative assembly in some policy areas and a full co-legislator in some restricted fields. The role of the European Commission within the EU is sometimes exaggerated by Member States hostile to extensions of Community competence; in fact, the Commission's role is limited to initiating policy, implementing measures adopted by the Council and ensuring that Member States fulfil their obligations under the Treaties. It is in a sense the civil service of the EU, but in many respects it is dependent upon national administrations for the actual day to day implementation of the policies of the Union. Moreover, like the European Parliament, the Commission has a very restricted role in the two intergovernmental pillars of the EU, concerned with foreign policy and cooperation in home affairs.

The fourth institution is the Court of Justice which has the task under Article 164 EC of ensuring that the law is observed. It has been assisted since 1989 by a Court of First Instance, creation of which was provided for in the Single European Act. The Court has been responsible for developing the EU legal system in ways that were doubtless not imagined by the founders of the Treaties. Much of Part III of this book will be concerned with explaining in detail those features which distinguish the European Union from an 'ordinary' international organisation, and which make the legal system operating in particular in relation to the 'Community' or 'first' pillar more akin to that of a federal state. This point will be sketched out initially in the overview of EC law contained in 1.5. The Court has also been active in ensuring that within the Community pillar itself the rule of law is applied, but it is almost entirely excluded from exercising a judicial function within the Second and Third Pillars (Common Foreign and Security Policy – Cooperation in Justice and Home Affairs – CFSP and CJHA), as well as in relation to the common provisions of the EU (Articles A–F TEU). Part IV examines the system of judicial control of the legality of legislative and administrative acts adopted by the institutions of the Union. This is one area in which the EU can rightly claim to have emulated in large measure the characteristics of the highly evolved legal systems of its Member States.

The institutions and structures of the European Community and the European Union are not to be confused with those of the Council of Europe, an intergovernmental body fostering cooperation between European states, and in particular with its most significant Treaty-based emanation, the European Convention on Human Rights and Fundamental Freedoms (ECHR). The institutions operating under the Convention, to which all the Member States are signatories, are the Commission and Court of Human Rights, and these are based in Strasbourg. The Court of Justice of the European Communities, and the Court of First Instance, are based in Luxembourg.

1.3 The Mission of the European Union

Broad statements of the aims of the European Community and the more recently created European Union are to be found in the Preambles and introductory sections of the basic Treaties. Article A TEU recalls the long standing commitment in the Preamble to the EEC Treaty to the creation of an ever closer union among the peoples of Europe, and identifies the creation of the Union as a new stage in this process. A reference to the federal mission of the Union was eradicated from the final version at the insistence of the UK delegation at the meeting of the European Council at Maastricht which finalised the Treaty on European Union. The Union has the following objectives (Article B TEU):

- 'to promote economic and social progress which is balanced and sustainable, in particular through the creation of an area without internal frontiers, through the strengthening of economic and social cohesion and through the establishment of economic and monetary union, ultimately including a single currency in accordance with the provisions of this Treaty;
- to assert its identity on the international scene, in particular through the implementation of a common foreign and security policy including the eventual framing of a common defence policy, which might in time lead to a common defence;
- to strengthen the protection of the rights and interests of the nationals of its Member States through the introduction of a citizenship of the Union;
- to develop close cooperation on justice and home affairs;
- to maintain in full the *acquis communautaire* and build on it with a view to considering, through the procedure referred to in Article N(2), to what extent the policies and forms of cooperation introduced by this Treaty may need to be revised with the aim of ensuring the effectiveness of the mechanisms and the institutions of the Treaty.'

The specifically socio-economic aspects of these aims are further elaborated in Articles 2, 3 and 3A EC. These identify the task of the European Community as being the promotion of harmonious and balanced economic development, of sustainable and non-inflationary growth respecting the environment, of a high degree of convergence of economic performance, of high levels of employment and social protection, of the raising of the standard of living and quality of life of citizens, and of economic and social cohesion and solidarity among Member States. The twin means for attaining this task are the creation of a common market and an economic and monetary union, and these are themselves to be achieved through the pursuit of the activities set out in Articles 3 (common market and common policies) and 3A (monetary union and single currency). So far, the law of the European Community has been, above all, the law of the common market (including the customs union) which has been developing steadily since 1958. For present purposes, we can take the common market referred to in Article 2 as practically identical to the 'internal market' defined in Article 7A EC, the achievement of which was the official central objective of the old European Economic Community between 1986 and the end of 1992. This provides that:

> 'The internal market shall comprise an area without internal frontiers in which the free movement of goods, persons, services and capital is ensured in accordance with the provisions of this Treaty.'

The goal appears, therefore, to be a free market ideal that, as far as possible, the territory of the fifteen Member States should resemble a single national market, where there is a level competitive playing field for all economic actors and where distortions of competition based on artificial legal barriers such as differences in consumer protection or environmental regulation will be eliminated.

Article 3 EC in turn gives more details on the activities which are to be pursued with a view to attaining this goal. These include the creation of a customs union, involving the abolition of internal customs duties on trade in goods and the erection of a common external tariff and a complementary common policy on external trade, the abolition of other obstacles to trade in goods, and the free movement of services, persons and capital between the Member States. These are essentially negative measures, in that they promote integration by removing existing barriers. Positive integration measures include the establishment of common policies, in fields such as agriculture and transport; the creation of these policies also reveals a certain *dirigiste* element in the thinking of the founders of the Treaty, alongside the commitment to the free market principles of the four freedoms. The commitment to a policy on the harmonisation of national legislation also demonstrates a recognition that deregulated markets alone will not bring about the creation of a single internal market which respects the interests of consumers and the environment, to name but two interests which may be sacrificed in unfettered free market competition. In addition, although subsequent amendments to the original Treaty have brought regional policy goals of social and economic cohesion and solidarity within the remit of the EU's prescribed activities, there is no clear commitment in Article 3 to a general social policy, as a complement to the economic policies described above. However, particularly with the effective conclusion of the lengthy legislative programme to complete the internal market by the end of 1992, the focus of law-making has shifted more into the fields of social policy, consumer policy and environmental policy.

The greatest substantive contribution of the Treaty of Maastricht to the attainment of European integration lies in its provisions on economic and monetary union, and its introduction of the aim of creating a single currency. The law on these aspects of the EU's activities is not as well developed as the law of the common or internal market, and discussion in this book will be confined to a brief presentation of the institutions of monetary union (4.17).

The goals of the EU lie, therefore, first and foremost in the socio-economic sphere. This book is concerned, however, with the constitutional and institutional foundations of the EU. It will seek, wherever possible, to demonstrate how principles of socio-economic integration underlie the work of the institutions, especially the Court of Justice. The study of EC law is above all the study of law in relation to integration processes. Consequently, a complete understanding of many of the constitutional and institutional principles identified and discussed in this book will only be possible once the reader has also acquired a deeper knowledge of the substantive economic and social law of the EU.

1.4 Key Terms

It will already be apparent from the preceding paragraphs that there is a distinctive language of European integration. This section aims to demystify certain key concepts, some of which have already been mentioned in passing such as *integration* and *federalism*. It also provides a brief account of some of the main political and theoretical positions taken on the process of European integration, although clearly a detailed discussion is these questions goes beyond an introductory book on the legal system of the EU such as this one (see the list of further reading for additional guidance).

The terms *federation* or *federal union* are commonly used to describe a sovereign state where power is divided between a central authority and a number of regional authorities. The basis for the division of power is generally to be found in a Constitution. Federal states are well known in the modern world: they include the United States, Canada and the Federal Republic of Germany. Sometimes federal states break up; this has happened recently in case of the Soviet Union and Yugoslavia. Within the European Community, *federalism* is propounded as one of a number of different methods for achieving the goal of an integrated Europe. Commonly *federalists* are seen as the 'radicals' advocating the rapid transition to a sovereign United States of Europe, with the relinquishing of sovereignty on the part of the Member States. A single central government would swiftly assume responsibility for the core activities typically pursued by a federal authority: foreign policy, defence and security, external trade and representation in international organisations, management of the currency, macroeconomic policy, and matters concerned with citizenship. Such a federal authority would incorporate the key features of the modern democratic state, including in particular a legislature elected on the basis of universal suffrage. A judicial authority would mediate conflicts within the federal authority and between the federal authority and the constituent states on the scope of their respective spheres of power, basing its resolution of disputes on a constitutional document.

A more pragmatic position has been taken by the so-called *neo-functionalists* who have advocated a more incremental and piecemeal approach to European integration in the spheres of both practical politics and integration theory literature. *Neo-functionalism* was probably the dominant account, offered in academic literature, of early integration processes, at least up to the mid-1960s when the European Community encountered significant opposition to the deepening of integration. In the political sphere, it also underlay the decision of the founding fathers of the Community such as *Jean Monnet* and *Robert Schuman* to abandon grand federalist projects and to promote instead the adoption of the ECSC Treaty which concentrated simply on putting two strategically important commodities – coal and steel – into the hands of a central authority outside national control. Subsequently they supported the EEC Treaty which, in particular in its original form, had a remit limited to economic integration. The Treaty also gave a powerful role in the determination of policy to the representatives of the Member States in the Council of Ministers. The idea behind neo-functionalism is that sovereign states may be persuaded in the interests of economic welfare to relinquish control over certain areas of policy where it can easily be proven that benefits are likely to flow from a common approach to problem solving. Power is transferred to a central authority which exists at a level above the nation state, and which exercises its powers independently of the Member States – a *supranational* body. However, that transfer of powers is viewed as just part of a continuing process. One level of integration will lead on to the next; a sectoral Treaty dealing with coal and steel leads on to a general Treaty covering all economic sectors; a *customs union* incorporating the removal of internal customs tariffs and the erection of a uniform external tariff leads on to a *common* or *internal market*, with comprehensive free movement for all commodities and factors of production. This in turn creates demands for some mechanism to eradicate the costs and obstacles to trade which result from shifts in the value of money between the different regions of the single market, involving either irrevocably fixed exchange rates, or even a single currency managed by a single central bank (a *monetary union*). Without serious damage to the weaker economies of the union, however, this cannot be effected without a convergence of economic policies, achieved either voluntarily, or through the transfer of macroeconomic powers to a central authority (an *economic union*), and without incorporating elements of a *regional policy* to ensure an equitable geographical distribution of resources (*economic and social cohesion*).

This process was termed '*spill-over*' by neo-functionalists, and as they have evolved, the European Community and later the European Union have indeed passed through a number of the stages described above, involving progressive transfers of power to them by the Member States. Spill-over has also operated in the extension of the powers of the old

European Economic Community out of the purely 'economic' field into other related areas such as environmental and social policy. It has also fuelled the debate about *political union* in the EU. Two aspects of this concept can be identified, one substantive and the other procedural. According to the substantive notion of political union, the EU should exercise political powers which are commensurate with its economic powers. For example, external trade competence should be linked to the introduction of foreign policy cooperation. A concept of citizenship of the Union should be introduced and then developed into a substantive expression of membership of a supranational polity. In its procedural meaning, political union demands that the methods by which the transferred socio-economic competence is exercised do not lead to a net decrease in democratic and popular participation in and control of decision-making processes. In the EU, this is associated with calls for the European Parliament to be given greater powers.

If the functionalist logic is followed to its conclusion the supranational authority will, at a certain point, merge into a federal authority as more and more powers are transferred, and as the mechanisms for exercising these powers become increasingly separated from the nation state level. In this scenario the sovereign powers of the nation state are shared between the centre and its component parts, and power is exercised at the federal level not by the Member States, but by the autonomous organs of the federation. This means, in practice, if the traditions of Western liberal democracy are to be maintained, governance by a democratically elected legislature and a government which derives its legitimacy from the electoral process. Within the EU, the European Parliament is in fact now a democratically elected body, but its legislative powers are restricted, and it has little power or influence in relation to the Second and Third Pillars of the EU. Power in truth is largely exercised by the representatives of the governments of the Member States, meeting as the Council. Pressure to alter this situation in order to remedy a *democratic deficit* within the EU is understandable and logical from a functionalist perspective.

To summarise, the essence of supranationalism is found in a gradual transfer of competences to the higher level, and in the evolution of a distinctive form of decision-making at the higher level where increasingly decisions are taken on a majoritarian basis, rather than by consensus. This form of supranationalism has been termed 'decisional supranationalism' by Weiler (1981), and has generally been an area in which the Community, and now the Union, has been quite weak, at least until the changes in the decision-making process introduced by the Single European Act and more recently the Treaty of Maastricht. It can be distinguished from a specifically legal facet to the supranational nature of the Community, which Weiler has termed 'normative supranationalism'. This concerns the authority of the Court of Justice to give binding and authoritative rulings on the nature and effects of EC law, and to fashion a legal system in which EC law takes precedence over national law. In that respect, the EC has evolved more rapidly, and it is argued by some that the work of the Court of Justice has upset the delicate balance between the supranational and *intergovernmental* elements of the Treaties.

An alternative account of the development of the EU is offered by *intergovernmentalism*. This term can be used to describe a basic political position on integration which stresses that the EU is primarily a creature of its component states and should limit itself either to the types of activities more commonly undertaken by international organisations founded on Treaties, which are characterised by cooperation between states rather than by the independent actions of autonomous bodies or institutions, or to the narrow economic sphere of creating a free trading area. There have been conflicts throughout the history of the EC and the EU between the proponents of federalism and intergovernmentalism as basic positions on how these bodies should evolve. The policies of Margaret Thatcher and Charles de Gaulle towards what was then the European Community fall into the category of intergovernmentalism, although they were each propounding rather different forms of *nationalism* as one of the key building blocks of their policies. The battle lines are frequently drawn over the concept of *national sovereignty*, with intergovernmentalists arguing in favour of a Community of states, or at most a *confederal union of states*, in which state sovereignty is preserved, not a 'union of peoples' as the Preamble to the EC Treaty puts it. Intergovernmentalists will obviously oppose any extension of the supranational powers of the EU, involving the shift of 'Union' matters into the 'Community' pillar, an increased range of Community competence (e.g. social policy), or an enhanced supranational element in the decision-making process through the strengthening of the powers of the Parliament and the extension of majority voting in the Council.

In similar terms to the political position described above, academic literature adopting an intergovernmentalist position is one which characterises both the EU itself and the policies it pursues as the outcomes of bargains between states. From the mid-1960s to the mid-1980s intergovernmentalism was the dominant theory of European integration, although after the decision by the Member States to proceed towards the completion of the internal market neo-functionalist accounts enjoyed a partial revitalisation. The Treaty of Maastricht offers no clear resolution of the competing intergovernmentalist or federalist tendencies. On the one hand, it significantly extended the remit of Community-style supranational integration with a concrete timetable for monetary union, but at the same time it appeared to re-empower the Member States with the three pillar structure described in 1.2 and the introduction of the principle of *subsidiarity* which subjects the exercise of competence by the EU institutions to a new test intended to show that EU action is both necessary and efficient (Curtin, 1993). However, the emergence of an unprecendented degree of popular dissatisfaction with 'Europe-building' during the process of the ratification of the Treaty of Maastricht has raised new challenges to the conventional accounts of the integration process, however it is characterised, but each of which see it primarily as something which is imposed from above and which is not the result of popular demand.

As academic accounts or theories of the process of European integration, what both neo-functionalism and intergovernmentalism have in common is that they provide explanations which are framed in terms of an *international relations* paradigm of relationships between sovereign states. An alternative approach is to treat the internal politics of the EU as if they were in fact the domestic politics of a state, and to use the insights of *comparative* or *national politics* rather than international relations as the basic building blocks of study. From the perspective of lawyers, what accounts such as those which characterise the EU as a *'multi-level governance system'* and which focus on the various actors within the policy-making process, is that it is possible to insert a realistic and balanced statement of the role of law and legal institutions in the EU system (Wincott, 1995a). Domestic politics accounts also fit well with the urgent need to provide a sound *constitutional* basis for the European Union, in view of its current crisis of *legitimacy* in the wake of the difficulties over the Treaty of Maastricht. Consequently, theorists of democracy and constitutionalism are increasingly turning their attention towards the European Union.

One of the generally assumed virtues of the EU legal order described in the next paragraph has been its unity, uniformity and cohesive force (Shaw, 1996). The extent to which these basic principles can be sustained in the light of the *widening* (enlargement) and *deepening* (acquisition of new areas of competence, some of which are not directly related to the original economic mission, and which fall under the intergovernmental pillars) is not wholly clear. The 1996 IGC may clarify some of the constitutional uncertainties of the EU as it stands at present. It may also introduce constitutional structures for *variable geometry*, *Europe 'à la carte'*, or *multispeed Europe*, in which some Member States proceed more quickly towards closer integration than others. The prospects for a small core of countries moving towards a single currency and monetary union before the others are ready or willing, provided in the Treaty of Maastricht, foreshadows this trend, which has been criticised as breaking up the essential unifying purpose of the integration project. The infamous UK *'opt-out'* from the Social Policy Agreement appended to the Treaty of Maastricht, negotiated by John Major at the last IGC, poses similar challenges to the claims that the EU has a single cohesive legal order.

1.5 An Overview of some Key Elements of the Legal Order of the EU

An overview of any legal system should start with its basic structure, generally to be found in a constitution and associated documents. This is all the more important in the case of a federal-type legal system, where the constitution contains important rules governing the balance between central or federal and regional or state authorities in the law-making sphere, and on the relationship between federal and state law. Neither the European Community nor the European Union is, or can be, of course, explicitly described as a federation, although the legal order which now exists displays certain of the characteristics of a federal system. Nor does it have a constitution as such, but the Court of Justice now describes the founding treaties as the European Community's 'constitutional charter' (Case 294/83 *Parti Ecologiste 'Les Verts'* v. *European Parliament* [1986] ECR 1339 at p. 1365) (see, for detailed discussion, Chapter 3).

However, much of the 'constitutional law' of the EU is contained not in the Treaties themselves, but in the judicial pronouncements of the Court of Justice which plays a pivotal role in the legal system, and which has a commitment to the pursuit of integration through law. It has consistently given a maximalist interpretation of the authority and effect of EC law, of the regulatory and policy-making competence of the institutions and of its power to control both the institutions and the Member States to ensure that 'the law is observed' (Article 164 EC). Inevitably, therefore, the study of EC law concentrates for much of the time on the work of the Court, but that focus should be tempered by an awareness that using a picture of the EU in which the edifice of EC law as interpreted by the Court is placed at centre stage tends to give the impression that the whole system is more advanced than in fact it is. It also tends to understate the importance of the legislative and regulatory activities of the EU political institutions, and to focus on EC law as a normative structure imposing duties on and granting rights to Member States and EU citizens, at the expense of its role, to give just one example, in creating a new supranational regional development policy leading to a substantial redistribution of public resources (Scott, 1995a: xi–xii). The rest of this overview is, nonetheless, devoted to a brief explanation of the main areas of work of the Court.

One of the most important aspects of the Court's contribution has been its characterisation of the relationship between EC law and national law. On this topic, and on the question of the effect of EC law within the domestic legal systems of the Member States, there is little clear guidance in the Treaties themselves. Article 5 EC provides:

> 'Member States shall take all appropriate measures, whether general or particular, to ensure fulfilment of the obligations arising out of this Treaty or resulting from action taken by the institutions of the Community. They shall facilitate the achievement of the Community's tasks.
>   They shall abstain from any measure which could jeopardize the attainment of the objectives of this Treaty.'

This provision has been described by AG Tesauro in Case C-213/89 *R* v. *Secretary of State for Transport, ex parte Factortame Ltd (Factortame I)* ([1990] ECR I-2433 at p. 2454) as the key to the whole system of remedies which exists for the enforcement of EC law. In terms of specific enforcement procedures, which can be seen as an extrapolation of the 'duty of

Community loyalty' in Article 5, Articles 169 and 170 EC make it possible for the Commission and other Member States to bring infringing Member States before the Court of Justice, and Article 171 EC gives the Court the power to make a declaration stating that there has been an infringement and requiring the Member State to take measures to put an end to the infringement. Financial penalties for non-compliance were introduced by the Treaty of Maastricht. These measures allow for the 'direct enforcement' of EC law. They give no hint, however, that the obligations undertaken by the Member States under the Treaties they have signed are relevant at any level other than that of international law, which is primarily a law between states with minimal applicability to individuals. Individuals do not have recourse to the provisions in Articles 169 and 170 either to enforce EC law directly against the Member States themselves, or to force the Commission or another Member State to do this on their behalf. In fact, in an exercise of remarkable judicial creativity (Mancini, 1989), the Court of Justice has consistently distanced the EU legal system from 'ordinary' international law, arguing that by accession to the EU the Member States have transferred sovereign rights to the Community, creating an autonomous legal system in which the subjects are not just states, but also individuals. The Court has given effect to this view by enunciating four key principles:

- EC law penetrates into the national legal systems, and can and must be applied by the national courts, subject to authoritative rulings on the interpretation, effect and validity of EC law by the Court of Justice; in other words, the duty of 'Community loyalty' or 'fidelity' provided for in Article 5 applies to courts as well as to other organs of the Member States such as the government and the legislature;
- in this context individuals may rely upon rules of EC law in national courts, as giving rise to rights which national courts are bound to protect (the principle of 'direct effect');
- in order to guarantee the effectiveness of this structure, EC law takes precedence over conflicting national law, including national constitutional provisions (the principle of 'supremacy' or 'primacy').
- the organs and constituent bodies of the Member States, including the legislative, executive and judiciary, are fully responsible for reversing the effects of violations of EC law which affect individuals. This may, for example, involve the courts ordering the government to pay damages for loss caused by breach of EC law.

The Court has given an extensive task to the national courts which are responsible for ensuring what is often termed the 'indirect enforcement' of EC law at the instance of individuals. It has stressed the binding nature of EC law, including not only the Treaties themselves, but also those acts of the institutions (regulations, directives and decisions), to which binding effects are ascribed in Article 189 EC. These can, where appropriate, be enforced by individuals in national courts, if their provisions are justiciable (i.e. sufficiently precise and clear). It has also stressed that the European Community itself is bound by norms of international law, in particular where they are contained in Treaties which the EC itself has concluded with third countries or international organisations as an international actor exercising legal personality, or where the EC has succeeded to the international Treaty obligations of the Member States. Finally, it has articulated a body of superordinate principles, 'general principles of law', which govern the activities of the EU institutions and of the Member States acting within the sphere of Community competence, and which include not only fundamental rights, but also procedural principles such as proportionality and legal certainty. These are not as such to be found in the Treaties but are in fact further products of the remarkable judicial creativity of the Court which has developed a body of individual rights and principles of administrative legality which ensure the application of the rule of law within the EU legal system. The Treaties, the acts of the institutions, binding norms of international law, the general principles of law, and the case law of the Court itself together constitute the body of sources of EC law.

The key to the structure of indirect enforcement lies in the organic connection between the Court of Justice and the national courts in Article 177 EC. This provides that national courts may, and in certain circumstances must, refer to the Court of Justice questions on the interpretation and validity of provisions of EC law where such questions are raised in the context of national litigation and the national court considers a reference necessary in order to enable it to give judgment. National courts must refer questions of doubt regarding the application of EC law to the Court in two situations: first, where the national court is one of last resort; second, where it is the validity of a rule of EC law which is in doubt. Only the Court of Justice has the power to invalidate a rule of EC law. The preliminary ruling procedure has limits, and it depends for its effectiveness on cooperation between national courts and the Court of Justice. It is not an appeal by the parties to the Court of Justice. The power to ask for a ruling lies solely with the national court, and the legislative and political authorities of the Member States may not interfere with the exercise of discretion. Correlatively, the Court of Justice does not have the power in the context of a preliminary ruling hearing to invalidate a provision of national law. It cannot even formally make a declaration of incompatibility with EC law, as it can in the context of Articles 169–171. It is limited to an interpretation of EC law. However, the manner in which the Court of Justice has often chosen to frame its rulings has given little choice to the referring court but to apply EC law in preference to national law, and in effect to invalidate provisions of national law. This duty flows from Article 5 for the national court, and it is a duty which gives rise to some difficulty in the context of the UK where the principle of parliamentary sovereignty leads judges conventionally to regard themselves as subordinate to the will of Parliament. The European Communities Act 1972 attempts, if only imperfectly, to resolve the difficulties raised by membership of the EU in conventional constitutional doctrine. In summary, therefore, the Court has constructed a system which comes close to the power conventionally held by the supreme court in a federal system, namely the power to invalidate state legislation which contravenes the federal constitution. Examples of the interaction of the various enforcement mechanisms, such as the litigation regarding the Merchant Shipping Act 1988 in the UK (*ex parte Factortame*) will be discussed in Chapters 7, 9 and 10.

In addition to controlling the exercise of sovereign power by the Member States, the Court also acts as the judge of the proper exercise of sovereign power by the European Community, and as an umpire in disputes regarding legislative authority between the institutions and between the EU's political organs and the Member States. This form of control likewise operates both directly in the Court and indirectly in litigation before the national courts. It will be seen from the above that individuals are not restricted in the national courts simply to asserting their EC law rights against the Member States. An individual may in addition question the validity of an act of an EU institution in the context of national litigation, and a national court which is minded to accept that allegation must refer a question to the Court for a ruling on validity. There are broadly two reasons why an individual might seek to challenge a rule of EC law. First, it may be unlawful because of its effects upon the complainant as an individual or part of group (e.g. a particular class of economic actors such as the producers of a particular commodity). In this context, the Court of Justice frequently makes reference to the fundamental rights of the affected group when ascertaining the legality of an EU act. Second, the complainant may argue that the act is in breach of some more general rule of legality or constitutionality: e.g. the manner in which the act was adopted was in breach of the Treaty rules, it may fall outside the competence of the institution which adopted it, or it may fall outside Community competence altogether.

It is also possible to mount such a challenge directly in the Court of Justice itself, although there are strict restrictions on the standing of individuals under the provisions of Articles 173 and 175 EC which provide for the judicial review of unlawful acts and the unlawful failure to act on the part of the institutions. Member States, the Commission, the Council and, within limits, the European Parliament may also use Article 173 in order to seek the annulment of EU acts. Through its decisions on such actions the Court of Justice has been concerned to construct a body of principles which delineate the powers of the institutions *inter se*, and of the Member States and the Community respectively. This is another area in which the Treaty, aside from setting out procedural rules which govern the legislative process and outlining minimum prerequisites of validity for EU acts such as a statement of reasons, does not provide much assistance to the Court. The tendency of the Court has been to interpret the powers of the Community broadly: the institutions are given certain tasks by the Treaties, and the Court has consistently held that they must be regarded as having either express or implied powers to carry out these tasks. Thus there is no explicit reserved area of sovereign powers for the Member

States. However, the precise delineation of the powers of the States and of the Union remains a difficult area, as Chapter 3 will show. The advent of the principle of subsidiarity as a new criterion defining the relationship between the EU and the Member States, which may be justiciable before the Court, introduces a new range of challenges for the Court of Justice.

The extent to which this picture of unity and cohesion can now be sustained was commented upon already in the 1.4, and is an underlying theme of many chapters, especially Chapter 3 dealing with the constitutional principles of the EU. The reality of the Treaty of Maastricht (Curtin, 1993), its impact during the first few years after it came into force, the prospects for the 1996 IGC, and the challenges of further enlargements all suggest that in ten years time the EU legal order may appear very different to how it is at present.

1.6   Legal Literature

The successful study of EC law requires regular consultation of the founding Treaties of the European Communities and the European Union, relevant secondary legislation and other official documentation, as well as the case law of the Court of Justice. There are a number of English language sources for all these materials. In addition to the publications by the Office of Official Publications of the European Communities, which are available through HMSO, the Treaties are available in (portable) private collections such as Blackstone's *EC Legislation* (Foster, 1995) and Rudden and Wyatt, *Basic Community Laws* (Rudden and Wyatt, 1994). These collections – which are regularly updated – also contain much of the basic secondary legislation, and where they do not, the texts are available in less portable form either in the European Community's *Official Journal*, Sweet & Maxwell's *Encyclopedia of European Community Law* or (annotated) in vol. 42A of Halsbury's *Statutes of England* (3rd edn). The latter publications also contain copies of the Treaties.

Every student hesitates before first confronting the mass of materials contained in the European Documentation Centre ('EDC') located, if the student is fortunate, in or near the Law Library which he or she regularly uses. First in line for consultation must be the *Official Journal of the European Communities* which contains in its 'L' series the legislative acts adopted by the institutions. The 'C' series contains preparatory documents, non-binding acts such as resolutions and recommendations, reports of the activities of the European Parliament, the Economic and Social Committee, and the Committee of the Regions and long lists of agricultural prices. Students should also get to grips with 'COM Docs', the documents issued by the Commission. Important documents such as the White Paper on removing barriers to interstate trade which forms the basis of the 1992 legislative programme are often issued as COM Docs (COM(85) 310).

Next, check whether the *European Court Reports* (*ECR*), which are the official Law Reports of the European Court of Justice, are held in the EDC, or with the other Law Reports. With these reports may also be typescript versions of recent Court of Justice cases, but often only in French (the working language of the Court is French). Alternatively, there may be a summary publication available in either French or English entitled the *Proceedings of the European Court of Justice*. The publication delay attributable to translation difficulties which constantly undermines the prompt production of the European Court Reports makes consultation of English language versions of recent cases occasionally difficult. At the beginning of 1994 many of these difficulties in relation to cases decided after that date were resolved by reducing the amount of material published in the *ECR* and by abandonning simultaneous publication in every language. The consequence has been that although more recent cases are already available, there still remained in mid-1996 a big gap in English for most of 1993. Cross-checking with Law Reports in *The Times*, *The Independent*, the (privately published) *Common Market Law Reports* (*CMLR*), the (general) *All England Law Reports* (*All ER*), especially the *EC* volume, and, where appropriate, specialist Law Reports such as the *Industrial Relations Law Reports* (*IRLR*), can often uncover an unofficial English language version.

Extracts from important cases are, of course, to be found in casebooks, a number of which have appeared in the field of EC law. The most useful and up-to-date is Craig and de Búrca (1995) which contains also a wide-ranging and stimulating selection of secondary literature, much of which is drawn from non-legal sources. Ellis and Tridimas (1995), which concentrates on EC public law, also offers a stimulating selection of materials.

Finally, the EDC also offers a wealth of complementary material in the form of the reports of the other institutions and EU bodies, publications such as the *Bulletin of the European Union* (cited hereafter as Bull. EU), *European Economy* and *Social Europe*. Each of these publications have useful supplements. Also frequently to be found in the EDC is *European Access*, a bibliographical journal, not itself an EU publication but which is an essential research tool for preparing projects in the field of EC law and policy. University and other libraries should also be able to provide assistance in accessing much of the EDC material (and much more besides) on CD Rom or online (see the Commission's World Wide Web server at http://europa.eu.int/).

Each chapter of this book will contain lists of further reading to which you should refer. There is also a general bibliography containing additional works. One of the main objectives of the book is to make the specialised literature more accessible. Much of the further reading will be found in the core journals in the field: the *European Law Review* (*ELRev*), the *Common Market Law Review* (*CMLRev*), the *Yearbook of European Law* (*YEL*), the *European Law Journal* (*ELJ*), the *Maastricht Journal of European and Comparative Law* (*MJ*), and *Legal Issues of European Integration* (*LIEI*). Of the general English journals, the *Modern Law*

Review (MLR) probably publishes the most material on EC law. Many subject specific journals now have European sections which offer more detailed coverage (e.g. *Industrial Law Journal (ILJ)*, *Journal of Social Welfare and Family Law (JSWFL)*). In the specific sphere of public law *Public Law (PL)* and *European Public Law (EPL)* are important resources. Any student pursuing a research project in EC law should consult these journals, as well as the usual legal journals indexes. Not to be forgotten also are the more detailed general textbooks available such as those by Kapteyn and VerLoren van Themaat (1989), Wyatt and Dashwood (1993) and Weatherill and Beaumont (1995), as well as the detailed expositions of individual fields of EC law in series such as those published by Oxford University Press and Wiley/Chancery Law Publishing.

Recent years have seen the publication of many new books on specific fields of EC law. Where appropriate, these are referred to in the further reading sections which follow the relevant chapters. Reference may also usefully be made to books which provide specific insights such as the views of the European Court judiciary (MacKenzie Stuart, 1977; Slynn, 1992), to a book such as Brown and Kennedy (1994), which focuses on the work of the Court. The general approach of many of these works is broadly doctrinal, or 'black letter', setting out and commenting upon the legal rules and structures, and the work of the Court of Justice. More sceptical, critical or contextual views of the role and nature of law European integration processes are, however, increasingly common and can be found in works such as those of Scott (1995a) who critiques the development of EU regional development policy, and Snyder (1990) who argues in particular from the contextualist perspective of international political economy. More general collections of essays include Snyder (1993a) and Shaw and More (1995). A number of works focus specifically on the Treaty of Maastricht including Dehousse (1994a), O'Keeffe and Twomey (1994) and, from a more political science perspective, Monar *et al.* (1993) and Duff *et al.* (1994). From a similar perspective of academic response to change and the attempt to relate to the political agenda, the 1996 IGC will soon be generating a parallel body of work. Those seeking EU/US comparisons of integration in a federal context can look to the massive Integration Through Law series published by Walter de Gruyter (Cappelletti *et al.*, 1986). This series, like a more recent series on human rights in the European Community published by Nomos (Clapham, 1991; Cassese *et al.*, 1991a, 1991b), represents the fruits of a research project based at the European University Institute (EUI), in Florence. The EUI also produces a number of series of working papers where new work on the EU and its legal order receives rapid publication.

As will be seen, much of the more recent work on EC law makes use of interdisciplinary approaches to legal studies. To this end, the final section of this chapter introduces some of the contributions in the fields of economics, political theory and policy studies which might assist you in making the most of the study of EC law.

1.7   Making the Most of Studying EC Law

In the other social science disciplines, periodical literature on the politics, governance, economics and sociology of the EU is to be found in a great variety of different journals. There are a number of more specialised journals including the *Journal of Common Market Studies*, *West European Politics* and the *Journal of European of European Public Policy*. However, in addition, students must consult general social science journals, using a bibliographical reference tool or periodical index. As with legal publishing on the EU, recent years has also seen an explosion in social science publishing. This survey can only draw attention to a number of useful basic tools. Works on more specific policy areas are referred to in the further reading sections of individual chapters.

Thorough historical surveys are to be found in Dinan (1994) and Urwin (1995), and a useful collection of historical documents is made available in Weigall and Stirk (1992). Many general books also begin with historical surveys of the emergence of the Community in the post-war transformation of Europe and of its evolution from the ECSC Treaty to the Treaty of Maastricht, structuring the discussion within some of the different theories which have been used to explain the integration process (see George, 1991; Holland, 1993; Pinder, 1995). A set of readings specifically focused on these theories is offered in Nelsen and Stubb (1994). Increasingly works aim to set the 'West European experience' of regional integration into a broader European or global context (e.g. Wallace, 1990; 1994; Bulmer and Scott, 1994; Crouch and Marquand, 1992). A similar approach has been taken to patterns of government and politics within the European arena (Hayward and Page, 1995) or the development of new constitutional principles and practices (Bellamy *et al.*, 1995; Bellamy, 1996).

Institutional aspects of the work of the EU are well covered in more general (Keohane and Hoffmann, 1991; Nugent, 1994) and more specific (Jacobs *et al.*, 1992; Edwards and Spence, 1994; Westlake, 1995) works. Good general surveys of the policies, politics and economics of the EU include El-Agraa (1994) Lodge (1993) Wallace and Wallace (1996). The Single Market Project provided a singular focus for publication activities (e.g. Crouch and Marquand, 1990) with a favourable analysis to be found in Cecchini (1988), which includes the results of Commission sponsored research, Cockfield (1994), whose view is that of the 'insider', and Wistrich (1994) who offers a federalist perspective on European integration. More sceptical views can be found in Grahl and Teague (1990), Cutler *et al.* (1989) and Bieber *et al.* (1988). A general survey of the impact of the internal market is offered by Swann (1992). The resurgence of work from the US on the EU is well represented by Sbragia (1992), Adams (1992) and the biennial series published by the European Community Studies Association entitled *The State of the European Community/Union* (Hurwitz and Lesquesne, 1991, Cafruny and Rosenthal, 1993, and Rhodes and Mazey, 1995).

Summary

This chapter introduces the study of EC law by providing the basic facts and introducing the key tools of analysis which students require. The mission of the EU is to promote integration in Europe, and both the legal and political systems of the EU should be understood in the context of this mission. The EC legal system is *sui generis* and has evolved in the hands of the Court of Justice into a supranational and quasi-federal system where EC law consistently 'trumps' national law.

Questions

1   What are the 'European Community' and the 'European Union'? Why are these terms misleading and what ambiguities can arise when they are used?
2   Using the Preamble and introductory sections of the Treaties of Paris and Rome, as well as the SEA and the Treaty of Maastricht, identify whether and how the basic aims of the EC and the EU have evolved since the beginning. What additional methods for promoting integration have been gradually given to the EC and the EU? To what extent is the integration function now taken over by the European Union (understood in the specific sense of the broader constitutional structure established by the Treaty of Maastricht)? (One of the objectives of this question is to involve you in a search for the relevant documentation in the available literature and in the EDC and the Library.)
3   Define the following terms:

   –   federalism
   –   supranational
   –   intergovernmental

   What do these definitions tell us about the nature of the EU and the EC?
4   What are the key features of the legal order of the EU?

Further Reading

Full publication details for works such as Snyder (1990) will be found in the Bibliography. At this stage you may find some of the works cited here difficult or inaccessible. You may find it useful to return to them once more when you have read further through this book.

Arnull (1994), 'Judging the New Europe', 19 *ELRev.* 3.
Caporaso and Keeler (1995), 'The European Union and Regional Integration Theory' in Rhodes and Mazey (1995).
Curtin (1993), 'The Constitutional Structure of the Union: A Europe of Bits and Pieces', 30 *CMLRev.* 17.
Everling (1992), 'Reflections on the Structure of the European Union', 29 *CMLRev.* 1053.

Harmsen (1994), 'A European Union of Variable Geometry: Problems and Perspectives', 45 *NILQ* 109.

Holland (1993), Ch. 1, 'Integration and the ideas of Jean Monnet: federalism versus intergovernmentalism'.

Koopmans (1991) 'The Birth of European Law At the Crossroads of Legal Tradition', 39 *AJCL* 493.

Mancini (1989) 'The Making of a Constitution for Europe', 26 *CMLRev.* 595; also published as Ch. 6 in Keohane and Hoffmann (1991).

Pinder (1995), Ch. 5, 'Institutions or Constitution'.

Snyder (1990), Ch. 1, 'New Directions'.

Weatherill (1995a), Ch. 1, 'From Community to Union'.

2 Evolving From Community to Union

2.1 Introduction

The title and the text of this chapter seek to emphasise the dynamic and changing nature of first the Community and then, later, the Union and to highlight the fact that the processes of integration within Europe have not yet reached a conclusion or final stage of evolution. A basic knowledge of the history of the EC and the EU offers a number of benefits to the student:

- it gives a context to contemporary events, demonstrating that the current debates on the integration process have a long pedigree, and that ideas such as monetary union or political union are not simply novelties dreamt up by Jacques Delors in the late 1980s;
- it puts the EU firmly in the context of other developments within and outside Europe, recognising the significance for the European Union of events such as the unification of Germany, the end of the Cold War, the break up of the Soviet Union, the emergence of new democracies in Eastern and East Central Europe, as well as the economic context of the global trading order under the 'new GATT';
- it highlights the ebbs and flows of the European Community and Union, which have coincided quite closely with the low and high points of the European economy since the Second World War;
- finally, the stop-start progress of political and economic integration emphasises the unparalleled contribution made by the Court at crucial points (Wincott, 1995a). Yet although the Court has been characterised as the 'engine of integration', when the events discussed in this chapter are reviewed subsequently in the context of developments in the EC legal system which form the main focus of this book and its companion volume, it will be seen that the work of the Court of Justice has not always run parallel to the political and economic evolution of the Treaties. In particular, sometimes there has been a fit and sometimes a misfit between political context and legal action; more often there appears to be a lag of some years between the point when work

begins towards a new goal in the sphere of politics and correspondingly significant progress in the construction of the EU legal framework.

2.2   The Roots of European Integration

Although it would be wrong to characterise current developments in
European integration as the direct descendants of earlier ideas and
proposals, it is nonetheless of interest that the idea of a unified Europe
is by no means new. The model of a Europe brought together not by
military conquest, but in common pursuit of higher goals of peace,
prosperity and stability has attracted the attention of thinkers since the
Middle Ages. An institutional form of federal unity in Europe was argued
for by prominent intellectuals of the Enlightenment such as Bentham,
Rousseau, and, later, Saint-Simon. More concrete progress was made in
the field of economic integration. The early period of capitalist organisation saw not only the transformation of the means of production and the
shift to industrialisation, but also the integration of national markets,
often achieved in parallel with national political unity. The next step was
the liberalisation of trade between sovereign states, where Britain took a
leading role with its commitment to free trade in the middle of the
nineteenth century. However, none of the proposals for increased cooperation between states in the economic field such as a Central European
customs union between the Hapsburg empire and the German states in the
1840s achieved real success, and there was a resurgence of nationalism and
protectionism in the late nineteenth century which eventually culminated
in the First World War.

The interwar years saw continued discussion of the ideal of European
integration as a better way forward for Europe than destructive interstate
rivalry, most notably within the forum of the Pan-European Union
founded in 1923 by the Austrian Count Richard Coudenhove-Kalergi. It
is perhaps significant that amongst the pre-war membership of the Union
were a number of politicians who played key roles in postwar Europe,
including Konrad Adenauer, later Chancellor of the Federal Republic of
Germany, and Georges Pompidou, later President of France. However,
the influence of the Union did not succeed in saving the only initiative
towards European integration of the interwar years put forward at the
governmental level, the Briand Plan of 1929–30, a proposal by the French
Foreign Minister for a confederal bond linking the peoples of Europe. The
logic behind French foreign policy and the Briand Plan was that of
achieving security for France against Germany by tying the latter firmly
into a European structure of cooperation. The theme of the 'Europeanisa-
tion' of Germany has been an enduring one which has enjoyed a
renaissance since unification in 1990. Despite the modest nature of the
proposals, the Briand Plan was never taken further because of scepticism
and hostility in Britain, Italy and Germany.

2.3   The Postwar Climate of Change

At the end of and just after the Second World War quite different attitudes
to the prospects for European unity were apparent. Even before the end of
the war, voices calling for a form of unity which prevented future wars
could be heard in the Resistance movements of the occupied countries of
continental Europe. Prominent figures in the Resistance movements such
as Altiero Spinelli, who re-emerged much later as a champion of European
federalism in the European Parliament in the late 1970s and early 1980s,
argued for a federal Europe with a written constitution, state institutions
such as a government and a Parliament, a judicial system and a common
army. Resolutions supporting these propositions were passed at a conference of Resistance representatives held in Geneva in July 1944. It was
believed at the time that support for European federalism would also come
from Britain, in particular from Winston Churchill, who was popular in
federalist circles following his dramatic offer to the French of the creation
of a Franco-British union in 1940. The major driving force behind that
offer was, moreover, Jean Monnet, who proved to be a key actor in
postwar developments.

Churchill's loss of the British premiership with the victory of the
Labour Party in the 1945 General Election, and the re-emergence of
prewar political leaders in many European countries at the expense of
Resistance leaders, were two factors which contributed to the failure to
translate the ideals of federalism into a concrete agenda for action. The
immediate imperatives of national economic rebuilding took precedence
over the proposal that postwar reconstruction should occur within an
entirely new political framework. The danger was present, therefore, that
as before the war the ideas of unity would not take root within the
institutions of the state, and that rallying calls such as Churchill's famous
speech in Zurich in 1946 and the resolutions of numerous federalist groups
gathered at the Congress of Europe at The Hague in 1948 would remain
simply extragovernmental expressions of a desirable, but unattainable goal
of integration within Europe. However, this view discounts a number of
features which distinguish the two situations. These included the increasing closeness of certain key personalities such as Jean Monnet to centres of
political power (Monnet had become head of the French Economic
Planning Commission), the willingness of federal idealists to countenance
incremental strategies for achieving integration (the ideas of functionalism
outlined in Chapter 1) and a greater global commitment to free trade and
economic cooperation, evidenced by the adoption of the General Agreement on Tariffs and Trade (GATT) and the creation of the International
Monetary Fund. Last but not least there was the need of the USA for
stability in Western Europe in the context of the Cold War which followed
hard on the heels of the Second World War and its consequent interest in
and partial sponsorship of ideas of Western European integration.

In 1947 the USA committed itself to the so-called 'Truman Doctrine'
which was a pledge of US support for 'free peoples who are resisting

subjugation by armed minorities or by outside pressures'. The Americans had an interest in preventing a destabilising power vacuum in Europe. One outcome of this doctrine was the Marshall Plan to provide economic aid for reconstruction to countries in Europe committed to ideas supported by the USA, aid which, because of the underlying political motivation of the provider, was shunned by the Soviet Union and its allies in central and eastern Europe. The allocation, administration and delivery of American aid became the initial preoccupation of the first international organisation in the economic sphere set up in postwar Europe – the Organisation for European Economic Cooperation (OEEC) set up in 1948. The OEEC was a strictly intergovernmental organisation which never succeeded in achieving any of its grander ideals of economic cooperation, but nonetheless it had a wide membership within Europe and North America (sixteen founder members) which grew much larger when it gave way in 1961 to the Organisation for Economic Cooperation and Development (OECD) which encompasses other Western style economies such as Australia and Japan.

The broad attractions of a loose intergovernmental form of cooperation were also evident at an early stage in the political field where the grandly styled but rather ineffective Council of Europe was established in 1949. The proposals for the Council of Europe grew out of the resolutions of the Hague Congress. Although the nature of the Council of Europe has always been bland (Urwin, 1995: 40), and it has consistently avoided controversial issues such as defence and security, it benefits from its symbolic role within Europe, including its role as a forum for discussion, and from the particular association it has acquired with political democracy and human rights. The most significant international instrument to come into being under the aegis of the Council of Europe is the European Convention on Human Rights and Fundamental Freedoms which came into force in 1953. Membership of the Council and signature of the Convention, while not demanding in the sense of requiring the signatory to relinquish a significant portion of state autonomy of action, have come to be benchmarks of acceptability amongst Western-style liberal democracies, achieved by countries emerging from dictatorship such as Spain and Portugal in the 1970s and more recently by the new democracies of central and eastern Europe. As membership of the European Union has come to appear increasingly attractive to a range of European countries, the Council of Europe has become a convenient stepping stone in the process of achieving membership. However, at no time has the Council departed from the intergovernmental consensus-based approach to international cooperation.

Finally, in the military field, cooperation took a distinctly Atlanticist turn with the conclusion in April 1949 of the North Atlantic Treaty tying together the North American states with the European parties to the 1948 Treaty of Brussels – France, the UK and the Benelux countries. Germany was later brought into the Western European Union after the failure of the initiative for a European Defence Community in 1954. In 1955 Germany joined NATO.

2.4   From Grand Ideals to Incremental Stages

A separate chapter in the evolution of integration in Europe was opened in May 1950 with the publication of the Schuman Plan, drawn up, on behalf of the French Foreign Minister Robert Schuman, by Jean Monnet. This Plan was the precursor of the European Coal and Steel Community (ECSC). The text of the Plan neatly encapsulates the small and large visions of European integration which have marked the evolution of the European Community (Weigall and Stirk, 1992: 58–9). The plan itself was shaped around the proposal to place French and German coal and steel production under a common authority (a 'High Authority') outside national control and open to the participation of other European countries. However, although its immediate preoccupation was with supranational control of these two commodities alone, its wider agenda was evident. It declared this to be only the first step in the federation of Europe, and asserted that 'Europe must be organised on a federal basis'. However, 'Europe will not be made all at once or according to a single plan. It will be built through concrete achievements which first create a *de facto* solidarity'. The ECSC therefore represents a clear example of the functional approach to integration.

This French proposal, attractive to Germany because it marked the first step towards recovering sovereignty over the Saarland, still then belonging to France, while allowing the fledgling Federal Republic to regain a place in the international community, attracted also the participation of the Benelux countries and Italy. Although the UK participated briefly in the negotiations leading to the conclusion of the ECSC Treaty, the plan to transfer control away from national governments to an appointed body proved unacceptable. Only a much smaller number of countries proved ready to participate in truly supranational international cooperation than in the looser arrangements of the Council of Europe.

The ECSC Treaty was concluded in Paris in April 1951, and contained an institutional structure rather different to that envisaged by the Schuman Plan itself, in particular with less strong elements of supranationalism. The actions of the High Authority at the centre of the institutional structure of the ECSC were to be tempered by a Council of Ministers, composed of representatives of the Member States, to give a greater intergovernmentalist input into the Community and to act as a political counterweight to the High Authority. Its task was to give its opinion to the High Authority which was charged with the principal decision-making power. The triad of political institutions was completed by a Common Assembly composed in the early years of representatives chosen by the national parliaments, and endowed only with consultative powers and a minimal role in ensuring the accountability of the High Authority. Some aspects of the institutional and decision-making structures were strongly supranational: decisions were to be taken and then implemented by the High Authority independently and action did not require a consensus of the Contracting Parties; furthermore, decisions of the High Authority were binding upon the Contracting Parties. However, the potential for independent decision on the part of the High Authority was restricted by the nature of the ECSC Treaty as a *traité loi*. The four-pronged institutional pattern, which was later adopted as a model for the European Economic Community (EEC) in 1957, was completed by a Court of Justice, charged with ensuring observance of the law.

The ECSC Treaty created a common market for coal and scrap (Article 4). This comprises the abolition of internal customs duties and quantitative restrictions on imports and exports, measures and practices which discriminate between producers, purchaser or consumers, government aids and subsidies and restrictive practices tending towards the sharing or exploiting of markets. These essentially free market principles were fetters upon the possible dirigiste tendencies of the High Authority which might have resulted from the influence of its first President, Monnet, who was known to favour a strong element of central planning in the economy. Interestingly, unlike the later EEC Treaty, the ECSC Treaty does not provide for a complete customs union for coal and steel as it does not create a common external tariff for imports from third countries. In practice, the Member States have created a system of uniform external protection to avoid anomalies between coal and steel products and other products.

The ratification of the ECSC Treaty by the national parliaments and the entry into force of the Treaty did not inexorably lead towards closer integration. The success of the ECSC Treaty was followed closely by a serious failure – the Treaty establishing a European Defence Community (EDC) and the draft Statute for a European Political Community. This initiative was also based on a French proposal aimed at managing the re-emergence of Germany on the international stage. The Pleven Plan put forward by the French Minister of Defence proposed to apply the methods of the Schuman Plan to the field of defence, allowing German rearmament, then being vigorously urged by the USA, within the context of a European Army. The Treaty establishing the EDC was concluded by the Six in May 1952 (the UK participated in early negotiations but then withdrew from the plan, despite Winston Churchill's championship of the concept of a European army in 1950), but then encountered serious difficulties at the ratification stage. However, even before ratification, the Parliamentary Assembly envisaged for the EDC was meeting and drafting, as required by Article 38 EDC, proposals for institutional reform to guarantee the democratic character of the Community in the form of a draft Statute for a European Political Community. Both plans collapsed when the EDC Treaty did not achieve ratification by the French parliament in August 1954. Some semblance of purely European cooperation in the defence field was rescued at the initiative of the UK, with the creation in 1954 of the Western European Union (WEU) bringing Germany into the security framework of the West. After years of obscurity, the WEU has enjoyed a strange renaissance since the mid-1980s offering a distinctive Western European voice in defence issues and as the basis for an expansion of European integration in the defence field. It is specifically incorporated into the Common Foreign and Security Pillar of the Treaty of Maastricht as an 'integral part of the development of the Union' (Article J.4(2) TEU) and is charged with the implementation of decisions of the Union which have defence implications. These questions are part of the agenda of the 1996 IGC, in particular in view of the impending expiry in 1998 of the Brussels Treaty on which the WEU is founded (Article J.4(6)).

Despite these setbacks further concrete progress towards European integration was made in the 1950s. This time the initiative for a '*relance européenne*' came from the Benelux countries, already tied together in tighter economic cooperation than the other members of the ECSC. The key to the new initiative was that economic integration should precede political integration, but that new instruments were needed to go beyond both the ineffectual OEEC and the sectorally-based ECSC. This broadening and deepening of the emphasis of economic integration is often said to be a classic example of the principles of 'spillover' outlined in 1.4. The proposal was for a general common market, and for specific measures in the emerging field of nuclear energy. Out of a discussion at Messina in June 1955 between the Foreign Ministers of the Six came the decision to convene a committee to elaborate one or more treaties to give effect to these proposals. The report of the committee, named after its Chairman Paul-Henri Spaak, a Belgian, was submitted and approved by the Foreign Ministers of the Six by May 1956 (Weigall and Stirk, 1992: Ch. 6).

The Spaak report called for the creation of a common market, which it defined as the result of the fusion of national markets to create a larger unit of production. This, it argued, would make for greater economic growth and an accelerated increase in the standard of living. The Report foresaw three main strands to the development of this common market: the achievement of a customs union and free movement of commodities and factors of production; the creation of a policy for the common market to ensure fair competition; and the adoption of measures to facilitate the transformation and modernisation of economies and enterprises, for example through investment aid and retraining of workers. What the Report did not propose were common educational or social policies, which were not regarded as necessary for the achievement of the common market. The institutional structure was based on that of the ECSC, with a Court, a Common Assembly, a Council of Ministers, and a central supranational authority, in this case termed the Commission. Once again the Commission was to be the pivotal political institution, but endowed with rather fewer powers than the High Authority under the ECSC Treaty. The Spaak Committee accepted that the many activities to be undertaken by the institutions for the achievement of these goals could not be regulated in detail in a Treaty, and that what was needed was not a *traité loi*, but a *traité cadre*, itself giving extensive law-making powers to the institutions, in particular to the Council. This Treaty was elaborated on the basis of the Spaak Report and signed in Rome in March 1957, along with a Treaty establishing a European Atomic Energy Community (Euratom). The process of parliamentary ratification proceeded smoothly and the Treaties entered into force on 1 January 1958.

The EEC represented a reversion to the vision of a Europe created by stages, with the common market as a stepping stone towards political union. As such, it is a remarkable triumph of common interest over diversity. The Six had very different motivations and goals in seeking the creation of the Community. France had long been pursuing a policy of preventing German domination of the continent of Europe. Germany saw supranational cooperation as the means to regain self-respect and standing in the international community. The Benelux countries sought to overcome the disadvantage of smallness in an increasingly global economy. Italy was looking for a new start and respectability. All the countries saw the potential for economic benefit: in particular, the Germans sought outlets for their manufactured products, and France insisted on an agricultural policy which protected its large agricultural sector. Italy fought for the inclusion of the free movement of workers in order to capitalise on one of its greatest assets – its labour. At an institutional level, too, the document represents a compromise between federalists and intergovernmentalists, and like any document which is the result of compromise, the EEC Treaty contains inconsistencies which articulate the delicate balance between giving independence of action to the supranational institutions and retaining Member State control over the direction of the Community.

2.5 The Non-Participants in Supranational Europe

The UK excluded itself from participation in the supranational project of the European Community from the outset of the negotiations for the ECSC Treaty. Soon after the ratification of the EEC Treaty, the UK spearheaded negotiations looking at the possibility of instituting some form of free trade arrangement between the Six and the other OEEC countries, but without a common external tariff or arrangements for the harmonisation of laws to prevent distortions of competition. A number of Member States were anxious about the dangers of watering down their achievements; opposition was strongest from the French, and the negotiations came to an abrupt end when they were vetoed by General de Gaulle, then President of France. As a result of this rebuff a number of OEEC countries formed a separate, but looser arrangement for economic co-operation, the European Free Trade Association (EFTA), concluded by the Treaty of Stockholm in January 1960. The founder members of EFTA comprised the UK, Denmark, Sweden, Norway, Austria, Switzerland and Portugal. They were subsequently joined by Finland and Iceland, but numbers were reduced by the departure of Denmark, the UK and later Portugal to join the European Community. EFTA often sought closer

economic relations with the Community, and in the 1992 these culminated
in the signature of the Treaty creating the European Economic Area
(EEA) which largely assimilated the relations between European Community and EFTA countries to internal European Community relations,
and applied the basic principles of the internal European Community
common market to those relations. This treaty, too, encountered difficulties in the ratification process when it was rejected by a referendum in
Switzerland. However, the failure of one state to ratify this Treaty did not
preclude it coming into force on 1 January 1994. Many of the members of
EFTA were also applicants for membership of the EU, and on 1 January
1995, the accession to the EU of Austria, Finland and Sweden reduced the
participants in the EEA arrangements to Norway, Iceland, and Liechten-
stein (3.13).

A change of attitude in the UK towards the European Community in
the early 1960s resulted in two requests for membership in 1961 and 1967,
which were vetoed or stalled by de Gaulle's opposition to British membership. Only after the departure of de Gaulle was the path opened to the
enlargement of the Community.

2.6   The Early Years

The years of the late 1950s and the early 1960s were years of economic
boom with unprecedented growth which made the tasks of the nascent
Community rather less daunting. The Treaty provided for a transitional
period of twelve years, divided into three stages each of four years, ending
on 1 January 1970. At the end of this period, the common market should
have been in place (Article 7(7) EC). Common economic interest dictated
that during the first two stages progress was smooth involving the
dismantling of tariffs and quota restrictions, the erection of a common
external tariff, the liberalisation of the free movement of workers and the
creation of a system protecting the social security interests of migrant
workers, the adoption of the initial regulations for the implementation of
the Community's competition policy, and the introduction of a system of
common farm prices and common organisations of the market which form
the basis of the Common Agricultural Policy (CAP). Up to this point the
Member States moved forward by consensus, since during the first two
stages the Treaty provided for decisions to be taken by the Council acting
unanimously. The Commission under Walter Hallstein, its first President,
played a key role in these achievements, initiating policy and brokering
agreements between the states, and there seemed little opposition at that
time to its full exploitation of the supranational potential of the tasks
which it had been assigned under the EEC Treaty. The Court of Justice
too was busy carving out a distinctive role for itself within the Community
system. In the ground breaking cases of *Van Gend en Loos* in 1963 (Case
26/62 [1963] ECR 1) and *Costa* v. *ENEL* in 1964 (Case 6/64 [1964]
ECR 585) the Court sought to distance the EC legal system from the

conventional structure of international law by identifying the importance of the relationship between EC law and individual citizens of the Member States, and by asserting the superiority of EC law over the laws of the Member States. The Court argued that there had been a transfer of sovereign powers by the Member States to the Community.

Meanwhile, however, the warning signs for the Community had been present since 1958 when General de Gaulle came to power as the first President of the Fifth French Republic on a fiercely nationalistic platform. His view that cooperation within Europe should take place within a confederal structure in which the Member States retained full sovereignty was put forward in the Fouchet Plan of 1961, an attempt to divert the process of political union to his own ends. This proposal for a 'union of states' based on strictly intergovernmental precepts came to naught after encountering opposition in particular amongst the smaller states. Nonetheless it was clear that the favourable political circumstances in which the Community had flourished would not last for ever. The crisis point came when De Gaulle was faced with the prospect of the Community entering the third stage of the transitional period at the beginning of 1966 when many important decisions would be taken by a qualified majority in the Council (see Table 4.1).

2.7   De Gaulle and the Luxembourg Accords

De Gaulle objected to qualified majority voting under the EEC Treaty as he felt that it would endanger French interests within the Community. Yet majority voting was due to apply to agricultural pricing decisions – one of the issues of keenest interest for France – from 1966. De Gaulle chose to make his stand, and to precipitate the most serious crisis in the history of the Community, not over majority voting as such but over a series of linked proposals put forward by the Commission in March 1965. These concerned the financing of the CAP through a system of own resources belonging to the Community rather than through contributions by the Member States, as well as increased Parliamentary input into the making of the budget. The Commission rightly saw these matters as linked: the CAP represents the main expenditure by the Community; 'own resources' (then coming from the revenue of the Common Customs Tariff (CCT), agricultural levies at the external borders and a percentage of the new common turnover tax levied by all Member States – Value Added Tax (VAT)) – were intended to give the Community financial autonomy; and greater control by the European Parliament was a necessary democratic counterweight as control over the budget increasingly escaped the scrutiny of national Parliaments. France was not in favour of a greater role for the European Parliament, and used the lack of agreement on the package as a whole (i.e. the unwillingness of the other Member States to follow its line) to justify withdrawing from the work of the Council from June 1965 to January 1966. This period is sometimes called the period of '*la politique de la chaise vide*' (empty chair politics), and the deadlock was broken only by an agreement between the Six known as the Luxembourg Accords.

It was agreed, in the case of decisions which were to be adopted by a qualified majority, but where very important interests of one or more Member States were at issue, that the members of the Council would attempt, within a reasonable period of time, to reach solutions capable of adoption by unanimity. The French delegation added that in its view such discussion should continue indefinitely until a unanimous decision was reached. The delegations accepted that there was no common view on what should be done if unanimity could not be achieved, but agreed at that stage that this disagreement should not prevent the normal work of the Community being taken up once more. The result, in practice, of the Luxembourg Accords was that there was no voting in the Council. Just as the Member States arrived at the stage where majority voting would be introduced, they baulked at the last hurdle. Thus De Gaulle had achieved his central objective of weakening certain supranational elements of the Community. The intergovernmental mode of decision-making based on consensus building prevailed over a federalist majoritarian approach as more and more of the Member States saw the attraction of maintaining the practice of unanimity. After the accession of the UK, for example the Accords allowed British politicians to maintain what they have been fond of calling the 'veto' over decisions of the Community which the UK does not like. This lies at the heart of repeated Government statements to the Westminster Parliament that British interests can always be protected by the use of the veto.

Although the Luxembourg Accords are essentially in the nature of informal understandings between sovereign states, and as such have no formal status within the EC legal system, they have proved remarkably enduring. No legal challenge can be mounted by any individual, institution or Member State to a refusal on the part of the Council to proceed to a vote. Even the Commission which makes the proposals on the basis of which the Council acts is impotent in such a case. The Accords were responsible for nearly twenty years of legislative stagnation within the Community where negotiations lasting up to ten years might be needed before agreement was reached on the simplest pieces of legislation. There is only one recorded instance of the Council riding roughshod over one Member State's assertion of a vital national interest in order to block qualified majority voting, and this was in May 1982 when the UK was seeking to oppose the adoption of agricultural prices. Furthermore, as the European Council became increasingly important within the Community's political structure, the practice emerged of passing on decisions which could not be taken in the Council to the European Council where their substance would be reduced to the lowest common denominator in the best traditions of political compromise. Commitments in the European Council to break the legislative deadlock by agreeing to relinquish the practice of decision-making by unanimity proved to be empty rhetoric. Since provisions of the Treaty already provided for qualified majority voting in certain instances but these were being ignored, what was needed to revitalise the Community was not merely an increase in the range of decisions which could be adopted by a majority, but also a new willingness actually to vote on the part of the Council. Not until the adoption of the Internal Market Programme in 1985 and the entry into force of the Single European Act on 1 July 1987 were these two conditions satisfied. After that, remarkably rapid progress was made in many fields in the adoption of legislation required for the achievement of the single internal market.

The failure of the functionalist theory of European integration to take full account of the effects of resurgent nationalism as demonstrated by De Gaulle is one example of the deficiencies of the theory which led to its widespread rejection as a tool of analysis of the Community in the 1970s. However, it would be wrong to lay too much responsibility at the door of De Gaulle. The saga of the Luxembourg Accords and subsequent voting practice in the Council is symptomatic of how the Community has evolved, at least until the adoption of the Single European Act. The pressures of a global economy in recession, the impact of the oil crisis, the loss of confidence and prestige on the part of the Commission after the departure of President Hallstein and the effects of enlargement to incorporate countries with ever more diverse interests were all factors which contributed to the years of stagnation.

2.8   The Years of Stagnation

The years following the 1965 crisis were marked not only by a protracted legislative stalemate, but also by a general loss of momentum on the part of the Community. The politics of incremental steps to European union would normally have demanded a significant reappraisal of the direction of the Community at the conclusion of the transitional period by which time the European Community was to be one, common market. Yet creating the common market proved to be much more complicated than simply legislating for a common external tariff and prohibiting internal barriers to trade and factor movements. In fact, the hidden barriers composed of the multiplicity of national rules which govern the trading environments in each of the Member States proved resistant to removal, and, as the European economy moved into recession in the mid-1970s, underwent a revival as the Member States shifted increasingly towards national protectionism. Consequently, to say that the common market was complete at the conclusion of the transitional period would be merely an empty rhetorical statement. Attempts to move on to the logical next step – the achievement of full economic and monetary union – were entirely fruitless. The Report of the Werner Committee in 1971 setting out a timetable for the achievement of monetary union by 1980 contained unrealistic goals. Currency instabilities in the 1970s destroyed a number of attempts to peg exchange rates during that decade. The Community was too vulnerable to wider economic changes to be capable of translating any amount of goodwill into concrete progress.

Moreover, commitments such as that made at the Paris Summit in October 1972 to convert the (economic) Community into a (political) European Union proved equally worthless, as the Member States were incapable of translating words into actions. The Tindemans Report of 1975 drawn up at the instance of the European Council was left on the table by the Member States. Much the same fate was suffered by the draft 'European Act' drawn up by Genscher and Colombo, the German and Italian Foreign Ministers, which resulted only in a Solemn Declaration on European Union adopted by the European Council at Stuttgart in June 1983.

The most significant source of progress towards political union between 1970 and 1985 was the gradual increase in the intensity of intergovern-mental cooperation in the foreign policy field and its subsequent institu-tionalisation as European Political Cooperation (EPC) in Part III of the Single European Act. Wherever possible, the Community has sought to present a common face to the outside world. However political coopera-tion of this nature has always been entirely voluntary on the part of the Member States and tended, then as now, to break down in the face of serious challenges to foreign policy cohesion such as the Argentinian invasion of the Falkland Islands in 1982 and the subsequent war between the UK and Argentina.

One proposal during this period does deserve greater attention and that is the Draft Treaty establishing a European Union (DTEU) adopted in 1984 by the European Parliament, as a counterweight to the initiatives of the diplomats and national politicians. In the climate of the time, when European Union was not high on the agenda of the Member States, the sponsorship of the DTEU by the Parliament could have been seen as a vain and impotent gesture on the part of an ineffective assembly. On the contrary, the DTEU played an important if indirect part in setting the agenda of closer integration for the second half of the 1980s.

The DTEU aimed not to sweep away the Community patrimony or *acquis communautaire*, but to build on existing achievements, albeit in an entirely new Treaty. The Treaty aimed to create a federal entity displaying the features of democratic accountability of its institutions, democracy in its decision-making processes, legitimacy through its respect for funda-mental rights, and political decentralisation. The DTEU is notable for being the first semi-official Community document in which the concept of subsidiarity appeared. Article 12(2) regulates the case of concurrent competence held by the Member States and the Union:

'The Union shall only act to carry out those tasks which may be undertaken more effectively in common than by the Member States acting separately, in particular those whose execution requires action by the union because their dimension or effects extend beyond national frontiers.'

There are remarkable similarities between this formulation and that ultimately inserted in the Treaty of Maastricht.

In keeping with the tradition of European integration, the DTEU envisaged a combination of 'common action' (i.e. supranational action by the institutions of the Union) and 'cooperation' (i.e. intergovernmental decisions taken by the Member States and implemented by them). The aim of the DTEU was to create a bicameral legislature with the European Parliament – elected according to a uniform electoral system – holding equal powers with the Council of the Union. The Commission was to retain the right of initiative and the right to put forward amendments. The Draft proposed the institutionalisation of the European Council. The general policy aims of the Union would have remained broadly the same, although social policies would have been strengthened.

The fate of the DTEU is discussed in 2.10 on the relaunch of the Community.

2.9 Widening and Deepening

It should not be thought that the DTEU was the only bright spot of the post-transitional period era. On the contrary, during the 1970s and early 1980s the Community went through a significant process of widening and deepening. It was widened through the process of enlargement from Six to Twelve by 1986. This would not have occurred if the candidate countries had not seen the Community as a positive force creating increased economic and political cohesion in Europe. The Community was also deepened in two dimensions – the substantive and the constitutional.

In the domain of substantive competences, despite difficulties which can be attributed at least in part to the Luxembourg Accords, the Commission was able to persuade the Council to embark upon new legislative programmes which were not envisaged in the Treaty itself. The Community developed policies on the environment and in the field of research and development without actually holding specific powers in these areas. Creative use was made in these fields of Article 235 EEC which provides a residual general law-making power for the purposes of the achievement of the objectives of the Community where specific powers are not granted elsewhere in the Treaty. It was not difficult to argue that the environment with its obvious cross-border dimension, and research and development where cross-border cooperation can significantly increase the level and effectiveness of investment, should thus be brought within the ambit of Community policy-making, although countries such as Denmark were not wholly happy about such extensions of Community competence.

Less successful was the argument for the launch of a Community social policy. The roots of a more activist policy lay in the declaration of the Paris Summit in 1972 that the Member States attributed the same importance to energetic proceedings in the field of social policy as to the realisation of economic and monetary union, thereby seeking to give the

Community a more human face. A Social Action Programme was
elaborated by the Commission and accepted by the Council in 1974, but
it resulted in few significant legislative measures.

In the process of the constitutionalisation of the EC Treaties, the 1970s
saw a number of significant developments. The Court of Justice confirmed
the supremacy of EC law, holding that national legislation may be
'disapplied' where it is contrary to Community law (Case 106/77 *Amministrazione delle Finanze dello Stato* v. *Simmenthal (Simmenthal II)* [1978]
ECR 629). It also extended the concept of direct effect to directives,
allowing individuals to rely upon directives in national courts in order to
claim their EC rights (Case 41/74 *Van Duyn* v. *Home Office* [1974] ECR
1337). In the field of external relations, the Court developed a theory of
implied powers in Case 22/70 *Commission* v. *Council (ERTA)* ([1971] ECR
263) which considerably extended the scope of the EC's competence to
conclude international agreements in place of the Member States. Finally,
in the context of interinstitutional relations, it was established that
legislation adopted by the Council would be annulled if the Council had
failed to consult the European Parliament had where it was required to do
so (Case 138/79 *Roquette Frères* v. *Council* [1980] ECR 3333). These are
just four examples of many which illustrate that while the EC's political
system partly stagnated, the Court of Justice vigorously pushed forward
the development of the EC's legal system, considerably strengthening the
hands of individuals claiming grievances against Member States alleged
not to have observed EC law and of the supranational institutions within
the Community structure, so that when the Community finally emerged
into a period of positive growth in the political arena it was with a vastly
changed legal system (see Chapter 3 on the constitutional development of
European Union).

2.10   The Relaunch of the Community

The strong support for European Union coming from the European
Parliament in the form of the DTEU was just one of the factors which
lay behind the achievement of an interstate bargain needed to relaunch
Europe. Indeed, the immediate impact of the DTEU should not be
overestimated, since when the Draft came before the European Council
at Fontainebleau in June 1984 it was not accepted, but shifted off for
discussion to an Ad Hoc Committee on Institutional Affairs, commonly
named after its Chairman, James Dooge of Ireland. One of the first acts of
the Dooge Committee was in fact to reject the DTEU as being too radical
and open-ended, and proposing unacceptable levels of institutional reform.

On the other hand, the Dooge Committee was generally in favour of
some reforms of the EEC Treaty, proposing, by a majority of its members
(the UK opposing), the convening of an intergovernmental conference to
prepare a draft European Union Treaty. The Committee also pointed out

that certain very basic things could be done to further the objectives of the Community, and these included the completion of the unfulfilled tasks under the EEC Treaty. This Report alone, however, would not have persuaded the UK and the other Member States sceptical of deeper integration to agree to significant reforms of the Treaty. Pressure came additionally from a number of different sources.

By 1984 François Mitterrand, then President of France, had become a firm proponent of taking the European Community project further. In general he was supported by Helmut Kohl, the German Chancellor and the other half of the firm Franco-German alliance which has existed at the heart of the European Community since the conclusion of a Treaty of Friendship between the two states in 1963. In the first half of 1984, France assumed the Presidency of the Community, and Mitterrand was determined to leave his mark. He kept up pressure on the UK by making constant reference to the possibility of creating a two tier Europe, with those Member States prepared to go further forging ahead in the creation of a European Union, leaving others such as the UK behind. This was opposed by the UK which did not want to risk falling behind as had happened once before in the 1950s. Mitterrand also engineered a resolution of the long-running dispute between the UK and the Community concerning the so-called British budget rebate, which recognised that the UK was a net over-contributor to the Community budget. Between the European Councils at Brussels in March and Fontainebleau in June 1984 the European Community hovered on the brink of breakdown. Eventually, at Fontainebleau, Margaret Thatcher accepted a compromise deal very similar to one she had rejected at Brussels, and she did not oppose the creation of either the Dooge Committee or a second Ad Hoc Committee on a People's Europe, chaired by Adonnino.

At the same time, a new President of the Commission was appointed, the French socialist Jacques Delors, who resolved to mark his occupation of the post by succeeding where previous Commission Presidents had failed in revitalising the Community and re-establishing the prestige of the Commission. In choosing the programme to complete the internal market as his flagship he went back to the economic and incrementalist roots of the Community to be found in the Schuman Plan and the Spaak Report, and found a proposal which offered something to everyone – Eurosceptics, federalists, European business leaders – in its promise to bring growth to the European economy. In his task, Delors was assisted by the nomination to the Commission by Margaret Thatcher of Lord Arthur Cockfield, a committed free market liberal. Cockfield, appointed Commissioner responsible for the Internal Market, put together at the request of the European Council the so-called 'White Paper' setting out a total of nearly three hundred measures which would need to be adopted to remove the physical, technical and fiscal barriers to trade in the Community. Already in January 1985 Delors started making speeches proposing the achievement of these objectives by the end of 1992 (two terms of office for the Commission) and when the White Paper came before the European

Council at Milan in June 1985 it was unanimously accepted. Where some Member States differed from the others was with regard to the necessity for institutional reform to make the White Paper a reality. The UK argued that it was possible to complete the internal market simply through informal improvements in the decision-making processes of the Council. However, anxious to bring some concrete achievement out of the Italian Presidency, the Italian Prime Minister called for a vote on the convening of an intergovernmental conference to discuss amendments to the Treaty necessary to implement the goals of the White Paper, and, uniquely within the history of the Community, the proposal for a conference was carried by a majority vote, with the UK, Denmark and Greece opposing.

Reluctantly, the UK participated in the conference, arguing for institutional reforms including majority voting and the strengthening of the European Parliament to be limited to those measures necessary to complete the internal market. Majority voting was successfully excluded by the minimalists from the contentious areas of fiscal harmonisation, the free movement of workers and social policy. Progress towards monetary union was kept out of the main body of the Treaty, with merely a reference being made to it in the Preamble. European Political Cooperation was included in the Treaty, but although it was given an institutional framework, it was maintained on a strictly intergovernmental basis excluding the operation of the Community rules themselves. Negotiation of what became the Single European Act proceeded exceedingly quickly, and was concluded at the European Council in December 1985 in Luxembourg, ready for signature in February 1986.

At the time, the UK believed that it had scored a significant victory in removing the impetus for a two tier Europe, in persuading the rest of the Community of the benefits of the free market, and in minimising the impact of institutional reforms. Criticisms of the Single European Act came from the European Parliament which felt cheated of any role in the negotiations and objected to the outright dismissal of its initiative, and from pro-European commentators who feared that the SEA, being more intergovernmentalist in nature, might lead to a significant watering down of the supranational content of the Community and its legal order in particular. Subsequent events have, however, proved such pessimistic prognoses to be wrong, and now require a broad reassessment of the significance of the SEA, which claimed in its Preamble to be, and ultimately turned out to be, a stepping stone on the road to closer European integration.

2.11   The Single European Act

The provisions of the Single European Act can be divided into five categories. First, and foremost, there are provisions amending the EEC Treaty, with a view to the achievement of the goals of the White Paper. These comprise principally:

- (What is now) Article 7A EC, which contains a definition of the internal market and setting the deadline of 31 December 1992;
- a new law-making power to be exercised by the Council acting by a qualified majority in cooperation with the European Parliament, giving the Council the necessary means to achieve the objective in Article 7A (Article 100A EC);
- a new legislative procedure (the 'cooperation procedure') creating a Parliamentary second reading of proposed legislation, after the Council has adopted a 'common position' by a qualified majority and the Commission has reviewed the amendments proposed by the Parliament on its first reading (now Article 189C EC).

Further amendments to the EEC Treaty were introduced by the second category of provisions which consolidate *de jure* some of the extensions of competence which had occurred *de facto* since the early 1970s. An example was the amendment to what is now Article 6(2) EC to allow the Council, acting by a qualified majority in cooperation with the European Parliament, to introduce rules designed to prohibit discrimination on grounds of nationality against nationals of other Member States. Specific competences were also introduced in relation to regional development, research and technological development, and the environment, each of which was further amended by the Treaty of Maastricht (see now Articles 130A–130T EC). Finally, in this context, there were minor amendments to the Treaty provisions concerned with social policy.

The third category of provisions allowed for an important addition to the institutional structure of the Community, through the creation of a Court of First Instance, to be attached to the European Court of Justice (Article 168A EC). This Court was set up by Council Decision and commenced work in 1989.

The last two categories of provisions did not amend the EEC Treaty itself. In other words, they did not form part of the supranational corpus of EC law, but operated in the conventional realm of international law. Title I of the Single European Act consolidated and institutionalised the activities of the European Council, until then merely an *ad hoc* and informal gathering of the Heads of State or Government of the Member States. It was now required to meet at least twice a year and the leaders were assisted by their Foreign Ministers and a Member of the Commission (conventionally the President) (see now Article D TEU).

Finally, Title III of the Single European Act put the practice of European Political Cooperation (EPC) on a much firmer footing. Throughout this Title, the Member States were referred to as the High Contracting Parties, thereby stressing the intergovernmental nature of EPC; however, there were linkages with the Community's institutional structure in so far as the Ministers of Foreign Affairs meeting within the context of EPC were chaired by the representative of whichever Member State held the Presidency of the Council. The Commission was 'fully associated' with the work of EPC (Article 30(3)(b) SEA) and the

Presidency was responsible for informing the European Parliament of the foreign policy issues currently at issue within EPC. The voluntarist nature of EPC was stressed by Article 30(1), which merely bound the High Contracting Parties to 'endeavour jointly to formulate and implement a European foreign policy' (see 2.15–2.16 for important changes to the nature of foreign policy cooperation introduced by the Treaty of Maastricht).

2.12   After the Single European Act

The immediate prognosis for the Single European Act was not good. It encountered harsh criticism on account of the vagueness of its wording, the many derogations which it allowed Member States, and its assertion that completing the internal market was somehow a new goal for a Community which since 1958 has always been committed to creating a common market (Pescatore, 1987). These criticisms, however, fail to take into account that progress for the Community must always take the form of delicate interstate bargains, which themselves may be transformed into more positive achievements by subsequent political events and by the willingness of the institutions and the Member States to implement the provisions in good faith. By 1985 the Community was suffering a serious crisis of legitimacy. It was seen by many to be a lame duck since it could never deliver on its grandiose aims, and the much vaunted common market was quite clearly a chimera. The Community lurched from one crisis to another, beset by budgetary indiscipline, agricultural spending spiralling out of control, and the lack of an obvious contribution which it could make to the pursuit of macroeconomic growth in Europe. In the event, the Single European Act revitalised the fortunes of the Community, as the Member States became involved in a project for which all had enthusiasm. The 'Christmas Tree' (i.e. overoptimistic) economic analysis (up to 5 million new jobs; an increase in 5–7 per cent of GDP) of the team of economists charged by the Commission with the task of estimating the macroeconomic benefits of the single market or, to put it another way, the 'costs of non-Europe', generally prevailed over more sober judgments of the negative effects of uncontrolled industrial restructuring on more vulnerable regions (Cecchini, 1988; Cutler *et al.*, 1989).

From most perspectives, the progress made by the institutions towards the completion of the 1992 programme was impressive. The Commission rapidly put forward proposals for the bulk of the three hundred or so measures envisaged by the White Paper. The Council streamlined its decision-making machinery, adopting an amendment to its working procedures to allow any one member of the Council, or the representative of the Commission who attends without a vote, to call for a vote on a measure. This, coupled with a new willingness not to seek to rely upon the Luxembourg Accords, led to a remarkable acceleration in the legislative process. However, very many important and contentious measures still needed to be adopted unanimously, and in this context the old practice of building 'packages' which offer something for everyone in return for compromises has continued. That was evident in July 1992 when the important fiscal harmonisation measures were agreed by the Council with the UK conceding the power of the Community to set VAT rates in return for concessions on a favourable taxation level for Scotch whisky, an important UK export.

The European Parliament meanwhile continued to make full use of the limited powers which were conceded to it, maintaining its fruitful alliance with the Commission in order to exercise maximum influence over the legislative procedure at both first reading and second reading. It sought to protect the use of the cooperation procedure by preventing the Council from using legal bases within the Treaty for measures which require a lower level of Parliamentary input. It did this by supporting Commission litigation in the Court of Justice and by bringing actions in its own name, seeking the annulment of measures enacted on the basis of the 'incorrect' legal basis. It enjoyed a mixed degree of success (on legal basis litigation see 5.2 and 5.17).

As progress was made quite rapidly towards the completion of the legislative goals set in the Single Market programme, extensive use was made of a new style of minimalist regulation by the institutions, which introduced essentially a new technique for harmonising the legislations of the Member States. In its case law on barriers to trade between the Member States, the Court of Justice had already made an important contribution to the goals of the internal market by holding that where a product is lawfully put on the market and sold in one Member State, it cannot normally be excluded from the market in the other Member States. Products must be allowed to benefit from production in one trading environment and sale in another, unless the Member State seeking to impede import or marketing can successfully argue that the rules which it is applying to the imported product (and to identical national products) are necessary for the protection of certain mandatory interests such as consumer protection, health and safety or the protection of the environment. The Commission then altered its policy on the harmonisation of national laws in order to incorporate this principle of mutual recognition. Measures put forward for adoption set only basic minimum standards for products which, if complied with, guarantee the right to free movement. This approach has obvious attractions for states such as the UK which have been pursuing a vigorous deregulatory approach at national level, and have argued for the adoption of this approach at Community level. The argument is that this approach sets the stage for products to compete freely in a wider market, with consumers effectively choosing the type of trading (and, therefore, regulatory) environment in which they would like products to be produced. Consumer lawyers have countered by pointing out the risk that hard won gains at national level in the field of consumer protection may be destroyed by a Community-wide deregulatory approach.

2.13   The Social Dimension of the Internal Market

The apparent victory of free market economics within the internal market did not wholly remain unnoticed by social policy-makers, trade unions and politicians on the political left. For example, while sponsoring the political and economic relaunch of the Community through the internal market programme, President Mitterrand constantly made clear his interest in creating a 'Social Europe'. However, his proposal for a 'European social space' in which basic principles for the protection of workers were to be introduced at a mandatory Community level languished at the bottom of the agenda until it was picked by the Belgian Presidency in 1987 with the proposal for a 'plinth of social rights'. Soon thereafter, in February 1988, some of the problems of the anticipated differential regional effects of the internal market – one of the other central 'social' concerns of the Community – were resolved at the Community level by an agreement in the European Council to restructure the European Regional Development Fund and the European Social Fund in order to channel more EC resources into regional development measures and away from the apparently bottomless pit of the CAP.

This was followed by the adoption by eleven of the twelve Member States (the UK dissenting) of a Community Charter of Fundamental Social Rights Workers at Strasbourg in December 1989. It contains a declaration on the part of the signatories that the implementation of the Single European Act must 'take full account of the social dimension of the Community', and a statement of basic social rights of workers including freedom of movement, the right to fair remuneration, the importance of the improvement of living and working conditions, and the right to adequate social protection. This purely declaratory measure, to which the Commission attached an Action Programme containing a resumé of the measures which it intended to propose, was supposed to revitalise the social policy of the Community, just like the Social Action Programme of the 1970s. The results of the initiative were just as disappointing, since the political will amongst the Member States proved lacking, and the EC Treaty remained weak on the social policy front, requiring in all cases except health and safety at work a unanimous vote for the adoption of social policy measures.

The Social Charter is not binding and it introduced no new law-making powers into the Treaty. It also declares – with explicit reference to the principle of subsidiarity – that implementation of many of the rights is the responsibility of the Member States, not the EC itself. This accords with the view of some Member States such as the UK, that the EC should be minimally concerned with social policy, which it alleges is irrelevant to the achievement of the internal market and a matter for resolution at national level. For the UK, social policy became almost a symbol of its reserved sphere of national sovereignty. A new phase in the history of social policy opened up with the Social Policy Agreement which was attached to the Treaty of Maastricht (see 2.15).

2.14   Towards a Treaty on European Union

Despite the failure of the Single European Act significantly to extend the overall ambit of the Community's activities, Jacques Delors did succeed after 1986 in keeping economic and monetary union and institutional reform on the diplomatic agenda. A positive note was maintained by the February 1988 agreement on budgetary discipline and reform of the structural funds. Soon afterwards in June 1988 the Hanover European Council reaffirmed the Community's commitment to the progressive realisation of EMU, and charged a committee chaired by Delors himself with the task of identifying the concrete stages needed to realise that aim.

The Delors Committee reported in April 1989. Its report identified the three basic attributes of monetary union: full currency convertibility, complete integration of financial markets and irrevocable locking of exchange rates. The Treaties already provided for the first two attributes to be achieved. The Report therefore concentrated on the third attribute, focusing on the need not only for exchange rates to be locked, but on the further step of the adoption of a single currency which would demonstrate the irreversibility of monetary union and remove the transaction costs of converting national currencies. However, without a convergence of economic conditions in the Member States and the adoption of certain common macroeconomic policies, even the locking of exchange rates cannot be successfully achieved. The Report therefore identified a crucial second stage in the achievement of monetary union in which budget deficits would be limited and European level institutions would be introduced which would gradually assume responsibility for monetary policy and exchange rate and reserve management. This would follow an initial stage (which began in July 1990) in which all the European Community currencies would be brought within the exchange rate mechanism ('ERM') of the European Monetary System (EMS) which controls exchange rate fluctuations, and in which fiscal coordination is gradually intensified. The final third stage would begin with the irrevocable locking of exchange rates and a European Central Bank taking over the role of national central banks.

The Report did not receive unanimous acceptance from the Member States; in particular, disagreement existed on when the various stages should begin, on whether transition from Stage Two to Stage Three would be automatic and fixed in advance, on whether all currencies would be replaced by the new currency and on whether the new Community banking institutions should be independent of control by politicians as they are in Germany. The UK favoured not a single currency, but a 'common currency' in which a hard, convertible ECU would be created which would compete with national currencies and might gradually supersede them. Against the opposition of the UK, the other eleven governments agreed at the Rome European Council in October 1990 that Stage Two would begin in January 1994, and this date was provided for by Article 109E(1) EC, as amended by the Treaty of Maastricht. The UK did agree, however, to the convening of an intergovernmental conference on Economic and Monetary Union and this started work in December 1990.

Some Member States were unwilling to allow the Community to continue along the path towards EMU without significant moves towards Political Union involving the extension of the competence of the Community, and the enhancement of the democratic accountability of its institutions. Chancellor Kohl, for example, knew that a Treaty under which the Member States transferred significant competence in economic and monetary policy-making to the Community would not be acceptable either to the German Parliament, the *Bundestag*, or to the *Länder*, unless the loss of democratic input into policy-making at national level were at least in part matched by an increase in democratic input at the Community level. President Mitterrand also supported further moves to Political Union. Consequently, a parallel intergovernmental conference on Political Union was convened to consider the competences of the Union, in particular competences in foreign affairs, defence and collective security, and the institutions necessary to make the Union operational.

The outcome of diplomatic hard bargaining was the Treaty of Maastricht, agreed by the Heads of State or Government in December 1991 and signed in February 1992. The Treaty formed the results of two separate bargaining processes, brought together only at the final stage. There was little interaction between the two conferences. After the departure of Margaret Thatcher and the arrival of John Major as British Prime Minister in late 1990, the UK was able to sign up to a Treaty laying down the stages for the achievement of EMU, while retaining the right as laid down in a Protocol not to proceed to participate in the third stage of monetary union (a similar Protocol is provided for Denmark, which might require a referendum before participation). However, in contrast to the positive progress on EMU the results of the debates on Political Union were much more modest changes. The IGC was unable to reach a single conclusion on the introduction of significantly enlarged competences and decision-making powers for the institutions in respect of social policy. Major refused to accept a new 'Social Chapter', and this was eventually concluded amongst the other eleven Member States as a separate Social Policy Protocol and Agreement outside the legal framework of the EC Treaty. Foreign policy also remained outside the structures of the Community proper, and, like the new field of cooperation in the internal fields of home affairs, immigration, asylum and the administration of justice, which codified existing informal arrangements, was given a separate intergovernmental 'pillar' operating alongside the supranational 'Community' pillar within the framework of an overarching European Union.

2.15 After the IGCs: the Struggle for Ratification of 'Maastricht'

The difficulties encountered in a number of Member States in gaining political and popular acceptance of the Treaty of Maastricht, as required by the various ratification processes in the different states, were unprecedented in the history of amendments to the founding Treaties of the European Communities. For a number of months, it was doubtful whether the Treaty of Maastricht would even come into force, as ratification by all Member States is required of any Treaties amending the original Treaties of Rome. These difficulties have proved extremely significant in that they have affected the progress that the 'new' European Union has made since its inception. The feeling of popular disempowerment and disillusionment felt in a number of Member States and expressed in the ratification referendums of Denmark and France has challenged the legitimacy of the process of European integration, and its institutional forms, in a manner which may well shape aspects of the 1996 IGC.

The entry into force of the Treaty of Maastricht was originally foreseen for 1 January 1993. It eventually came into force on 1 November 1993, following protracted ratification procedures in particular in Denmark, France, Germany and the United Kingdom. Even in those Member States where ratification was relatively straightforward in political terms, complex constitutional amendments were required on matters such as the transfer of powers to the institutions of monetary unions, and giving effect to the concept of Union citizenship. It was the first Danish referendum in June 1992, in which – contrary to the urgings of all the main political parties – ratification was rejected by a majority of 47,000 votes, which threw the ratification process seriously off balance. For example, it was agreed in the UK to postpone further parliamentary debate regarding ratification until after a second (at then, as yet unplanned) Danish referendum. Hoping to relaunch 'Maastricht', as well as to benefit from internal divisions amongst opposition politicians, Mitterand called a strictly unnecessary referendum in France which led to a very narrow (51.05 per cent to 48.95 per cent) popular vote in favour in September 1992. This too contributed to the feeling that something was seriously amiss both in the content of the Treaty itself, and in the procedures whereby it had been agreed amongst the politicians.

Responding to the malaise, the European Council meeting in Edinburgh in December 1992 under the UK Presidency attempted to meet Danish concerns about political sovereignty halfway, without actually reopening the text of the Treaty, by accepting certain declarations, particularly on Economic and Monetary Union. The compromise achieved was of dubious legal status, but the position taken has never been formally challenged in any way. The European Council also discussed in detail the implementation of the subsidiarity concept introduced by the Treaty, stressing that part of the concept which is concerned with 'closeness of the citizen'. That has been a significant leitmotiv of political rhetoric on EU governance ever since then, along with the principles of 'openness' and 'transparency'.

Picking up the pieces in Denmark, a new coalition government, supported by most opposition parties, led a successful campaign for ratification in a second referendum in May 1993. The 'yes' vote was 56.8 per cent. When the matter returned to the UK Parliament, however, an atmosphere of hostility to Maastricht almost prevailed, particularly when Conservative Euro-sceptic rebels entered an unholy alliance with opposition parties which objected to Major's failure to accept the Social Policy Agreement. Only the calling of a vote of confidence by Major on 24 July 1993 secured the passage of the Bill.

Meanwhile, in Germany a different type of ratification problem had emerged. Political ratification procedures, including extensive constitutional amendments, were completed in December 1992. However, a number of objectors to more intensive integration brought a constitutional challenge to the conformity of the Treaty with the newly amended Basic Law before the Federal Constitutional Court in Karlsruhe. This delayed ratification by some eight months, and although the Court ultimately ruled against the applicants it delivered a judgment which appears to place strict limitations upon the constitutional possibilities of European Union, when they are set against the background of the German Basic Law and the prerequisites of German sovereignty (*Brunner* [1994] 1 CMLR 57). The German challenge to European constitutionalism is discussed in 3.3.

2.16   The Treaty of Maastricht

The basis of the integration process since 1993 is now the European Union, established by Article A TEU; it represents

> 'a new stage in the process of creating an ever closer union among the peoples of Europe, in which decisions are taken as closely as possible to the citizen.'

This latter point is a reference to the principle of subsidiarity, further defined in Article 3B EC (see 1.4 and 1.5). That provision also confirms that the Community is a body with only 'limited powers' conferred on it under the Treaties. At the insistence of the UK a reference to the 'federal vocation' of the Union was removed and in Article F(1) TEU an explicit commitment is made to the Union respecting the national identities of the constituent states. Article F(2) seeks to protect citizens further by providing a (non-justiciable) guarantee of the protection of fundamental rights as 'as guaranteed by the European Convention for the Protection of Human Rights and Fundamental Freedoms' and as they result from the constitutional traditions common to the Member States, as general principles of Community law'. Article A also sets out the structure of the Union, which is based on the European Community, with its strongly supranational institutional systems, 'supplemented by the forms of cooperation established by this Treaty'. These, as noted above (see also Fig 1.1), are the two pillars of foreign policy (Common Foreign and Security Policy – CFSP) and home affairs (Cooperation in Justice and Home Affairs – CJHA). The unity of these separate pillars is, however, protected by Article C TEU which provides that the Union shall be served by a 'single institutional framework' which builds on the existing Community institutional framework. Article C also seeks to preserve the '*acquis communautaire*', that is the body of achievements within the framework of 'Community' treaties. The EEC Treaty is renamed the European Community Treaty.

Titles V and VI of the Treaty of Union set out the provisions on CFSP (second pillar) and CJHA (third pillar). The CFSP provisions build on Part III of the Single European Act, but with significant extensions. An element of defence and security policy is introduced within the scope of CFSP. The prospect of an eventual common defence policy and a common defence is foreseen by Article J.4 TEU, which also calls upon the WEU, enjoying its late revival in importance, to implement actions of the Union which have defence implications. This has been agreed by the Member States notwithstanding that some Member States have a policy of neutrality, and not all are members of the WEU. The second innovation is in Article J.3 which provides for joint action to be agreed upon where appropriate by a qualified majority. This significantly strengthens the supranational character of CFSP at the expense of intergovernmentalism. Such joint actions appear to be binding in that they 'commit the Member States in the positions they adopt and in the conduct of their activity' (Article J.3(4) TEU), although it is not clear what sanctions for non-compliance might be. The European Council is given a particularly important position in defining the 'principles' and 'general guidelines' of CFSP (Article J.8(1) TEU). A Political Committee of Political Directors from the Member States monitors the day to day international situation, and provides the essential back-up to the political decision-making. In contrast, the Commission and especially the Parliament have a very restricted role in relation to CFSP.

The provisions on Justice and Home Affairs are concerned with issues of immigration and asylum policy, police cooperation, judicial cooperation and the residence of third country nationals within the EU. Interstate cooperation in this context might typically involve either the conclusion of international agreements between the Member States or the formulation and implementation of joint positions or actions (Article K.3(2) TEU). The relationship with the competence of the EC strictly defined is a difficult question, and matters are complicated by the creation of a number of bridges ('*passerelles*') allowing for the accretion of competence in this field by the EC institutions (Article 100C(6) EC and Article K.9 TEU) on the unanimous agreement of the Member States in Council, and the ratification of any such agreement by the Member States. As with CFSP a 'Coordinating Committee' of senior national officials (Article K.4 TEU) plays an important role in coordinating and guiding general CJHA policy, and the Commission and the Parliament are correspondingly restricted. Under both intergovernmental pillars, the Court of Justice has essentially no role to play, unless it is explicitly given one in relation to Conventions concluded within the framework of CJHA.

The provisions on EMU (Articles 3A, 4A, 102A–109M EC and additional Protocols) lay down the timetable for the achievement of monetary union and the convergence conditions for the national economies which will be needed to be satisfied if the shift to irrevocably fixed exchange rates is not to be accompanied by damage to some of the EU economies. Stage Two began on 1 January 1994, and Stage Three should begin on 1 January 1997 or, if delayed by the Council, 1 January 1999. The number of participating currencies will depend upon the achievement of the convergence criteria, and the decisions of the UK and Denmark under their respective 'opt-out' Protocols. The Treaty provides for a European Monetary Institute which is taking monetary policy forward to the third stage when it will be superseded by a European Central Bank (ECB), operating within a European System of Central Banks. Significantly, the Treaty opted for the 'German' approach, with an independent central bank, set apart from short-term political pressures. Decisions in relation to progress to monetary union are to be taken by majority votes in many instances.

Other amendments to the European Community Treaty itself come within the context of Political Union. These include a new form of legislative procedure popularly termed 'co-decision' which further extends the powers of the Parliament, but at the expense of increasing the complexity of the already burdensome procedures (Article 189B EC). Such measures are signed jointly by the Presidents of the Council and the Parliament. This procedure applies in a significant number of cases, although existing procedures are also retained. The duration and mandate of the European Commission was synchronised with that of the European Parliament, and the membership of the Commission is now approved by the Parliament. This approach was taken for the first time with the arrival of a new Commission at the beginning of 1994, when Hearings of individual Commissioners-elect were held by the Parliament. Many underwent quite harsh scrutiny. This increases the accountability of the Commission, although there were no changes in the Treaty to the accountability of the unelected and secretive Council. The Treaty also enshrines the right of citizens to petition the European Parliament, and empowers the Parliament to set up Committees of Inquiry to investigate allegations of maladministration by the Community institutions. The appointment of an Ombudsman was also provided for, and after some delay an appointment was made by the Parliament in 1995. One final important institutional innovation is the creation of a Committee of the Regions to represent the particular interests of the Regions.

The substantive changes to the European Community Treaty outside the field of EMU are relatively modest. A concept of Union citizenship was introduced, but the attributes of citizenship are relatively insignificant in comparison to the attributes of national citizenship. They comprise principally the right of free movement, the right to stand and vote in municipal elections and elections to the European Parliament anywhere in the Union (new Articles 8–8E EC), as well as certain rights to consular protection. Social policy within the Treaty itself underwent certain minor amendments, with the more significant amendments proposed by the Dutch Presidency being relegated to a Protocol and Agreement giving the UK its so-called social policy opt-out. This delegates to the Member States other than the UK, by agreement of all Member States, the power to adopt social policy measures using the procedures and institutions of the European Community. Vocational training is now regulated in more detail by the Treaty itself, and it is joined by general provisions on education, culture, health policy, consumer protection, industrial policy and development aid policy. Further amendments to the provisions on economic and social cohesion (including the creation of a Cohesion Fund), research and development policy and environmental policy were introduced. Legislative measures in all these policy areas, where the EC holds concurrent powers with the Member States, are subject to the principle of subsidiarity enshrined in Article 3B EC, which prescribes a test of the efficiency and necessity of EU action. In the sphere of the internal market and the external trade policy of the EU, changes are limited to introducing in certain fields the 'co-decision' procedure, and to altering certain aspects of the negotiation of external agreements with third countries.

In the final provisions to the Treaty of Maastricht, changes to the procedures for revising the Treaties were introduced, and the convening of a conference of government representatives in 1996 to review progress towards political union was provided for. While the Commission considered the progress towards Political Union contained in the Treaty to be modest, it considered it to be a worthwhile victory to persuade the Member States to commit themselves in advance to review progress.

One distinctive feature of the Treaty of Maastricht, which is perhaps explicable by reference to difficulties in the negotiating process, is the proliferation of declarations and Protocols attached to the Treaty. Some of these were strictly necessary (e.g. Protocol on the Statute of the European System of Central Banks and of the European Central Bank), but others were attached for the simple reason of appeasing certain Member States (e.g. Protocol on ownership of second homes in Denmark; Declaration on the outermost regions of the EC) or, more sinisterly, of correcting a Court of Justice judgment perceived by the Member States to go too far in extending the impact of EC law or to impose excessive burdens (e.g. Protocol on the *Barber* judgment, concerned with limiting its temporal impact upon retirement pension schemes).

The remaining paragraphs of this chapter are concerned with providing a brief review of the development of EU policies – internal and external – since the coming into force of the Treaty of Maastricht, with the intention thereby of focusing attention on the major outstanding challenges facing the integration project in the last years of the twentieth century.

2.17   Internal Policy After the End of 1992

Since the end of 1992, by which time the internal market legislative programme had largely been completed on schedule, the emphasis in internal policy has shifted towards the management of the internal market, the continued progress towards the liberalisation of public procurement and highly regulated markets such as telecommunications, and the enhancement of flanking policies such as those on economic and social cohesion, social affairs and employment, industrial affairs, the environment and transport. However, the Commission's legislative programmes have sought to reflect the need to implement the subsidiarity principle, with an emphasis on fewer, less complex and less restrictive legislative measures. This is partly in response to the influential Sutherland and Molitor Reports on the Internal Market and Legislative Simplification, respectively (5.10). Perhaps the most important omission from the legislative structure of the internal market is a measure on the removal of internal border controls on movements of people, required by Article 7A EC, although the Commission has now put forward specific proposals. There is an overlap between 'EC' action in this sphere, and 'EU' action under the third pillar (see 2.19). The Commission has also sought to ensure the concentration of the institutions on the stabilisation of the EU finances, and on the fight against fraud, which is particularly problematic in the agricultural field.

In contrast to earlier periods of development of the European Community, the Court of Justice has been relatively cautious in its approach to the interpretation of the Treaties and secondary legislation. This may be related to the impact of the Treaty of Maastricht, particularly the clear attempts to restrict the role of the Court on the part of the Member States, and fears that an over-bold approach during the mid-1990s might lead the Member States in the 1996 IGC to impose further restrictions on the powers of the Court. There have not been wholesale revisions of earlier case law, but, as will become clear during the course of the chapters which follow, it has more frequently been the case that the Court has not seized opportunities for 'pro-integrationist' or 'pro-Union' interpretations which it might have taken in the past when its case law was subject to less close political scrutiny than it has been in recent years.

2.18   Progress towards Economic and Monetary Union

Optimism, even when it emerged that the Treaty of Maastricht was facing ratification difficulties, that the path to increased integration via monetary union was much more solid than that offered by political union was blown out of the water in 1992 and 1993 by the crisis in the ERM. This resulted initially in the withdrawal of sterling on 'Black Wednesday' (16 September 1992) as a result of international currency pressures, and then, even more seriously, in the effective collapse of the ERM in July–August 1993 when pressure specifically on the French franc forced the bands within which currencies should circulate to be widened from 2.25 per cent to 15 per cent. Thus, just as currencies should have been converging and becoming more closely 'locked' together in preparation for the second stage of monetary union which began on 1 January 1994, they were effectively blown apart. Only the Deutschmark and the Dutch gilder are now tied together within narrower bands and the timetable for the third stage now seems implausible. Monetary Union, with the irrevocable locking of exchange rates, is unlikely before the end of the century, even though in December 1995 the European Council resolved to give the anticipated single currency the rather colourless name of 'Euro', a decision derided by the UK Prime Minister Major as 'irrelevant'.

Progress on the convergence criteria other than exchange rates has been equally problematic. These concern budget deficits, public debts, long-term interest rates, and inflation rates. Only Luxembourg and Germany, of those states most interested in monetary union, seem likely to be able to comply. In the second stage of EMU, with the creation of the European Monetary Institute (the forerunner of the central bank), which is situated in Frankfurt, the emphasis has shifted towards the analysis and management of economic policy. Member States are now being tied to ever more binding guidelines on the management of economic policy, including a power on the part of the Commission to monitor budget deficits in the Member States and to recommend to the Member States that they should remedy the position if these are deemed 'excessive'. Even so, these mechanisms seem unlikely to deliver convergence in the face of continued economic and fiscal difficulties faced by most Member States.

2.19 The 'Third Pillar', the Schengen Agreements, and Immigration and Asylum Policies

Slow progress has been made since 1993 in the implementation of the 'Third Pillar'. In terms of the creation of a framework for internal free movement of persons, and a common external policy on immigration, asylum, visas and border control, the formal Cooperation in Justice and Home Affairs has yet to supplant fully existing systems of cooperation based on intergovernmentalism. A smaller number of states operate now a system of open borders based on the Schengen Agreements of 1985 and 1990. This excludes the UK, and also falls outside the framework of the EU. Other conventions on Europol, the crossing of external borders and certain aspects of asylum laws have not yet been brought into force, although *de facto* asylum practices in particular have become more restrictive in recent years in many European countries, and there has been some convergence of such practices. The frequently informal basis for the intergovernmental contacts which underlie such practices has been much criticised as threatening civil liberties. CJHA has not lived up to the hopes that it might provide a structured environment within which the EU Member States could face up to the demographic and political challenges posed by movements of people within and across continents. The types of 'joint action' foreseen in the third pillar have been disappointing: the most far-reaching proposals concerning action on racism and xenophobia were vetoed by the UK in late 1995.

2.20   External Trade and the Conclusion of the Uruguay Round

Since the Treaty of Maastricht was signed, the external trading environment of the EU has changed dramatically with the conclusion of the GATT 'Uruguay Round', the extension of global trading regulation into new fields such as trade in services, and the creation of the World Trade Organisation. The EU and its Member States have participated jointly in the international agreements relating to the WTO. For the Commission, which had sought to assert the exclusive power of the EU to participate without the Member States, a ruling by the Court of Justice confirming the continuing rights of the Member States was a major disappointment (see 3.12). Meanwhile the substantial completion of the internal market programme has enhanced the EU's position as a global trading force, and 1994 saw the enactment of most of the legislation needed to complete the external dimension of the internal market in terms of creating a common external frontier in relation to third country products.

2.21   The Development of the Common Foreign and Security Policy

As with CJHA, the operation of CFSP has not entirely lived up to the challenges that the EU has faced. Since 1993, in particular with the upheaval in the Balkans, these challenges have been substantial. Largely ineffectual action in Bosnia has been accompanied by a serious challenge to the authority of the EU, and the binding force of its legal order, posed by the unilateral economic sanctions imposed by Greece on the Former Yugoslav Republic of Macedonia. The ineffectiveness of EU action was also highlighted by the serious political problems in Rwanda. Frequent inability to obtain an appropriate consensus on joint action has been exacerbated by difficulties regarding the funding of such action as has been agreed, with serious doubts as to whether appropriate budgetary and consultative mechanisms involving the European Parliament have been put in place. Overall, doubts can be raised as to whether or not CFSP is any more effective in building a common identity in foreign policy matters for the EU than the more intergovernmental approach of European Political Cooperation which preceded it was for the EC.

2.22 Responding to Changed Political and Economic Circumstances in Europe

Whatever the level of internal popular disillusionment, it remains the case that the EU represents a substantial pole of attraction for many of the states of Central and Eastern Europe (as well as the states of the Mediterranean); they see membership as the logical conclusion of the process of political and economic transformation which began with the removal of the Iron Curtain and the break up of the Soviet Union. The EU cannot ignore these challenges, particularly if it wishes to avoid the accusation that it is a 'rich country club'. Faced with a number of applications for membership, the EU has sought to draw on the experience of the past by identifying stages of cooperation and integration with the EU through which applicants may pass on the way to membership. This is the approach taken in particular with the four so-called 'Visegrad' countries (Poland, Czech Republic, Slovakia, and Hungary) which can make out perhaps the best case for relatively prompt membership, based on the modernisation of their economic and political systems, and their capacity for economic growth and prosperity. These countries are currently linked to the EU through 'Europe Agreements' establishing bilateral free trading areas with the EU, and amongst themselves by the Central European Free Trade Area agreement. It is possible that they may pass in due course through the EEA, as a closer 'waiting room' for membership. Bulgaria and Romania also have Europe Agreements, but are not such immediate candidates for membership.

Further east there are additional candidates for membership, such as the Baltic states, currently linked to the EU by Partnership and Cooperation Agreements. Other countries carved out of the former Soviet Union, including Russia itself, also have similar agreements which do not provide for the same degree of economic integration as a Europe Agreement. Relations with the countries of the former Soviet Union are focused not only on the accepted need to widen the EU, but also on the need to foster the maximum degree of political stability in a highly volatile geographical area, particularly around the Black and Caspian Seas.

2.23 Towards the 1996 IGC

Internally, the greatest challenge which faced the EU soon after the ink was dry on the ratification processes for the Treaty of Maastricht was the preparation of the next Intergovernmental Conference, foreseen in Article N TEU to review the operation of that Treaty. This began in March 1996 in Turin. During the course of 1995 preparations became increasingly intense: the Council charged a Reflection Group, composed of representatives of the Member States, the Commission and the European Parliament with drawing up reports highlighting important agenda items and identifying the main areas for discussion. Each of the institutions also submitted a separate report. At one level the agenda is substantive, in that it concerns specific policy areas – particularly those of the EU second and third pillar – where reform might be desirable. Also to be addressed are questions concerning the institutional configuration of the EC and the EU, the law-making processes, the role of the Commission and the Parliament, and even the role of the Court of Justice. There exists also the possibility of providing through the Treaties in a formalised way for some form of multispeed Europe, perhaps in relation to areas like environmental policy where future Member States may find full compliance with standards imposed almost impossible, and overburdensome. Many of the questions addressed by the IGC can be gathered under the broad rubric of 'efficiency'. At a deeper level, the IGC is concerned, however, with much more fundamental questions about the legitimacy of the EU institutions, and even the *raison d'être* of the entire integration project in its current form. The existing treaties urgently need reform and simplification to make them into some sort of accessible constitutional document. Beyond the rhetoric of transparency and 'closeness to the citizen' much used in recent years, genuine citizenship involvement and commitment with the EU does need to be facilitated, in order to ensure that more support does not ebb away. Some suggest inventing a new working method for the EU, abandoning

> 'the traditional Monnet-Hallstein method of the "benign conspiracy". According to this method the EU operates with a process of small, gradual, technical adaptations without publicly clarifying the long-term political objectives. In the post-Cold War context the direct external threat to Western Europe has disappeared, and the whole of Europe is now involved in a democratic renaissance. In this context the old 'benign conspiracy' is not only inadequate but directly counter-productive . . .' (Gustavsson, 1996: 223).

Consequently, the process of reform itself is also under scrutiny, since the type of hidden and exclusionary debate which marked the pre-Maastricht IGCs, if repeated once more, is quite likely to lead at the end to popular rejection of compromise solutions agreed between politicians. One way of proceeding was suggested by the Parliament in its 1994 Resolution on the Constitution of the European Union (OJ 1994 C61/155), which would have involved the Parliament itself and the national parliaments in a constitution-building process. It was rejected, in favour of the use of the 'traditional' intergovernmental method (3.4). Ultimately, therefore, the 1996 IGC is involving the political elites of the Member States in the attempt to draw a fine balance between preserving the practices of interstate negotiation fundamental to international relations, and enabling popular participation and empowerment so as to ensure that the results of the interstate bargains are not lost at the very end.

Summary

1 The unification of the nation states of Europe has been a consistent theme in political thinking for many centuries. Only since the Second World War has significant progress been made towards realising the ideals of a unified Europe.

2 In postwar Europe, a number of intergovernmental organisations were set up, attracting a wide membership. These included the Council of Europe, the OEEC and the WEU. Tighter supranational forms of integration attracted fewer members; the original ECSC, EEC and Euratom were composed of just six members.

3 The ECSC emerged out of a French proposal to put key strategic commodities under international control. It was followed by the unsuccessful initiative for a European Defence Community, and then the relaunch of economic integration in the form of the EEC and Euratom. The thinking behind these proposals was guided by neo-functionalism.

4 The early years of the European Community were years of economic boom and great progress was made towards completing the customs union within the agreed timetable. Less progress was made towards the completion of the common market. In 1965–66, the Community encountered a serious crisis when France withdrew from participation in protest at the move to qualified majority voting.

5 The Luxembourg Accords which brought this crisis to an end effectively committed the Community to consensus-based decision-making, a pattern which was broken only after the adoption of the Single European Act in 1986.

6 Thereafter came years of stagnation, with a legislative blockage in the Council. This was exacerbated by a period of deep economic recession in Europe, and an increase rather than a decrease in protectionist measures erected by Member States. No proposals for advancing the structures of integration, for example through monetary union, had a serious chance of success.

7 Meanwhile, the Community had enlarged, and was consolidating its activities in certain areas, such as the CAP. Integration was largely led by the Court of Justice, which developed a strongly supranational case law.

8 The relaunch of the Community came in 1985–86, with a conjunction of factors, including the arrival of a new dynamic President of the Commission (Delors), the commitment of key political leaders such as Mitterrand and Kohl to further integration, and the realisation that the Community must revitalise itself in order to survive.

9 The adoption of the 1992 Single Market Programme and the amendments to the Treaty of Rome through the Single European Act 1986 have proved catalysts for a recovery of prestige and effectiveness of the Community, with a huge increase in the rate of adoption for legislation.

10 While progress continued on the completion of the single or internal market, economic and monetary union and political union returned to the agenda. A committee chaired by Delors put forward a step-by-step proposal for the achievement of monetary union.

11 Twin intergovernmental conferences were convened in 1990 on EMU and Political Union and were concluded at Maastricht in December 1991. The Treaty of Maastricht was ratified nearly a year late, after encountering significant popular opposition in the UK, Denmark and France.

12 The Treaty of Maastricht introduced a new framework for European integration: the European Union. Two additional pillars concerned with intergovernmental cooperation in foreign affairs and home affairs now flank the 'Community' pillar, which itself has been strengthened principally by the introduction of provisions intended to bring about EMU before the end of the century.

13 Progress in existing and new policy fields in the EC/EU has been slow since the ratification of the Treaty of Maastricht. EMU in particular seems unlikely to be achieved within the timetable foreseen. Cooperation in Justice and Home Affairs has yet to become properly established; the Common Foreign and Security Policy has not provided the answers to the challenges faced by the Member States in the foreign policy field.

14 The Treaty of Maastricht provided for an intergovernmental conference to be convened in 1996 to review the experience of operating that Treaty. This IGC faces particular challenges concerned the legitimacy of the integration project as presently constituted.

Questions

1 In what ways does the early history of the Community illustrate the strengths and weaknesses of the ideas about European integration discussed in Chapter 1?

2 How did the crisis of 'empty chair politics' affect the subsequent evolution of the Community?

3 Is it fair to describe the UK as an 'awkward partner in Europe' (George, 1990)?

4 Is the deepening of the European Union through the Treaty of Maastricht and progress towards economic and monetary union the correct response to the pressures currently affecting the process of European integration?

5 How should the 1996 IGC seek to overcome the difficulties which faced the ratification of the Treaty of Maastricht?

Further Reading

Anderson, den Boer, and Miller (1994), 'European Citizenship and Cooperation in Justice and Home Affairs', in Duff *et al.* (1994).
Dinan (1994), *Ever Closer Union? An Introduction to the European Community*, Chs. 1–6.
Duff (1994), 'Ratification', in Duff *et al.* (1994).
Gustavsson (1996), 'The European Union: 1996 and Beyond – a Personal View from the Side-line', in Andersen and Eliassen (1996).
Hayward (1995), 'Governing the New Europe', in Hayward and Page (1995).

Hirst (1995), 'The European Union at the Crossroads: Integration or Decline?' in Bellamy *et al.* (1995).

Kapteyn (1996), *The Stateless Market*, Routledge, London.

Laffan (1993), 'The Treaty of Maastricht: Political Authority and Legitimacy', in Cafruny and Rosenthal (1993).

Pescatore (1987), 'Some Critical Remarks on the Single European Act', 24 *CMLRev.* 9.

Pinder (1995), *European Community. The Building of a Union*, Oxford University Press, Oxford.

Taylor (1995), *EMU 2000? Prospects for European Monetary Union*, Chatham House Papers/Royal Institute of International Affairs, Cassell, London.

Teasdale (1993), 'The Life and Death of the Luxembourg Compromise', 31 *JCMS* 567.

Urwin (1995), *The Community of Europe. A History of European Integration since 1945*, 2nd edn, Longman, London.

Wallace (1994), *Regional Integration: The West European Experience*, The Brookings Institution, Washington, DC.

Ward (1996), 'The European Constitution and the Nation State', 16 *OJLS* 161.

Wincott (1995a), 'Political Theory, Law and European Union', in Shaw and More (1995).

3 Constitutional Fundamentals of European Union

3.1 Introduction

Earlier paragraphs (especially 1.4, 1.5, 2.16 and 2.17) have referred to the more detailed discussion of the constitutional fundamentals of European Union contained in this chapter. Here we gather together some of the strands of constitutional development highlighted above and look to see whether something more like a coherent whole can be identified. We shall also seek to identify any relevant constitutional values which underpin the institutional and substantive development of the European Union. This chapter also sets the stage for the ones which follow, where certain legal structures and relationships lying at the heart of the EU system are discussed in more detail. Constitutional principles form the foundation for both the institutional and substantive law of the European Union. While the constitutional structure may so far remain incomplete, this chapter attempts to organise a rather diverse and sometimes diffuse collection of principles under a number of important headings which address issues such as federalism, democracy and the rule of law. As a very broad range of issues are raised, inevitably the discussion in some places is brief. The reader will find it useful to cross-refer, now and later, between this chapter and those which follow to gain a better insight into how deeply these constitutional fundamentals are embedded into the institutional law of the EU.

This chapter will also highlight the extent to which the debate about constitutionalism in the EU is a political debate; the ways in which both the 'descriptive' questions (does the EU have a constitution, and if so what is it composed of?) and the 'normative' questions (should the EU have a constitution, and if so what should it comprise?) are answered partly depends upon much larger debates about the politics of European integration. For those purposes, it is useful to refer back to the different academic and political positions on European integration processes sketched out in 1.4. Nor should the role of law and legal institutions be overstated: constitution-building is to a large extent a matter of politics, and dependent upon the development of a meaningful politics within the EU (Bellamy and Castiglione, 1996).

A final introductory point to be made is that 'constitution-building' has been firmly on the agenda throughout Europe, at least since the end of the Cold War. The countries of Central and Eastern Europe, as well as those of the former Soviet Union have moved at different speeds towards systems of liberal constitutional democracy which have borrowed heavily from historical American and European models. The European Parliament too has been preoccupied with constitution-building for the European Union, beginning soon after the first direct elections with the Spinelli initiatives, continuing through the Draft Treaty on European Union (2.8 and 2.10), and taking up similar issues once more in the wake of the Treaty of Maastricht with an initiative for a European Constitution (2.23). These preoccupations influenced that institution's responses to the challenges posed by the 1996 IGC and highlight the enduring character of concerns about constitutionalism within the European Union. However, in the recent past the whole debate about constitutionalism has become irrevocably intertwined with the problems of the 1996 IGC and the current context of integration in Europe.

3.2 A Constitution for the European Union?

It is useful to distinguish between two separate meanings of the term 'constitution' when it is applied to states. At one level, a constitution is the bundle of legal rules and practices which underlie the exercise and control of state power, and which structure the form of government within a state. At another level, a constitution is a formal document or set of documents, achieving the same objectives. The United Kingdom has an 'unwritten' constitution in the first sense (although, of course, the vast majority of the rules are to be found in written form), but lacks a set of formally identified 'constitutional' documents in the latter sense (a 'written' constitution). However, the vast majority of modern states have such a formal constitutional document or documents.

While it is self-evident that the EU is not a state, it is nonetheless a *sui generis* type of 'union' or 'confederation' of states, which displays, as we have already seen, certain 'federal' characteristics which mark it out as binding together its constituent Member States in close relationships with the central institutions within a legal order. It is also an entity which exercises many of the traditional functions of government, albeit within limited fields, and to which, according to the Court of Justice, sovereign powers have been ascribed. The EU undoubtedly, therefore, needs a constitution of the first type, namely a set of basic groundrules which govern these functions and powers, which deal with the apportionment of power to various organs and the relationships between these organs. These groundrules or principles are necessary to secure the rule of law, and to secure some level of legitimacy, in the sense of popular or social legitimacy, through democratic means of participation, and also as a vehicle for the expression of values which are embodied in the idea of European Union.

It will be apparent already from earlier paragraphs that the Court of Justice believes that the EU has a constitution in this sense. In particular it has referred, as we have seen, to the founding treaties of the European Communities as its constitutional charter. As the Court of Justice is first and foremost the Court of the 'Community', not the Union, this is an obvious approach to take. However, it is important not to ignore the Treaty of Maastricht itself as providing a constitutional foundation. Most of this chapter is devoted to identifying the basic contents of the EU constitution, which is based around the three pillar structure established by the Treaty of Maastricht. However, to highlight the fact that the constitutional structure is not yet complete (a Europe of 'bits and pieces' – Curtin, 1993) and remains in a dynamic state of flux, it is probably better to refer to the EU having a set of 'constitutional principles', rather than a 'constitution' as such.

Indeed, in view of the fact that the constitutional structure is so far incomplete – a point reinforced by the fluidity of some of the boundaries that currently exist between the different pillars of European Union constituted by the Treaty of Maastricht – it is probably correct to say that the EU does not at present have a constitution in the second, formal sense. Whether it should have such a constitution has been a question which, in recent years, has aroused a good deal of discussion and controversy, especially in the German literature (cf. 3.3) (e.g. Weiler, 1995a; Grimm, 1995; Habermas, 1995; Schuppert, 1995). There are arguments of efficiency, transparency and legitimacy which lend weight to the argument that a single such document expressing a set of coherent principles would bring the EU 'closer to the citizen', as Article A TEU indicates it should be. On the other hand, the very idea of 'constituting' the EU in this way may reinforce the strength of the EU in a way which remains unacceptable to Member States jealous of their own sovereignty and of their own autonomous rights within the international system of nation states.

3.3   The German Challenge to European Constitutionalism

The sovereignty argument lies to a large extent behind the strongest challenge in recent years to the possibilities of European constitutionalism, the challenge which emerged out of the decision of the German Federal Constitutional Court which formally cleared the way for Germany to ratify the Treaty of Maastricht, but which in truth raised some very difficult questions about the nature – present and future – of the European Community and the European Union (*Brunner* [1994] 1 CMLR 57 (unofficial English translation)).

The German Court opened the door to a scrutiny of the Treaty of Maastricht when it accepted the contention that the right of German citizens to participate in elections to the German parliament (the *Bundestag*) guaranteed by Article 38 of the German Constitution (the 'Basic Law') might be infringed by the Treaty. Article 23 of the Basic Law authorises the transfer of sovereign powers by the legislature to the European Union, but this is only permissible in so far as the transfer does not alter the 'identity of the constitutional order' of the Federal Republic – that is the central principles which are protected against repeal by Article 79(3) of the Basic Law. These are the principles of democracy, the rule of law, the essential content of the fundamental rights, and the federal basis of Germany. In setting the limits of German participation in the EU using these building blocks, the Federal Constitutional Court painted a picture of the EU which drew heavily on classic concepts of national sovereignty, and which saw the EU and its legal order as fundamentally a creature of international relations and international law, based on Treaties which are controlled by the Member States, and lacking the *sui generis* features of 'supranationalism' which the Court of Justice has always claimed for it.

Democracy in the EU is guaranteed, according to the Federal Constitutional Court, not through the European Parliament, but through the national parliaments. This is because there is no single European people, and since democracy comes 'from the people', the European Parliament cannot in that sense secure democracy; it can only play a 'supporting' role ([1994] 1 CMLR 57 at p. 87). Instead, national parliaments represent national peoples. The use of the concept of 'people' in that way has been heavily criticised in some quarters (e.g. Weiler, 1995a; 1995b; see 3.6). However, from that foundation comes the limitation upon the sovereign rights which the EU may exercise. They are not the sovereign rights of a state, but of a limited 'confederation' or 'association' of sovereign states ('*Staatenverbund*'). Consequently, the Community has only limited competences – only limited competences may be transferred by a sovereign state. Authorisations given by the Member States must be given in a precise and limited way, such that the actions of the EU are foreseeable, and the EU must stay within its 'integration programme' ([1994] 1 CMLR 57 at p. 89). Most devastatingly for the Court of Justice, however, the Federal Constitutional Court held that the Community lacks what is called a 'competence-competence', that is the power to determine what are the scope of its competences. That must lie elsewhere: implicitly, with the Federal Constitutional Court (and other national constitutional courts), since it confirmed explicitly that acts of the EU institutions would not be applicable within the territory of the Federal Republic of Germany if they exceeded the limits of the competences conferred upon them by the Member States. By this means, the German Court explicitly linked its judgment back to a series of earlier judgments – termed a rebellion – handed down by the German courts specifically in relation to the question of fundamental rights which appeared, by mid-1980s, to have been quelled with the Federal Constitutional Court ceding authority to the Court of Justice (6.7). It would appear that with the larger 'constitutional' claims of European Union, the dangers of possible conflicts between the Court of Justice and the Federal Constitutional Court have emerged again with added urgency.

Many of the assertions about the EU contained in the *Brunner* judgment can, and have been, challenged by reference to the constitutional specifities of Germany, or as representing a one-dimensional picture of the EU legal order which takes insufficient account of either the dynamic nature of the EU itself (Smits, 1994), or indeed the increasingly uncertain concept of national 'sovereignty' (e.g. MacCormick, 1995). However, it has served an essential function in giving a backdrop to serious consideration and debate about the future of European Union, in particular of an EU in which a single currency with economic and monetary union is a serious, if still relatively distant, possibility. It raises questions about the continuing need to take both sovereignty (de Witte, 1995) and the nation states (Ward, 1996) seriously. In that sense, it is acknowledged as having 'rendered an important service to European integration' (Herdegen, 1994: 249).

3.4   Constitution-building in the European Union

Assuming that the difficulties identified in *Brunner* could be overcome, and if a formal constitutional document were to be adopted, how would it be brought into being? Two alternatives immediately present themselves which highlight the transitory position between 'Community' and 'Union' which the EU in its present form currently occupies. At present, the basic constitution-building process of the EC/EU comprises international negotiations between representatives of sovereign states (in a so-called intergovernmental conference or IGC), the unanimous conclusion of a Treaty amending or adding to the existing Treaties, followed by a ratification process in which *all* the Member States must ratify the Treaty agreed upon according to their respective constitutional requirements (Article N TEU, replacing Article 236 EEC). Throughout, the process of negotiation requires 'common accord'. The formal involvement of the EU institutions is also sparse: the Commission may propose the amendment of the Treaty; the Council must deliver an opinion in favour of convening an IGC after consulting the Commission and the European Parliament (and, where appropriate, the European Central Bank), before the formal negotiation process can begin. However, once begun the negotiations are matters of intergovernmental bargaining. Moreover, at the national level, there may be little or no involvement of bodies other than the government during the negotiations themselves, so that when any amending Treaty is subsequently presented to the national Parliament or the electorate for ratification through vote or referendum, it is as a *fait accompli* on a 'take-it-or-leave-it' basis with no possibility for piecemeal change. This further distances the citizen (and the national political fora) from the process of change of the EU Treaties. The experiences with the Danish referendum in which the Treaty of Maastricht was rejected demonstrates that any intergovernmental consensus may not always receive the approval of national political organs. As a result the whole ratification process of the Treaty was jeopardised and only saved by very careful political footwork on the part of the Danish government and the other EU governments, in particular at the European Council meeting convened in Edinburgh in December 1992.

The lessons to be derived from this experience and from the problems encountered in relation to the ratification of the Treaty of Maastricht are clear. The 'traditional' mode of constitution-building for the EU, although firmly grounded in international diplomacy, the states system and international law, cannot necessarily deliver a satisfactory outcome because, whatever the content of Treaties agreed between governments, the process is one which excludes many interested parties, including ordinary citizens in particular.

The second means of constitution-building derives from federal constitutionalism rather than international relations. Reflecting the American constitutional experience, this is often termed the 'Philadelphia' model, and would involve a constitutional convention for something like a 'United States of Europe', in which a new constitutional settlement is determined directly by the representatives of the people elected to such a convention by direct or indirect suffrage. The European Parliament has sought to promote the adoption of a variant of this method of constitution-building, sometimes by seeking to appeal to national parliaments over the heads of governments. Such a change would undoubtedly herald a quantum increase in the power and influence of the European Parliament both over the procedure of amendment (as it is the sole existing popular representative institution of the EU), and over decision-making powers in any subsequent 'state' or 'union'. A shift to such a 'federal' approach to constitution-building lies behind the Parliament's 1994 initiative for a European Constitution to be enacted jointly by the Parliament and the Member States (2.23).

Clearly the practical politics of European integration tell us that whatever the 'legitimacy dividend' of such a means of constitution-building, it would not be acceptable to the most influential actors involved at this stage. Moreover, and perhaps paradoxically, the history of the development of European integration, and the progressive adoption and implementation of new Treaties, tends to show that it is often the apparently small steps which have offered the most realistic chance of incremental progress towards deeper integration (and therefore federal goals). This argument could be made in relation to the content and subsequent impact of the Single European Act (Bermann, 1989). It may also be one reason why in its opinion on the 1996 IGC, the European Parliament renounced the earlier radical constitutionalism it was espousing and accepted that the means whereby the IGC would inevitably proceed would be through an international Treaty. However, the Parliament and many observers stressed that, whatever the *form*, the *content* of the process would involve constitution-building and must therefore take heed of relevant values of democratic participation, and openness and accountability.

In that context, it might useful for the political entities involved to take heed of the third method of constitution-building which has proved extremely important hitherto for the EU, namely the role of the Court of Justice in identifying and implementing constitutional principles (what is often termed the 'constitutionalisation of the Treaties'). The work of the Court should certainly not be viewed with rose-tinted spectacles in the belief that it offers some type of general panacea for other (political) deficits in the EU. Nonetheless, reading together the existing Treaty texts and the relevant case law of the Court, it is possible to identify some key principles which would form a useful foundation for any subsequent constitution-building exercise, whatever form it might take. The following paragraphs attempt to do just that by highlighting some key achievements (although some achievements can be seen to be more apparent than real) and certain important lacunae; they offer a foundation for more detailed discussion in the chapters which follow. One important point which will emerge throughout is the role of the Court of Justice as a *constitutional court*, that is, as an institution providing authoritative statements and determinations on the exercise of governmental power under the rule of law in the EU. To the critics of the Court that means something like a government of judges; its supporters would say that the Court has essentially been applying the logic of the Treaties.

The approach taken in this chapter is to organise the material under a set of headings or questions against which the EU system is now increasingly being tested – what Eleftheriadis (1996: 41) has called the principles of the 'substantive constitution':

– is the EU a democratic system and how should democratic principles be instrumentalised in the context of the EU?
– who are the 'citizens' of the EU, and what role should they be given?
– to what extent is the EU a federal system, and how are the principles and practices of federalism policed within that system?
– are justice and the rule of law adequately protected within the EU?
– what position does or should the EU take within the global economic and political systems?
– does the EU now offer a single coherent system of government?
– has there been an irreversible process of (economic, legal and even political) integration between the Member States of the EU, and what core of stability lies at the heart of that process?
– to what extent – if at all – does the EU have an 'economic constitution' which sets a normative framework for the type of economic order which it supports?

3.5   A Democratic System?

At risk of over-simplification it can be stated that democracy means government by the people for the people. Without wishing to pre-empt the detailed debates about the institutions and the work which they do in subsequent chapters, it is useful to highlight at the outset the difficulties which the EU has as regards the upholding of basic principles of democracy so defined. Article F(1) TEU refers to democracy in the Member States, but says nothing about democracy in the EU itself. Whether the 'democratic deficit' is seen as insufficient input on the part of the European Parliament, or too great a disempowerment of national parliaments as a result of the transfer of powers to the EU and the increased use of qualified majority voting, its existence and the problems which arise as a result in terms of sustaining the legitimacy of the actions taken at EU level cannot be denied. The bare statement in Article A TEU about decision-making in the European Union occurring 'as closely as possible to the citizen' is largely rhetorical flourish. It might also be said to be more to do with the EU's federal vocation (see 3.7) than its democratic vocation; that is, it has more to do with the level at which power is exercised, not the manner.

Within the political systems of the states which comprise the EU, the exercise of governmental and state power is legitimated through democratic processes involving citizen participation (although it should not be thought that those states themselves do not in some ways also have 'democratic deficits'). One of the most important of these processes is the electoral process. Within the EU, only the European Parliament is directly elected; the Commissioners are appointed by the Member States, as are the members of ancillary advisory bodies such as the Economic and Social Committee (ECOSOC) and the Committee of the Regions, through the medium of the Council. The representatives of the national governments who meet in the Council can be regarded as legitimated in their function of exercising governmental power through the national electoral processes. The system is still self-evidently incomplete, a point acknowledged by the majority of the Member States who have generally supported a gradual empowerment of the European Parliament within the EC system. The Court likewise has long recognised the pivotal role of the Parliament. In Case 138/79 *Roquette Frères* v. *Council* ([1980] ECR 3333 at 3359) it stated that the power of the Parliament to participate in the legislative process through 'consultation' (5.4)

'represents an essential factor in the institutional balance intended by the treaty. Although limited, [such power] reflects at Community level the fundamental democratic principle that the peoples should take part in the exercise of power through the intermediary of a representative assembly.'

It has repeated this point on numerous occasions since, even though the Parliament does now in certain circumstances have a more direct and effective input into the legislative process than the form of consultation at issue in *Roquette*. Despite the imperfections of the system, what this point illustrates is that each of the institutions in the EU makes some contribution to the level of democracy – including national and subnational institutions which are involved. In view of some (e.g. Mancini and Keeling, 1994), the Court of Justice has made one of the most important contributions.

So, for example, it should not be thought that power is exercised in any way arbitrarily within the EU, that there exist no checks and balances in the system, or that there is no 'separation of powers', even if there is no separation of legislative, executive and judicial roles in the classic sense. Within a system such as the EU, each institution, including the Court of Justice must play some role in relation to questions of democracy, legitimacy and also institutional efficiency. An important concept is 'competence', and the system of limited powers which the Treaty establishes and the Court of Justice is required to enforce. The separation of powers between the institutions is recognised by Article 4 EC which proclaims that:

> 'Each institution shall act within the limits of the powers conferred upon it by this Treaty.'

Similarly, Article 173 provides that 'lack of competence' is a ground for the annulment of measures adopted by the EU institutions. Consequently, the Court of Justice can police these provisions, and uphold what it calls 'institutional' or 'interinstitutional balance', in particular in the context of challenges to the powers of particular institutions to act under the Treaty, brought before it either by the other institutions or by the Member States. Many of these challenges seek to identify the correct 'legal basis' for measures adopted under the Treaties, or to show that a particular institution has overstepped its proper powers. The Court has also developed a concept of 'loyal' or 'sincere' cooperation between the institutions, which governs the manner in which they may exercise their powers.

Some examples will show the important contribution of the Court of Justice.

- In order to protect interinstitutional balance the Court recognised that the European Parliament could be both a defendant and a plaintiff in actions for annulment of illegal acts brought before it, even though the EEC Treaty before the Treaty of Maastricht made no reference to this possibility (see 5.17). The Parliament was given the power to take action before the Court in order to 'protect its prerogatives' (Case C-70/88 *Parliament* v. *Council (Chernobyl)* [1990] ECR I-2041; see now Article 173 EC). The Court has specifically recognised the contribution made by the Parliament as the representative of the people, and opted for a general principle that where genuine alternatives exist under the Treaty system, there should be a preference for the legal basis for any given measure which gives greater input from the Parliament.
- In 1994 the Court of Justice annulled an anti-trust cooperation agreement with the United States concluded by the Commission,

acknowledging that the power to conclude such an agreement lay, under the system established by the Treaty, with the Council not the Commission (Case C-327/91 *France* v. *Commission* [1994] ECR I-3641).

- Where an institution has determined in advance the way in which it will exercise a power which is conferred upon it by the Treaties or by relevant secondary legislation, it cannot retreat from the position it has publicly taken. We can take an example from the enforcement of the competition rules of the Treaty (Articles 85 and 86 EC) which prohibit various forms of anti-competitive conduct by undertakings and groups of undertakings. In the past the Commission has taken a more generous position than was strictly required by the case law of the Court in its public statements on the question of what 'access' to the 'file' which the Commission has compiled on the case an undertaking accused of a breach of the competition rules may have. The Court of First Instance held that the Commission was bound by that statement to provide the level of access it had 'promised' (Case T-7/89 *Hercules* v. *Commission (Polypropylene)* [1991] ECR I-1711.

- A similar lesson emerges from the Court of First Instance's treatment of the Council's attempts, in the post-Maastricht search for greater transparency, openness and therefore legitimacy within the EU, to create a new policy of public access to its documents, appearing to step away from the almost total secrecy which had hitherto dominated its decision-making processes (4.7). It established a decision-making structure for the release of documents on request by a member of the public which allowed it a discretion in determining what was secret and what it was not in the public interest to disclose. When a journalist and his newspaper sought to put the policy to use, they were refused access to the documents they wanted. A challenge before the Court of First Instance was successful on the grounds that having established a discretion, the Council must at least turn its mind on a case-by-case basis to whether documents should be released. A continued blanket ban on public access would not be a proper exercise of the discretion (Case T-194/94 *Carvel and Guardian Newspapers* v. *Council* [1995] 3 CMLR 359).

Significantly, what the Court of First Instance did not say in *Carvel* was that there is a general principle of 'transparency' in the Community legal order, and that it binds the Council (and indeed the other institutions). The existence of such a principle has been suggested by AG Tesauro in a case in which the Netherlands challenged the legal basis of one of the Decisions which form the basis for the document release policy (Case 58/94 *Netherlands* v. *Council* (30.4.96)). Potentially the recognition of such principle – whether by the two EU Courts or by the Member States in an amendment to the Treaties – would represent a fundamental change in the nature of European government (Curtin, 1995), to one in which citizens could play a much more meaningful role.

3.6   Union of Peoples or Union of People? Citizenship and Identity in the EU

It is often said that the European Union cannot have a concept of 'citizenship' because it does not have a 'people'. There is no European 'demos' in the way that there is certainly a German 'volk'. People do not by and large identify themselves as 'European' in the same way that they identify themselves by reference to the Member State of which they are citizens, or by reference to the region in which they are resident or from which they originate. The point is emphasised by Article F(1) TEU which provides that:

> 'The Union shall respect the national identities of its Member States, whose systems of government are founded on the principles of democracy.'

The argument which links citizenship to a 'people' also lies at the heart of the way in which the German Federal Constitutional Court sought to highlight the limits of European integration processes in its judgment on the ratification of the Treaty of Maastricht (3.3). In contrast to this essentially ethnic approach to the question of citizenship, some commentators have suggested alternative approaches to 'membership' of the Community or Union, based on concepts of political loyalty, constitutional patriotism, or an ethic of multiculturalism (Tassin, 1992; Habermas, 1994; Weiler, 1995a; 1995b). Indeed, these types of questions about identity have been on the political agenda since as long ago as 1974. Whatever form of 'membership' is chosen it will need to be one which is sufficiently flexible to respond to future geopolitical changes in the configuration of the European Union, involving in particular new countries acceding in the East. This will change the context of 'identity' in Europe.

Developing a concept of citizenship – that is, membership of a political entity identified as the European Union – is probably essential to its future health and stability. At the moment the EU is gradually altering, or perhaps better broadening, its essential core: it is changing from being a functionally defined economic association where the primary goals are the creation and sustenance of an internal market, through a stage of constitutional evolution in which the principle of the rule of law is fully integrated into the legal system, into a mature governance system in which the Member States and the EU institutions share political and legal authority, and in which citizens perform a vital legitimating role. Some steps have already been made towards identifying the citizens of the European Union, and towards endowing them with certain rights. So far, these steps have been limited.

The existing status of the 'citizen of the Union' is based on a combination of Treaty provisions and Court of Justice case law. The Treaty of Maastricht introduced into the EC Treaty a new section (Part Two of the Treaty), establishing a concept of 'Citizenship of the Union':

'Every person holding the nationality of a Member State shall be a citizen of the Union' (Article 8(1)).

The reference to the nationalities of the Member States is important. It states clearly the limited nature of EU citizenship. However, it should not be thought that EU has no input into questions of immigration and asylum – i.e. highly political questions about who can come in and on what basis. The role of the Third Pillar (CJHA) as the basis for coordination and common action in this field is vital, but these are so far questions which fall outside the scope of the EC Treaty.

The rights and duties of EU citizens as defined in Article 8 are first and foremost those conferred or imposed by the EC Treaty (Article 8(2)). The following provisions go on to confer some specific rights including:

- the 'right to move and reside freely within the territory of the Member States, subject to the limitations and conditions laid down in this Treaty and by the measures adopted to give it effect' (Article 8A);
- the right to vote or stand in municipal elections for those citizens residing in Member States of which they are not nationals (Article 8B(1)) (Council Directive 94/880 on the exercise of the right to vote and stand in municipal elections OJ 1994 L368/38);
- the right to vote or stand in European parliamentary elections for the same group of citizens (Article 8B(2)) (Council Directive 93/109 on the exercise of the right to vote and stand in European parliamentary elections OJ 1993 L329/34);
- EU citizens finding themselves in the territory of a third country where their own country is not represented have the right to diplomatic or consular protection by any Member State which is represented there (Article 8C);
- the right to petition the European Parliament and to apply to the Ombudsman established under Article 138E (4.12).

It will quickly be seen that this catalogue of citizenship rights is exceedingly limited and hardly comparable with domestic conceptions of citizenship. In fact, one of the key concessions made to Danish sensibilities after the first referendum which narrowly rejected the Treaty of Maastricht, was a declaratory confirmation by the European Council that nothing in the provisions of the Treaty of Maastricht in any way displaces national citizenship.

What is notable is that citizenship of the Union is founded on the concept of free movement – a right which EU nationals hold and exercise *vis-à-vis* the Member States, not on rights which citizens exercise first and foremost *vis-à-vis* the European Union or the European Community. Moreover, it is a right which they already have, either by virtue of the various provisions of the EC Treaty which uphold the principles of the internal market (Articles 7A, 48, 52 and 59), or pursuant to a series of

Directives enacted in 1990 to confer rights of residence on a number of residual categories of persons who are not economically active (or are not the members of the families of those who are), such as pensioners, students, and those of independent economic means. Article 8A seems to add nothing new, in particular since it is subject to the proviso concerning measures to be enacted by the Council to give effect to the right of free movement. This allows the Council to continue to uphold the principle enacted in the 1990 Directives that those who are not economically active (or members of the families of the same), should be capable of supporting themselves without becoming a burden on the host state, and should have adequate health insurance. The Court of Justice has already confirmed the 'subsidiary' or 'residual' character of the free movement right in Article 8A, emphasising that it will apply a specific provision of the Treaty wherever one is available (Case C-193/94 *Skanavi and Chryssanthakopoulos* (29.2.1996).

The original Spanish Memorandum proposing the introduction of a concept of citizenship for the European Union suggested that rights for European citizens would constitute an important and indeed essential core. That suggestion was not wholly adopted. For example, the protection of the fundamental rights of EU citizens is to be found elsewhere in the Treaty system, in Article F(2) TEU:

> 'The Union shall respect fundamental rights, as guaranteed by the European Convention for the Protection of Human Rights and Fundamental Freedoms signed in Rome on 4 November 1950 and as they result from the constitutional traditions common to the Member States, as general principles of Community law.'

This is an example of how citizenship rights can be scattered across the treaties. However, unlike Articles 8–8E EC, this provision stands outside the jurisdiction of the Court of Justice. Nonetheless it does achieve the enactment into constitutional principle (albeit not justiciable principle) of the existing case law of the Court of Justice which ensures the protection of the fundamental rights of citizens in exactly those same terms. This will be discussed in detail in Chapter 6. The point should be emphasised, nonetheless, that EU citizens are not covered by a single clear and identifiable catalogue of rights which they may exercise *vis-à-vis* both the EU institutions themselves, and also the Member States where they act within the limits of EU competence.

Clearly, therefore, it is essential to look beyond the formal provisions on citizenship to see how and to what extent these citizens are constituted as 'members' having a stake in the European Union as a political union. Returning to the importance of free movement rights for the development of EU legal order, these have long been given a quasi-constitutional status by the Court of Justice in its case law. Not only has the Court placed extensive interpretations on key concepts such as that of the 'worker' under Article 48 EC, but it has also extended the protection of EC law to a number of other categories of persons not specifically named in the Treaties. Article 6 EC, the guarantee of non-discrimation on grounds of (EU) nationality, has played a vital role in this context as a constitutional principle. Two key cases will highlight the point amply. The plaintiff in Case 186/87 *Cowan* v. *Le Trésor public* ([1989] ECR 195) was mugged on the Metro when he was visiting Paris as a tourist. He was denied compensation from the French criminal injuries compensation scheme, on the grounds that he was a UK national. The Court of Justice brought Mr Cowan within the scope of the protection of the Treaty, finding that as a tourist he was a recipient of services who had exercised his right of free movement, and therefore was implicitly covered not only by the provisions on the free movement of services, but also by the general right to non-discrimination in Article 6. Hence a compensation scheme which arbitrarily excluded non-nationals was contrary to the principles contained in the Treaty.

The second example concerns migrant students: the plaintiff in Case 293/83 *Gravier* v. *City of Liège* ([1985] ECR 593) was a French national who wished to study strip cartoon art at university in Belgium. The Court held that by virtue of (what was then) Article 128 EEC which established an outline competence for the Community in relation to vocational training, she too fell within the scope of the Treaty (wishing to undertake a vocational training course in another Member State), and was therefore entitled to the protection of Article 6 EC. Hence she was entitled to access to the course on a non-discriminatory basis and could not be charged a fee which was only imposed by Belgian universities on non-nationals. In these cases, provisions of the Treaty which originally had a 'market' orientation, have been used for a broader constitutional purpose. *Cowan* and *Gravier* are constituted at least as 'market' citizens of the European Union.

The Court of Justice has not, however, been entirely consistent. Case C-168/91 *Konstantinidis* v. *Stadt Altensteig* ([1993] ECR I-1191) concerned a self-employed masseur of Greek nationality living in Germany. He complained that the German authorities were infringing his EU rights in their official mistranslation (transliteration) of his name (from Greek letters into Roman ones), such that 'Christos' became 'Hrestos'. The Court of Justice concluded that in such circumstances the German authorities were not entitled to insist on a spelling of the applicant's name in such a way as to misrepresent its prononciation since 'such distortion exposes him to a risk of confusion of identity on the part of his potential clients'. What is notable about this case is that the Court focused specifically on the economic considerations, highlighting the role of Konstantinidis within the EU system as a 'market' citizen. In contrast, AG Jacobs, in a very wide-ranging opinion, concentrated on a fundamental rights argument in which he argued that the migrant worker (or professional) should be able to rely on a *prima-facie* claim as a 'European citizen' to a basic standard of rights protection, irrespective of whether the protection he or she received was granted on a non-discriminatory basis (6.8).

The extent to which the market citizenship of European *Economic* Community has now been transmuted both by the introduction of Articles 8–8E EC, and by the creation of the European Union and the move towards closer political union, is a rather moot point. It also draws us back to the discussion of principles of democracy in 3.5. Democracy, and associated questions of political accountability, and broad legitimacy, remain rather problematic questions. Moreover, as we noted in 3.5, the action brought before the Court of First Instance to secure disclosure of Council documents by a journalist and a newspaper (Case T-194/94 *Carvel and Guardian Newspapers* v. *Council*) was decided on a very limited point about Council discretion, and not on the basis of fundamental principle. The figure of the citizen remained an obscure one in that case. The conclusion must be drawn that a mature concept of political citizenship for the European Union still remains to be developed in the future, and that there is more to the 'rhetoric' than the 'reality' (Lyons, 1996).

3.7   A Federal System?

Federalism has formed an important current in much thinking about European integration; although self-evidently the EU is not a federal state, nonetheless power is now in fact divided between the Union and the Member States in a manner which partially mimics a federal system. Moreover, as many writers have stressed, federalism is potentially a very broad concept capable of describing any type of governance system involving a divided power structure (Lenaerts, 1990: 263; Koopmans, 1992; Fischer and Neff, 1995). In that spirit, it can be shown that a number of important constitutional principles of the EU seek to organise the exercise of political and legal authority in a way which is not wholly dissimilar to the basic framework of a federal state with a federal authority and constituent states. Certainly, the organisation of the relationship between EC law and national law, outlined in 1.5 and discussed in detail in Chapters 9 and 10 demonstrates the hallmarks of a federal system. EC (federal) law is a higher source of normative authority than national (state) law, and takes effect within the national legal systems (from the point of view of the Court of Justice) without need for intermediate action by the Member States. Where appropriate, rules of EC law are enforceable in the national courts, and take precedence over contradictory national rules. The Court of Justice asserts its authority as a superior court, able in effect to determine the 'constitutionality' of provisions of national law, through its jurisdiction of interpretation (Article 177 EC), as well as its enforcement jurisdiction (Article 169). In that system, Article 5 EC plays a key role, instituting a multifaceted duty of loyalty binding the states, and all (superior and inferior) state authorities, of whatever nature.

The system is, however, incomplete or underdeveloped as a federal system, for example in relation to the vertical division of powers. Federal constitutions classically opt for one of two solutions to the problem of the vertical division of powers (between federal authority and constituent states). Either the powers of the federal authority are specifically defined, with the residue of powers falling to the constituent states, or the powers of the states are specifically defined with the residue of powers falling to the federal authority. In each case, some powers may be shared. Whatever principle is adopted, it can be policed by the constitutional court. Within their respective spheres, the federal authority and the constituent states will be free to exercise the powers attributed to them, subject to the respect of overarching constitutional principles. Moreover, typically a federal constitution will, as a minimum, give to the federal authority key powers relating to foreign policy, external and internal security policy, macro-economic policy, and monetary policy (including the power to issue currency), as well as sufficient powers to ensure the preservation of an effectively functioning internal market.

As a result of the sometimes rather *ad hoc* way in which the EC and now the EU has developed over a number of years, the powers now attributed to the Union, the Community and the EU institutions by the Treaties (and the manner in which they can be exercised) are partly the result of historical accident. Hence the EU has broad powers relating to the creation and maintenance of the single internal market, including powers to bring about the harmonisation of national legislation, and also in relation to foreign trade policy. The Treaty of Maastricht introduced the powers to create a single currency and a monetary union, although the process whereby that may occur is by no means automatic and is conditional partly on the willingness of the Member States, as well as certain economic contingencies. The EC Treaty also confers competences on the Community which must be shared with the Member States in fields such the environment, economic and social cohesion, consumer protection, social policy, education and vocational training, and culture. The range of these powers can be seen from a reading of Article B TEU, and Articles 2, 3 and 3A EC. Significantly in terms of the autonomy of action of the European Community, that body (but not the European Union) is given 'legal personality' (Article 210 EC), which consequently gives it the capacity to act on the international sphere by concluding international treaties – bilateral and multilateral – and by participating where appropriate in international organisations.

Since the Single European Act, many (but not all) of the activities to be undertaken by the Community can be pursued using legislative powers which can be exercised on a (qualified) majoritarian basis, bringing the EU closer in form to a federal political system (although the legislative power vested primarily in the Council and only secondarily in the European Parliament offers a model of legislative action which differs somewhat from a conventional federal legislative format involving a balanced bicameral legislative authority). In contrast, of course, broader foreign policy issues not related to trade fall under the intergovernmental pillar of Common Foreign and Security Policy, where the approach is more akin to the international relations between sovereign states than the internal affairs of a federal state. Likewise, questions of internal security are not subject to the supranational 'Community' method, but are largely determined by intergovernmental principles and practices.

As an alternative to looking at the express terms of the Treaties in order to see which activities the EU may or must pursue and to ascertain what powers are conferred on the institutions for the purposes of achieving the objectives of the Treaty, is it possible to identify any general principles which structure the vertical division of powers? Article A TEU talks of decisions being taken as closely as possible to the citizen, but offers no more guidance on the concrete question of division. The reference to 'closeness to the citizen' is generally taken to infer a reference to subsidiarity as a broad *political* principle drawing inspiration from the heritage of that term in certain traditions of European political and social philosophy. But the absence of any clear consensus about exactly what that heritage implies for the future of the EU means that this reference is not particularly helpful. Article 3B EC lays down some key legal principles:

> 'The Community shall act within the limits of the powers conferred upon it by this Treaty and of the objectives assigned to it therein.
>
> In areas which do not fall within its exclusive competence, the Commuity shall take action, in accordance with the principles of subsidiarity, only if and in so far as the objectives of the proposed action cannot be sufficiently achieved by the Member States and can therefore, by reason of the scale or effects of the proposed action, be better achieved by the Community.
>
> Any action by the Community shall not go beyond what is necessary to achieve the objectives of this Treaty.'

The reference to the principle of *limited* powers and objectives is clear. It consigns in EC law the established principle of 'attributed' powers, recognising under public international law that the state is where the primary source of sovereignty lies (a point stressed by the Court of Justice in Opinion 2/94 *Accession by the Community to the European Convention on Human Rights (ECHR)* (28.3.1996). In that sense, Article 3B is certainly not a federalist principle. The application of the principle of *proportionality* also appears relatively straightforward. Even the application of the principle of 'subsidiarity' (here understood as a *legal* principle, to which Article B TEU also refers) to the *exercise* of those limited powers appears unproblematic until it is recalled that it actually presupposes a pre-existing division of powers. The terms of Article 3B in fact presume the existence of a distinction in EC law between powers ascribed '*exclusively*' to the Community and those '*shared*' (or held '*concurrently*') with the Member States. Thus, although the interpretation and application of Article 3B, in particular the efficiency criterion which it establishes in relation to the exercise of powers, must be vital to the federal evolution of the EU, it does not provide all of the answers (see the discussion in 3.10).

Furthermore, the application of the principles outlined above is made more complex by the wide formulation given in a number of places in the EC Treaty both to the powers granted to the institutions, and to the objectives set for the European Community. The Court of Justice has also partially undermined the principle of the attribution of powers through its case law giving an extensive interpretation both to the range and the nature of the Community's powers (3.9).

3.8 Exclusive and Shared Competence

Despite the reference to exclusive competence in Article 3B EC, the balance of exclusive and shared powers is not easy to determine in EC law. Indeed, the adoption of Article 3B has brought this lack of clarity to the fore, a point illustrated by the absence of any consensus amongst academic commentators as to exactly when Article 3B subsidiarity applies (see for example the differencs of view in Toth, 1994 and Steiner, 1994). Some provisions do make clear that the Community and the Member States share a particular power; for example, Article 129A EC declares that the 'Community shall contribute to the attainment of a high level of consumer protection . .'. In similar terms Article 127 reads:

> 'The Community shall implement a vocational training policy which shall support and supplement the action of the Member States, while fully respecting the responsibility of the Member States for the content and organisation of vocational training.'

The Treaty itself is not always so clear in its meaning. Few would doubt the exclusivity of Community competence in fields such as the customs union, agriculture or the social security of migrant workers, where the EU has established a single dispositive regime regulating a particular field, primarily through the medium of a type of measure termed the 'Regulation' (6.12). In a concept which is similar to the notion of the supremacy of EC law, Member State competence is deemed to be 'pre-empted' by the effect of such Community powers. In such fields, Member States may no longer validly exercise their own legislative powers. This concept is discussed in more detail in 9.13, but a good example can be taken from Case 48/85 *Commission* v. *Germany* 9 [1986] ECR 2549) which concerns the common market in wine:

> 'As the Court has pointed out on a number of occasions, it is one of the fundamental characteristics of a common organization of the market that in the sectors concerned the Member States can no longer take action through national provisions adopted unilaterally. . . Their legislative competence can only be residual; it is limited to situations which are not governed by the Community rules and to cases where those rules expressly give them the power to act.'

The possibility of pre-emption can also arise in other areas, such as the internal market, where the Community has sought to create a single trading environment through the adoption of measures, particularly in the form of 'directives' (6.13) which bring about the harmonisation or approximation of national laws but frequently do not institute a single supranational rule in substitution for the national rules. We shall consider further the problems arising in this context in 9.13.

Problems of exclusivity also arise in the external sphere, and are discussed in 3.12. In that context, the practical problems which arise are twofold: the effect of national measures which cut across areas of exclusive Community competence, for example, in the field of the common commercial policy (external trade policy), regulated under Article 113 EC, and the extent to which the EU may validly regulate in the field of external relations in particular through participation in international agreements. In recent years, as the EU has extended its international activities, it has increasingly entered fields where shared competence is the norm, and where it must consequently act cooperatively with the Member States. However, in relation to the common commercial policy, the Court declared in Case 41/76 *Donckerwolcke* v. *Procureur de la République* ([1976] ECR 1921) that 'full responsibility was transferred to the Community by means of Article 113(1)'.

3.9   Limited Powers and Implied Powers

At first glance, the activities of the Community are closely circumscribed by the law-making powers which are ascribed to the institutions by individual provisions of the Treaties, which must be exercised for the specific purpose of achieving a particular policy goal. Articles 3B and 4 EC appear to make this point very clearly. In practice, the work of the EU has evolved in a more dynamic fashion as a result of two main legal factors, which have operated in conjunction with the constant pressure from the Commission and the Parliament upon the Council to extend the range of the Community's activities. These factors are:

- the development by the Court of Justice of a theory of implied powers, again in both the internal and external spheres;
- the existence within the EC Treaty of a number of more general law-making powers, namely Articles 6(2), 100, 100A and 235 EC, and the creative use of these powers by the institutions.

The second factor is not so much a constitutional principle, as an important element of the practical politics of the institutions; as such it will be considered in more detail in Chapter 5. The application of a theory of implied powers is crucial, however, to the constitutional fundamentals of European Union, as they have been identified in this chapter.

The concept of implied powers, as applied in EC law, aids the effectiveness of the work of the institutions. It allows the EU to take decisions where no specific power is given, but where an obvious duty or task exists under the Treaty. Article 235 EC, which gives a residual legal basis allowing for the adoption of measures aimed at the pursuit of the objectives of the Treaty, in circumstances where the Treaty fails to provide specific powers is an example of the concept of implied powers. In addition, the Court of Justice has also applied a general doctrine of implied powers both internally and externally, to facilitate the evolution of Community competence. We shall review the internal and external dimensions here, as both have contributed to the development of the general principle.

In the internal sphere, the concept of implied powers has been applied in particular to extend the scope of the Commission's power of decision. In Case 281, etc./85 *Germany et al.* v. *Commission (Migration Policy)* ([1987] ECR 3203) the Court was required to interpret the meaning of Article 118 EC. This gives the Commission the task of 'promoting close cooperation between the Member States in the social field'. On the basis of this provision, the Commission adopted a decision requiring Member States to communicate information regarding their policies on migrant workers from third states. A number of Member States challenged the competence of the Commission to adopt such a decision, arguing that such a measure should have been adopted by the Council on the basis of Article 235, if it fell within the competence of the Community at all. The Court held:

'where an article of the EEC Treaty – in this case Article 118 – confers a specific task on the Commission it must be accepted, if that provision is not to be rendered wholly ineffective, that it confers on the Commission necessarily and *per se* the powers which are indispensable in order to carry out that task.'

Accordingly, the Court found for the Commission as regards its power to adopt a binding decision, although it disagreed in some respects with that institution's interpretation of the scope of Article 118.

The Court has also applied the doctrine of implied powers in order to extend the Community's external powers and to create an extensive, if not complete, parallelism between internal and external competence. The development of implied powers in the external sphere is closely linked to the determination of the 'exclusivity' of the Community's external powers (see 3.7 and 3.12). The Community has always had an 'express' power to conclude agreements, but only in limited areas. But there are a number of principles laid down by the Court of Justice under which the Community can and has acquired external competence, even exclusive external competence (e.g. fisheries conservation), even in the absence of express powers in the Treaty. The position was summarised by the Court as follows in Opinion 2/91 *Re ILO Convention* ([1993] ECR I-1061 at p. 1076):

'Authority to enter into international commitments may not only arise from an express attribution by the Treaty, but may also flow implicitly from its provisions . . . . [I]n particular . . . whenever Community law created for the institutions of the Community powers within its internal system for the purpose of attaining a specific objective, the Community had authority to enter into the international commitments necessary for the attainment of that objective even in the absence of an express provision in that connection.'

The doctrine of implied powers has become less significant in the field of external relations, as amendments to the original Treaties have gradually conferred more express powers on the institutions. For example, the Community now has express powers in the fields of research and techno-logical development (Article 130M EC) and environmental policy (Article 130R(4) EC). Other new provisions have given the Community a power to 'foster co-operation at the international level'; this appears to include implicitly again a power to enter into agreements. An example of a measure adopted by the EU under its implied powers, but now covered by specific provisions of the EC Treaty is Council Regulation 1360/90 establishing the European Training Foundation (OJ 1990 L131/1). The aims of the Foundation are to act as a vehicle for the delivery of aid in the form of assistance for vocational training from the Member States of the European Community (and certain other third countries) to the new democracies of central and eastern Europe. The political justification for the Member States acting together in this way, rather than separately, is that it enhances the effectiveness of the aid. The legal justification was that the Community had an external competence in relation to vocational training which matched its internal competence (Article 128 EEC), but the legal basis of the regulation was Article 235 EC. Articles 126 and 127 EC, which supplanted Article 128 EEC, expressly identify an external dimen-sion to EU policy on education and vocational training respectively, making the adoption of such measures a matter of express rather than implied powers.

3.10 Application of the Principles of Subsidiarity and Proportionality

The introduction of the principle of subsidiarity into both the EC Treaty and the Treaty of Maastricht has provoked a massive outpouring of academic comment and speculation, including work which specifically identifies subsidiarity as a constitutional principle, but little by way of tangible change at the constitutional level has so far occurred. This brief discussion will distinguish between subsidiarity as a political principle guiding the development of the EU as a whole, and subsidiarity as a legal condition of the validity of certain types of EC measures. It will also review shortly the role of subsidiarity in the legislative process.

As a political principle, closely allied in certain respects to concepts of federalism, subsidiarity enjoys a relatively long history. Its roots lie primarily in Catholic social philosophy. Subsidiarity crystallised as a term describing a particular way of understanding social relations in Papal doctrine during the interwar years. It expressed a specific concern with the role of the state, and postulated the individual as the base unit of society. Wherever possible individual self-determination should be ensured, and only where decisions can more effectively be taken by groups which are subsidiary to the individual (family, community, locality, region, nation state, federal union) should this occur. Within these hierarchies or networks, the collectivity holds a responsibility for the wellbeing of the individual (the principle of subsidiarity). The position in Catholic social doctrine is summarised by Peterson (1994: 118) in the following terms:

'Small social groups should be autonomous and sovereign in a pluralist society, yet united in a common morality which stresses duty and harmony. They should be assisted in their activities by a state which neither substitutes for social groups nor is shackled by their demands, but which serves the public good and provides legal order'.

In similar terms, Kersbergen and Verbeek (1994: 222) argue that

'one has to appreciate that in Catholic social doctrine subsidiarity is intrinsically linked with other fundamental principles, such as personalism, solidarity, pluralism and distributive justice, that – taken together – have found their most profound expression in the continental christian democratic version of the welfare state, the social market.'

In postwar Germany, subsidiarity, although not explicitly adopted in the Constitution or Basic Law, has constituted an underlying theme dominating the evolution of federalism as a way of breaking loose from the shackles of corporatism under national socialism, in which private interests were co-opted coercively into the processes of the state. It protects the autonomy of the *Bundesländer* in a system of cooperative federalism in which the individual states and the federal *Bund* share certain key political powers.

Subsidiarity, therefore, has a rich, complex and sometimes contradictory heritage, in which it is deeply embedded into state/society relations. So far, in both rhetoric and practice in relation to the EU, this heritage has largely been ignored as subsidiarity is primarily viewed as structuring the EU/Member State relationship. Remarkably, in the aftermath of the Maastricht negotiations, subsidiarity has shown itself to be a plastic concept, offering the basis of an argument to all possible sides:

'The German Länder have used it to put pressure on Chancellor Kohl and . . . Jacques Delors, in order to protect their own autonomy in the advent of increasing understandings between Bonn and Brussels. The British government led by John Major felt attracted by it, because it seemed a perfect instrument to prevent the European Community from snatching away national sovereignty. At the same time, Jacques Delors grasped subsidiarity as a means of temporarily soothing these fears, well aware that the adoption of such a dynamic and moral concept would not by definition preclude future enlargements of the Community's responsibilities' (Van Kersbergen and Verbeek, 1994: 226).

However, that aspect of subsidiarity which de-emphasises the nation state, proposing models of decision-making which imply radical decentralisation towards local and regional authorities, may ultimately be difficult to ignore as subsidiarity becomes increasingly well-established in thinking about the European Union. Subsidiarity may come, in time, to inform not only the EU/Member State axis, but also the full range of social and political relations from the local to the transnational.

The more limited ambition of subsidiarity within the post-Maastricht European Union is evident from the terms of Article 3B(2) EC, which contains an essentially procedural definition focused on questions of efficiency. It emerges equally clearly from the detailed discussion of the instrumentalisation of subsidiarity in a number of documents: the Presidency Conclusions issued after the Edinburgh European Council in December 1992; various communications and reports subsequently published by the Commission, especially those concerned with inserting the principle into the legislative process (COM(93) 545; COM(94) 533); and the 1993 Inter-Institutional Agreement on Procedures for Implementing the Principle of Subsidiarity (EC-Bull, 10-1993, p119; on interinstitutional agreements see 5.16). The Presidency Conclusions in particular offer a detailed manual on how subsidiarity should be used within the EU legal order (see the sections reprinted in Ellis and Tridimas, 1995: 75–78).

The test of comparative efficiency for Community legislative action introduced by Article 3B(2) cannot really be considered in isolation from the final paragraph of that Article 3B which requires Community action to be 'proportionate': that is, not to go beyond what is necessary to achieve the objectives of the Treaty. That idea can be reduced to the question of *how* the Community should act, and is closely linked with the subsidiary nature of Community action, that is, *whether* it should act. The community is limited to taking action which seeks to achieve an objective which cannot be *sufficiently* achieved by the Member States, *and* which can be *better* achieved by the Community, 'by reason of the scale or effects of the proposed action'. In this domain, subsidiarity is perhaps better described as a 'regulatory principle' (Dehousse, 1994b: 109) than as a 'constitutional principle'. It should also be noted that the inclusion of Article 3B within the EC Treaty, rather than in the common provisions of the Treaty on European Union means that it is primarily aimed at Community competences, rather than the broader sweeper of the Union's powers. In other words, it is applicable in circumstances where the supranational 'Community' method is at issue, rather than the intergovernmentalism of the EU.

The nature of the terms contained in Article 3B is such that it is more appropriate to examine the subsequent practice of the institutions, especially the Commission which plays a key role through its role of legislative initiative, rather than subject the language of the article to an exhaustive and probably unrewarding semantic analysis. In any case, it has been suggested (Dehousse, 1994b) that there is an inherent ambiguity between the 'sufficiency' criterion and the 'better achievement' criterion, resulting perhaps from the legislative history of the provision. This suggests that too strict a textual analysis may yield little fruit. It is perhaps for the Commission that the application of subsidiarity and proportionality has had the most significant and tangible consequences in terms of its legislative activities: following its declaration to that effect at the Edinburgh Summit, it has withdrawn a number of proposals, and declined to submit new proposals in areas or in forms which it now considers inappropriate (i.e. too intrusive into national diversity, unnecessarily restrictive). In some fields, it has chosen a form of legislative measure which is less restrictive of national discretion, or opted for a 'soft' measure such as a recommendation rather than a formally binding directive. It has also engaged in a programme of 'legislative review' which has led to the simplification and codification of some legislative instruments, most notably in the field of the common external customs tariff. The Commission's legislative review programme will be examined in more detail in 5.10.

One point which should appropriately be reviewed in a chapter on constitutional principles is the question: 'is subsidiarity justiciable?' (Toth, 1994; Bermann, 1994: 390–403; Partan, 1995). Formally, the answer is 'yes'. Article 3B falls within the provisions of the Treaty which are subject to the binding and authoritative jurisdiction of the Court of Justice. Arguably the Court of Justice could soon be faced with the argument that a particular Community legislative measure is unlawful because it breaches the principles stated in Article 3B. The exercise of the review jurisdiction will undoubtedly be a difficult task for the Court, since it may have to take care not to trespass into areas of political discretion or to embark upon a review of socio-economic circumstances which carry it outside the province of the judicial role. Some authors suggest that the Court should confine itself to simple questions of process: have the institutions adequately turned their minds to the question of subsidiarity in considering whether and how to legislate or otherwise to take action (e.g. Bermann, 1994). Even if this approach is the one chosen by the Court in relation to direct challenges to *Community* measures, that may not be the end of the influence of the principle before the Court. For while showing a reluctance to invalidate EU level legislative measures, it may simultaneously recognise the influence of subsidiarity in sustaining the legitimacy of diverse national measures. It is already becoming evident in fields such as the free movement of goods that the influence of the subsidiarity principle can be seen in the Court's case law. For example, the Court has set stricter limits to the capacity of Article 30 EC to provide a general all-purpose constitutional norm for challenging all types of national measures which might potentially restrict interstate trade, however vestigially (Cases C-267, 268/91 *Keck and Mithouard* [1993] ECR I-6097). Subsidiarity has also shaped the balance of enforcement powers in the field of competition law, with the Commission adopting a Notice seeking to encourage greater decentralised enforcement of Articles 85 and 86 by national courts, and with the Court of First Instance giving general support to the Commission's approach (Case T-24/90 *Automec* v. *Commission (Automec II)* [1992] ECR II-2223).

3.11   A Just System?

It might seem repetitious to reiterate here the point about the fundamental importance of the Court of Justice and the EU legal order to the systems and processes of European integration. The point is implicit throughout this book. It is useful, however, to emphasise the specific importance of the law to the constitutional debate about European Union. The Court of Justice is given the task of ensuring that 'in the interpretation and application of this Treaty the law is observed' (Article 164 EC). Looking beyond this provision, the question must be asked: is the European Union a 'just' system, and to what extent are principles of 'justice' observed within that system? In this discussion of justice, the discussion is primarily structured around the status and importance of the *individual* in the EU legal order; questions of inter-state equity are not considered, although the question of inter-regional redistribution is touched upon briefly.

The question of 'justice' is not necessarily solely a 'legal' or 'normative' one. It is a perfectly valid question to ask the extent to which the EU promotes (or prevents) the achievement of forms of economic or social justice. This will be briefly considered below. We shall also examine questions of justice as they arise in the guise of the availability of remedies for individuals and the protection of individual rights, and in particular fundamental human rights.

The point has already been made in this chapter that the construction and the constitutionalisation of the legal status of the individual in EC law occurs to a large extent as a function of the federalisation of the EU legal order. That is, provisions of EC law may in certain circumstances confer rights on individuals, *against the Member States*, which national courts are bound to protect. This raises the status of the right of access to law as a right for EU citizens. As the Court of Justice put it in Case 222/84 *Johnston* v. *Chief Constable of the Royal Ulster Constabulary* ([1986] ECR 1651 at p. 1682):

'the requirement of judicial control stipulated by [Article 6 of Directive 76/207] reflects a general principle of law which underlies the constitutional traditions common to the Member States. That principle is also laid down in Articles 6 and 13 of the European Convention for the Protection of Human Rights and Fundamental Freedoms.'

The point is elaborated by Advocate General Darmon in the same case: 'the right to challenge a measure before the courts is inherent in the rule of law' (at p. 1656).

Specific questions of justice arise when the vindication of these rights is sought: in principle, remedies are a matter for national law, subject to the twin proviso that the remedies available are no more restrictive than those available in similar circumstances for the protection of rights under national law and the conditions to which such remedies are subject should not be such as to make it practically impossible to obtain a remedy. These notions are often abbreviated as the principles of non-discrimination and effective remedies (these are discussed in more detail in Chapter 10). It remains a controversial point just how far EC law can and should be intruding into the domains of the national legal orders in this context. Beyond such essentially procedural questions, broader societal questions of access to justice (availability and cost of lawyers; costs of legal proceedings; legal aid; etc.) remain matters within the control of the Member States (although limited legal aid for proceedings before the Court of Justice, including Article 177 EC reference proceedings is available).

Individuals also have rights of action before the Court of Justice itself, in this case to challenge directly acts or omissions of the EU institutions (see 1.5 and Chapter 12). A variety of forms of action and remedies are available, of which the most important are the action for annulment and the claim for compensation in respect of harm caused by unlawful actions of the institutions. The Court of Justice has frequently reiterated the importance of the rule of law for the institutions:

'It must first be emphasized . . . that the European Economic Community is a Community based on the rule of law, inasmuch as neither its Member States nor its institutions can avoid a review of the question whether the measures adopted by them are in conformity with the basic constitutional charter, the Treaty. . .' (Case 294/83 *Parti Ecologiste 'Les Verts'* v. *European Parliament* [1986] ECR 1339 at p. 1365).

In principle, therefore, individuals should be fully protected against arbitrary or other unlawful actions of the EU institutions. However, the right of action for individuals is in practice exceedingly limited: under the terms of Article 173 EC, a 'natural or legal person' may seek the judicial review of either (a) a decision addressed to them; or (b) a decision addressed to them by which they are directly and individually concerned;

or (c) a decision, which although in the form of a regulation, is of directly and individual concern to them. Neither the Court of Justice nor, more recently the Court of First Instance which has assumed primary jurisdictional responsibility for these provisions, has given a notably broad interpretation of provisions (for recent reviews see Craig, 1994; Arnull, 1995a; Neuwahl, 1996). Its approach has attracted considerable criticism over the years, particularly in the light of its willingness to encourage challenges to national legislation and national rules in national courts, and the lack of a clear theoretical underpinning to its approach to the question of access (Harlow, 1992a). The constitutional imbalance seemed to appear even starker after the Court of Justice's ruling in Cases 6, 9/90 *Francovich* v. *Italian State (Francovich I)* ([1991] ECR I-5357) in which it held that national governments could be held liable in damages for failure to implement a Directive, and that failure meant that those individuals who would have benefited from the implementation could claim damages for loss caused to them (van Gerven, 1994b). However, in subsequent cases the Court has sought explicitly to draw a parallel between the two cases, but not without causing a great deal of controversy. In its ruling in Cases 46, 48/93 *Brasserie du Pêcheur* v. *Germany, R.* v. *Secretary of State for Transport, ex parte Factortame Ltd (Factortame III)* ([1996] 1 CMLR 889) the Court held the United Kingdom government could in principle be liable for loss caused to Spanish fishing boat owners who were forced out of business by the adoption of discriminatory provisions in the Merchant Shipping Act 1988 which had been held to be contrary to Article 52 EC (freedom of establishment).

A second vital aspect of the 'justice' of the EU system concerns the respect for individual rights, especially fundamental rights. The protection of fundamental rights was discussed briefly in 3.5 and will be revisited in more detail in Chapter 6. Plainly, what is at stake here is not only an adequate judicial system of protection and a set of principles which put individuals at the centre of that system, but also the need for empirical assurance that those authorities acting within the realm of the powers conferred on the EU and EC (not only the institutions, but also the Member States where they are executing EC decisions) are in fact achieving a sufficient level of respect for fundamental rights. The absence of many positive findings of violations of EU fundamental rights by the Court of Justice does not wholly reassure that necessary standards are always being achieved, because there may be other reasons why certain types of problems are not being subjected to judicial resolution. It is partly for this reason that the proposal has been mooted that the EU should build on its formal commitment to the human rights standards enshrined in the European Convention on Human Rights and Fundamental Freedoms (ECHR) contained in Article F2 TEU and the case law of the Court of Justice, and seek accession to that Convention, thereby submitting the Court of Justice to a higher judicial authority in the form of the (Strasbourg) Court of Human Rights. The chances of accession occurring in the near future were significantly reduced by the approach taken by the

Court of Justice in Opinion 2/94. Asked whether the Community could accede to the ECHR without need for treaty amendment, it gave a negative reply. It also refused to consider what formal mechanisms might be appropriate to subject EC law and its courts to the authority of the ECHR institutions (Opinion 2/94 *Accession by the Community to the ECHR* (28.3.96)).

Concluding this brief discussion of issue of justice in the judicial sphere, it is appropriate to highlight the double-edged relationship between the Court of Justice and the issue of the legitimacy in the EU. Paradoxically, the very success of the Court, and its achievement of a relatively high level of compliance on the part of the actors over which it holds judicial authority, while partially reversing the worst effects of the EU's lack of democracy in the popular sense by providing a stable and largely predictable order of principle and policy, has sometimes taken weight from arguments aimed at correcting that lack of democracy as detractors have pointed to the worst 'excesses' of government 'by European judges'. Even so, the Court's authority has rarely been seriously challenged, although it has been clear that ever since the controversy over the Treaty of Maastricht heightened awareness of the provisions of the Treaty and the requirements of EC law (without necessarily increasing levels of understanding), domestic politicians in a number of Member States (especially the United Kingdom) have been prepared to call publicly for the role of the Court of Justice to be reduced.

The promotion and pursuit of justice in the socio-economic sphere raises more intangible questions which do not permit of straightforward answers in any political system, and especially not in the EU. At the level of rhetoric, Article 2 EC commits the Community to the task of promoting a 'high level of employment and of social protection, the raising of the standard of living and quality of life, and economic and social cohesion and solidarity among the Member States.' Beyond the rhetoric, Article 6 EC offers one important and concrete principle: the right to non-discrimination on grounds of nationality for EU citizens. This principle finds specific expression in many of the provisions on the internal market, and elsewhere in EU legislation. With the exception of Article 119, which guarantees the right to equal pay for men and women, the Treaty is otherwise devoid of justiciable social rights; those rights which it does convey are primarily to be understood according to a market logic. EU action in other vital human rights fields – has also been confined to the realm of 'soft law' – that is non-binding and declaratory commitments. A good example are the 1990 Resolution of the Council and the Member States on the fight against racism and xenophobia (OJ 1990 C157/1). Implementation of that resolution has now largely been taken into the sphere of CJHA – outside the narrow realm of EC law – although in an important new development the Commission has decided to include a 'non-discrimination clause' in any new or continuing policy initiatives, such as those taken under its vocational training or educational programmes (*CREW Reports*, 1996, vol. 16, no. 1/2, pp.3–5).

The paucity of justiciable rights is not, of course, the end of the story. Particularly since the mid-1980s and the first major revision of the Treaty of Rome by the Single European Act to include provisions on 'economic and social cohesion', the EU has been actively pursuing regional development policies whereby it targets funding towards less developed regions out of its structural funds. These provisions are not based on concepts of individual justice or equity, but on solidarity and equity as between *regions*. It could also be argued that the logic of these policies, as with EU policies on unemployment, growth and vocational training, to cite other redistributional policies, is primarily 'economic' and not 'social' in inspiration. The objective is to offset the worst effects of the impact of the internal market in areas of underdevelopment or where employment opportunities have been sucked away by the effects of market pressures on outdated industries. In the United Kingdom, long-standing leftwing opposition, on ideological grounds, to the EU has tended to be replaced in recent years by a sometimes unguarded enthusiasm for many of the policies coming 'from Europe', in that they have provided some of the few new regulatory structures for the United Kingdom which trades unions, for example, are convinced take sufficiently seriously the interests of less advantaged sectors of society. However, the continuing underdevelopment of the EU's social policies in comparison to its internal market policies indicates that over-enthusiasm for the European project on those types of ideological grounds is likely to be misplaced.

3.12   A Polity in a Global System?

Constitutions are not just internal documents; they also mediate the relationship between the entity 'constituted' and the outside world. In this paragraph, therefore, we are concerned with sketching out the impact of constitutional principles on the external relations system of the EU, in its bilateral relationships with other states or international organisations (e.g. the Council of Europe – see Article 230 EC) and in multilateral relationships which arise within global systems such as the General Agreement on Tariffs and Trade (GATT) and the World Trade Organisation (WTO).

While the EU itself has no formal international legal personality, each of the three European Communities exercises powers both in the internal and external spheres (e.g. Article 210 EC). As we noted in 3.9, a number of provisions of the EC Treaty provide explicitly for the formulation of policies in the external sphere, including those involving the conclusion of international treaties. The common commercial trade policy (Article 113 EC) is an obvious example; Title XVII of Part Three (development cooperation) and Part Four of the EC Treaty (association of overseas territories and countries with special relationships with Member States, including ex-colonies and dependencies) could also usefully be cited in this context. Article 238 provides for the conclusion of associations with States or international organisations 'involving reciprocal rights and obligations, common action and special procedure'. Where international agreements are to be concluded, Article 228 EC provides for a single method for negotiation and conclusion. The essential structure requires the Commission to negotiate on behalf of the EC, acting under authorisation from the Council, with the Council itself concluding the agreement. In many fields the Council will act by a qualified majority, unless an equivalent internal act would require unanimity, in which case parallelism is preserved. Parallelism is not, however, the principle governing the treatment of the European Parliament, which is normally only *consulted* on the conclusion of agreements (Article 228(3) EC). A number of exceptions are made, of which the most important cover agreements with important budgetary implications for the EU and agreements entailing the adoption, internally for the purposes of giving effect to the agreement, of a measure falling under the procedure of European Parliament–Council co-decision. These are subject to European Parliament *assent*.

The exercise of the EC's external powers is substantially shaped by the approach which the Court of Justice has taken to the interpretation of the scope of those powers. In this context the doctrine of implied powers has been extremely important, since it allowed the early development of parallel internal and external competences in relation, for example, to transport and the environment. Likewise, since the question of *exclusivity* is not expressly dealt with by the Treaty, the role of the Court has been vital. Notably the field of external trade policy offers a number of Court of Justice rulings which declare the exclusivity of Community *external* competence. From the early 1970s onwards, in a series of landmark rulings, the Court of Justice was able to enhance the autonomy of action of the fledgling European Community in the sphere of international economic relations. In Case 22/70 *Commission* v. *Council (ERTA)* ([1971] ECR 263 at p. 276) the Court declared, in relation to the common commercial policy, that the existence of

> 'these Community powers excludes the possibility of concurrent powers on the part of the Member States.'

The power to implement the common commercial policy – through international treaties including multilateral arrangements, and through unilateral actions by the institutions – lies exclusively with the Community (Opinion 1/75 *Re the Draft Understanding on a Local Cost Standard* [1975] ECR 1355). Although the situation of exclusive competence is very much the exception outside the field of the common commercial policy, the conservation of fisheries and competition policy, the Court is of the view that:

> 'The exclusive or non-exclusive nature of the Community's competence does not flow solely from the provisions of the Treaty but may also depend on the scope of the measures which have been adopted by the

Community institutions for the application of those provisions and which are of such a kind as to deprive the Member States of an area of competence which they were able to exercise previously on a transitional basis.' (Opinion 2/91 *Re ILO Convention* [1993] ECR I-1061 at p. 1077)

For agreements lying across the competences of the EC and the Member States, the phenomenon of the 'mixed agreement' concluded by both parties has developed. The very significant agreements stemming from the conclusion of the GATT Uruguay Round and underpinning the operation of the WTO were concluded in the form of mixed agreements, following the advice of the Court of Justice (Opinion 1/94 *GATT/WTO* [1994] ECR I-5267). One of the main reasons for this is that the common commercial policy does not include most aspects of trade in services, as opposed to goods. Indeed, shared competence leading to mixed agreements has very much been the norm in recent years. Wherever there is shared competence, the Member States and the Community are both bound by an obligation of cooperation, both in the processes of negotiation and conclusion, and in the fulfilment of commitments entered into (Opinion 1/94 [1994] ECR I-5267 at p. 5420).

There are particular problems of cooperation which will result from the joint participation of the Member States and the Community in an international organisation which stems inevitably from the limited nature of the latter's external competence (see Sack, 1995). These were discussed by the Court of Justice in Case C-25/94 *Commission* v *Council (FAO)* (19.3.96). The United Nations Food and Agriculture Organisation (FAO) was the first international organisation of which the EC formally became a 'member organisation'. The management of the right to vote in the FAO Council – which deals with subjects which cut across both national and Community competences – is dealt with in an unpublished Arrangement dating from 1991 between the Council and Commission 'regarding preparation for FAO meetings, statements and voting' which establishes a coordination procedure between the Commission and the Member States to decide on the exercise of responsiblities or on statements on a particular point. Section 2.3 deals with questions where there is shared competence: the respective roles of the Member States and the Community are determined according to where the 'thrust' of the measure lies. In the absence of agreement between the Commission and the Member States the matter will be decided according to the procedure provided for in the Treaty and the agreed practice. In the absence of agreement on this basis, the matter will be referred to the Committee of Permanent Representatives (COREPER). In the *FAO* case, the Court found that Arrangement to be binding on the institutions, and concluded that in the particular instance which concerned fishery conservation matters (covered by Cases 3/76 etc. *Kramer* [1976] ECR 1279), the Council had acted in breach of that Arrangement by opting for a Member State vote. In contrast to the form of cooperation organised for the participation in the FAO, specific procedures for the organisation of cooperation in relation to the WTO are laid down by Council Regulation (Council Regulation 356/95 OJ 1995 L41/3).

In terms of ensuring the constitutionality of external actions, Article 228(5) confirms the obvious point that agreements cannot be concluded which go against the terms of the Treaty; for such agreements to be adopted, prior Treaty amendments must be brought about under Article N TEU. The role of the Court of Justice at an early stage is guaranteed by Article 228(6) which allows any Member State or institution to obtain the opinion of the Court of Justice on an, as yet, unconcluded agreement (see Opinion 1/94 above). Agreements once concluded (or, more precisely, the acts of the Council which give effect to them internally) must be challenged using the Article 173 annulment procedure.

Article 228A provides a special procedure in respect of the adoption of measures giving effect to common positions or joint actions adopted under the Common Foreign and Security Policy (the Second Pillar of European Union), specifically where these require the imposition of economic sanctions on third countries. This highlights the vital external role of the EU, notwithstanding its lack of formal international status. Article B TEU in particular commits the Union to the objective of asserting 'its identity on the international scene, in particular through the implementation of a common foreign and security policy including the eventual framing of a common defence policy, which might in time lead to a common defence'.

The EU is committed to respect for international law. Provisions of international agreements concluded by (or binding on) the EC are part of EC law and may, in appropriate circumstances, be invoked before national courts as giving rise to enforceable rights for individuals (e.g. Case 104/81 *Kupferberg* [1982] ECR 3659). This has been particularly the case with appropriately phrased provisions of the agreements linking the EU and other 'associated' states. The Court has also held that the provisions of the European Convention on Human Rights and Fundamental Freedoms may be enforceable within the EU legal order, as general principles of EC law, an approach now given formal constitutional sanction by Article F(2) TEU. However, the Court has consistently held that provisions of the GATT are not capable of judicial enforcement, in order, for example, to invalidate an EC measure via the reference procedure in Article 177, because they are not of a nature to confer rights on individuals (Cases 2/4/ 72 *International Fruit Company NV* v. *Produktschap voor Groenten en Fruit* [1972] ECR 1219). Most controversially, the Court of Justice refused to accept the argument from Germany that provisions of the EC's importation and production regime for bananas were contrary to the GATT (Case C-280/93 *Germany* v. *Council* [1994] ECR I-4873), and as a consequence is facing arguments that the EU is degenerating into a 'banana republic' because of the refusal of the Court to develop adequate principles of 'foreign policy constitutionalism' (Petersmann, 1995: 1164). The Court of Justice judgment flew in the face of a GATT internal dispute settlement mechanism conclusion (a so-called GATT Panel) that certain aspects of the regime contravened GATT non-discrimination principles. In terms of the development of EU constitutionalism, it is arguably time for the Court of Justice to renounce what is perhaps a rather overprotective approach to the role of GATT in the internal legal order of the EU.

3.13   A Single Coherent System of Law?

The early seminal writings on the Community legal order place great store by its unity and uniformity. A quotation from Dagtoglou neatly illustrates this point:

'The European Community's legal order simultaneously presupposes and creates unity – and vice versa. The Community is above all a 'Community based on law' in the sense that the relations between the Community's subjects are relations between subjects of law and 'lega-lised' to a high degree under the control of the Court . . . For this reason Community law is important as a unifying factor' (Dagtoglou, 1981: 40).

Against the picture which Dagtoglou paints, it is possible to discern parallel trends in the constituting Treaties and in the Court's own case law in which EC law is by no means such a 'unifying' or centralising factor (Shaw, 1996). In the eyes of many, the Opinion which the Court of Justice handed down on the incompatibility of certain institutional aspects of the Agreement on the creation of a European Economic Area (EEA), especially as regards the creation of a court and a separate legal order, represented a high watermark in the evolution and authority of a single and autonomous Community legal order, characterised by a close link between law and legal processes and the inexorable march onwards of 'integration'. According to Weatherill it marked a 'zenith' in the 'Court's description of the Treaty structure as a Constitution' (Weatherill, 1995a: 184). From that high water mark, the Court has since retreated in a number of areas of its case law; moreover, the history of the development of the EC, now EU, Treaties since the amendments introduced by the Single European Act in 1986 indicates that picture is now much more complex, and that a number of variable elements must now be regarded as deeply implanted in the EU legal order.

As a result of the accession of most of the (EFTA) countries originally involved in the EU in January 1995 (see 2.5), the creation of the EEA lost much of its practical importance; however, as an essay in creating a novel and enhanced form of cooperation between the EU Member States and third countries partially modelled on, but not quite attaining, the level of integration *within* the EU, its legal importance should be underlined. The Agreement in its original form provided for the establishment of a Court combining judges from the EEA countries and from the Court of Justice, policing a type of legal order which would have partially merged with that of the EC/EU itself, but no longer under the sole authoritative control of the Court of Justice. The Court took exception to this institutional configuration, when it was asked about the compatibility of the Agreement with the EC Treaty (Opinion 1/91 *EEA Agreement* [1991] ECR I-6079), and on the way to reaching its conclusion passed a number of comments upon the nature of (what was then) the EEC, comparing it to the EEA. Provisions of the EC Treaties on competition and free movement are not ends in themselves, but mere means for attaining deeper ends, namely 'concrete progress towards European unity' (para. 17 of the judgment). The EEC Treaty, although an international treaty, is the 'constitutional charter of a Community based on the rule of law'. Moreover,

> 'as the Court of Justice has consistently held, the Community treaties established a new legal order for the benefit of which states have limited their sovereign rights, *in ever wider fields*, and the subject of which comprise not only Member States but also their nationals.' (emphasis added) (at p. 6102)

The progressive character of the Community's competence seems constitutionally crystalised by that ruling. In contrast, the EEA system is characterised as based on an 'ordinary' international treaty, which does not provide for the transfer of any sovereign rights to the intergovernmental institutions. Given the absence of homogeneity between the EEA and the EEC systems, the Court found that the proposed system of courts could have undermined the autonomy of the Community legal order 'respect for which must be assured by the Court of Justice pursuant to Article 164 of the EEC Treaty'. As a consequence of the Court's ruling, a revised draft was submitted for the Court's approval which proposed a separate court for the EFTA states only, but with the Court of Justice itself given an authoritative role in relation to the interpretation of the EEA, even in relation to EFTA national courts. The Court was able to approve the revised but rather complex dispute settlement procedures (Opinion 1/92 *EEA Agreement (No. 2)* [1992] ECR I-2821). For this reason, amongst others, it is difficult to accept that the EEA achieves its aim of creating a 'dynamic and homogeneous' area 'based on common rules and equal conditions of competition' (Preamble to EEA Treaty); rather, the terms 'Byzantine structures' and 'variable geometry' (Cremona, 1994) have been coined to describe this unusual experiment in broadening the Community experience with economic integration, through a form of cooperation which is more akin to accession than other forms of association, but which still differs in both legal form and economic substance. Furthermore, early indications highlight doubts about the development of a parallelism between the interpretation of the EEA Agreement by the EFTA court and the Court of Justice's approach to the EC Treaty (Kronenberger, 1996).

Notwithstanding the Court's approach to the questions it was asked in Opinion 1/91, it has in fact been possible to see increasing elements of what might be broadly termed 'variability' or 'differentiation' in the Treaty structures, legislative measures and even Court of Justice case law, probably since the adoption and entry into force of the Single European Act in 1986, and certainly since the conclusion of the Treaty of Maastricht in November 1991 (Harmsen, 1994). Taken together, the evidence would appear to indicate that while it has lost little if any of its overall authority, the EU legal order should be understood as a little less homogeneous than it was, as tolerating a wider diversity of institutional arrangements, and as requiring a lower degree of substantive uniformity in its relationship with national law.

Three examples from the Single European Act can usefully be cited to show the impact of 'variability' in a number of fields. The SEA provided the first institutional structures for the existing practices of European foreign policy cooperation (European Political Cooperation), but excluded this field of intergovernmental cooperation from the jurisdiction of the Court of Justice, an approach adopted in Title V of the Treaty of Maastricht and extended also to the field of Cooperation in Justice and Home Affairs (Title VI of the Treaty of Maastricht). Even within the narrower 'Community' field, something akin to a 'subsidiarity' principle was added to the new provisions on environmental policy, so that action by the Community was permissible only 'to the extent to which [the objectives of environemntal policy] can be attained better at Community level than at the level of the individual states' (Article 130R(4) EEC). This provision presaged the introduction of Article 3B EC by the Treaty of Maastricht. Finally, Article 100A(4) EC introduced a new element of flexibility in legislative approaches to harmonisation measures, perhaps as a trade-off for the arrival of qualified majority voting in respect of many of the harmonisation measures needed to give effect to the internal market programme. Even after the adoption of harmonisation measures under Article 100A, Member States may continue to apply national provisions 'on grounds of major needs', such as consumer protection or the protection of the environment. The Commission is given a power to police the operation of this provision, where necessary through recourse to the Court. This represents of a significant shift in tone as regards the ideology of harmonisation: uniformity is no longer the objective, but rather a sufficient degree of convergence to ensure the enhancement of broad internal market objectives. Likewise both legislative techniques of harmonisation (which increasingly adopt a minimum level of harmonisation allowing Member States to continue to apply stricter national rules) and judicial interpretations of the effects of harmonisation measures (which downplay the 'pre-emptive' impact of such measures on the legislative competence of the Member States – see 9.13) support a similar understanding of the broad objectives of the economic integration process.

The evidence in relation to the development of the legal order has to be reviewed in the light of a broader political debate about the direction, intensity and speed of continued progress towards integration. This debate could be summarised by highlighting tension between 'increased differentiation' or 'stronger uniformity'. Likewise there is a tension between 'deepening' (i.e. enhancing the structures existing between the current Member States) and 'widening' (i.e. pursuing the historic vocation of making the EU accessible to other European countries which wish to adhere to its institutional structures and political and economic objectives). It is now widely acknowledged that a much larger Union encompassing the countries of Central and Eastern Europe which have recently adopted free market economic and liberal democratic constitutional systems, as well as the very small countries of the Mediterranean such as Malta and Cyprus, cannot operate using an institutional framework designed for a relatively homogeneous Community of Six in the 1950s, and that the much greater levels of variation in economic development may require a very gradual imposition of the disciplines of the internal market upon countries such as Poland or Hungary. Within the Union itself, deep differences in perspective between the 'continental' core and the United Kingdom which continued a policy of semi-detachment into the mid-1990s have highlighted the lack of a cohesive overall sense of direction.

There has been little consensus about the precise use of terminology, but as the Member States and the institutions have continued to review the structures and concepts of European Union in the aftermath of the Maastricht Treaty ratification debacle, and in the lead up to the 1996 IGC, broadly three forms of variability or differentiation can now be identified, all of which can be exemplified by reference to more or less recent developments in the EC/EU. The lowest level of variability ('multi-speed') acknowledges the reality that the Member States may not all achieve what are common and agreed objectives at the same time. The use of transitional periods, particularly in accession agreements, is a good example, as are variable speeds in relation to VAT harmonisation. There is nothing constitutionally disruptive about 'multi-speed' integration. The other two forms of variability are more problematic: 'variable geometry' is a label now generally attached to a (permanent?) division within the EU between a 'hard' core and 'soft' periphery, with the hard core proceeding more rapidly towards greater integration and refusing to be held back by those standing on the periphery. This is one way of conceiving of the arrangements for Economic and Monetary Union under which there can be an irreversible locking of exchange rates for a small number of countries which achieve the convergence criteria, leaving out those countries which do not. It can also be applied to the Schengen system, under which a core group of countries have proceeded under separate international treaty to remove substantially all the internal borders between their countries. Much of the political rhetoric from many French and German politicians in the run-up to the 1996 IGC concerned the desire not be restricted in the pursuit of deeper integration by lagards such as the United Kingdom.

In some ways, there is only a small gap between variable geometry so defined, and the even looser model of a 'Europe *à la carte*' where countries pick and choose freely from a menu of policy areas in which they do or do not wish to be involved in integrative structures and processes. The EMU derogations for Denmark and the UK can be characterised in these terms, as can the UK's 'opt-out' from an enhanced social policy which is established by the Protocol and Agreement on Social Policy attached to the Treaty of Maastricht. The key difference appears to be between the creation of groups of countries following different but settled paths (in which a settled pattern of institutional and legal arrangements can also be envisaged), and the infinite possibilities of numerous Member States opting into and out of particular policies, perhaps as a function of internal political developments, potentially disrupting all possibility of the type of cohesive and relatively clear legal framework which marked the early years of the European Community project. At the time of writing at the very beginning of the 1996 IGC, these questions were the subject of intensive political and legal discussion, but remained substantially unresolved. In particular, there remains the very large question of how, if at all, the Court of Justice will be able to preserve at least the level of constitutional cohesiveness which currently characterises the system of the EU (Harmsen, 1994).

A separate question concerning the cohesiveness of the legal elements of integration arises in relation to the thesis that there is a gradual convergence between European legal systems (including those belonging to states currently outside the EU) in the fields of both public and private law (Markesinis, 1994; Schwarze, 1995), and a movement towards a *ius commune* for Europe which does not depend solely upon the exercise of legislative authority by the EU institutions. While the question of whether this is occurring is undoubtedly highly controversial (cf. Legrand, 1996), there is no doubt about the specific role of EC law in the development of a higher degree of functional (if not philosophical) convergence in certain areas of private, economic and administrative law. It has also greatly enhanced the status and relevance of comparative law in the modern legal world (Markesinis, 1993).

3.14   An Irreversible System?

Implicit in much of the discussion in the previous paragraph was the uncertainty that hangs over the very continued existence of the EU in the long term. The negotiated withdrawal of Greenland from the EU in 1985 emphasises the possibility that membership is not an irreversible status for Member States; but what of the system and structures themselves?

In Opinion 1/91 the Court was asked to consider whether Article 238 EC (which provides for associations between the Community and third states) could be amended to permit the type of EEA court envisaged by the original draft Treaty. In a passage which has been widely commented upon by those working in the field the Court held:

'Article 238 of the EEC Treaty does not provide any basis for setting up a system of courts which conflicts with Article 164 of the EEC Treaty and, more generally, with the very foundations of the Community.

For the same reasons, an amendment of Article 238 in the way indicated by the Commission could not cure the incompatibility with Community law of the system of courts to be set up by the agreement' [1991] ECR I-6079 at p. 6111).

Some have suggested that this passage means that the Member States are no longer the 'masters' of the Treaties which they once were, and there are certain fundamental principles which the Court of Justice would uphold even if the Member States were specifically to provide for their removal from the Treaties. Such 'supra-constitutional' principles might include the judicial role and authority of the Court of Justice itself, as well as liberal constitutional principles such as democracy and the rule of law. More cautious voices have pointed to the Court's own reaction to its exclusion from considering or interpreting certain sections of the Treaty of Maastricht which do not amend the EC Treaties. These include Article B TEU which sets out the objectives of the Union. In Case C-167/94 *Grau Gomis* ([1995] ECR I-1023) the Court unequivocally denied its authority to take a preliminary reference from a national court on that provision. According to Arnull (1995b: 611), Article L TEU (which precludes the jurisdiction of the Court of Justice)

'does more than merely establish that new areas of activity are not to be reviewed by the Court. It prevents the Court from adopting an expansive interpretation of its pre-existing powers under the first pillar [the EC Treaties] so as to bring within their scope action taken under the second and third pillars [CFSP and CJHA]. To that extent, the case law on Article L, albeit meagre, endorses the view that the Member States remain free to amend even the most fundamental provisions of the Treaties, including those concerning the powers of the Court.'

In the absence of a fundamental change of direction by the Member States, the concept of the *acquis communautaire* does introduce an element of internal stability and irreversibility into the system. Article B TEU declares the maintenance 'in full' of the *acquis communautaire* to be an objective of the EU, strengthening the argument that the introduction of the second and third pillars of the Union should be seen as progressive developments, leading perhaps to a subsequent reintegration of the 'Community' and intergovernmental 'methods', rather than as aspects of a hidden agenda to water down what has already been achieved. The *acquis* is likewise cited in Article C TEU; the institutions of the Union are committed to the respect for and duty to build upon the *acquis communautaire*. Literally, the *acquis* (or 'Community patrimony') could be seen as the whole body of legal provisions adopted under the Treaties by all of the institutions since the very inception of the Treaty. This is unrealistic, since clearly legislative fashions change, the objectives of the EU have developed, and scientific and technical knowledge has evolved. All of these factors mean that provisions may have to be amended, simplified or brought up to date from time to time. So the *acquis* must be seen as a narrower concept, linked to a set of legislative measures which give expression to the fundamental objectives of the internal market; it is defined by the Commission in a White Paper which addresses pragmatically the difficulties encountered by the countries of Central and Eastern Europe in their preparation for accession to the EU (COM(95) 163). Those countries linked by 'Europe Agreements' to the EU must gradually assimilate the *acquis* even *prior* to their accession to the EU. To help them select the relevant measures of EC law and to fix priorities, the Commission has defined the *acquis* in the following terms:

'Treaty articles and secondary legislation . . . [which] directly affect the free movement of goods, services, persons or capital. It is legislation without which obstacles to free movement would continue to exist or would reappear.'

One criticism of this approach is that it appears to prioritise the economic objectives of the EU over its social objectives to secure better living and working conditions, and to give effect to solidarity between the Member States.

3.15   An Economic Constitution?

The vital role of economic integration at the heart of the EU legal and political order (to be seen also in the approach of the Court of Justice) must always be stressed when studying EC law, although there is clearly a good deal of debate about the meaning of that role (1.4). One of the key contributions of the Court of Justice to the constitutionalisation process has been its interpretation of the key provisions granting specific freedoms (goods, labour, services, enterprise and capital) contained in Articles 9-73H EC (Titles I-III of Part Three of the EC Treaty) (6.6). Another important constitutional principle is contained in Article 7A EC, the general clause which contains a definition of the internal market. Not all of the 'economic' provisions of the Treaty should, however, be regarded as having a 'constitutional' character. It is perhaps premature, for example, to ascribe constitutional force to provisions on economic and monetary union laying down a timetable which realistically cannot be met.

On the other hand the general principles of economic and monetary union through the Treaty of Maastricht, with provisions on certain factors of economic convergence, institutional structures for a monetary union and single currency, and a constitutionalised relationship between monetary institutions and political and legal ones, can probably safely be described as constitutional. Moreover, it is probably the case that the future of the 'economic constitution' of the EU lies above all in this sphere (Harden, 1994: 616–620).

So far, however, the concept of an 'economic constitution' in the EU has had a specifically Germanic meaning, drawing heavily on a constitutional debate about the relationship between economic structure (based on a particular vision of free market competition) and formal constitution which has occurred particularly in relation to the Basic Law in Germany (Gerber, 1994). It has been argued further that the internal market is more than a functional framework for *interstate* trade, but a manual for government of the economy which determines *how* we do business (e.g. on the basis of fair and free competition).

A comprehensive review of all of these questions would presuppose a detailed knowledge of the economic and social law of the EU, and falls outwith the scope of this chapter and this book. The general consensus based on the Court of Justice's most recent case law on the internal market, in particular the free movement of goods and the capacity of Member States to regulate their economies, is that the Treaties as presently constituted do not offer the basis for an Economic Constitution (cf. Chalmers, 1995; Streit and Mussler, 1995; Joerges, 1994). On the other hand, there is substantial support for the view that the 'economic' orientation of the Treaties has often represented an important fetter upon the development of 'social' policies (e.g. employment policy; social integration; consumer protection), because structural deficiencies in the Treaties (the absence of the relevant legal provisions) has coalesced in an unholy alliance with the lack of political will demonstrated by a number of Member States.

3.16 Conclusion

The debate about the form and content of EU constitutionalism is proving to be an important aspect of the maturing of the EU political and legal order. The complexity of many of the issues passed over briefly in this chapter demonstrates that one of the major difficulties inherent in the *status quo* is that what passes for a constitution at present is insufficiently transparent, to the extent that the degree of accountability and legitimacy of the political institutions is frequently inadequate. Finally, it should now be apparent that the constitutional principles of the EU do not operate in a vacuum. The EU itself does not operate as a discrete and separate entity, but can only be properly understood in the context of the other places where public and state power is exercised, in particular at the level of the Member States.

Summary

1   It is important to set out in a single chapter those elements of an 'EU constitution' which can currently be identified.

2   At the present the EU has a constitution in the practical sense of having rules of an authoritative nature which determine the exercise of governmental powers, and which govern the relationships between the EU institutions and the Member States. It does not have a single formal document which can be identified as a 'constitution'. At the present stage of its development, the EU constitution is developed primarily through processes of international negotiation which produce treaties, supplemented by the interpretative role of the Court of Justice.

3   The German Federal Constitutional Court has raised serious doubts about EU constitutionalism, based on an analysis of sovereignty, democracy and citizenship in the EU.

4   The level of democracy in the EU can be regarded as inadequate, although the Court of Justice does supervise interinstitutional relationships with an eye to maximising the input of the Parliament in most circumstances, and to ensuring interinstitutional balance.

5   The citizenship rights of EU nationals are dispersed across the Treaty, and are based on a concept of free movement rather than a human rights foundation.

6   The federalism of the EU system is secured through a system of divided powers in which the EU has limited competences. Principles of exclusive competence and implied powers assist the EU institutions in making full use of the powers conferred upon them. The principle of subsidiarity in Article 3B is vital to an understanding of the scope of EU powers.

7   The Court of Justice secures the rule of law in the EU.

8   The external relations of the EU are to a large extent mediated through the EU constitutional system. The EU has important powers in the external sphere.

9   To an ever increasing extent, elements of diversity and fragmentation are penetrating into the EU legal order. A notion of multiple geometry is very clearly visible in the Treaty of Maastricht, especially the provisions on EMU.

10   As the Member States are still the 'masters' of the Treaties, the developments towards integration are theoretically reversible. However, the concept of the '*acquis communautaire*' introduces additional solidity into the system.

11   In so far as the EU has an 'economic constitution' it is based on the internal market, and, in the future, the development of Economic and Monetary Union.

Questions

1   In what respects is the EU constitutional framework incomplete?

2   Why is the concept of 'competence' important? How limited is Community competence?

3   To what extent is the EU constitution built on a rights foundation?

4   Why is the Court of Justice called a 'constitutional court'?

Workshop

You are the legal adviser to an EU constitutional convention, formed of delegates from each of the national parliaments. Draw up a draft of the first 20 'basic' articles of the EU constitution. What subjects should be covered? What types of principles should be incorporated? You should draw, where appropriate and useful, upon the existing provisions of the EU Treaties.

Further Reading

Bankowski and Scott (1996), 'The European Union?', in Bellamy (1996).

de Búrca (1996), 'The Quest for Legitimacy in the European Union', 59 *MLR* 349.

Cremona (1994), 'The "Dynamic and Homogeneous" EEA: Byzantine Structures and Variable Geometry', 19 *ELRev.* 508.

Dashwood (1996), 'The Limits of European Community Powers', 21 *ELRev.* 113.

Dehousse (1994b), 'Community Competences: Are there Limits to Growth?', in Dehousse (1994a).

Eleftheriadis (1996), 'Aspects of European Constitutionalism' 21 *ELRev.* 32.

Emiliou (1992), 'Subsidiarity: An Effective Barrier Against "the Enterprises of Ambition?"', 17 *ELRev.* 383.

Everling (1994), 'The *Maastricht* Judgment of the German Federal Constitutional Court and its Significance for the Development of the European Union', 14 *YEL* 1.

Harden (1994), 'The Constitution of the European Union', *PL* 609.

Koopmans (1994), 'The Quest for Subsidiarity', in Curtin and Heukels (1994).

Laffan (1996), 'The Politics of Identity and Political Order in Europe', 34 *JCMS* 81.

Lodge (1994), 'Transparency and Democratic Legitimacy', 32 *JCMS* 343.

Lyons (1996), 'Citizenship in the Constitution of the European Union: rhetoric or reality?', in Bellamy (1996).

MacCormick (1993), 'Beyond the Sovereign State' 56 *MLR* 1.

MacLoed, Hendry and Hyett (1996), Ch. 3, 'The Powers of the Communities'.

Nentwich and Falkner (1996), 'Intergovernmental Conference 1996: Which Constitution for the Union?', 2 *ELJ* 83.

Schmitter (1992), 'Representation and the Future Euro-polity', 3 *Staatswissenschaft und Staatspraxis* 379.

Schuppert (1995), 'On the Evolution of a European State: Reflections on the Conditions of and the Prospects for a European Constitution', in Hesse and Johnson (1995).

Walker (1996), 'European Constitutionalism and European Integration', *PL* forthcoming.

Weatherill (1995a), Ch. 5, 'Pre-emption and Competence in a Wider and Deeper Union'.

Weiler (1994a), 'Fin-de-Siècle Europe', in Dehousse (1994a).

Weiler (1995a), 'Does European Need a Constitution? Reflections on Demos, Telos and the German Maastricht Decision', 1 *ELJ* 219.

Part II

The European Union at Work

4 The Institutions of the European Union

4.1 Introduction

This chapter examines the composition, and basic powers, functions and organisation of the institutions of the EU. Discussion of the institutions at work is reserved for consideration in Chapter 5.

The institutional structure of the European Community established by Article 4 EC was, from the beginning, *sui generis*. The same institutional structure is now embedded into the European Union (Article C TEU), although as we shall see it remains uncertain to what extent the institutions we shall study here are institutions of 'the Union' or 'the Community' (5.8). The institutional structure resembles neither the typical governing structure of an international organisation, in that its institutions exercise sovereign powers transferred by the Member States, nor (yet) the institutional framework of a modern parliamentary democracy. It is, for example, not possible to identify a clear separation of powers between the legislative and the executive functions (Lenaerts, 1991a). The legislative function is presently divided between the Council and the Parliament, with inputs from the Commission and from a number of subsidiary bodies. The executive function is largely held by the Commission, but often under delegated powers from the Council which retains control through a committee structure, and such powers can only properly be exercised with the active cooperation of the Member States. There is no single legislative or executive procedure which can be described in simple terms. Reference must always be made to the Treaties to ensure that the institutions are acting within their powers as required by Article 4 EC. Within these limits, however, the institutions have broad autonomy of action, and may establish their own Rules of Procedure, which once created must be observed. The Court of Justice exercises a supervisory control over the division of powers between the institutions, as it does over the division of powers between the EU and the Member States.

The four cornered structure – Commission, Council of Ministers (now renamed Council of the European Union and termed 'Council' in this book), Parliament and Court of Justice, assisted by the Economic and Social Committee – envisaged by the original Treaties of Paris and Rome was described briefly in Chapter 1. A number of constitutional principles which govern their work have also been identified in Chapter 3. The institutions of the three founding Treaties have been merged since 1967, although the powers conferred by each Treaty upon the various institutions continue to differ. The discussion of the powers of the institutions in this chapter is focused on the powers granted by the EC Treaty. Since the Treaty of Maastricht this structure has now expanded; the Court of Auditors, which ensures financial discipline and prudentiality within the EU, has been given the status of an institution, and a Committee of the Regions has been established to make an additional advisory input into the legislative process (Article 4 EC). The essential institutional structure for EMU was also established. Under Article C TEU, the EU is served by a single institutional structure, based on that established for the EC itself, but supplemented in particular by the European Council (Article D TEU), and by the provisions of the TEU itself which guide the work of the three political institutions and the Court of Justice (Article E TEU).

Since the inception of the European Community, although the basic outline of the political institutions has remained largely the same, the details of the structure have altered considerably. Changes have been the product both of the enlargement of the EU which has necessitated the enlargement of the institutions and changes in their working patterns, and of the evolution of the functions and activities of what is now the EU. The pattern of development has frequently been one of the *de facto* development of new activities and interinstitutional relationships, followed by subsequent *de jure* recognition of the changes in an amendment to the constitutive Treaties. At no point does a study of the Treaties alone give a complete picture of the institutions at work.

The new bodies which have emerged inside and outside the existing framework, while making the pattern of policy-making at the EU level ever more complex, have not always brought improvements in the efficiency, transparency or accountability of the activities of the EU. The balance of power between the institutions has altered in significant ways. For example, the intergovernmental element in the decision-making process, represented by the Council of the European Union, has exercised a more dominant role than envisaged in the founding Treaties, and has tended to prevail over the supranational element, represented by the Commission and the Parliament. This is not just because the Council has largely retained the core legislative power, but because its influence has been strengthened by the following key developments:

- the evolution of the European Council;
- the emergence of the distinctive role of the Presidency;
- the establishment of the intergovernmental structures of political cooperation, and cooperation in home affairs matters;
- the work of the Committee of Permanent Representatives (COREPER); and
- the evolution of a structure of committees of national representatives which advise, assist and sometimes control the Commission ('comitology').

In sum, the Council has expanded 'upstream' in such a way as to influence the initiation of policy, and 'downstream' so as to exercise more control over the implementation of policy. The expansion of its roles has been largely at the expense of the Commission.

The European Parliament, while unable to overcome the dominance of the Council, has gradually emerged as a more significant political actor. It has worked to maximise its most important powers through:

- its increasing input into the legislative and budgetary processes, which ensures an element of democratic legitimacy for the EU;
- its powers of supervision and control over the other political institutions which promote executive accountability.

Despite the evolution of the other institutions and the proliferation of other bodies (including in very recent years a number of regulatory and executive agencies which may in the future come to assist and even compete with the Commission in relation to the management of EU policies), however, the Commission still retains a pivotal role within the institutional structure. Consequently, a discussion of the political institutions needs to begin by considering the composition, duties and tasks of the Commission.

4.2 The European Commission: Composition and Basic Character

The European Commission was originally intended as the 'bonding element' within the supranational institutional structure of the EU (Urwin, 1995: 81). It would drive forward the motor of integration, recommending policies for action, administering the Treaties and acting as a guardian and watchdog of the 'Community' interest. It grew out of the High Authority, created by the ECSC Treaty, which has greater powers of decision under the more detailed provisions of that Treaty. The Commission is based in Brussels, although it has an important outpost in Luxembourg.

In legal terms, the Commission is a college of twenty Commissioners – at least one from each Member State – chaired by a President. By convention, two Commissioners are drawn from each of the five larger Member States (France, Germany, Italy, Spain and the UK), and one from each of the ten smaller states. The Commissioners are appointed by common accord of the Member States (Article 158 EC), although in practice governments rarely oppose each other's nominations. By convention also, the UK's two Commissioners come from the two main parties –

Conservative and Labour. In theory, the President was in fact supposed to be appointed from amongst the Members of the Commission. In practice, the name of the President emerged before that of the other Commissioners, and this practice has now been given legal force in Article 158 EC as amended by the Treaty of Maastricht. The Member States will now nominate the President, after consulting the European Parliament, and the nominated person will be consulted in the process of nominating the rest of the Commissioners. The new Commission is then subject to a vote of approval as a body by the European Parliament, and only after this will the President and Commissioners be appointed by common accord of the Member States. This is one of the features of the Treaty of Maastricht which renders the Commission a more politicised and less purely bureaucratic and administrative body. It may be seen increasingly as a prototype European government. The sense of the appointment of an accountable body of politicians was given greater strength when the new Commissioners due to enter into office at the beginning of 1995 were subjected to lengthy, and in some cases quite rigorous, hearings before a European Parliament committee.

The term of office of the Commission was also extended from four to five years by the Treaty of Maastricht, and by transitional arrangements in Article 158(3) intended to synchronise the mandates of the European Parliament and the Commission, the Commissioners who came into office in 1993 were replaced or reappointed from January 1995. The current composition of the college of Commissioners may be altered by the IGC which began in March 1996. In particular in view of impending further enlargements, Member States may be forced to sacrifice the principle of each state having at least one Commissioner, and the large states having two. This will make the Commission a less unwieldy and probably more effective political body.

According to the Treaty, the qualities of the Commissioners are their general competence and an independence which is beyond doubt (Article 157(1) EC). Although appointed by the Member States, the Commissioners are not national representatives. Their independence is guaranteed by Article 157(2) which prohibits them from taking instructions from any government or other body, from taking any action incompatible with their duties, and from engaging in other occupations, and which enjoins them to act during and after their term of office with integrity and discretion. They give a solemn undertaking at the beginning of their term to respect the obligations of office. In return, they are protected from dismissal except for failure to fulfil the conditions required for the performance of their duties or serious misconduct, in which case the Court of Justice may compulsorily retire an errant Commissioner (Article 160 EC). In practice, the controls are greater, since the possibility of non-renewal in post at the expiry of a term of office may be sufficient occasionally to remind a Commissioner that ultimately he or she owes the appointment to the exercise of national discretion. Margaret Thatcher's well publicised refusal to renominate Lord Cockfield, the architect of the Commission's White

Paper on the completion of the internal market, for the second Commission presided over by Jacques Delors is a good example of the use of the renewal of the mandate as an instrument of discipline.

At the beginning of the term of office, the President allocates policy portfolios to the other Commissioners. The President's nominally free hand in this task is fettered by the need to balance national interests, which jealously demand the allocation of important and prestigious portfolios to their Commissioner(s), and by the general competence and reputation of the nominees. Not all the policy portfolios carry the same workload, or degree of policy coherence. Each Commissioner is assisted by a *cabinet*, composed of officials personally appointed by the Commissioner, which operates outside the formal bureaucracy of the Commission. The *cabinets* are headed by the *Chefs de cabinet*, who meet on a regular basis to prepare the work of the Commission itself. These meetings fulfil something of the same role in relation to the Commission as the Committee of Permanent Representatives (COREPER) in relation to the Council (4.10). A unique insight into the working of the Delors *cabinet* was provided by an important recent study of the man and his work (Ross, 1995).

Most of the day to day work of the Commission is done by a body of European civil servants who are employees of the institution. Those 'Eurocrats' concerned with policy and executive functions number around 10,000, assisted by a similar number in technical and support posts. Contrary to popular demonology about 'Brussels', this represents a small bureaucracy both in relation to the tasks which it is required to undertake and in comparison to the size of the national civil services. Eurocrats are normally appointed on the basis of entry examinations or, increasingly, come on secondment from national administrations, and while officially there are no national quotas, in practice a balance must be maintained, particularly in the more senior posts. The Commission is divided into twenty-three departments or Directorates-General ('DGs'), plus a number of special units and services such as the Secretariat General, the Legal Service, the Statistical Office and the Translation and Interpretation Services. Amongst the most important DGs are DG III (Internal Market and Industrial Affairs), DG IV (Competition), DG V (Employment and Social Affairs), and DG VI (Agriculture). Others, such as DG XXIII (Enterprises' Policy, Distributive Trades, Tourism and Social Economy) have a less clearly defined and coherent policy remit. The size of the DGs varies, as does their degree of influence and input into the policy-making process. There is no clear match between the DGs and the policy portfolios of the Commissioners. Some find themselves reporting to two or more Commissioners in respect of the various aspects of their work. Some Commissioners must liaise with two, three or more DGs. This mismatch, which can make for difficult relationships between the DGs and the Commissioners and their *cabinets*, coupled with the rigid organisational structure and the lack of overall policy oversight within the Commission, means that policy-making is often fragmented and lacking in coherence.

Since the Treaty of Maastricht, the Commission, like the other political institutions, has been preoccupied with the question of openness and transparency, and has invested a number of services, offices, groups, committees and DGs with varying degrees of responsibility for the development and implementation of policy on information and communication. In particular, the Commission has made increasing usage of the benefits of new technology to make available large numbers of documents through its internet server (http://europa.eu.int/), to supplement its paper-based information services which function primarily through the national offices of the Commission, through the Spokesman's Service which works with the press in Brussels and through DGX which has overall responsibility for the internal coordination of information and communication activities.

As a college, decisions must be taken collectively by the Commissioners, who meet every week in private session. The Commission takes decisions by a simple majority vote, but Members are bound by a principle of collective or collegial political responsibility, even if they opposed a particular decision. To facilitate the decision-making process, and prevent administrative overload, the Commission's own internal Rules of Procedures allow for a 'written procedure', whereby copies of draft decisions are circulated in advance to the Commissioners, and are adopted without discussion if there is no opposition. The Commission may also delegate the power to take 'clearly defined measures of management and administration' to individual Commissioners (Article 27 of the Rules of Procedure); delegation of certain decision-making functions to senior members of the Commission staff is also permissible.

The observance of both the Rules of Procedure, and general principles of administrative fairness and consistency, mean that the Commission must always comply carefully with the limitations set down by these procedures. This is well illustrated by the *BASF* case. In December 1988 the Commission adopted a decision finding a violation of Article 85(1) by a number of chemical firms alleged to be members of a cartel in the PVC sector. Heavy fines were imposed. The firms successfully challenged the decision before the Court of First Instance in Cases T-79/89, etc. *BASF* v. *Commission* ([1992] ECR II-315), which held that the decision was so vitiated by defects of form and procedure as to be 'non-existent' (12.2). It found that the measure had been altered in a way which went beyond the correction of grammatical, orthographical or typographical errors after it had been adopted by the Commission; this was a breach of the principle of the inalterability of administrative measures (Case 131/86 *United Kingdom* v. *Council (Battery Hens)* [1988] ECR 905). The Commission itself had considered only the French, German and English versions of the draft decision; it had left the Commissioner for competition policy matters to adopt text of the decision in the other languages of the case (Dutch and Italian). Finally, the Court of First Instance established that there was a problem over the timing of the taking of the decision, since some versions appeared to have been authenticated by Peter Sutherland – whose mandate expired on January 5 1989 – at a time when there was no text ready for notification or publication. The most controversial finding of the Court of First Instance was that concerned with 'non-existence'; this could have meant that all previous decisions of the Commission could be challenged, since no time limit applies to the challenge of non-existent acts. This aspect of the case was overturned by the Court of Justice on appeal in Case C-137/92 P *Commission* v. *BASF* ([1994] ECR I-2555), which found that there was no case for applying this extreme sanction, recalling that

'acts of the Community institutions are in principle presumed to be lawful and accordingly produce legal effects, even if they are tainted by irregularities, until such time as they are annulled or withdrawn' (p. 2647).

However, the Court of Justice agreed with the first instance finding of irregularities, stressing the vital importance of the collegial responsibility of the Commissioners:

'Compliance with that principle, and especially the need for decisions to be deliberated upon by the Commisioners together, must be of concern to the individuals affected by the legal consequences of such decisions, in the sense that they must be sure that those decisions were actually taken by the college of Commissioners and correspond exactly to its intention' (p. 2650).

It rejected the Commission's view that it need only make clear its intention to take certain action without needing to be involved in the drafting and finalisation process:

'Since the intellectual component and the formal component form an inseparable whole, reducing the act to writing is the necessary expression of the intention of the adopting authority' (p. 2651).

The Court confirmed the primacy of the principle of inalterability, and the paramount necessity for authentification of acts in the form provided for in the Rules of Procedure (signatures of President and Executive Secretary), as a guarantee of legal certainty (see 6.5). Consequently, the Court annulled the decision.

The independence of the Commission makes it uniquely qualified to give a 'European perspective' upon the progress of European integration, although in practice it is of course never entirely separated from national or sectoral pressures and lobbies. It has developed a role as the mediator and conciliator between disparate and conflicting interests, in particular within the Council, and has operated as the broker in the resolution of numerous intractable disputes such as those over budgetary contributions and financial discipline within the EU.

The powers and tasks of the Commission are set out in Article 155 EC:

'In order to ensure the proper functioning and development of the common market, the Commission shall:
- ensure that the provisions of this Treaty and the measures taken by the institutions pursuant thereto are applied;
- formulate recommendations or deliver opinions on matters dealt with in this Treaty, if it expressly so provides or if the Commission considers it necessary;
- have its own power of decision and participate in the shaping of measures taken by the Council and by the European Parliament in the manner provided for in this Treaty;
- exercise the powers conferred on it by the Council for the implementation of the rules laid down by the latter.'

In practice, the role of the Commission is best described by dividing it into the four basic functions examined in the following paragraphs:

- the formulation of policy;
- the execution and administration of policy;
- the representation of the interests of the EU;
- the guardianship of the Treaties.

The more limited powers of the Commission in relation to CFSP and CJHA are covered in 5.8.

4.3   The Policy-Making Function

There are three main mechanisms whereby the Commission develops the policy of the EU. It makes proposals for action; it drafts the budget which determines the allocation of resources (5.13); and it takes policy decisions within the limited powers it is granted by the Treaties.

Proposals for action take either a 'small' or a 'large' form. 'Small' initiatives are draft legislative acts prepared by the Commission for adoption by the Council (acting, where, appropriate with the European Parliament) under the law-making powers of the Treaties. Almost all the provisions of the Treaty which grant a law-making power to the Council begin 'on a proposal from the Commission. . .'. The Commission has a broad discretion in putting forward policy proposals, although some limits are imposed by the Treaty itself. For example, when making proposals for the adoption of measures in relation to the completion of the internal market, the Commission has been required by Article 7C to take into account the difficulties faced by weaker economies as they prepared for the internal market. Article 100A(3) EC further requires all proposals made for measures concerned with the completion of the internal market under that provision which concern health, safety, environmental protection and consumer protection to take as a base a high level of protection.

'Large' initiatives are Commission proposals for EU action within a broad field. Perhaps the best known is the Commission's White Paper *Completing the Internal Market*, but others include the *Social Action Programme* issued as the basis for action to implement the Community Social Charter, and the so-called *Delors II* plan, on the restructuring of the EU's finances for the achievement of European Union (5.12).

The Commission has a limited power of decision under the Treaty. Some powers are granted explicitly by the Treaty, others are implicit in its system. One example is Article 118 EC which gives the Commission the task of promoting close cooperation between the Member States in various fields of social policy including employment, labour relations, working conditions, vocational training and social security. In Cases 281, etc./85, *Germany et al.* v. *Commission (Migration Policy)* ([1987] ECR 3203) the Court of Justice held that where the Commission is granted a specific task under the Treaty, it must be regarded, implicitly, as having the power to take steps to achieve this task, including the power to adopt binding measures such as decisions. The Commission is also responsible for developing the competition policy of the EU, which involves not only the enforcement of the prohibitions in Articles 85 and 86 EC on anticompetitive and monopolistic conduct against individual undertakings (a function better characterised as enforcement rather than policy implementation: 4.6), but also the development of general policy initiatives aimed at dismantling rigidities in public sector markets such as telecommunications. To this end it has an important power of decision under Article 90(3) EC. Use of this power to issue directives has been upheld by the Court of Justice on several occasions (Cases C-271, etc./90 *Spain et al* v. *Commission* [1992] ECR I-5833). Other original legislative powers include Article 48(3) EC giving the Commission the power (which it has exercised) to lay down regulations establishing the principles on which retired migrant workers may continue to reside in the host state. However, the majority of the Commission's legislative or regulatory powers are not original, but are delegated to it by the Council. This has occurred extensively in the field of agriculture under Article 43 EC, in relation to customs law, and to a more limited extent in the field of competition law.

In the development of policy, the Commission's internal bureaucracy is assisted by internal working groups and Advisory Committees composed of national experts, or civil servants representing national interests, by networks of experts, and by 'Euroquangos' such as CEDEFOP, the EU's centre for the promotion of vocational training. Closely linked to the Commission is an ever-growing network of agencies and other similar bodies which exercise quasi-regulatory and advisory functions (4.14). The Commission – like the other political institutions – is also subject to intense lobbying by national and EU-based interest groups (Harlow, 1992b; Mazey and Richardson, 1994; Andersen and Eliassen, 1996b; see 5.9).

4.4   The Executive and Administrative Function

Since the bureaucracy of the EU is extremely small, and largely centrally-based, it relies for the most part for the implementation of policies upon the administrations of the Member States, and, where appropriate, the network of agencies referred to in 4.3. The examples of 'direct implementation' of EU policies by the Commission are few, and can more accurately be characterised as activities of the Commission aimed at protecting the legal fabric of the EU such as the enforcement of the competition rules and the rules on state aids (see 4.6). The Commission's role in the 'indirect implementation' of the major policy areas such as external trade, customs, agriculture and social security for migrant workers is likewise supervisory, and consists in large part in the making of rules which the national administrations must observe, and then ensuring that they are observed. The duty of loyalty to the European Community contained in Article 5 EC requires national administrations to cooperate in the implementation of EU policies.

In laying down the rules for national administrations to follow, the Commission is commonly exercising a power delegated by the Council under Article 145 EC. As amended by the Single European Act, this provision envisaged the creation by the Council of a clearer structure for the long-standing practice of delegating powers to Commission subject to the supervision of committees of national representatives chaired by a representative of the Commission. This structure is known as 'comitology', and is one mechanism whereby the Member States have extended their input into EU activities beyond the legislative role of the Council itself (see 5.11).

In its executive role, the Commission manages the finances of the EU, and supervises both revenue collection and expenditure. More than half of the funds go to the European Agricultural Guidance and Guarantee Fund, the Guarantee Section of which is charged with implementing the agricultural price support system established under the Common Agricultural Policy. The Commission also administers the structural funds of the EU aimed at ensuring economic and social cohesion, namely the European Social Fund, the European Regional Development Fund and, more recently, the Cohesion Fund. The management of smaller incentive funds, such as, for example, the programme of grants available under the SOCRATES scheme to encourage higher education student and staff mobility, is now frequently contracted out to outside bodies which are responsible to the Commission for the proper management of the funds.

4.5   The Representative Function

The supranational composition and role of the Commission make it uniquely qualified to fulfil the function of representing the interests of the European Union on the wider global stage. The Commission President is recognised as an important international statesman, attending international conferences, acting within international organisations and speaking on behalf of the EU, often in conjunction with the leader or foreign minister of the Member State which holds the Presidency of the Council, who tends to focus on the political representation of matters falling within the Second and Third Pillars of European Union. As third countries increasingly choose to deal with the EU rather than individual Member States, the Commission's role in establishing diplomatic missions in third countries and accrediting diplomatic missions from those countries is becoming more important (MacLoed *et al.*, 1996).

The Commission also has the task of recommending the opening of negotiations with third states and of conducting negotiations leading to the conclusion of international agreements on behalf of the EC under the procedures in Article 228 EC.

4.6 Guardian of the Treaties

The Commission is the guardian of the legal framework of the Treaties, a role explicitly conferred by Article 155 EC. Its significance is such that it will be discussed fully in a separate chapter (Chapter 7). The Commission has a general power under Article 169 EC to refer to the Court of Justice alleged violations by the Member States of the Treaties and of the rules adopted thereunder. It has additional specific enforcement powers, for example in relation to state aids (Article 93 EC) and the control of the anti-competitive activities of public undertakings and undertakings entrusted with the performance of public services (Article 90 EC). It may in some circumstances authorise Member States to depart from the strict rules of Treaty; for example, it may authorise the Member States to restrict imports of third country products in free circulation in other Member States under Article 115 EC. It also supervises the right of the Member States to apply national measures to protect environmental and health and safety policies under Article 100A(4) EC, even where the EU has adopted harmonising measures.

Under Council Regulation 17 adopted in 1962, the Commission was granted numerous enforcement powers in relation to Articles 85 and 86 EC, which proscribe anti-competitive and monopolistic conduct on the part of undertakings within the EU. In exercising these powers, the Commission is subject to the control of the Court of Justice over the legality of its procedures.

4.7 The Council of the European Union: Composition and Basic Character

The Council is composed of representatives of the Member States, at ministerial level 'authorised to commit' their government (Article 146 EC).

The Council represents the intergovernmental element within the institutional structure of the EU. Indeed, it is, in many respects, the main institution of the 'Union'. It meets, generally, in Brussels, where its Secretariat is based (in the recently built *Justus Lipsius* building). The Presidency of the Council circulates on a six monthly rotation between all of the Member States – a long established practice which is coming under challenge as the EU grows larger. The President sits in the chair at Council meetings (see also 4.11). The Council meets when convened by the President, or at the request of one of its members or the Commission. As this implies, a member of the Commission with appropriate responsibilities normally attends Council meetings, although without a vote. The membership of the Council is not static. Although there is a body conventionally designated the 'General Council' composed of the Foreign Ministers of the Member States, which discusses issues of general concern to the EC and especially the EU, much of the practical work of the EU is undertaken by the 'technical' Councils, that is sectoral and specialised Councils. These include the 'Internal Market Council', composed of trade and industry ministers with special responsibility for the completion and management of the internal market and the 'Agriculture Council', composed of Agriculture ministers who oversee the development and implementation of the CAP. The fragmentation of the Council weakens its effectiveness, as there is insufficient general policy coherence within the legislative activities of the EU, although this function is fulfilled in part by the Commission, the European Council, the Presidency and even the Council's own bureaucracy or Secretariat which, while smaller than the Commission's, is increasingly influential. The Council is also assisted by its own Legal Service.

The tasks of the Council are set out in Article 145 EC. They are to ensure the coordination of the general economic policies of the Member States, to take decisions and to delegate implementing powers to the Commission. There is a tension between the first two tasks, in that they illustrate the sometimes irreconcilable dual role of the Council: to act as the forum for the representatives of the Member States, and to act as the principal decision-making body for both the European Community and the European Union. The Council also has the power under Article 152 EC to request the Commission to undertake any studies the Council considers desirable for the attainment of the objectives of the Community, and to submit to it any appropriate proposals. Used extensively this power could significantly limit the policy-making function of the Commission.

It is not possible to know exactly what happens within the Council. Indeed, the Council remains the least known of the EU institutions (cf. Westlake, 1995; Hayes-Renshaw, 1996). It deliberates in secret and no full record of its business is published. As it does not have a permanent political presence in the same way as the Commission, it has not established informational channels to the same degree. Press Releases and briefings by national ministers have often been the only sources of information, apart from the published record in the Official Journal of legislative acts which the Council passes, or resolutions which it adopts. In the aftermath of the Treaty of Maastricht, as openness and transparency moved onto the political agenda, the Council introduced reforms to allow for limited public sittings, publication of voting records, and a policy of limited access to its internal documents (reviewed in Case T-194/94 *Carvel and Guardian Newspapers* v. *Council* [1995] 3 CMLR 359: 3.5). These changes have been implemented primarily through *internal* amendments to the Council's Rules of Procedures in 1993, which establish secrecy as a general principle for Council action subject to exceptions. These are managed through specific rules governing public access to Council documents; what *Carvel* established was the need for an individual case-by-case assessment of requests made by the public. This is backed up by a Code of Conduct applying to Council and Commission documents, introduced in 1993 and amended in 1995 (Bull-EU 10/95), covering also access to Council minutes. Secrecy remains strongest in the intergovernmental fields of EU policy, notably the Second and Third Pillars. The current situation has been described as unsatisfactory by a number of commentators, as it rests on internal discretionary measures of the Council in particular, and lacks a fundamental rights foundation through a 'right-to-know' (e.g. Lodge, 1994; Curtin, 1995).

The members of the Council are not politically accountable to any EU institution for their acts. The Parliament can and does ask questions of the Council, but the answers given are not always full or helpful. However, a convention is developing that the Presidency presents its programme of action for the next six months for debate in the Parliament. The level of accountability at the national level varies between the Member States. The Danish Parliament – the *Folketing* – exercises the tightest control, with the Danish representatives on the Council being frequently required to delay EU decision-making processes in order to consult at a parliamentary level. Scrutiny within the UK Parliament is not as strict. This unsatisfactory situation persists although a number of governments, that of the UK included, insist that the democratic legitimacy of the EU is anchored through the role of national Parliaments, and a number of statements to that effect are to be found in Declaration no. 13 on the role of national Parliaments in the European Union, annexed to the Treaty of Maastricht.

The Council is subject, like all the institutions, to the rule of law. This largely leaves its legislative discretion unfettered, although there are a number of overriding principles which legislative acts may not violate (5.2; 6.4 *et seq.*). This can lead to the annulment of legislative acts adopted by the Council, or to actions for damages (see Part IV). Within narrow limits the Council is also responsible for a failure to act in the legislative field. In Case 13/83 *Parliament* v. *Council* ([1985] ECR 1513) the Parliament successfully challenged the failure of the Council to create a common transport policy using Article 175 EC. Although the Court of Justice would not substitute itself for the legislature and lay down what form such a policy should take, the case was widely interpreted as a rap on the knuckles for the Council for dilatory exercise of its legislative function.

Article 148 EC provides for simple majority voting, unless the Treaty provides otherwise. A simple majority is constituted by the votes of 8 countries out of 15. In practice, the Treaty almost always provides for unanimity or a so-called qualified majority, the latter becoming increasingly the norm. Qualified majority voting (QMV) means that under Article 148(2) EC, the votes of the Member States are weighted as in Table 4.1.

A qualified majority requires there to be at least 62 votes cast in favour of a measure out of 87, where the Council's deliberation is based on a proposal from the Commission. In other cases (e.g. under CFSP and CJHA where there is limited usage of QMV), the 62 votes must include the votes of at least 10 Member States. The weighting of votes in QMV departs in part from the theory of the equality of all states in international law, although the weighting does not fully reflect population differentials – the less so, the larger the number of Member States belong to the EU. The voting power of Germany was not strengthened after unification although it is now much the biggest Member State. Before the latest enlargment, the weighting of the voting and the minimum requirement had the effect of allowing what would normally be at least three dissenting Member States to block a measure. In view of that enlargement, rather than remake the whole structure, the European Council adopted the so-called *Ioannina Compromise* whereby a minority of Member States with a total number of votes between 23 and 25 may temporarily block a decision due to be taken by QMV. In such a case, the Council then tries to reach a solution which can be adopted by a least 65 votes. The reluctance of the Council (and the Member States) to commit themselves fully to QMV has been one of the consistent themes of institutional development in the EC and now the EU.

Table 4.1   Qualified Majority Voting

Austria	4
Belgium	5
Denmark	3
Finland	3
France	10
Germany	10
Greece	5
Ireland	3
Italy	10
Luxembourg	2
Netherlands	5
Portugal	5
Spain	8
Sweden	4
United Kingdom	10
Total	87

4.8 The Council Acting as an Intergovernmental Body

On certain occasions, in particular where the subject-matter of the meeting falls outside the scope of Community competence, the representatives of the Member States will meet on an intergovernmental basis. The best known instance of this, and the one which has been 'formalised' longest, is foreign policy cooperation, institutionalised initially in the form of European Political Cooperation (Part III of the Single European Act) and then superceded by the Common Foreign and Security Policy (CFSP) (the second pillar of European Union). This is rather wider in scope and a little more supranational in nature than EPC with some provision for QMV. Intergovernmental cooperation between the Member States also grew up to coordinate policies on immigration, asylum, police cooperation and other home affairs matters. The Trevi Group and the Ad Hoc Group on Immigration in which the Member States met to discuss these matters were replaced by the more formalised arrangements of Justice and Home Affairs in Title VI TEU (Third Pillar of European Union) (see also 4.10).

The institutional structures have also provided a framework for inter-governmental cooperation in certain areas which once lay at the margins of Community competence such as policy on culture, education and health. Measures adopted in this field were commonly designated 'Decision of the Representatives of the Governments of the Member States, meeting in the Council'. An example is the Resolution of the Ministers for Culture Meeting within the Council of June 7 1991, on the development of the theatre in Europe (OJ 1991 C188/3). Since the Treaty of Maastricht, such a resolution can now be adopted within the context of the EC's own limited new competence in relation to culture (Article 128 EC). Even as the competence of the Community expands, and certain areas are brought within the second and third pillars of the Union (e.g. measures on racism and xenophobia), still there are areas of cooperation and collaboration which prove themselves apt for the 'Decision of the representatives . . . .' formulation. A recent example is the Resolution of the Council of the European Union and of the respresentatives of the Governments of the Member States, meeting within the Council of June 1995 on the employ-ment of older workers (OJ 1995 C228/1). Measures of this nature should be characterised as 'soft law' which is not binding, but largely exhortatory in content and nature (6.16).

4.9 The European Council

The most prominent and most powerful form of intergovernmental cooperation within the EU is the European Council. The practice of summit meetings between the leaders of the Member States has long existed. Regular meetings have occurred since 1974, and the European

Council was finally formalised in Article 2 of the SEA, now superceded by Article D TEU. This provides that the European Council should meet at least twice a year and that it should be attended not only by the Heads of State or Government, assisted by their Foreign Ministers, but also by the President of the Commission and one other Commissioner. It is given the task of providing the EU with 'the necessary impetus for its development' and of defining 'the general political guidelines thereof'. It is required to submit a report after each meeting to the European Parliament, and make a yearly written report on the progress achieved by the EU.

The European Council has remained formally outside the structures of the European Community (i.e. the supranational pillar), not subject to the control of the Court of Justice. Conversely it has no legal power to act in pursuance of the Community's objectives or power of decision (Case T-584/93 *Roujansky* v. *European Council* [1994] ECR II-585). Of course, there would be nothing to prevent the Heads of State or Government meeting as the Council of the European Union; however, one of the strengths of the European Council, which has increasingly come to fulfil a troubleshooting role in pushing forward the process of European integration and resolving the conflicts between the Member States at the highest level, lies precisely in its informality.

During the crisis over the ratification of the Treaty of Maastricht, the European Council probably gained an even higher status than before, with a number of skilful compromises being worked out which eventually put the ratification process back on course. Indeed, European integration processes without the European Council have now become unimaginable, although such a crucial role for the Member States in policy formulation was not envisaged by the founders of the Treaties. In practice, the European Council is not simply an opportunity, as it is sometimes portrayed in the British media, for the leaders of Member States reluctant to press further with European integration to halt the entire process. For example, Margaret Thatcher found the regular meetings of the European Council to be occasions when she could not always resist pressure for conformity, as with the agreement over the British budget rebate at the Fontainebleau summit in June 1984 (see 2.10). Furthermore, a skilful Commission President such as Jacques Delors was able to exploit alliances with pro-integrationist leaders such as President Mitterrand of France in order to carry forward the objectives of the Community. An example of this is the budgetary discipline settlement agreed at the special meeting in Brussels in 1988. The essence of the European Council's function, more than any other EU body, is compromise. Leaders, whose domestic fate in elections will be judged largely according to their economic success, need to find a balance between promoting the 'good' elements of integration, whilst hindering the 'bad' ones. That means choosing between those EU proposals which are perceived, from the perspective of the domestic agenda, as excessively intrusive or insufficiently beneficial, and those which are not.

4.10 The Committee of Permanent Representatives (COREPER)

In addition to the help it gets from 'above' in the form of the resolution of serious conflicts at the level of the European Council, the Council also receives assistance from 'below' in the form of the preparatory work of the Committee of Permanent Representatives (COREPER), which is provided for in Article 151 EC. The Permanent Representatives are in effect the Ambassadors of the Member States to the Community, who are based in Brussels and who provide a continuity of presence which political representatives cannot. COREPER meets at two levels: COREPER I (deputy Permanent Representatives) whose remit covers more technical matters and COREPER II (Permanent Representatives themselves) who discuss the more controversial political matters, identifying the differences of view which the Council itself must settle at a political level. The workings of COREPER and the Council are further facilitated by working groups and committees which meet on a regular or *ad hoc* basis to discuss policy proposals at an early stage.

Formally, COREPER facilitates Council deliberations by permitting the division of the Council agenda into two parts. Part A contains items on which a unanimous view has been obtained within COREPER. These points can be agreed without discussion. Part B contains the points on which a decision cannot be reached without further discussion and probably compromise within the Council itself. These matters are regulated by the Council's own Rules of Procedure, which themselves represent, however, a fetter on the extent to which the Council can delegate effective authority to COREPER (see Case 68/86 *United Kingdom* v. *Council (Agricultural Hormones)* ([1988] ECR 855) where the Court declared a Directive to be void, as the Council was in breach of its own Rules of Procedure in adopting a Directive by a written vote when two Member States (the UK and Denmark) were known to be against it). The Court has also confirmed that COREPER, despite its increasingly significant contribution to the institutional life of the EU, is not an institution in the formal sense of the word, as its role is limited by the terms of Article 151 EC, and cannot therefore take 'decisions' in a legal sense (Case C-25/94 *Commission* v. *Council (FAO)* (19.3.96)).

Operating parallel to COREPER under the two 'outer' Pillars of European Union are two further committees which assist the Council in its work in relation to CFSP and CJHA respectively. These are:

- the Committee of Political Directors (Article J.8 TEU) which monitors the international situation, contributes to the definition of policies by delivering opinions to the Council, and monitors the implementation of policies in the field of foreign and security policy generally; and
- the Coordinating Committee (Article K.4 TEU, and known as the Article K.4 Committee) which has a role in coordinating CJHA policy,

giving opinions to the Council and preparing of the Council's discussions under CJHA. It also has a specific 'Community' role under Articles 100C and 100D EC, in relation to the coordination of visa policy and any other policy area which the Member States choose to bring over the bridge or *passerelle* from CJHA into the European Community proper.

4.11   The Presidency

The Presidency of the Council of the European Union circulates at six monthly intervals between the Member States, originally according to an alphabetical arrangement based on the title of the country in the national language (Belgique, Danmark, Deutschland, Ellas (Greece), etc.). In the present round of Presidencies, which began in January 1993, the Member States were reversed in pairs, to ensure that they alternate between the January–June slot and the July–December slot. In the first half of the year, the everyday work of the EU is dominated by the CAP; in the second half of the year, it is the budget which normally dominates the agenda. Adjustments consequent upon the fourth enlargement have altered the earlier arrangement to give the Presidency for the first time to Austria in the second half of 1998 (by which time the IGC and any consequences it gives rise to should be dealt with), to Finland in the second half of 1999, and to Sweden in the first half of 2001. The future of the Presidency in its present form has been in question for some time, as further enlargement will make the rotation principle unwieldy, reduce the influence of the larger and most internationally respected Member States, and raise the possibility of several small (or indeed exceedingly small states) succeeding each other over a period of years. Reform of the arrangements for the Presidency was therefore an item placed at an early stage on the IGC agenda, but there is no simple solution which respects the formal equality in international law of sovereign states.

On paper the task of the Presidency of the Council is a modest one. It is to convene and chair meetings of the Council, and to sign, on behalf of the Council, legislative and other acts adopted by the Council, or by the representatives of the Member States meeting within the Council. The Presidency acts as the Chair within all the fora convened within the EU structures, in the largest sense. This includes not only the General Council, the Sectoral Councils, the European Council and COREPER I and II, but also other fora of intergovernmental cooperation such as CFSP and CJHA. In practice, however, the Presidency has become a great deal more significant, usurping in part many of the policy-making and mediation functions of the Commission. The country holding the Presidency usually sees it as an opportunity to leave a distinctive mark upon the EU scene, and to be seen by the outside world as synonymous with the EU itself. It prepares and presents a programme of action for the Presidency and prioritises particular measures which it would like to see passed in the Council. This it can achieve by controlling the agenda of the Council, in conjunction with the Council's own Secretariat. The state holding the Presidency now works closely in a triumvirate with those immediately preceding and succeeding it, to seek to ensure some policy continuity. This important *de facto* development is referred to in the Treaties only in the context of CFSP (Article J.5(3) TEU).

The key role of the Presidency can be illustrated through some examples. The Dutch Presidency of the second half of 1991 was given the onerous responsibility of brokering the outcome of the intergovern-mental conferences on Economic and Monetary Union and Political Union, and the agreement within the European Council on the text of the Treaty of Maastricht. The uneven progress of the ratification process in late 1992 was influenced by the somewhat ambivalent attitude of the UK Presidency, although ultimately the Edinburgh European Council in December 1992 proved to be a triumph of diplomacy. Not all Presidencies contain such important events in the calendar of integration, but Member States do vie with each other to have the most 'productive' term of office, although not all share the same idea of what this means. It is not clear to what extent the EU has benefited from the tendency of the Presidency to match the Commission's functions as mediator and broker of compromise deals, as initiator of policies, and as representative of the EU towards the outside world (although the Presidency does have a particular role in relation to the EU Second and Third Pillars).

4.12 The European Parliament: Composition, Basic Character and Powers

The European Parliament is composed of 626 directly elected representa-tives of the peoples of the States brought together in the EU. The number of MEPs elected in each Member State is set out in Table 4.2 (Article 138(2) EC).

The Members of the European Parliament are elected in a five yearly cycle, with the first direct elections having been held in 1979. Not until 1999 will the whole of the EU as it is presently constituted vote together, because the fourth enlargement was confirmed after the 1994 elections. Since 1989, there has been a centre-left majority in the Parliament, with the Socialists as the largest single grouping with around 220 seats, followed by the European People's Party (Christian Democrats) with around 170 seats. However, given the powers of the Parliament there is no governing party political coalition in the conventional sense. There is at present no uniform electoral procedure, and the UK is out of step with the other Member States in so far as it continues to elect the representatives for mainland Britain (Scotland, Wales and England) on the basis of single-member constituencies with a first-past-the-post system. Proportional representation is used in Northern Ireland. It is the task of the European

Table 4.2   Membership of the European Parliament

Austria	21
Belgium	25
Denmark	16
Finland	16
France	87
Germany	99
Greece	25
Ireland	15
Italy	87
Luxembourg	6
Netherlands	31
Portugal	25
Spain	64
Sweden	22
United Kingdom	87
Total	626

Parliament to draw up proposals for a uniform electoral procedure, and, since the Treaty of Maastricht, to give its assent to any provisions adopted for this purpose by the Council, which must act unanimously. However, any changes to the existing system will need to be ratified by the Member States according to the national constitutional requirements, and so far the UK has remained trenchantly opposed to adopting a system of proportional representation based on multi-member constituencies. So far, the European Parliament has merely adopted a resolution on a uniform electoral procedure which would allow the UK to retain up to two thirds of its seats elected on a single member basis (OJ 1993 C115/121). The Council has not yet acted on the proposals.

The origins of the European Parliament are extremely modest. Designated the 'Assembly' in the original Treaties (a term for which Margaret Thatcher retained a great fondness), the Parliament was composed simply of delegates nominated by the national Parliaments and endowed with a narrow range of consultative and supervisory powers. Until the changes introduced by the Single European Act, the only input into the legislative process which was given to the Parliament (a name which it gave itself from 1962 onwards, and which was formally recognised in the Single European Act), was to be consulted by the Council on proposals made by the Commission. It has had mild supervisory powers over the Commission, including the right to put questions to the Commission (Article 140 EC) and the right to discuss the annual general report submitted by the Commission (Article 143 EC). It has also held from the beginning a draconian power of censure over the Commission, namely the power, by a two-thirds majority vote, to require the Commission to resign as a body.

However, although threatened, this power has never been used, and in any event there would be nothing to prevent the Member States reappointing the same Commissioners.

Since then, the Parliament has grown in size as consequence of enlargement, changed its character through direct elections, and acquired an important range of new powers. Clearly, there has always been a strong case for developing the role of the Parliament within the system of the EU, both in terms of its input into the decision-making process, and in terms of its control and supervisory power over the other institutions. The EU suffers from a serious 'democratic deficit' (see 3.5), in so far as it exercises sovereign powers transferred by the Member States, but without the same degree of legislative input by an assembly of representatives elected by universal suffrage, and without the executive accountability of the Commission or the Council to such a body. Ironically, so long as the Parliament remained a non-elected body with 'dual mandate' members (national Parliament and European Parliament), the case for more powers could be defeated, by pointing to the low calibre and the low level of commitment of its members, who were generally more committed to their role as members of national Parliaments. Even now, some critics point to the absence of a coherent transnational party structure, the relatively low level of popular interest in the Parliament, and its alleged tendency to adopt positions on European integration which are out of step with popular feeling as reasons for continuing to limit the powers of the Parliament. The real reason may have more to do with the jealous protection of national sovereignty. The institution of a proper, effective European Parliament endowed with the full range of legislative and supervisory powers associated with parliaments in liberal democracies would mean acknowledging that the EU had in truth reached the stage of something approaching a federation. At present, however, democracy is suffering, since power has been effectively taken out of the hands of national Parliaments, and given to Ministers who are not collectively responsible to any representative body. A step towards the enhancement of a 'European' party system was introduced in Article 138A EC which asserts the importance of political parties at the European level as a factor promoting integration, since they contribute to forming a European awareness and to expressing the political will of the citizens of the Union.

The Parliament has the power to organise its own work by adopting Rules of Procedure (Article 142 EC). It has regularly amended these Rules in order to give maximum effect to its role in the institutional structure (e.g. OJ 1995 L293/1; Nicoll, 1994). For example, in relation to its input into the legislative process, it has maximised the effectiveness by creating a committee structure in which the range of political views within the Parliament are represented, with 20 individual Committees responsible for preparing draft amendments to legislative proposals which are placed before the plenary session. Furthermore, to facilitate its work and in order to enable it to manage its workload, the Parliament has since 1988 been able to agree an annual legislative programme with the Commission (5.9).

The Parliament also acts on its own initiative in certain policy areas. The best known example is the setting up of a Committee concerned with institutional reform after the first elections in 1979 which drew up the DTEU. The business of the Parliament is managed by its President and Vice-Presidents (now 14 in number), who are elected from amongst the MEPs (Article 140 EC), and by the so-called Enlarged Bureau, on which the President and Vice-Presidents are joined by the Chairs of the Committees. The final say is held by the Plenary session of the Parliament, which meets eleven times a year. The current work of the Parliament is hampered by its geographical fragmentation: in accordance with established agreements between the Member States, plenary sessions are held in Strasbourg and occasionally in Luxembourg, but most of the Parliament's bureaucracy and support staff are located in Luxembourg, and Committee meetings are held in Brussels. There is longstanding conflict between the Parliament and certain Member States, since the Parliament would prefer to be relocated in a single city, but that desire was again frustrated by the European Council meeting in Edinburgh in December 1992 which largely preserved the status quo.

At present the European Parliament holds the following powers under the EC Treaty, in addition to those with which it was endowed under the original Treaties and described above. By Budgetary Treaties of 1970 and 1975 amending Articles 203–4 EC, the Parliament was given the status as co-budgetary authority with the Council, although its power, in practice, to affect how the resources of the EC are spent remains limited (5.12 and 5.13). The Commission is responsible to the Parliament in respect of accounting for expenditure. The Single European Act significantly increased the powers of the Parliament by giving it the power of assent (and therefore of veto) over the accession of new members (now Article O TEU) and the conclusion of association agreements with third states (now Article 228(3) EC). The Single European Act also introduced the cooperation procedure which allows the Parliament to give a second reading, and to propose further amendments, to certain legislative acts (5.5). Finally, the Single European Act extended the range of provisions where an opinion of the Parliament is required.

The Treaty of Maastricht took Parliamentary involvement in the legislative procedure one step further. The assent provisions were expanded to include the adoption of a uniform electoral procedure (Article 138 EC), aspects of citizenship of the Union (Article 8A EC), reorganisation of the structural funds (Article 130D EC), certain aspects of the supervision of the ECB (Article 105(6) EC) and the amendment of the Statute of the ECB (Article 106(5) EC). It gave the Parliament a power which parallels that given to the Council by Article 152 EC to request the Commission to submit proposals to it on matters which it considers EU legislation to be necessary (Article 138B EC). In addition to widening the instances in which the cooperation procedure is to be applied (e.g. environment, vocational training), the Treaty also introduced what is termed 'Council–Parliament' co-decision as a new legislative procedure (see 5.6). Many (but not all) provisions where the cooperation procedure previously applied were 'upgraded' to co-decision.

The Treaty of Maastricht also significantly enhanced the position of the European Parliament as the guardian of the interests of citizens of the Union, although the impact of these powers has been slow to be felt. Article 138C EC empowered the Parliament to set up temporary Committees of Inquiry to investigate alleged instances of maladministration on the part of the other institutions or bodies established under the Treaties, but the first such Committee was not established until December 1995 to look at alleged contraventions or maladministration under the Community transit system (OJ 1996 C7/1). Article 138D EC formalised a longstanding informal right on the part of all persons resident in the Union to petition the Parliament, individually or collectively, on any matters coming within the Community's field of activity which affect them directly, a right repeated for EU citizens in Article 8D.

The same provision also refers to Article 138E EC which provides for the appointment of an Ombudsman by the Parliament to receive and investigate complaints of maladministration by the EU institutions, but delays meant that the first Ombudsman (Jacob Magnus Söderman) was not inaugurated until September 1995. The Decision of the European Parliament necessary to lay down the detailed rules and regulations on the performance of the Ombudsman's duties was adopted, after the Commission had given an opinion and the Council had given its approval, in March 1994 (OJ 1994 L113/15). Delays then attended the formal appointment of the first incumbent, because of a failure within the Parliament to agree upon a name. In due course, difficulties arising as a result of the overlaps arising between temporary Committees of Inquiry, the Committee on Petitions which deals with petitions, and the work of the Ombudsman will need to be resolved (see for preliminary discussions: Marias, 1994; Magliveras, 1995).

The range of powers held by the Parliament in relation to the intergovernmental activities of the EU in the sphere of foreign policy has always been very limited (Bieber, 1990). Article 30(4) Single European Act merely required the Parliament to be kept informed concerning European Political Cooperation, although in practice there was a greater level of contact, channelled through the Presidency, which has reported to the Parliament regularly and held meetings with the Committee on Political Affairs. The level of involvement was little changed by the introduction of the new provisions on Common Foreign and Security Policy by the Treaty of Maastricht (Article J.7 TEU) or the new pillar of Justice and Home Affairs (Article K.6 TEU) (5.8).

It still not possible, even after Maastricht, to characterise the Parliament as a fully operational democratic legislature; it has, for example, not received increased powers in the context of either the ECSC or Euratom Treaties. It is, however, important to stress its symbolic role within the EU political system. It has become the platform on which statesmen and women from inside and outside the EU choose to address their thoughts on European integration. The address given by Queen Elizabeth II to the European Parliament in May 1992 constituted an historic event from the perspective of both the UK and the Parliament itself in its search for greater international recognition.

4.13   The Economic and Social Committee (ECOSOC) and the Committee of the Regions

The idea of the ECOSOC, and, since the Treaty of Maastricht, the Committee of the Regions, is to provide for the formal representation, within the institutional structure, of disparate economic, social, and regional interests. The ECOSOC originated in a similar body – the Consultative Committee of the European Coal and Steel Community (Article 18 ECSC). Under Article 193 EC the ECOSOC is given advisory status, and this in practice means being consulted by the Council and Commission where the Treaty so provides (e.g. Article 100A), or where those institutions consider it appropriate (Article 198 EC). In practice, it also issues 'own initiative' opinions, and this practice is formalised by Article 198 EC, as amended.

The 222 members of the ECOSOC are allocated between the Member States on a basis which is broadly proportionate to size and population. They are appointed by the Council, on the nomination of the Member States, for four years, with appointments renewable. The members are appointed in their personal capacity and must not be bound by any mandatory instructions. This is strengthened by Article 194 EC which insists that the members of the ECOSOC must be 'completely independent in the performance of their duties, in the general interest of the Community'.

The interests to be represented are listed, on a non-exhaustive basis, in Article 193 EC. They include representatives of producers, farmers, carriers, workers, dealers, craftsmen and professional occupations and representatives of the general public. In practice, members are divided into three categories: I – employers; II – workers; III – others, including agricultural interests, professional associations and consumers. The ECOSOC is organised in specialised sections (e.g. agriculture, transport, etc.) which prepare draft reports on legislation for consideration in plenary session.

The Treaty of Maastricht established a Committee of the Regions, composed of representatives of regional and local bodies (Articles 198A–C EC). Like the ECOSOC, the Committee has 222 members, divided on the same basis amongst the Member States. The provisions on the appointment of members by the Council and the organisation of the work of the Committee largely parallel those governing the ECOSOC. Like the ECOSOC, the Committee undertakes much of its work in commissions and subcommissions. It is to be consulted where the Treaty so provides, and where the Council and Commission so decide. It may also issue own initiative opinions, and is to be advised of instances where the ECOSOC is to be consulted, but it is not, with the possibility that it might then decide to submit an opinion, believing there to be significant regional interests affected (Article 198C EC). The provisions on EU policy in the field of culture introduced by the Treaty of Maastricht (Article 128 EC), as well as the revised provisions on economic and social cohesion (regional policy) (Articles 130A–E EC) provide for the consultation of the Committee of the Regions but the amended provisions on environmental policy do not, despite the obvious links with regional policy (Articles 130R–T EC).

4.14   Agencies and Other Bodies Established under the EU Treaties

Since 1990 there has been a proliferation of independent agencies endowed with specific functions or limited delegated powers under the EU Treaties. They vary greatly in composition, nature and scope of powers (although almost all have separate legal personality), and many of them are only just beginning their work. Long disputes between the Member States over the location of some of the most important agencies have caused delays. Some however are longstanding such as CEDEFOP (European Centre for Development of Vocational Training, 1975) which has recently relocated from Berlin to Thessaloniki in Northern Greece, and the Foundation for the Improvement of Living and Working Conditions (1975), located in Dublin in Ireland. Amongst the most important of the new bodies are Europol and the Europol Drugs Unit (The Hague, in the Netherlands), the European Training Foundation (Turin in Italy), responsible for the delivery of training aid to the countries of Central and Eastern Europe, the European Environment Agency (Copenhagen, in Denmark), the European Agency for the Evaluation of Medicinal Products (London), and the Agency for Health and Safety at Work (Bilbao, in Spain). Perhaps the most significant regulatory powers are those given to the Office for Harmonisation in the Internal Market (Trade Marks and Designs) (the Community Trade Mark Office, by another name) (Alicante, also in Spain). This body will implement EU trade mark law under the Trade Mark Regulation (and in future a regulation on design and models), and will have legal, financial and administrative autonomy. It will raise its own revenue from fees, as will the Medicinal Products Agency. The arrival of these new bodies marks a significant shift in the pattern of regulation in the EU, as a departure from reliance upon the current structures based on the unwieldy and opaque 'comitology' which is sometimes unable to integrate the necessary technical expertise, and upon soft instruments such as mutual recognition. However, regulatory agencies themselves give rise to difficulties such as problems of control, accountability and independence, as well as the extent to which the powers of the EC and EU may validly be delegated in this way (Everson, 1995; Lenaerts, 1993).

Europol and the Europol Drugs Unit are rather different types of bodies to the others discussed in this paragraph. They derive their authority, and their work, from the competence of the EU under the third pillar (CJHA). Europol, when it is finally formally established, will be based on a convention adopted under Article K.3 TEU, and duly ratified by the Member States. The precise status of Europol will remain indeterminate until the Member States finally decide whether or not its actions will be subject to the review of the Court of Justice – a matter on which the United Kingdom has taken a different view to the other Member States.

4.15   The Court of Auditors

Under the Treaty of Maastricht, the Court of Auditors acquired the status of an institution. Accordingly, the provisions (Articles 188A–C EC) which govern its establishment, composition, tasks and duties were shifted into the Chapter on the institutions, having previously been linked solely to the budgetary provisions. It has been in existence since 1977, and consists of fifteen members – one from each Member State – who are persons qualified to serve on a body which has the task of carrying out the audit of EU finances, and whose independence is beyond doubt. They are appointed for six year terms by the Council. The European Parliament, which has particular budgetary responsibilities, is consulted on the appointments. The protected legal status of the members of the Court of Auditors during their term of office resembles that of the members of the Court of Justice, although they can be deprived of their office by the Court of Justice (Article 188B(7) EC).

The Court of Auditors has an auditing and supervisory task, and not, despite its name, a judicial role. It extends not only to the revenue and expenditure of the EU itself, but also to all bodies set up by the EU, unless other arrangements have been made. By providing a statement of assurance regarding the reliability of the accounts and the underlying financial transactions conducted by the EU, the Court of Auditors assists the Parliament in giving the Commission a discharge in respect of the implementation of the budget. Previously somewhat of a Cinderella institution within the EU structures, the role of the Court of Auditors have come increasingly to the fore as the EU budget has grown and diversified into new areas, as the fight against waste and fraud within the EU has intensified, and as the academic study of the practice of audit has evolved (Harden *et al.*, 1995).

4.16   The European Investment Bank (EIB)

The European Investment Bank has separate legal personality, although it is governed by the provisions of the EC Treaty (Articles 198D–E). It was established by the original Treaty of Rome, and it has a particular function to provide investment loans to assist the funding of projects aimed at promoting regional development within the EU, and projects of particular interest to two or more Member States. Its revenue is derived from money subscribed by the Member States and money which it raises on the international capital markets. The management of the Bank is entrusted to a Board of Governors, a Board of Directors and a Committee of Management.

4.17   The Institutions of Economic and Monetary Union

The institutions of Economic and Monetary Union (EMU), established by Article 4A and Title VI of the EC Treaty replace the earlier institutions such as the European Monetary Cooperation Fund. They are based in Frankfurt in Germany. On completion of EMU the most important bodies will be the European System of Central Banks (ESCB), composed of the European Central Bank (ECB), which will have separate legal personality, and the national central banks (Article 106 EC). Details are contained in the Treaty and in the associated Protocols and Declarations. According to the Treaty timetable the ECB should come into being in 1997, or 1999 at the latest, a timetable which is generally acknowledged to be overoptimistic following the tensions within the European Exchange Rate Mechanism and its partial collapse in 1992 and 1993. Eventually, the European Central Bank should have the exclusive right to authorise the issue of banknotes within the EU (Article 105A EC). Preparation for the work of the ESCB and the ECB is being undertaken by the European Monetary Institute (EMI) established under the transitional provisions of Article 109F EC, which took over from the existing Committee of Governors of Central Banks. The transition to monetary union, and the associated coordination of national policies, is also assisted by a temporary Monetary Committee with advisory status (Article 109C(1) EC) which will be dissolved and replaced on transition to the third stage of monetary union by an Economic and Financial Committee (Article 109C(2) EC). The institutions of monetary union under the Treaty of Maastricht are built on a model of central bank independence, but one which will not necessarily ensure adequate accountability and legitimacy for these institutions. It might, on the contrary, exacerbate the EU democratic deficit (Gormley and de Haan, 1996).

4.18   The Court of Justice and the Court of First Instance

Since 1988 the so-called 'Community judicature' has comprised two courts sitting in Luxembourg: the Court of Justice, and, attached to it, and empowered to hear only certain categories of case, the Court of First Instance (Article 168A EC and Council Decision 88/591 OJ 1988 L319/1).

The Court of First Instance is not really a separate entity from the Court of Justice (it is 'attached' to it), but to a certain extent the two courts are beginning to develop separate identities, as they work on different fields of EC law and become engaged with slightly different sets of priorities. The division of jurisdiction between the two courts has evolved gradually over the years such that the Court of First Instance now hears all direct actions brought by natural or legal persons the EU institutions (including staff cases). Appeal lies on points of law from the Court of First Instance to the Court of Justice itself. The Court of Justice hears all references for preliminary rulings submitted by national courts (Article 177 EC), and actions brought by the institutions or Member States against each other.

Each court now has fifteen judges (one from each Member State), and the Court of Justice is assisted by nine Advocates General, who submit opinions on each of the cases heard by the Court. The Court of Justice is often influenced by the views of the Advocate General, whose opinions frequently contain detailed discussion of the background to the legal issues at issue which is not to be found in the judgments themselves, often backed up by comparative research which has been essential to the development of EC law. In some fields, important developments in the law have emerged from 'dialogue' between the Court and the Advocates General (for more details see Vranken, 1996). Advocates General have the same status and privileges as judges. The Court of First Instance does not have Advocates General, but a member of the Court may adopt that role where the Court considers it necessary.

The Judges and Advocates General of the Court of Justice are chosen from persons 'whose independence is beyond doubt and who possess the qualifications required for appointment to the highest judicial office in their respective countries or who are jurisconsults of recognised competence' (Article 167 EC). The qualification to be a judge of the Court of First Instance is likewise independence, and 'the ability required for appointment to judicial office' (Article 168A(3) EC). The members of both courts are appointed by common accord of the Member States for six years, with partial replacement every three years (Articles 167 and 168A EC). Each court elects a President.

Further provisions governing the operation of the Court of Justice and the Court of First Instance are contained in the Statute of the Court of Justice appended to the founding Treaties, the Rules of Procedure of the two courts which are approved by the Council, and the Council Decision establishing the Court of First Instance referred to above. Procedures before the two courts differ somewhat from those before a court in the United Kingdom (see Edward, 1995). Amongst the most distinctive features of the ways the courts work are:

- a greater use of written, as opposed to oral, submissions; the written procedure is more important than the subsequent oral procedure;
- all judgments are collegiate, with no single judge benches, and no dissenting judgments;

- the advisory role of the Advocate General (before the Court of Justice);
- the role of the *juge rapporteur* appointed by the President of the Court, who draws up the Report for the (oral) Hearing and the initial draft of the decision which is then discussed by the judges in secret;
- the judgments of the Court of Justice in particular are very brief, and often lack the full reasoning associated with the judgments of courts in the UK;
- this brevity is not so apparent in the judgments of the Court of First Instance where there is normally no Advocate General; moreover, one of the particular functions of the Court of First Instance is to provide a forum which can give a detailed resolution of often complex submissions of fact and law on, for example, a Commission finding of an infringement of the competition rules;
- multilingualism: there are twelve official languages, one of which will be the language of the case, but the Court of Justice itself will normally work in French.

The Court of Justice sits in plenary session, or in chambers of five or three judges. In order to make the work of the Court more effective, and to limit the role of the plenary session to that of deciding the most important cases, it now sits in plenary session in cases to which an institution or a Member State is party, only where a request is made by one party. Most preliminary rulings are also heard by chambers. The Court of First Instance normally sits only in chambers of three or five judges.

The basic task of the Community judicature is simple: it is to ensure that the law is observed (Article 164 EC; see also Article 31 ECSC). Articles 169–186 and 215 EC govern the most important types of action which can be brought before the courts and the types of rulings which it may give. Reference should be made to 1.5 for an outline of the basic work of the Court.

The Treaty of Maastricht brought a number of important changes to the jurisdiction of the Community judicature. Amendments were made to include the new institutions of Economic and Monetary Union, in particular the European Central Bank, within the system of judicial review. Judicial review was extended to cover the acts of the European Investment Bank and the Parliament which have legal effects, and formally to confer limited standing rights on the Parliament. Provision was also made for financial penalties to be imposed on Member States which fail to comply with judgments of the Court of Justice establishing an infringement of the Treaties or rules adopted thereunder (Article 171 EC), although this provision has yet to be used.

At first glance, the role of the Court of Justice, like the other institutions, is limited by the principle of 'attributed powers'. As a creature of Treaty, the Court of Justice can only hear actions and give remedies where provided for in the constitutive Treaties; however, it is arguable that with the evolution of the institutional structure and the range of competences and activities of the EU the overriding duty of the Court to ensure the rule of law should be regarded as more important than the strict limitations of the Treaties. In fact, the Court of Justice made a number of innovations within the jurisdictional structure of the Treaties, allowing acts of the European Parliament to be subject to judicial review and giving it a limited power to bring actions against the acts of the other institutions. These *de facto* developments were formally recognised by the Treaty of Maastricht. Arnull (1990a) has argued that in fact the Court of Justice has an inherent jurisdiction which requires it where appropriate to fill in gaps in the system of legal remedies under the Treaties. In his view, in extending its jurisdictional scope, the Court is acting no differently to the other institutions which have *de facto* extended their powers in response to political imperatives. Such comments must be read, however, in the light of explicit limitations on the scope of the Court's jurisdiction. By Article L TEU, the Court has no jurisdiction over the common provisions of the Treaty of Maastricht (Articles A–F TEU), Title V (CFSP) and Title VI (CJHA), unless the Member States expressly provide for a judicial role in conventions adopted under Article K.3(2)(c) TEU.

The reform of the Community judicial architecture has come firmly onto the agenda of the IGC (Arnull, 1995b). Like the other institutions, the Court of Justice lived and worked through 1995 under the shadow of the IGC. Like the other institutions, it too produced a report on the functioning of the Treaty on European Union which served as part of the material considered by the Reflection Group. The reaction of the Court of Justice (and of the Court of First Instance which produced a separate report differing in certain respects from the approach taken by the Court itself), is notable because of the proposals for fettering the role of the Court of Justice, both by restricting the range of its activities and limiting certain aspects of its current adjudicatory discretion, which have come from a number of directions including the government of the United Kingdom.

The Court of Justice was necessarily limited in any criticisms it could make of the Treaty structure under which it operates, but it did point to the unsatisfactory level of judicial protection given to individuals under the Second and Third Pillars of the EU. Some of the most significant comments by both Courts are directed to the structure of the Community judicature. The Court of Justice opposed any suggestion that references under Article 177 EC should be dealt with other than by itself. It does suggest, however, that some appeals from the Court of First Instance might be subjected to a 'filtering system'. The Court of First Instance advocated the limited use of single judge courts – a possibility which would represent a significant departure from the collegial nature of the current system. Both courts also suggested changes to their composition. For the Court of Justice the problem arises because of possibility that its plenary session (involving all the judges) might, as a result of further enlargements, become unmanageably large and 'cross the invisible boundary between a collegiate court and a deliberative assembly'. At the IGC the

Member States may need to accept that not all Member States should in the future have judges – in the same way that the composition of the Commission might be revised. Other possibilities are a plenary consisting only of the President and the Presidents of the various Chambers. The Court of First Instance would more enthusiastically welcome the possibility of an increase in its membership, as it largely sits in chambers, not in plenary. Such an increase is essential, as just two years after its creation the Court of First Instance was already receiving more new cases each year than it could handle, thus leading to increasing delays in the dispensing of justice. That said, not all those who observe both EU courts would agree with the proposal for more judges. According to Koopmans (1991c: 24),

> 'One of the worst methods for increasing judicial productivity is to enlarge the number of Judges and Advocates-General.'

The effect of creating too large a judicial structure in Luxembourg is destabilising in the view of some. Even so, no concrete support has yet been lent to a longstanding suggestion that the Community judicial architecture should be reworked along regional lines (Jacqué and Weiler, 1990).

What has been notable about the Court of Justice during its nearly fifty year history – and this point will be evident already from the previous chapters – has been its judicial activism. This has been most obvious in its role in 'constitutionalising' the Treaties (see Chapter 3), and in 'federalising' the relationship between EC law and national law (1.5). In the 1970s in particular, commentators were fond of pointing to the Court's 'teleological' or 'purposive' methods of interpretation (see the extracts in Ellis and Tridimas, 1995: 563–569; Kutscher, 1976; Tridimas, 1996). On occasion its interpretative methods have led it to be severely criticised for being over-activist, and giving judgments which go against the text (Rasmussen, 1986; 1992; Hartley, 1996). But it is more frequently the case that academics and practitioners in the field have leapt to its defence (Cappelletti, 1987; Weiler, 1993; 1994a; Arnull, 1996). What has intrigued political scientists more than anything about the Court has been the level of compliance on the part of Member States with its judgment which it has attracted – what some have termed 'legal integration'. Over the years this has lent to the legal order a 'federalist' and 'constitutionalist' aura which has often stood in stark contrast to the political and economic order (Burley and Mattli, 1993). As each of the chapters of this book will make clear, the time is perhaps past for the Court to be viewed as a 'heroic' figure in the development of the EU. Its importance is probably no less than it ever was. It certainly works now in a stronger glare of not always approving publicity. But it is now the case the Court more than ever occupies a place in constantly evolving dialogue with each of the institutions, offering a specifically 'legal' voice within a ever-changing policy process.

Summary

1   The role and tasks of the institutions are not exhaustively stated in the Treaties. Regard must also be had to constantly changing interinstitutional dynamics.
2   The Commission is the pivotal political institution. It has policy-making, executive, enforcement and representative functions.
3   The Council still carries the primary legislative function, although increasingly it shares that function with the European Parliament. It is also the body which represents the national interest, and tends towards intergovernmentalist methods, relying on the achievement of consensus. It has seen an increase in its influence, in particular through related bodies and structures: the European Council, COREPER, comitology etc. The Presidency of the Council has also evolved into an important motor of the EU integration process.
4   The Parliament is gradually evolving into a legislature, ensuring democracy and accountability within the EU, with a particular brief for protecting the interests of citizens.
5   The interests of employers, unions, consumers and other corporatist interests are protected by the Economic and Social Committee (ECOSOC). Regional interests are protected by the Committee of the Regions introduced by the Treaty of Maastricht.
6   Other institutions or bodies with increasing importance within the institutional structure include the Court of Auditors, various independent agencies endowed with a variety of delegated powers, and the institutions of monetary union.
7   The Court of Justice and the Court of First Instance ensure the rule of law in the EU. They have acquired a central role in maintaining the momentum of integration.

Questions

1   Identify the mechanisms whereby national interests are recognised and represented within the institutional structures of the EU. To what extent does the influence of national interests extend outside the Council into other bodies as well?
2   Would you agree with the suggestion that the EU does not possess an institutional structure which easily facilitates overall coherence of policy formulation and policy implementation?
3   To what extent has the Council usurped the roles of the other institutions?
4   Which institution would you consider to have changed most since the establishment of the EU, and in what ways?
5   What mechanisms exist to enable the institutions to take the concerns of citizens seriously, and how effective are these?

Workshop (for Chapters 4 and 5)

Formulate a set of proposals for the reform of the EU institutions which make them:

(a) more democratic and accountable in composition and working methods; and

(b) more effective in accomplishing their tasks under the Treaty.

Further Reading

Alter (1996), 'The European Court's Political Power: The Emergence of an Authoritative International Court in the European Union', *W. Eur. Pols.* (forthcoming).

Dashwood (1994a), 'The role of the Council of the European Union', in Curtin and Heukels (1994).

Edwards and Spence (eds.) (1994), *The European Commission*, Longman, London.

Everson (1995), 'Independent Agencies: Hierarchy Beaters?', 1 *ELJ* 180.

van Gerven (1996), 'The Role and Structure of the European Judiciary now and in the future', 21 *ELRev.* 211.

Hayes-Renshaw (1996), 'The Role of the Council' in Andersen and Eliassen (1996a).

Hayes-Renshaw and Wallace, 'Executive power in the European Union: the functions and limits of the Council of Ministers', 2 *JEPP* 559.

Koopmans (1991c), 'The Future of the Court of Justice of the European Communities', 11 *YEL* 15.

Lodge (1996), 'The European Parliament', in Andersen and Eliassen (1996a).

Scorey (1996), 'A new model for the Communities' judicial architechture in the new union', 21 *ELRev.* 224.

Westlake (1994), *A Modern Guide to the European Parliament*, Pinter, London.

Westlake (1995), *The Council of the European Union*, Cartermill/Longman, London.

5 The European Union and its Institutions at Work

5.1 Introduction

This chapter introduces the work of the European Union, focusing on the ability of the institutions to make binding legal acts, and the processes whereby such acts are adopted, on raising and spending of revenue, and on the key mechanisms which have evolved to make these activities more effective and to extend the role of the EU in the economic, social and political spheres. Where appropriate the political and economic context of the legal structures of the EU are highlighted. The chapter concludes with a discussion of interinstitutional relationships, examining the vital role of the Court of Justice in this context. Reference is also made, where appropriate, to the role of the 1996 IGC in relation to institutional processes. A good summary of the institutional *status quo* in mid-1995, coupled with suggestions for changes, is to be found in the Commission's Report for the Reflection Group, composed of representatives of the Member States, charged with the task of preparing the IGC agenda (Commission, 1995a).

5.2 The Legal Acts of the Institutions

The essential differences between the 'methods' employed under the 'Community' pillar and the intergovernmental pillars of the European Union have already been highlighted in this book. This paragraph discusses the essential prerequisites for legal acts adopted by the institutions under the Community pillar, which are subject, of course, to the binding jurisdiction of the Court of Justice. There are certain basic conditions which a valid legal act of the institutions must satisfy. These are in part contained in the Treaty, and can in part be derived from the case law of the Court of Justice. The principle of judicial control is made clear in Article 173 EC which declares:

> 'The Court of Justice shall review the legality of acts adopted jointly by the European Parliament and the Council, of acts of the Council, of the Commission and of the ECB, other than recommendations and opinions, and of acts of the European Parliament intended to produce legal effects vis-à-vis third parties. . . .

on grounds of lack of competence, infringement of an essential procedural requirement, infringement of this Treaty or of any rule relating to its application, or misuse of powers.'

The basic requirements can be reduced here to four core principles. The first requirement is that the institution adopting an act must have *competence* or the legal power to act. This principle is easily derived from the two principles of 'limited' powers binding both the EU as a whole (Article 3B EC), and the institutions specifically (Article 4 EC) (see 3.5 and 3.7). It is evidenced, on a case-by-case basis, by showing that a legal act has a valid legal basis, and reference must normally be made in the recitals (or preamble) of the act to the concrete enabling power. This is generally to be found in the Treaty itself, or, in the case of delegated legislation, located in an enabling legislative act. However, legal basis not only shows that the EU and a specific institution or institutions have competence. In addition, under the Treaty system, because of the way in which the powers of the institutions are organised, it may be that the choice of legal basis affects the degree of input of a particular institution. Consequently, the choice of legal basis is an important element in the legislative process.

According to the Court of Justice legal basis is a matter of law:

'the choice of the legal basis for a measure may not depend simply on an institution's conviction as to the objective pursued but must be based on objective factors which are amenable to judicial review' (Case 45/86 *Commission* v. *Council (Generalised Tariff Preferences)* [1987] ECR 1493 at p. 1520).

An incorrect reference or a general reference to the Treaty as a whole is insufficient. Although an explicit reference is not absolutely necessary, the absence of such a reference will render a measure capable of challenge if the parties concerned and the Court of Justice are left uncertain as to the precise legal basis in fact used (Case 45/86 *Commission* v. *Council (Generalised Tariff Preferences)*). Problems continue to abound in relation to the identification of the 'correct' legal basis, problems which the Treaty itself often causes, as the Court has acknowledged:

'Under the system governing Community powers, the powers of the institutions and the conditions on their exercise derive from various specific provisions of the Treaty, and the differences between those provisions, particularly as regards the involvement of the European Parliament, are not always based on consistent criteria' (Case 242/87 *Commission* v. *Council (ERASMUS)* [1989] ECR 1425 at p. 1452).

A number of specific interinstitutional questions raised by the problem of legal basis are discussed in 5.17. Challenges to the legal basis of measures are, of course, not the sole prerogative of interinstitutional litigation: the question of legal basis is also frequently raised both Member

States in actions brought against the EU institutions (where such arguments are often closely linked to arguments about the scope of Community competence: e.g. Case 281, etc./85 *Germany et al.* v. *Commission (Migration Policy)* [1987] ECR 3203 and Case C-426/93 *Germany* v. *Council (Statistical Registers)* [1995] ECR I-3723 discussed at 3.9). Litigation opposing the Member States and the institutions has also frequently raised the crucial question of the relationship between general and specific legal bases (5.14), that is, between provisions of the Treaty offering powers in relation to specific fields (e.g. agriculture), and those offering general legislative powers.

The legal basis of measures may also be challenged by individual litigants in cases brought against the EU institutions, or against other individuals or public authorities in actions begun in the national courts where EU measures are at issue (e.g. Case C-405/92 *Etablissements A. Mondiet* v. *Armament Islais* [1993] ECR I-6133, concerning the correct legal basis for an EU measure banning the use of driftnets of more than 2.5km in length).

Second, every legal act must contain an adequate statement of reasons. The duty to give reasons is a principle of 'transparency', and to use the language of Article 173 EC, it is an 'essential procedural requirement'. Article 190 EC requires regulations, directives and decisions adopted by the Council, by the Commission or by the Council and Parliament jointly to refer to any proposals and opinions required to be obtained under the Treaty, and to contain a statement of reasons. A statement of reasons facilitates the process of judicial review, allowing any interested parties, and the Court where appropriate, to discover at a glance the circumstances which enjoined the adopting institution to act (see Case 24/62 *Commission* v. *Germany (Brennwein)* [1963] ECR 63). The intensity of the duty to give reasons depends upon the type of act adopted (a general legislative act requires less specific reasons than an individual act, such as one which imposes a pecuniary sanction on an undertaking for breach of the competition rules) and the circumstances in which an act is adopted. Where the institution must act urgently, a cursory statement of reasons may be sufficient (Case 16/65 *Firma Schwarze* v. *Einfuhr- und Vorratstelle für Getreide und Futtermittel* [1965] ECR 877). Similarly in complex areas like agriculture where there is frequently a highly fragmented and much amended body of legislation, the duty to give reasons has arguably been emptied of its 'substantive value' (Barents, 1994: 112). In such a field, even the objective of transparency may no longer be achieved. Closely linked to the giving reasons requirement is Article 191 EC which makes provision for the entry into force of binding acts of the institutions, and for their publication in the *Official Journal* and notification to addressees as appropriate. These principles can be similarly construed as means of facilitating review of measures.

Suggestions have been made that the giving reasons requirement might be extended beyond to transparency to encompass a right of participation (Shapiro, 1992; discussed in Craig and de Búrca, 1995: 107–112). Particularly as regards the executive and administrative work of the Commission, it could be argued that there is a close link between the duties which are frequently incumbent upon the Commission to hear the arguments put by those who are affected by its measures (especially, but not only in the field of competition law) (the principle of *audi alteram partem*), and the reasons then given for any measure which ensues. It is also linked to principles of participatory democracy referred to in Chapter 3. Recent case law of the Court of First Instance may indicate that it is moving in the direction of pushing the Commission into greater dialogue with those concerned by its administrative actions. In Case T-95/94 *Chambre Syndicale Nationale des Enterprises de Transport de Fonds et Valeurs and Brink's France Sarl* v. *Commission* (28.9.95), in the context of a complaint made by the applicants regarding Commission approval for certain state aids paid by France, the Court of First Instance held that the obligation to state reasons may in certain circumstances require an exchange of views with the complainant, and this obligation had not been discharged in the present case. However, the status of the dialogue principle is not yet fully enshrined in EC law.

The third precondition for EU legal acts involves respect for the principles of subsidiarity and proportionality set out in Article 3B EC. There is as yet little evidence, as was shown in 3.10, of how the principle of subsidiarity might be applied as a condition of a valid legal act. In contrast, the principle of proportionality, although only relatively recently formally constitutionalised, is a well-established general principle of EC law which the Court applies in a number of fields to control actions by both the EU and the Member States (de Búrca, 1993a). It means, essentially, that the means adopted should be appropriate to the end sought, such that 'a public authority may not impose obligations on a citizen except to the extent to which they are strictly necessary in the public interest to attain the purpose of the measure' (Hartley, 1994: 155). Proportionality is discussed further in 6.5. In the same paragraph, other so-called 'general principles' of EC law are discussed. Valid EU acts must not infringe these principles. Fourth and finally, therefore, even an act satisfying the first three core principles identified here may still infringe against a range of additional principles which bind the lawmakers of the EU – as the text of Article 173 EC makes clear ('. . . any other rule of law . . .') (see 6.4–6.9).

5.3   Introducing the Law-Making Process

There is no single law-making process for the adoption of measures under the EC Treaties. Indeed, as the Commission's Report to the Reflection Group makes clear, it is possible to identify 22 different legislative processes, highlighting a situation of excessive complexity. A complete picture of the law-making process can only be derived from a detailed study of the Treaties. There are, however, three basic patterns to which the majority of provisions in the EC Treaty which grant a law-making power to the Council of Ministers conform. The simplest procedure involves the Council acting, either by a qualified majority, or unanimously, on a proposal from the Commission, and after consulting, where required, the Parliament and/or the Economic and Social Committee (ECOSOC). This model dates from the original Treaty of Rome, but is still used for certain provisions, and has been introduced in new areas of competence where the Member States have sought to minimise parliamentary input. It is termed here the 'old procedure', and is discussed in 5.3. It could also be termed the single reading procedure, although there are variants in which the Parliament is not consulted at all. The Single European Act introduced the cooperation procedure and this is examined in 5.4. Most recently, the Treaty of Maastricht introduced what is popularly termed 'Council-Parliament co-decision', a form of joint legislative action by the Council and the Parliament. This is discussed in 5.5. In 5.6 the small number of cases where the assent of the Parliament is required will be discussed.

Both the cooperation and co-decision models, as with most cases under the 'old' procedure, require the Commission to initiate legislation. The right of proposal is important. The Commission maintains control over the proposal until its adoption or rejection by the Council. This is confirmed by Article 189A EC. The Commission may amend its proposal at any point during the law-making process, and the Council requires unanimity in order to amend a Commission proposal, regardless of whether the law-making power under which it acts requires only a qualified majority for the adoption of an act (formerly Article 149(1) EEC). In Case 355/87 *Commission* v. *Council (Italo-Algerian Maritime Transport)* ([1989] ECR 1517) the Commission objected to what it saw as the abuse of the Council's right of amendment. It argued that the Council had reversed the effect of its proposal. The Court found for the Council by holding on the facts that both the measure adopted and the proposal were designed to achieve the same objective, without ruling on the greatly differing submissions made by the two institutions on the scope of the right of amendment. The Commission can, of course, prevent the Council from adopting an amended version of its proposal to which it objects by withdrawing it from consideration.

A minority of law-making powers under the Treaties differ significantly from these patterns; these are generally, but not solely, concerned with the institutional configuration of the Union, and with arrangements relating to Economic and Monetary Union. For example, Council has some powers to adopt legal measures without the need, apparently, for the participation of any of the other institutions in the decision-making process. Two examples are Articles 213 EC, which requires the Council to lay down the conditions under which the Commission may collect statistical information and carry out checks required for the performance of the tasks with which it has been entrusted, and Article 217 EC, under which the Council shall determine by unanimity the rules governing the languages of the institutions.

Alternatively, a provision may give an institution other than the Commission the right of initiative. For example, Article 168A(2) EC makes provision for the transfer of additional categories of cases to the Court of First Instance. It requires the Council to act, on the request of the Court of Justice, and after consulting the European Parliament and the Commission. Here the Commission's role is merely consultative. Likewise, it is the European Parliament which is responsible for drawing up initial proposals for parliamentary elections according to a uniform election procedure in all Member States, to be decided upon by the Council acting unanimously after obtaining the assent of the Parliament itself. Finally, it is upon the initiative of the Commission *or a Member State* that the Council may unanimously decide under Article K.9 TEU to transfer certain areas of competence currently falling under CJHA within the scope of the Community proper (Article 100C EC). However, the latter two examples are not strictly speaking 'legislative' matters; in both cases, the decisions of the Council require ratification by the Member States according to their respective constitutional requirements.

5.4 The 'Old' Procedure

The simplest form of the old procedure involves a Commission proposal and a Council decision. This form of procedure is illustrated by Article 51 EC which provides for adoption of measures by the Council aimed at securing the social security rights of migrant workers, or to give a recent example introduced by the Treaty of Maastricht, by Article 73C(2), which allows the Council, acting on by a qualified majority on a proposal from the Commission to adopt measures on the movement of capital to or from third countries in relation to a number of types of transactions. Not infrequently, measures adopted using, for example, the cooperation procedure also make provision for certain types of amendments to be adopted by the Council acting alone and by a qualified majority, on a proposal from the Commission.

More frequently, consultation with the European Parliament, and/or ECOSOC, the Committee of the Regions, and in a few cases even the European Central Bank, is mandated by the Treaty. Despite all the changes introduced by the Single European Act and the Treaty of Maastricht, it is still the case that the majority of measures which the Parliament has to deal with fall under this rubric. Examples include cases of both qualified majority voting and unanimity. Article 128 EEC on vocational training was one of the few examples of ECOSOC consultation without Parliament consultation, but this anomalous provision has now been replaced by Article 126 EC. The old-style procedure retains a strong attraction for the Member States as evidenced by a number of provisions introduced by the Treaty of Maastricht. Examples here include Article 100C(1) EC, which allows the Council to determine, unanimously, on a proposal from the Commission, and after consulting the European

Parliament, the categories of third countries nationals who require a visa in order to enter the EU, and Article 130S(2), which provides for some measures in the field of the environment (e.g. those of a fiscal nature) to be adopted by the Council acting unanimously on a proposal from the Commission and after consulting the Parliament and the ECOSOC. A number of variants on the old style are included in the EC Treaty, as amended; an example is Article 8A(2), which provides for the adoption of measures to give effect to the general right of residence for EU citizens set out in Article 8A(1) EC by the Council acting unanimously, on a proposal by the Commission, and after obtaining the assent of the European Parliament.

The old style is used for two of the Treaty's important general law-making powers which will be discussed below in 5.10, namely Articles 100 and 235 EC, which both require a unanimous decision of the Council. A few instances remain in the Treaty where the old style procedure is used in conjunction with a qualified majority (Article 43 EC – agricultural policy; Article 113 EC – external trade policy), but in most instances law-making powers requiring only a qualified majority in the Council were altered by the SEA to increase parliamentary input from consultation to coopera-tion.

Consultation of the Parliament or other bodies means just that; there is no obligation on the part of the Council to follow the opinion. However, the Council must actually receive the opinion, not simply ask for it (Case 138/79 *Roquette Frères* v. *Council (Isoglucose)* [1980] ECR 3333). A measure adopted by the Council before it receives the Parliament's opinion can be annulled for breach of an essential procedural requirement; but the fact that the Council definitively adopts a measure just five days after receiving the Parliament's opinion in circumstances where it has indicated that there is a degree of urgency and the Parliament itself has taken several months over delivering the opinion does not of itself make that consultation a 'sham' (Case C-417/93 *Parliament* v. *Council (TACIS)* [1995] ECR I-1185).

Nonetheless, the Parliament must normally be given sufficient time to adopt its opinion; this can take some time, since the draft opinion is first worked on within the Parliament's committee structure, before it comes to the plenary session for adoption. In a recent case the Court of Justice was asked to consider the impact of 'urgency' on the consultation process: must the Council always wait for the Parliament to deliver its opinion? The answer is 'not always'. Case C-65/93 *Parliament* v. *Council (General-ised Tariff Preferences)* ([1995] ECR I-643) involved a proposal to extend into 1993 the 1992 system of generalised tariff preferences, which was sent to the Parliament on 22 October 1992. The Council requested urgency, and the Parliament accepted this request, setting the matter down for debate and decision at a plenary session on 18 December 1992. However, the session was adjourned before the matter could be discussed, and since there was no possibility of reconvening an emergency Parliament session before the end of the year, the Council went ahead and adopted the

Regulation on 21 December 1992 in order to meet the end-of-year dead-line. The Parliament failed in its action for annulment, since, although there had been no consultation in a formal sense, the Parliament itself had failed to observe the essential duty of 'sincere cooperation' which structures interinstitutional relationships, as much as it does those between the Member States and the institutions. Consequently, the Parliament was not entitled to complain of the Council's failure to await its opinion before adopting the contested Regulation.

As this shows, effective consultation always depends on the goodwill of the parties. Relations between the Council and the Parliament are not perfect. Despite the *Roquette* case, the Parliament regularly documents instances where the Council takes at least a preliminary decision before receiving the Parliament's opinion, although its failure to win the *TACIS* case may indicate that it has little hope of successfully taking action before the Court on this matter. On the other hand, the Council had a practice, when applying Article 113 EEC (the pre-Maastricht version did not require consultation of the Parliament), of consulting it voluntarily in any event. The Council also reconsults the Parliament in cases where it proposes to change the legal basis of a measure, in particular where this changes the procedure under which it is adopted. An example is provided by the Titanium Dioxide Directive which gave rise to litigation discussed in 5.12, where the legal basis was changed from Article 100A EEC (internal market – cooperation procedure) to Article 130S EEC (environment – simple consultation).

Reconsultation must likewise occur where the Council departs markedly from the text on which the Parliament has given its opinion. The Court has expressed the requirement to reconsult thus:

'[The duty to consult] includes a requirement that the Parliament be reconsulted on each occasion when the text finally adopted, viewed as a whole, departs substantially from the text on which the Parliament has already been consulted, except where the amendments essentially correspond to the wishes of the Parliament itself' (Case C-388/92 *Parliament* v. *Council* [1994] ECR I-2067 at p. 2085).

This point has been tested in a quite few cases arising in the field of road transport policy, beginning with Case C-65/90 *Parliament* v. *Council (Cabotage Regulation)* ([1992] ECR I-4593) where the Court held that where there was a lapse of three years between the Parliamentary opinion and the adoption of the regulation, and the Council had adopted a substantially different proposal, reconsultation was required. In a case such as *Harmonized Road Taxes* (Case C-21/94 *Parliament* v. *Council* [1995] ECR I-1827), where the Parliament has gone back as far as 1989 to identify a Directive on the harmonisation of road transport taxes which was adopted on the basis of a text substantially different to the one on which an opinion was given, it is making little concrete difference to the policies which are being adopted. Instead it is giving notice of its serious intention to ensure the protection of its prerogatives, however uncomfortable that might be for both the Council and the Commission in a sensitive and highly politicised field like road transport.

5.5   The Cooperation Procedure

The introduction of the cooperation procedure essentially appended a second reading of proposed legislation in the European Parliament onto the existing consultation procedure. It usually operates in combination with ECOSOC consultation. This not only gives the Parliament a 'second bite at the cherry' in the process of formulating EU legislation, but it also involves it in a more complex interactive process with the Council. The details of the cooperation procedure, originally introduced by Articles 6 and 7 SEA and now to be found in Article 189C EC, are set out in Figure 5.1.

The principal law-making powers in the EEC Treaty covered by the cooperation procedure after the adoption of the Single European Act included Article 100A (measures for the completion of the internal market) Articles 49, 54(2), 56(2) and 57 (measures for the achievement of free movement of workers, providers of services and the self-employed), and Article 118A (health and safety of workers). With the exception of Article 118A, each of these law-making powers has now, after the Treaty of Maastricht, been 'upgraded' to Council-Parliament co-decision. Table 5.1 sets out the most significant Treaty provisions in which Article 189C EC is now used.

The cooperation procedure is also used in the context of the Social Policy Protocol agreed by all the Member States with the exception of the United Kingdom (Article 2(2)).

The introduction of the cooperation procedure was important because it revealed the first signs of Council accountability to the Parliament. The Council has the obligation under Article 189C(b)(1) EC to inform the Parliament of the reasons which led it to adopt its common position. The Parliament has objected on numerous occasions that the Council has adopted a cavalier attitude towards this vitally important aspect of the cooperation procedure. Rarely does the Parliament obtain what it ideally wants, namely a specific reaction to each of the amendments it proposed on first reading. In order to prevent the second reading becoming cumbersome, the Parliament has, in its Rules of Procedure, restricted the range of amendments which can be considered on second reading in general terms to a return to its position on first reading or changes to the original draft contained in the Council's common position. Formally, if the common position amounts to a significant change from the original draft put before the Parliament, reconsultation (i.e. a new first reading) should be required. Occasionally there has been a dispute between the Parliament and the Council as to whether it is reconsultation or a second reading when the measure comes back to the Parliament, although the

Figure 5.1 The Cooperation Procedure – Article 189C EC

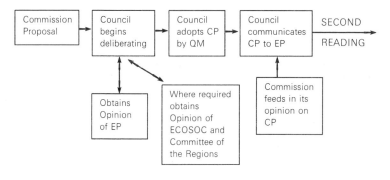

FIRST READING

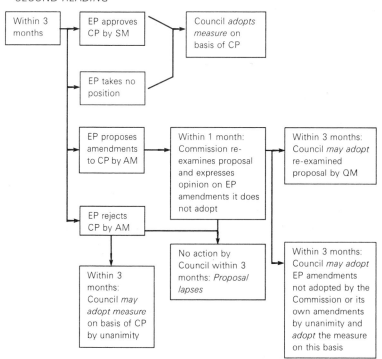

SECOND READING

ABBREVIATIONS

CP = Common Position
AM = Absolute majority of
     MEPs = 626/2 + 1 = 314

SM = Simple Majority of MEPs voting
QM = Qualified Majority
EP = European Parliament

Table 5.1   The cooperation procedure under Article 189C EC

EC Treaty Article	Nature of power
6	Elimination of discrimination on grounds of nationality
75	Common transport policy
84	Common transport policy
103	Multilateral surveillance of economic policies to ensure closer coordination
104A and 104B	Equal access to financial institutions
105A(2)	Issuing of coins
118A	Health and safety of workers
125	Implementing decisions on the work of the European Social Fund
127	Vocational training policy
129	Incentive measures in the public health field
129D	Trans-European networks
130E	Implementing decisions in relation to the European Regional Development Fund
130S(1)	Environment: actions to achieve Community objectives in Article 130R
130W	Development cooperation: actions to achieve Community objectives in Article 130U

latter body has been prepared to back down in order to avoid blocking the passage of measures which it is in favour of. Rejection of the common position by the Parliament has no formal consequence under the cooperation procedure, but the Commission has indicated its willingness to withdraw its proposal in such circumstances, to prevent the Council legislating against the will of the Parliament. In reality, it has not always done so, as the dispute between the institutions over the 'Sweeteners' Directive amply demonstrated, when the Commission was shown to be reluctant to withdraw a proposal after the Parliament had rejected a common position for only the second time ever in 1992 (Earnshaw and Judge, 1993). This in turn highlighted the urgent need for the introduction of Council–Parliament co-decision which gives the Parliament a negative power of veto.

5.6   Council–Parliament Co-decision

Article 189B EC introduces the new legislative procedure, termed 'co-decision' by most commentators, but not by the Member States themselves, who shied away from using the term in the Treaty of Maastricht. Measures adopted under the new procedures are signed by the Presidents of both the Parliament and the Council, and consequent amendments have been introduced into the judicial review procedures of the Treaty to recognise the co-responsibility of the two institutions. Essentially, the co-decision procedure, as set out in Figure 5.2 constitutes a more complex attempt to achieve Parliament and Council consensus on a common legislative text, although one important departure from the earlier structures is that when the Commission makes its proposal it sends it simultaneously to the Parliament and Council as twin branches of the legislative authority.

In addition to the second reading procedure, which is largely identical to that used in the context of the cooperation procedure, a Conciliation Committee and a possible third reading are grafted on. The Conciliation Committee may be convened where the Parliament intends to reject the Council's common position on the proposed measure. It *must* be convened if the Council fails to adopt *all* the Parliament's amendments to its common position. In the context of a failure to agree within the Conciliation Committee, the Council retains a positive final say, in that it can seek to adopt a text based on its common position; the Parliament has only a negative final say, in that it can block the adoption of the Council's preferred text. This may create a destabilising element in the whole procedure, and the Parliament will come under great pressure not to cause a legislative blockage. The Parliament's Rules of Procedure supplement the Treaty text by giving the President the power to invite the Commission to withdraw its proposal and to invite the Council not to adopt a position.

Table 5.2 sets out those fields in which Article 189B co-decision applies under the EC Treaty as amended.

The Conciliation Committee is composed of the members of the Council (or, as happens more frequently, a representative from CORE-PER) and an equal number of representatives of the Parliament. Within the Committee, agreement can be reached only where a qualified majority of the members of the Council (with the exceptions of Articles 128 and 130 EC: see Table 5.2) and a simple majority of the representatives of the Parliament are in favour (i.e. eight members). The task of the Commission in the final phase of the co-decision procedure is to participate in the work of the Conciliation Committee and to promote the achievement of agreement between the Parliament and the Council. The Commission's legislative role is thus reduced in the context of the co-decision procedure, as it loses its traditional role as intermediary between the Parliament and the Council. The Rules of Procedure of the Parliament determine the delegation of members of the Parliament to the Committee, and their responsibility to the Parliament as a whole. The delegation is formed separately for each act to be considered by the Conciliation Committee, and it is the political groups within the Parliament which are responsible for appointing the members. Of the fifteen members of the Parliamentary delegation, three are permanent members of the delegation chosen for twelve months from amongst the Parliament's Vice Presidents, two are the Chair and *rapporteur* of the parliamentary committee responsible for the

Figure 5.2 Council/European Parliament Co-decision: Article 189B EC

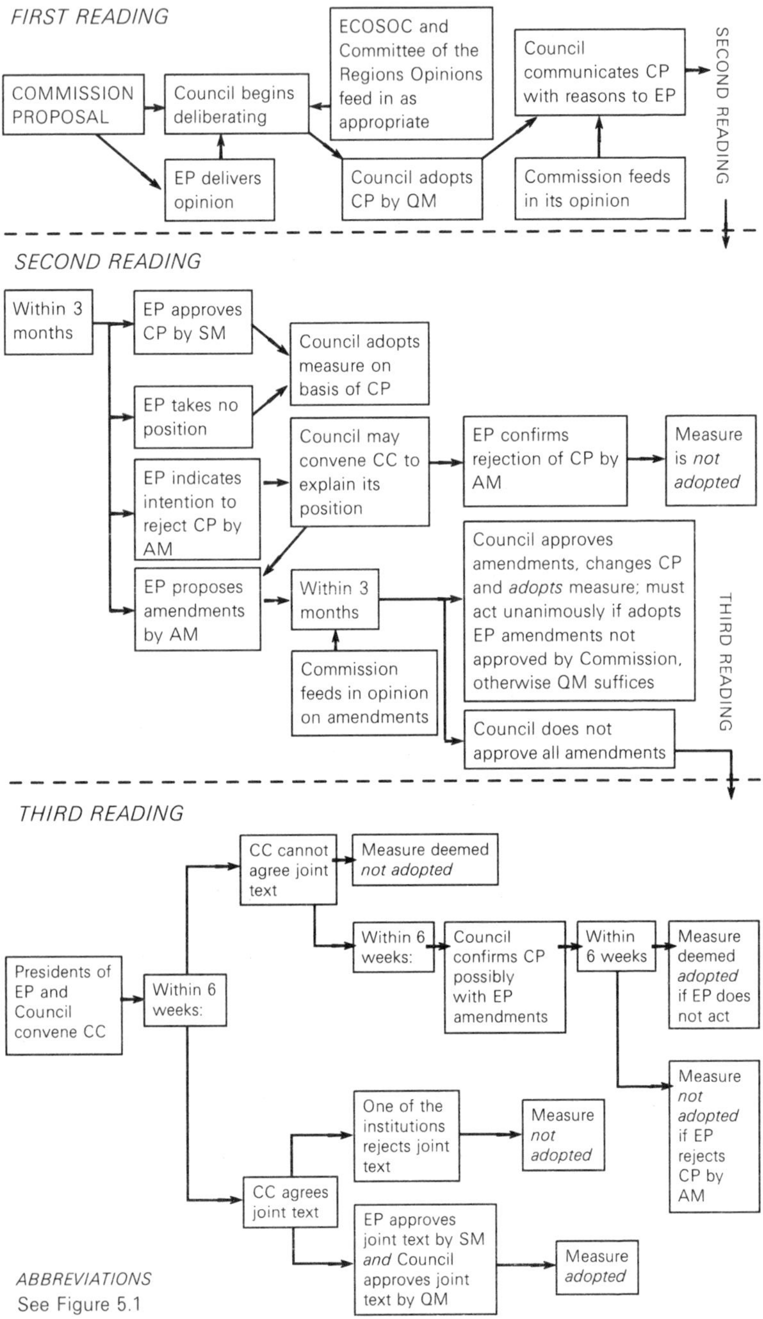

ABBREVIATIONS
See Figure 5.1

Table 5.2 Co-decision under Article 189B EC

Treaty Article	Nature of power
49	Free movement of workers
54(2)	Right of establishment for the self-employed
56(2)	Coordination of laws for the special treatment for foreign nationals
57(1)	Mutual recognition of professional diplomas
57(2)	Conditions of access and right to exercise a profession
66	Freedom to provide services
100A	Internal market
100B	Mutual recognition of national standards, by reference to Article 100A
126(4)	Incentive measures in the educational field
128(5)	Incentive measures in the cultural field
129(4)	Incentive measures in the public health field
129A(2)	Consumer protection
129D	Establishment of policy guidelines for trans-European networks
130I	Research and development multi-annual framework programme and finance
130S(3)	General action programmes in the environmental field

Note:
An oddity of the Treaty of Maastricht is that it provides for the use of co-decision in combination with Council unanimity (rather than qualified majority) in the areas of culture (Article 128 EC) and research and development (Article 130I EC). The rigidities of Council decision-making where unanimity must be achieved may render the co-decision procedure rather a fruitless exercise for the Parliament in that context.

legislation, and the remaining ten are chosen from among the members of the various parliamentary committees responsible for the legislation.

The details of the work of the Conciliation Committee were established following an interinstitutional conference held in Luxembourg in October 1993, involving all three political institutions. The arrangements are contained in an interinstitutional agreement of 25 October 1993 on 'the phase preceding the adoption of a common position by the Council and on the arrangements for the proceedings of the Conciliation Committee under Article 189B' (OJ 1993 C331/1). These arrangements determine that the chair at meetings of the Conciliation Committee is shared between the Presidency of the Council and the President (or Vice President) of the Parliament. The Committee is also serviced jointly by the secretariats of the two institutions. It meets *in camera*, and seeks, within six weeks, to draw up a joint text representing a compromise version of the legislation over which the two institutions have disagreed. Potentially any text may be placed on the table – including matters which were not originally amended by the Parliament.

So far the Conciliation Committee procedure has been used in under half the cases where co-decision is the mandated legislative procedure. So far the Conciliation Committee has only been convened once during the second reading because of a threatened Parliamentary rejection of the Council's common position. This occurred in relation to the directive on the engine power of two- or three-wheel motor vehicles. The Parliament subsequently confirmed its rejection, and a text was finally approved in January 1995, after the Conciliation Committee had been convened a second time during a third reading (Directive 95/1/EC; OJ 1995 L52/1). The Parliament achieved its essential political objective which was the removal of a ban on very high powered motorbikes.

Other high profile usages of the Conciliation Committee method where the Parliament has seriously flexed its legislative measures have included:

• the draft Directive the liberalisation of voice telephony, which the Parliament rejected after a failed conciliation process when the Council insisted on confirming its common position, after having been invited not to do so by the Parliament. Disputes about this proposal had become closely linked to what is termed the 'comitology' question (see 5.11), namely the issue of the involvement of the Parliament in implementing measures; this directive was reproposed by the Commission and was adopted in late 1995 in a form acceptable to the Parliament (Directive 95/62/EC on the application of open network provision to voice telephony OJ 1995 L321/16);
• Directive 94/62/EC on packaging and packaging waste (OJ 1994 L365/10), adopted after a difficult conciliation process requiring an extension of the six week time limit.

The introduction of the co-decision procedure was very much the result of political compromise. Even so, and despite the intense complexity of the procedures introduced, first experiences with co-decision were judged by many to be a success. In particular, the intensification of dialogue between the Parliament and the Council is considered a positive asset for the EU (Earnshaw and Judge, 1995). They also highlight a point which was already well known: that the Parliament will exhibit skill in maximising the utility of the opportunities for influence it has been given, through the way it moulds its own internal procedures and the informal pressures which it brings to bear on the other institutions.

5.7   The Assent Procedure

One of the changes introduced by the Treaty of Maastricht was a marked increase in the number of fields in which the assent of the Parliament is required. As Craig and de Búrca (1995: 128) put it, this is 'the true form of

Table 5.3 The requirement of parliamentary assent

Treaty Article	Nature of power
8A(2)	Facilitation of the right of free movement for EU citizens
105(6)	Granting the ECB tasks relating to the prudential supervision of credit and other financial institutions
106(5)	Amendments to the Statute of the ESCB
130D	Definition of the tasks, priority objectives and organisation of the Structural Funds
138(3)	Uniform electoral procedure for the European Parliament
228(3)	Association agreements, and other international agreements establishing a specific institutional framework, with significant budgetary implications or entailing the adoption of an act falling to be adopted under Article 189B (co-decision)
O TEU	Accession of new Member States

co-decision'. This began with association agreements and the accession of new Member States under the Single European Act, and has now been extended to 'legislative' fields outside external relations (see Table 5.3). In all cases except Article 138(3) on the uniform electoral procedure, where an absolute majority is required, assent requires a simple majority of members present and voting.

5.8 Common Foreign and Security Policy (CFSP) and Cooperation in Justice and Home Affairs (CJHA)

There are no 'legislative' processes under the second and third pillars of the EU in the sense in which we have discussed here the various structures under the EC Treaty and the different types of inputs which the institutions may make. The processes are largely, but not entirely intergovernmental in nature, with most direct inputs coming from the Member States and structured through the institutional framework of the Council. The 'outputs' of the policy-making processes, although capable of having binding effect in certain circumstances, are not subject in the same way to the jurisdiction of the Court of Justice (see 4.18).

The policy-making process in the context of CFSP is principally based on processes of mutual information and consultation amongst the Member States leading, in appropriate cases, to coordination of international action, the taking of common positions and the adoption of joint actions in appropriate cases. QMV may be used as the basis for votes in the context of joint actions under Article J.3 TEU; in other cases, the Council acts by unanimity. For the purposes of ensuring continued cooperation between the Member States, the Political Committee (see 4.10) plays a key role. The European Council and the Presidency – again representing in various ways the interests of the Member States – also play key roles in the processes. The former determines general guidelines of policy (Article J.8(1) TEU), and the latter has a representative role (Article J.5 TEU) as well as the task of consulting the Parliament – which is consigned to a minor institutional role in the context of CFSP (Article J.7 TEU). It may ask questions of the Council and make recommendations and is required to hold an annual debate on the progress in implementing the CFSP. The role of the Commission is rather more substantial: it is entitled to be 'fully associated' with the work carried out on CFSP (Article J.9 TEU), and can refer questions and proposals relating to CFSP to the Council (Article J.8(4) TEU).

The provisions governing CJHA broadly parallel those on CFSP. Once again, the Commission may make some direct inputs through a right of initiative in limited areas (but not a right of proposal) (Article K.3(2)) and the right to be 'fully associated' with work under this pillar (Article K.4(2)), and to a lesser extent the European Parliament can make indirect inputs through the right to be consulted on 'the principal aspects of activities' undertaken under CJHA (Article K.6 TEU). Once again it may ask questions, and must hold a debate on policy progress. Under CJHA, the Commission also has the very specific right to initiate debate on whether certain matters should be taken over the so-called *passerelle* (bridge) into the Community pillar of the Union (Article K.9). In certain areas under CJHA the use of QMV is envisaged, particularly for measures implementing so-called 'joint actions' or conventions drawn up under Article K.3(2). Otherwise unanimous voting is mandated (Article K.4(3)).

5.9   Law-making and the Policy-making Process Reviewed

It is broadly agreed that the time has come for a streamlining and simplification of the EU's legislative processes; the 1996 IGC may offer a suitable opportunity for action. In any case, the IGC was specifically given the task by Article 189B(8) EC of considering whether the co-decision procedure should be applied in a wider range of questions. In fact, co-decision is already estimated to account for 25 per cent of the volume of legislative activity undertaken by the Parliament.

It must be concluded that while the legislative processes of the European Union are now vastly different and more complex than those established in the original Treaties, they remain strongly intergovernmental in nature. This contributes to the generally high level of secrecy which surrounds the law-making process, and to the absence of transparency. The increase in complexity has not overcome the lack of accountability on the part of the Council for the manner and type of decisions it takes. EU legal acts are bargained for and negotiated, rather than debated openly.

The Conciliation Committee has not increased openness – in that it meets in secret – although it does offer increased efficiency (arguably) and increased legitimacy (definitely) by making the Parliament into something closer to a co-legislator. Moreover, one of the practices which the Council has used over the years to 'resolve or circumnavigate difficulties and disagreements' (Nicoll, 1993: 562) is the practice of inserting 'entries' or declarations 'in the minutes'. Very often these are simply a way of giving some recognition to a strongly held position taken by one delegation which is not directly reflected in the formal public output of a Council meeting. Rarely are these declarations made public, and they have a very uncertain legal status (see 6.16). However, they do have a significant impact upon the work of the Council, one which does not enhance the status or accountability of the EU legislature. The transparency of the legislative process is only slightly enhanced by the cooperation which now occurs between Commission and Parliament in relation to the former's 'work programme' each year. This programme is now formally submitted to the Parliament, and is now combined with a review of the work of the previous year (Work Programme for 1996, COM(95) 512; European Parliament and Commission Joint Declaration on the legislative programme and other activities for 1995 OJ C225/1).

Some areas such as environmental policy have a confusing plethora of different procedures which apply to different areas of EU activity in that field, ranging from simple parliamentary consultation to co-decision. Significant areas of Community competence are also still excluded from the new procedures, including agricultural policy, indirect taxation and the system of Community own resources, as well as the general legislative powers in Articles 100 and 235 EC. The general lack of agreement between the institutions on essential elements of the law-making process has resulted in a proliferation of disputes being submitted to the Court of Justice for resolution in the legal sphere, in particular in the matter of legal basis (5.17).

The democratic deficit is only very partially offset by alternative mechanisms whereby different interests can ensure input into the legislative process (4.3). Although the intensity and effectiveness of lobbying in the EU has increased dramatically since the early 1980s, it remains only a partial substitute for a 'genuinely' democratic and legitimate legislative process (Harlow, 1992b). As the EU has grown in importance, as a policy-maker and producer of legislative outputs, so it has become the target for ever larger numbers of lobbyists, operating through a variety of private and public channels for interest representation. In some ways, the involvement of different interests in the EU policy-making process is structured or channelled, either through ECOSOC and, more recently, the Committee of the Regions, or through the huge network of advisory committees where national interests are represented, often through the work of experts on whom the Commission relies quite heavily (Buitendijk and van Schendelen, 1995). There also exist numerous more or less effective European level interest representation groups, of which the best known are UNICE (representing employers and business), ETUC (representing employees and their organisations), CEEP (representing public sector enterprises), BEUC (representing consumers) and COPA (representing agricultural interests).

These groups, along with numerous other bodies such as the EC Committee of the American Chamber of Commerce (one of the most effective lobbyists), European level organisations in particular sectors (e.g. chemicals, the car industry, pharmaceuticals), individual firms, local and regional government, the voluntary sector and charities all seek to exercise influence upon the Commission, Members of the European Parliament, Council delegations and even the Economic and Social Committee. Involvement of a variety of actors in the policy process is in many ways extremely healthy; the Commission often relies upon its contacts for particular types of technical expertise. Inevitably, however, an urgent debate has arisen in recent years over the management of interest representation, to ensure some degree of fairness, probity and transparency. Progress in the management of interest representation has been slow, with the Parliament perhaps showing more willingness than the Commission to order the situation through a register of lobbyists. Some of the most concrete proposals for an informal code of conduct have come from lobbyists themselves, who are anxious not to lose credibility (see McLaughlin and Greenwood, 1995).

Even a brief discussion of the issue of private interest representation at the EU level serves to emphasise how misleading it is to analyse the legislative processes of the EU in isolation from a broader view of the policy-making process, extensively investigated by political scientists and policy analysts in particular (see the list of further reading). While recalling the continuing debates between those who ascribe varying degrees of importance to the respective roles of the EU institutions and the sovereign Member States (see 1.4), it is useful to point out a growing tendency amongst those who concentrate upon the institutions not only to show the Commission as pivotal, in particular in its capacity to show leadership, but also to acknowledge the types of inputs into the policy-making process that the Court may have and how the process is often shaped by an interaction between the Commission and the Court. The *cause célebre* in this context tends to be the Court's decision in *Cassis de Dijon* (Case 120/78 *Rewe-Zentrale AG* v. *Bundesmonopolverwaltung für Branntwein* [1979] ECR 649) in which it developed an important 'mutual recognition' principle in the context of the free movement of goods which played a not inconsiderable role as an underlying factor in the effectiveness of the single market programme. Another high profile example is the Court's decision in the *Philip Morris* case (Cases 142 and 156/84 *BAT and Reynolds* v. *Commission* [1987] ECR 4487) on the application of the EC competition rules to mergers between companies, which was undoubtedly an important factor in the Council reaching a long postponed agreement on a Regulation giving the Commission special powers on the supranational control of mergers.

5.10 Legislation Post-Maastricht: the 'Simplification' Programme

One low profile offshoot of the subsidiarity principle introduced by the Treaty of Maastricht and elaborated by the European Council at its December 1992 meeting in Edinburgh (3.10) is a programme of legislative review and 'simplification' (Maher, 1995; Wainwright, 1994). The work of the Commission in this area can also be traced back to the Sutherland Report, the independent report sponsored by the Commission to examine how the full benefits of the internal market could be secured in practice after 1992 (see 2.17) and, more recently, to the Commission's White Paper on Growth, Competitiveness and Employment of 1993 (Bull. EC Supp. 6/3). The application of the subsidiarity principle questions whether the EU should legislate in certain areas at all: hence after Edinburgh, a number of proposals were withdrawn, and others were changed in nature. The Commission has also radically reduced the numbers of proposals that it makes. Subsidiarity can also be linked to transparency, and to the argument that EU legislation needs to be 'recast' or 'simplified' (and occasionally 'repealed') to make the EU more transparent and therefore accountable in its work. There has also been a programme of 'consolidation', which has occurred in areas such as customs and agricultural law where multiple amendments not always coupled with the necessary repealing measures have left an excessively complex tangle of legislative measures. Other areas to which the Commission has turned its attention in the search for simplification have included the EU regulation of water, foodstuffs and vocational qualifications. Since December 1994, an Inter-institutional Agreement between the three political institutions specifically to ensure an accelerated working method for the official codification of legislative texts has been in place (OJ 1996 C102/2) (for further details on such agreements see 5.16). The work of the Commission in this area is now termed the 'SLIM initiative' (Simpler Legislation for the Internal Market), formally launched in March 1996.

5.11 Comitology and the Delegation of Powers

The legislative process should not be examined in isolation from the extensive structures of 'comitology' which determine the manner in which many powers arising under primary legislative instruments are exercised in practice. The term comitology refers to the practice within the Council of delegating implementing powers by primary legislation to the Commission, to be exercised in conjunction with committees ('*comités*' in French) of national civil servants chaired by a representative of the Commission, which wield varying degrees of influence over the executive process. There are over 200 such committees in existence. Whether one regards the practice of comitology as an enhancement of the effectiveness of the EU's institutional structure, or as a bureaucratic mechanism which rids EU decision-making of its last vestiges of democratic accountability is a moot point. What cannot be doubted is its importance, as well as the inevitability in practice of some sort of delegated powers system to enable the effective execution of EU policies. The exercise of delegated powers by the Commission is clearly foreseen in Article 155 EC which refers to the Commission exercising the powers 'conferred on it by the Council for the implementation of the rules laid down by the latter'. That provision was later supplemented by an amendment by the Single European Act to Article 145 EC which expressly acknowledges the authority of the Council to delegate implementing powers to the Commission, and provides in its third indent for these powers to be subject to the control of national representatives, a formal recognition of a *de facto* system described as 'possibly one of the most significant organic developments in the EU's institutional structure' (Bradley, 1992: 720).

The practice of delegation of powers within the EU has long been recognised by the Court of Justice. In Case 25/70 *Einfuhr- und Vorratstelle* v. *Köster* ([1970] ECR 1161) the Court acknowledged that the Council was empowered to delegate executive powers to either the Commission, or indeed to itself. In the considering the delegation of executive powers in relation to the common organisation of the market in cereals to the Commission, to be exercised according to the 'management committee' system (see below), the Court held:

> 'It cannot therefore be a requirement that all details of the regulations concerning the common agricultural policy be drawn up by the Council according to the procedure in Article 43. It is sufficient for the purposes of that provision that the basic elements of the matter to be dealt with have been adopted in accordance with the procedure laid down by that provision. On the other hand, the provisions implementing the basic regulations may be adopted according to a procedure different from that in Article 43, either by the Council itself or by the Commission by virtue of an authorisation complying with Article 155' (at p. 1170).

Moreover, the concepts of 'implementation' and 'implementing rules' have been interpreted quite broadly by the Court, to give a wide discretion to the Commission, especially in the field of agriculture (Case 23/75 *Rey Soda* v. *Cassa Conguaglio Zucchero* [1975] ECR 1279).

The comitology system recognised in *Köster* was formalised in Article 145 EC in terms which leave much discretion with the Council:

> [The Council shall. . . . .] 'confer on the Commission, in the acts which the Council adopts, powers for the implementation of the rules which the Council lays down. The Council may also reserve the right, in specific cases, to exercise directly implementing powers itself. The procedures referred to above must be consonant with principles and rules to be laid down in advance by the Council, acting unanimously on a proposal from the Commission and after obtaining the Opinion of the European Parliament.'

More detailed rules were enacted in a framework measure (Council Decision 87/373 OJ 1987 L197/33) which establishes that comitology can now take three basic forms, with a number of variants. The least intrusive Committee is the Advisory Committee (Procedure I), to which the Commission submits a draft of the measures it proposes to adopt. The Commission must take 'the utmost account' of the opinion delivered by the Committee, but is not prevented by a negative opinion from adopting the measure. Under Procedure II, the draft is considered by a Management Committee, which has the power, by a qualified majority, to delay the adoption of the measure by the Commission, during which time the Council itself can adopt a different decision by a qualified majority. The most restrictive type of Committee is the Regulatory Committee (Procedure III), where the support of a qualified majority of the committee is required for the Commission draft. If there is not sufficient support, the power of decision reverts to the Council, but if this institution does not act within three months, the Commission may adopt the act. The three procedures themselves incorporate a number of variants, and the delegating power granted by the Council will specify which procedure and variant applies in each case.

Comitology in this form is not supported by the Commission, which feels its discretion is excessively limited by Member State interference; this argument derives strength from an argument that the intention of the third indent of Article 145 was to intensify the separation of powers within the EU by consolidating the executive function within the Commission, not to intensify the powers of the Member States. The Parliament likewise is opposed since it fears that its prerogatives under the legislative process are restricted by forms of delegation of powers to the Commission under which the Council and the Member States retain control, but which bypass the legislative role of the Parliament. The sidelining of the Parliament had, of course, been enshrined by the Court ever since *Köster* which explicitly acknowledged that the original legislative procedure need not be followed for the implementing measures. Despite that precedent, the Parliament attempted to challenge the Council's Decision formalising the structures of comitology (Case 302/87 *Parliament* v. *Council (Comitology)* [1988] ECR 5615), but its attempt failed on the procedural question of its standing to bring annulment actions under Article 173 EC before the Court of Justice (a position on standing the Court later reversed), rather than an examination of the merits of its arguments. There matters rested for some time, although to protect the Parliament's interests, the Commission agreed that draft measures going before the Committees will be forwarded to the Parliament for information.

The comitology question returned to the institutional agenda with added force in the wake of the introduction of the co-decision legislative procedure by the Treaty of Maastricht. As a 'co-legislator' the Parliament was able to argue very forcefully that it should not be wholly excluded from the executive process, given that the Council, as the other co-legislator, is intimately involved in it, by virtue of the terms of Article

145. Using what powers it had under the Conciliation Committee process to seek improvements in its situation, the Parliament eventually rejected the draft voice telephony Directive precisely over its dissatisfaction with the comitology issue (see 5.5). This drastic action led the Council to the negotiating table to produce a *modus vivendi* agreed in December 1994 between the three institutions on comitology and measures adopted using the co-decision procedure (OJ 1996 C102/1) (a form of 'interinstitutional agreement': see 5.16). This puts on a more formal footing the Parliament's 'right' to receive all draft general implementing acts at the same time and under the same conditions as to the relevant committee. The Commission has committed itself to take account of the Parliament's comments and to 'keep it informed at every stage of the procedure of the action which it intends to take'. The Council's commitment, in the event of the matter being referred to it, is not to adopt an implementing measure without first consulting the Parliament, and taking due account of its views. It should seek 'a solution in the appropriate framework' with the Parliament. This was a matter set down for review at the 1996 IGC.

Increasingly, the EU institutions look to new bodies to take on implementing or regulatory tasks in relation to EC law. The validity of such delegations to 'bodies established under private law, having a distinct legal personality and possessing powers of their own' has been long recognised by the Court of Justice (Case 9/56 *Meroni* v. *High Authority* [1957–58] ECR 133 at p. 151), but equally the Court has made clear that delegations to such bodies may not grant the same wide discretionary powers which may be handed to the Commission:

'To delegate a discretionary power, by entrusting it to bodies other than those which the Treaty has established to effect and supervise the exercise of such power each within the limits of its own authority, would render . . . . ineffective' the 'fundamental guarantee' of 'the balance of powers which is characteristic of the institutional structure of the Community' ([1957–58] ECR 133 at p. 152).

Hence, the general limitation on agencies and other similar bodies is that their work should be limited to preparatory work, gathering and monitoring of information, research and coordination. Ultimately, they should improve the effectiveness of the Commission's own work, but at this stage of their existence, their genuine autonomy is limited by the impact of the *Meroni* judgment and the concept of interinstitutional balance.

5.12   The Finances of the European Union

The finances of the European Union, and the expenditure of those finances, involve much more than dry legal rules and procedures (for a good summary see Commission, 1995b). Both the income and expenditure sides of the EU budget have proved to be sites of intense political conflict which have mirrored the overall debates about the direction of European integration. For example, the crisis of the 'empty chair' in 1965–1966, which came closest to precipitating a complete breakdown in the work of the European Communities, was to a large extent a clash about the question of financing (see 2.7). The political conflicts have generally been viewed as reducible to two key issues: the division of the 'cake' between the Member States, and the relationships between the poorer and richer Member States, and the struggle for power between the various institutions, in particular between the Parliament – representing the 'federal' element in the EU – and the Council – representing the governments of the Member States.

The regime for financing the European Communities envisaged by the original Treaties of national contributions – the traditional method of funding international organisations – is now entirely supplanted by the 1970 and 1975 Budgetary Treaties, the 1984 agreement on the UK budget rebate, the 1988 agreement between the Member States on the restructuring of the budget and the reallocation of revenues (the so-called 'Delors I package' – see 2.13), and the 1992 decisions reached at the Edinburgh European Council which were based on the so-called 'Delors II package' (see Bull.-EC 12/92). That package was devised to update the financial structure and resourcing of the EU in order to make it possible to achieve the goals of Maastricht, providing a financial perspective from 1993 to 1999 (*From the Single Act to Maastricht and Beyond: the Means to Match our Ambitions* COM(92) 2000). In 1996, the budget of the EU stood at nearly 90,000m ECUs, subject to a ceiling that it could not exceed 1.22 per cent of GNP in the EU, and is due to rise to no more than 1.27 per cent of GNP by 1999. The rapid rise in the EU budget since the Treaty of Maastricht tends to give the lie to claims that subsidiarity means less intervention by the EU; what it probably means is intervention in different forms, and a widespread recognition that the move gradually towards economic and monetary union requires the EU to have something which approximates a little more closely to a 'pre-federal' budget.

Since 1988, the Member States and the EU institutions have sought to defuse conflict over the question of how much money is available to spend by adopting the method of medium term 'perspectives', based on political decisions about how the activities in the EU are likely to change within that time period. The method worked quite well between 1988 and 1992, to the extent that there was sufficient slack and flexibility in the system to allow the EU to respond quite effectively to the challenges posed by the changes in Central and Eastern Europe where it has sought to play a lead role in delivering and coordinating aid aimed at facilitating transformations to liberal constitionalism and market capitalism.

The European Union is now financed by a system of 'own resources', that is revenue to which it is entitled as of right, rather than national contributions. Contributions can, of course, be withheld; own resources cannot. This should mean that the money accrues to the EU automatically, irrespective of the relative wealth or poverty of the Member States. The EU's revenue has four components:

- customs duties charged on goods at the EU's external frontiers;
- levies charged on agricultural products at the external frontiers;
- a proportion of the VAT levied by the Member States up to a ceiling of 1 per cent;
- since the 1988 budget agreement between the Member States, a fourth resource calculated according to national GNP, which makes up the shortfall between the three 'traditional' own resources and the Community's necessary expenditure.

Unlike the VAT element, the fourth resource is progressive, not regressive; that is, it is a tax proportionate to the wealth of the Member States, whereas the VAT element has a tendency to penalise the poorer Member States where the VAT base on which it is calculated gives rise to disproportionately high contributions from poorer Member States. Such states have a greater level of consumption in relation to production. The fourth resource was also needed as the proportion of customs duties and levies within the total EU revenues has been dropping as customs duties have gradually been reduced in the move towards global free trade, and as the EU has become increasingly self-sufficient in agricultural resources. Consequently, there was a need to find additional resources for additional EU activities (especially policies on economic and social cohesion) without adding (and indeed reducing) the VAT element. Proposals for a fifth resource, based on a tax directly levied by the EU perhaps on energy consumption, have not as yet been accepted by the Member States.

The legal basis for an alteration to the basis of the EU's revenues is Article 201 EC. It is for the Council to lay down provisions on revenue, acting unanimously on a proposal from the Commission and after consulting the European Parliament; however, such provisions are merely themselves recommendations to the Member States which must then be ratified or accepted by them according to their respective constitutional requirements. In reality, the revenue side of the budget depends heavily upon the conclusion of interinstitutional agreements between the three political institutions. The most recent agreement dates from October 1993, and provides an essential buttress to the unilateral decisions on EU financing taken by the European Council at the Edinburgh Summit (Interinstitutional Agreement on budgetary discipline and improvement of the budgetary procedure, OJ 1993 C351/1).

In addition to the Common Agricultural Policy (CAP) and the structural funds, the EU spends its revenue on the buildings, staff and other administrative costs of the EU institutions and other policies including development aid, research and development support, educational and vocational training support programmes. The 1988 overhaul affected expenditure as well as revenue. It brought a major shift in emphasis from the CAP towards the structural funds, a shift mandated both by the increasingly widespread acceptance that the level of support going to the CAP was now too great, and by the commitment in the Single European Act to the development of regional policies. Limitations on spending on the CAP have been brought about both by structural reforms within the CAP itself (especially controls on production levels) and by cutting down on the price support system on which it is based. Agriculture now accounts for rather under 50 per cent of the expenditure of EU, although this is as much a result of growth elsewhere in the budget, as real constraints on agricultural spending.

One area where the financing of EU activities in recent years has given rise to particular problems in recent years has been that of the Common Foreign and Security Policy (CFSP). Formally, there is a budgetary process only for each of the 'Communities'. In reality, certain activities falling under the 'Union' pillars do require expenditure. Administrative expenditure for CFSP-related institutional activities are charged to the EC budget (Article J.11(2) TEU). Operational expenditure (e.g. for joint actions) should come either from the same source (in which case the budgetary processes described in 5.10 will apply to any expenditure, thus indirectly involving the Parliament in CFSP) or from contributions from the Member States. This takes the EU back to the old problem of contributions: Member States may be slow to pay their dues, as occurred in relation to EU aid to Bosnia, thus reducing the effectiveness of CFSP actions. An alternative which has been used in the past, but which has caused great friction between the Commission and the Parliament, has been the redirection of EU funds already committed elsewhere to CFSP purposes. An effective budget line for CFSP was only entered into the EU budget for 1995.

As the financial resources available to the EU have become greater, so the problem of ensuring the protection of those resources against fraudulent misuse has become more urgent. The role of the Court of Auditors has increased in recent years somewhat, to increase its role in highlighting financial irregularities. Frauds have become increasingly common not only in relation to agricultural expenditure, but also other forms of financial support provided by the EU institutions, under its structural programmes (social policy, regional policy, trans-European networks).

Although Article 209A EC, introduced by the Treaty of Maastricht, expressly assimilates the financial interests of the EU to the financial interests of the Member States, requiring Member States to counter fraud by means of the same measures which they take to counter fraud against their own interests, and requiring coordination by Member States, progress in this area has been quite slow. One problem has been the lack of a secure legal basis within the EC Treaty for securing the financial interests of the EU. This has resulted in the adoption of a CJHA convention under Article K.3(2)(c) TEU on criminal penalties which requires separate adoption by the Member States (Council Act of 26 July 1995 drawing up a Convention for the Protection of the Financial Interests of the European Communities OJ 1995 C316/48), supplemented by reference to matters falling directly within Community competence (administrative controls and penalties) by a Council Regulation of December 1995 on the same topic (OJ 1995 L312/1) (adopted on the basis of Article 235 EC). Unlike the budget itself, measures to protect the financial interests of the EU require unanimity on the part of Council. In recent years, the Commission has sought to use the fraud problem instrumentally both in order to maximise its own influence as an executive body, and in order to operate as a stimulus for the intensification of integration in areas such as criminal law which have traditionally been fields where national sovereignty has been paramount (Passas and Nelken, 1993; Mendrinou, 1994).

5.13   The Budgetary Process

It is one of the constant complaints of the Parliament that there is no institutional parallelism between the revenue and expenditure sides of the Community finances. Revenue raising remains in the hands of the Council and the Member States, with Parliamentary input largely limited to consultation (Article 201 EC); expenditure falls under the joint control of the Parliament and the Council. The budgetary process is governed by Article 203 EC, as amended by the Budgetary Treaties of 1970 and 1975. The present provisions need to be read in the light of the 1988 and 1993 interinstitutional agreements which introduced an element of medium-term financial planning into the budgetary process and thereby significantly reduced the potential for conflict between the institutions in the context of agreeing each annual budget. In the agreement the basic outlines of the next four budgets (financial perspective) were agreed in advance, and any revisions required the cooperation of the Commission and the consent of the Council and the Parliament.

Under the provisions of Article 203 the Commission draws up a preliminary draft budget for the next calendar year on the basis of expenditure estimates made by each of the institutions. The draft budget – and all amendments which follow – must be within the financial perspective established at Edinburgh, and amended to take account of the fourth enlargement in January 1995. This draft is then sent to the Council for amendment and approval, on a qualified majority, before 5 October. The Parliament then has 45 days to consider the draft budget as established by the Council.

For these purposes, a distinction must be made between compulsory and non-compulsory expenditure within the budget. Compulsory expenditure (CE) is that which results necessarily from obligations under the Treaty or acts adopted thereunder – for example, spending on the CAP. Non-compulsory (NCE) is other, discretionary, expenditure. In considering the budget, the Parliament has more restricted powers over CE than over NCE. It can, by a majority of members, propose amendments to NCE. These amendments will stand if they are not rejected or modified by the Council, acting by a qualified majority, within 15 days. In the latter event, when the budget returns to the Parliament for second reading, it can, within 15 days, in effect reinstate its amendments by a majority of its members and a three fifths majority of the votes. In the case of CE, the Parliament can merely propose modifications, acting by a majority of votes. Where these increase the total expenditure of an institution, the modifications will be included in the budget only if they are positively accepted by the Council within 15 days. Modifications which do not increase the total expenditure of any institution must be positively rejected by the Council within 15 days; otherwise they are included in the budget. It will be apparent, therefore, that the Parliament's real control over the content of the budget is not so great as might appear from its designation as joint budgetary authority. However, the distinction between CE and NCE needs to be read in the light of the 1993 Interinstitutional Agreement. Most significantly for the Parliament, this Agreement provides for a conciliation procedure between the Council and the Parliament in relation to CE, in the event that the Council wishes to depart from the preliminary draft budget. It also redefines the concept of CE, specifying that all expenditure on structural policies including the Cohesion Fund, and internal policies is NCE where the Parliament has the final say. Finally, it ring-fences NCE, protecting it against encroachment in the event of increases in the level of CE.

In the event of great dissatisfaction with the draft budget, the Parliament does have the power to reject it as a whole for 'important reasons', provided it acts by a majority of its members and two-thirds of the votes cast. It has done this twice – in 1979 and 1984. In this event, a new draft budget must be prepared by the Commission. Provision is made in the budgetary process for the spending to continue on a pro rata basis in the event of the non-adoption of the budget before the beginning of the year – a problem endemic in the mid-1980s. Supplementary budgets also sometimes have to be adopted, if unexpected contingencies cannot be covered out of the commitment appropriations.

The President of the Parliament also has the final power to declare the budget adopted at the conclusion of the budgetary process. This can in turn lead to disputes, since in 1985 the Parliament adopted a budget for 1986 containing what the Council considered to be proposed expenditure in excess of the 'maximum rate' set each year by the Commission, and used as a rule to restrict expenditure growth. The act of the Parliament was successfully challenged by the Council before the Court of Justice, the budget annulled, and the 1986 budgetary process reopened in the middle of the year (Case 34/86 *Council* v. *Parliament* [1986] ECR 2155). In 1995, the Council once more successfully sought the annulment of the adoption of the budget by the President of the Parliament (Case C-41/95 *Council of the EU* v. *European Parliament* [1995] ECR I-4411). The budget adopted in December 1994 for 1995 contained a higher increase in non-compulsory expenditure than was possible without an agreement between the Council and the Parliament. The Council also argued that the Parliament had exceeded its powers regarding compulsory expenditure by introducing amendments, and that it had violated the principle of sincere cooperation between the institutions. The Parliament's argument rested on the alleged apparent acquiescence of the Council to the Parliament's actions, through verbal assurances and behaviour which apparently approved the approach taken by the Parliament. The Court did not share the Parliament's view of the actions of the Council, and in particular its President. It annulled the act approving the budget, on the grounds that it was taken at a time when the budgetary procedure had not yet been concluded, holding that the Parliament had indeed violated the principle of cooperation with the institutions by which it is bound.

5.14   The Range of Community Powers

In Chapter 3, the principles which govern the existence and exercise of 'Community competence' (in particular, the concepts of limited powers, implied powers and exclusivity) were discussed in outline, as constitutional fundamentals of European Union. The existence of a number of general legislative powers (Article 6(2), 100, 100A and 235 EC), which greatly extend the legislative potential of the EU was also highlighted, for further discussion here.

Article 100 EC provides a general power for the adoption of directives aimed at harmonising national laws which 'directly affect the establishment or functioning of the common market'. Article 100 requires unanimity on the part of the Council of Ministers, and the consultation of the Parliament and the ECOSOC. It was used, for example, as the legal basis for a 1975 Directive harmonising national laws relating to the protection given to workers in the event of collective redundancies (Council Directive 75/129 OJ 1975 L48/29). The motivation for the directive was that the differences in standards of protection between the Member States affected the functioning of the common market, allowing companies operating in Member States with lower standards a competitive advantage over those in states with high standards of protection. Much the same justification can be used for a measure adopted under Article 100A. The Court's interpretation of Article 100 has been a classic example of its approach to the relationship between specific and general legal bases. In Case 68/86 *United Kingdom* v. *Council (Agricultural Hormones)* ([1988] ECR 855), it rejected an argument that a Directive laying down rules governing the production and marketing of certain types of meat should have been adopted under Article 100 as well as Article 43 EC (CAP). Article 43 alone was a sufficient legal basis, and it was wrong to create a dual reference where a specific legal basis would be sufficient.

Article 100A EC differs from Article 100 in that it provides for QMV in the Council and involves, since 1993, the Parliament–Council co-decision procedure. Unlike Article 100, Article 100A provides for the adoption of any type of 'measures', not just directives; it also structures the use of legislative power by requiring Commission proposals, where relevant, to be based on high levels of health, safety, environmental and consumer protection (Article 100A(3) EC). However, the scope of Article 100A is limited in that it cannot be used to adopt tax harmonisation measures, or measures in the fields of free movement of persons or rights and interests of employed persons (Article 100A(2)). In that respect, it is less easy to characterise it as a 'general' legal basis. The restriction on the use of Article 100A(2) in relation to the free movement of workers is partly offset by Article 6(2), which provides a general power for the Council to adopt measures which eradicate discrimination based on grounds of nationality. This power, too, has been broadly interpreted by the Court of Justice, using a strand of argument drawn from its work on implied powers (3.9). In Case C-295/90 *Parliament v. Council (Students' Rights)* ([1992] ECR I-4193), the Court concluded that although Article 6(1) appears to refer, in a narrow way, to the elimination of discrimination, measures adopted under paragraph 2 of that provision

'should not necessarily be limited to regulating rights deriving from the first paragraph of the same article, but they may also deal with aspects the resultion of which appears *necessary* for the effective exercise of those rights' (p. 4235) (emphasis added).

Consequently, it was the correct provision to use as the legal basis for a Directive covering free movement rights for students, who, by virtue of the Treaty provisions on vocational training, fall within the scope of protection of EC law.

The delimitation of Article 100A in relation to specific legal bases, especially those concerned with environmental policy, has become intimately entangled with problems of interinstitutional balance and the relationship between different types of legislative procedure. They are discussed in more detail in 5.17. The Court's treatment of the provision has, nonetheless, confirmed that it is a residual legal basis. In Case C-271/94 *Parliament v. Council (Edicom)* (26.3.96), the Court refused to accept that Article 100A was the correct legal basis for a Council Decision on interadministration telematic networks for statistics relating to the trading of goods. Such networks should, since the adoption of the Treaty of Maastricht, be established using Article 129D(3) EC, which provides for the creation of Trans-European Networks. The Court made clear its preference for Article 129D(3) as a *more specific* provision than Article 100A.

Furthermore, the Court has recently confirmed the potential breadth of Article 100A in a case brought by Spain to challenge its use as the legal basis for a Council Regulation on the creation of a supplementary patent protection for certain medicinal products. Although there are limitations on the EU's powers to regulate property and property rights, the Court nonetheless concluded that this aspect of the unification of national intellectual property laws through the creation of a uniform EU system was necessary for the purposes of the completion of the internal market

(Case C-350/93 *Spain* v. *Council (Patent protection for medical products)* [1995] ECR I–1985).

Article 235 EC is the most general legislative power in the Treaty. It is not limited in scope, for example, to harmonisation measures. It provides:

> 'If action by the Community should prove necessary to attain, in the course of the operation of the common market, one of the objectives of the Community and this Treaty has not provided the necessary powers, the Council shall, acting unanimously on a proposal from the Commission and after consulting the Assembly, take the appropriate measures.'

An example of the use of Article 235 in order to extend the range of EU activities is Council Regulation 2137/85 of July 25 1985 establishing the European Economic Interest Grouping (EEIG) (OJ 1985 L199/1). The EEIG provides a specifically 'European' vehicle for companies, professional partnerships and other types of business association to cooperate with each other at a transnational level unrestricted by the limitations of any one national law.

To facilitate law-making activities under Article 235, the Court of Justice has given the individual elements of this Article a consistently broad interpretation. For example, in Case 242/87 *Commission* v. *Council (ERASMUS)* ([1989] ECR 1425) the Court held that the pursuit of a 'People's Europe' was one of the objectives of the Community. Nowhere was such a goal explicitly to be found in the Treaties then in force but the Court read it into the system of the Treaty. Moreover, it is implicit in the Court's case law that it will not seek to restrict *de facto* extensions of competence into the areas covered tangentially rather than explicitly by the EU (see Case 8/73 *Hauptzollamt Bremerhaven* v. *Massey-Ferguson* [1973] ECR 897). This is legitimate since that no measure would have been adopted under Article 235 if all the Member States had not been in favour.

To restrict overenthusiastic reliance upon Article 235, and to encourage the Council to make full use of other law-making powers, the Court has also confirmed the genuinely residual nature of this legal basis. The Council may have resort to Article 235 EC only when a more specific power elsewhere in the Treaty is lacking (Case 45/86 *Commission* v. *Council (Generalised Tariff Preferences)*). The Council cannot, for example, have recourse to Article 235 in order to avoid using a legal basis requiring only a simple majority of votes (see Case 242/87 *Commission* v. *Council (ERASMUS)* which concerned the relationship between Article 128 EEC (vocational training) and Article 235) or one which provides for the use of the cooperation procedure (see Case C-295/90 *Parliament* v. *Council (Students' Rights)* which concerned the relationship between what was then Article 7(2) EEC [now Article 6(2) EC] and Article 235). In other words, it is notable that the Court has often paid greater attention to delineating the distinction between Article 235 and the other more specific powers under the Treaty, in order to limit recourse to this relatively restrictive legal basis, than it has to restricting the incremental growth of

Community competence through the gradual adoption of novel measures such as the EEIG Regulation, or the early environmental measures based on this Article. Specific powers have now been given under the Treaty allowing for the adoption of many of the measures for which, in the early days, recourse to Article 235 was required (e.g. Articles 130R–T EC, as amended), as well as new competences in the fields of education, public health, culture and consumer protection. There is some evidence that in light of these specific powers, and of that aspect of the principle of subsidiarity which operates as a fetter on legislative activities, that recourse to Article 235 has been less common in the years immediately following the Treaty of Maastricht. In contrast, when faced with the question whether Article 235 EC could accommodate the accession of the European Community to the European Convention on Human Rights and Fundamental Freedoms, the Court argued that it could not be used in effect to create an *institutional* novelty within the EU system (see 6.9).

5.15   Interinstitutional relationships in the EU

Much of this chapter has aimed at showing that law-making and policy-making in the EU often owe as much either to high level political agreements achieved within the European Council or between the various institutions, or to day-to-day structures of informal cooperation between and within the institutions as they do to the formal texts of the Treaties. In an evolving EU, disputes between the institutions are as inevitable as disputes between the EU and its Member States. Comitology, as described above, is just one example of an evolving institutional structure which continues to 'set institution against institution' (Bradley, 1992: 721). In so far as disputes exist between the EU's more and less supranational institutions (e.g. between the Commission and the Council), disputes between the institutions may also conceal an element of dispute between the interests of the Member States and those of the EU.

This was clearly the case with the dispute which arose between the Commission and the Council – representing the Member States – concerning voting arrangements in the United Nations Food and Agriculture Organisation (FAO) (Case C-25/94 *Commission* v. *Council (FAO)* (19.3.96)) (on the involvement of the EU in FAO see 3.12). The dispute arose because the Council insisted that for the purposes of a vote in the FAO on certain fisheries conservation measures the Member States should exercise their votes through the Presidency rather than the Community voting as a single member of the FAO. In an area (as here) where there is shared competence between the Member States and the Community, the institutions and the Member States 'must take all necessary steps to ensure the best possible cooperation' on the management of the right to vote. Here, that duty to cooperate had been fulfilled through an arrangement between the Council and the Commission on the exercise of the right to vote, and the Court essentially committed the Council to observing the provisions of that arrangement, and found the Council to be in breach of the provision which determined that the 'thrust' of an FAO measure would determine whether the right to vote would be enjoyed by the Community or the Member States. Consequently, in formal terms a dispute between the EU institutions and the Member States was subsumed into a dispute about the terms and effect of an 'agreement' between two of the institutions representing the 'intergovernmentalist' and 'federalist' elements of the EU.

A number of corrective mechanisms have emerged within the EU's political and legal systems whereby disputes may be resolved. These exist in addition to the normal channels of compromise and negotiation which mark the activities of any complex political organisation. A general duty of interinstitutional cooperation which is capable of being derived from Article 4 EC, and which was obliquely referred to by the Court in the 1995 Budget case (Case C-41/95 *Council* v. *Parliament*), is of great importance in this context (Bieber, 1984). The following paragraphs examine in more detail two of the most important corrective mechanisms: the proliferating phenomenon of interinstitutional agreements (e.g. 3.10, 5.6, 5.10, 5.12, 5.13), and the tendency to 'legalise' certain aspects of interinstitutional relations by submitting them to the Court of Justice for resolution according to the provisions of the Treaties. In this context, disputes about the legal basis of legislation represents perhaps the most important – but not the sole – trigger for such litigation.

5.16   Interinstitutional Agreements

Interinstitutional agreements involving the Council, the Commission and the Parliament are not a new phenomenon. They date back to the early 1960s, in the form of various types of practical measures agreed upon bilaterally between the Parliament and the Commission, and the Parliament and the Council, to increase the effectiveness of the Parliament's work. Trilateral agreements date back to the mid 1970s, with a joint declaration on the institution of a conciliation procedure between the Parliament and the Council in relation to legislation (OJ 1975 C89/1). It is, however, since the mid-1980s and especially since the adoption of the Treaty of Maastricht, that the practice of adopting such agreements and declarations has accelerated rapidly. Overall, it is difficult to be exact about the precise number of such measures, since not all have been officially published and there is no exact definition of what actually constitutes an 'interinstitutional agreement', nor any fixed procedure by which an interinstitutional agreement comes into being.

In addition to the interinstitutional agreements on the work of the Conciliation Committee (see 5.6), on legislative codification (5.10), and on the budgetary process and EU finances (see 5.12 and 5.13) already specifically discussed in this chapter, the most important agreement of the 'new' generation is that on *Implementing the principle of subsidiarity*

(Bull. EC 10/93), which is supplemented by an interinstitutional declaration on democracy, transparency and subsidiarity (Bull. EC 10/93) (3.10). Since 1993, the Parliament has also been pressing for interinstitutional agreements on the implementation of CFSP, CJHA and EMU, in each case in order to enhance its institutional input.

Interinstitutional agreements fall within the category of 'soft law' (see 6.16), and as such are more akin to political declarations of intent than formal legal commitments binding in a precise textual sense. That is not to say that they lack all legal effects, but it may be that they operate quite satisfactorily in the political realm as the basis of interinstitutional cooperation even while doubts exist as to their exact legal relevance or status. What is certain is that interinstitutional agreements cannot alter or modify the basic Treaties or secondary legislation (i.e. they must be constitutional), but they may operate to complement existing procedures. They may also be internally binding on the institutions (Case C-25/94 *Commission* v. *Council (FAO)*) (3.12), or binding externally in the sense of generating a legitimate expectation on the part of third parties such Member States. It was suggested, in the context of 1996 IGC, that interinstitutional agreements should both be given a formal position within a 'hierarchy' of norms of EC law, and that their use and form should be institutionalised and specifically authorized, perhaps along the lines of Article 138C which provides for the provisions governing European Parliament Committees of Inquiry to be determined by 'common accord' between the three political institutions (Decision of the European Parliament, the Council and the Commission on the detailed provisions governing the exercise of the European Parliament's right of inquiry, OJ 1995 L78/1). That would have the effect of increasing the level of legitimacy which attaches to this form of institutional cooperation.

5.17   Litigation Between the Institutions

The most drastic, public and formal way of bringing about the resolution of an interinstitutional dispute is to submit it to the Court of Justice. The legalisation of interinstitutional relationships in this manner is illustrative of the key role which the Court of Justice has played in the policy-making process. The involvement of the Court will normally take the form of an action brought under Article 173 EC for the annulment of an act taken by one or more institution (measures adopted by co-decision are signed jointly by the Presidents of the Council and the Parliament, and are seen as joint acts). Exceptionally, however, circumstances may arise where one institution takes action against another for failure to act, where there is a duty on the latter to act (Article 175 EC) (e.g. Case 13/83 *Parliament* v. *Council (Transport Policy)* [1985] ECR 1513). Much of the litigation between the institutions is concerned with the legal basis of EU measures (5.2), but some cases have raised other principles of EC law such as the duty of cooperation between the institutions (5.13), and the requirements of 'consultation' in the context of the legislative process (5.4).

One important obstacle to the involvement of the Parliament in inter-instituitonal litigation was that it was not cited as a potential plaintiff or defendant in the original version of Article 173, although it was, from the beginning, given standing under Article 175. In order to extend the scope of judicial protection, the Court of Justice was required to recognise the standing of the Parliament to bring an annulment action based on Article 173 (12.3). Although this point is now of largely academic interest following the alteration of this Article by the Treaty of Maastricht to extend *locus standi* to the Parliament, it is worth reconsidering briefly the two contradictory cases in which the Court first denied and then accepted the principle that the Parliament had the right to pursue an action before the Court, at least in order to protect its prerogatives – notwithstanding the strict wording of the Treaties. It should be noted that neither the Court, through its judicial legislation, nor the Member States in their amendments to the Treaty, have recognised a generalised right of action on the part of the Parliament in order to protect the general interest such as is accorded by Article 173(1) to the Council, the Commission and the Member States.

In Case 302/87 *Parliament* v. *Council (Comitology)* (5.11) the Court dismissed the Parliament's action as inadmissible, refusing to draw parallels between Article 173 and Article 175, or between the right of others to bring the Parliament before the Court in respect of allegedly unlawful acts (which it had already recognised in Case 294/83 *Parti Ecologiste 'Les Verts'* v. *Parliament* [1986] ECR 1339) and the right of the Parliament itself to bring an action. It suggested that the interests of the Parliament could be adequately protected by the Commission's ability – in the general interest – to take action in respect of any measure. The Court's decision was heavily criticised by commentators (Weiler, 1989; Bradley, 1988). Just over a year later the Court reversed its position (Case C-70/88 *Parliament* v. *Council (Chernobyl)* [1990] ECR I-2041), allowing the Parliament to bring an action, this time to challenge the legal basis used by the Council to adopt a measure regarding the marketing of foodstuffs affected by radiation. The Parliament successfully argued here that the measure should have been adopted on the basis of Article 100A EC rather than Article 31 Euratom. The Court acknowledged its right to bring an action in order to protect its prerogatives (e.g. involvement in the cooperation procedure, or the right to be consulted). In *Chernobyl* it was the right to be involved in the cooperation procedure which was at issue (Article 31 Euratom requires merely consultation of the Parliament) and it must have been significant for the Court's judgment that in this case the Commission did not support the Parliament's views and therefore had no incentive to protect the rights of the Parliament, as the Court had suggested in *Comitology* was the appropriate course of action. The Court held:

'The absence in the Treaties of any provision giving the Parliament the right to bring an action for annulment may constitute a procedural gap, but it cannot prevail over the fundamental interest in the maintenance and observance of the institutional balance laid down in the Treaties establishing the European Communities' ([1990] ECR 2041 at p. 2073).

The effect of the *Chernobyl* judgment was to recognise more fully the specific identity of each of the institutions, and to acknowledge the need for a legal mechanism to be available to each institution in order to ensure that its prerogatives are not harmed in the dynamic process of integration. It is the logical conclusion to the process of recognition of the Parliament in the institutional structure of the EU begun in the *Isoglucose* cases, which concerned the issue of consultation (5.4). However, it should not be thought that even now the Parliament has an unlimited right of standing. In Case C–156/93 *Parliament* v. *Commission (Micro-organisms)* ([1995] ECR I-2019) the Court held that the Parliament has no right of standing under Article 173 to attack the *reasons* on which the Commission is based, unless it can show that these in some way affect its prerogatives.

The phenomenon of interinstitutional litigation also illustrates how the intensely political issue of the choice of a legal basis can be reduced in large measure to the scenario of a legal dispute between institutions, where procedural rules rather than substantive political choices appear to predominate. The most dramatic example of this scenario is offered by the Court's shifting approach to the interrelationship between Articles 100A and 130S as legal bases for measures in the field of environment. In Case C-300/89 *Commission* v. *Council (Titanium Dioxide)* ([1991] ECR I-2867) the Commission (with the support of the Parliament) challenged the decision of the Council to use Article 130S EC as the legal basis for Directive 89/428/EEC approximating national programmes for the reduction and eventual elimination of pollution caused by waste in the production of titanium dioxide. The Directive had an admittedly dual function, namely to protect the environment (Article 130S) and to harmonise national measures which had an impact upon the completion of the internal market. From the latter perspective the measure would fall within the remit of Article 100A, thus requiring only a qualified majority vote in the Council and the use of the cooperation procedure (at that time). In contrast, Article 130S was an 'old-style' legislative power, requiring unanimity in the Council and involving only the consultation of the Parliament. The Court ruled out a dual reference to both articles, since this would in practice defeat the very purpose of the cooperation procedure, which is to expand the influence of the Parliament, and held that such a measure must be based on Article 100A alone. The effect of this decision appeared very significantly to limit the scope of application of Article 130S, and to assert the dominance of the procedural imperatives of the cooperation procedure over the substantive resolution of the appropriate content of an environmental protection measure.

In Case C–155/91 *Commission* v. *Council (Waste Directive)* ([1993] ECR I-939), however, the Court took a different view of the precise focus of Directive 91/156 on waste disposal. Again the legal basis chosen by the Council was Article 130S, but this time the Court held that the chief purpose of the Directive was to safeguard the management of the environment through the safe disposal of waste throughout the EU. Questions of free movement (and hence the issue of the internal market for waste) were *merely ancillary* to the central focus of this Directive. The Court reached a very similar conclusion in a subsequent case brought by the Parliament to challenge the use of Article 130S as the legal basis for Council Regulation 259/93 on the supervision and control of shipments of waste within, into, and out of the EU (Case C–187/93 *Parliament* v. *Council (Transport of Waste)* [1994] ECR I-2857). Since these cases were decided, of course, the relationship between Articles 100A and 130S has changed somewhat: both provisions now provide for QMV, although Article 100A is a co-decision provision and Article 130S involves the cooperation procedure. These changes, coupled with the modification of the Court's approach in the two *Waste* cases indicates that in future decisions involving Article 100A may be less motivated by procedural factors (see Case C-271/94 *Parliament* v. *Council (Edicom)* discussed in 5.14), and that the main arguments used will be whether the 'internal market question' is merely ancillary to the measure, and whether there exists a *lex specialis* which should be used as the legal basis.

However, it remains unlikely that the unanimity requirement in Article 235 will, or indeed should, ever be altered. As the Court repeated its arguments on the protection of the cooperation procedure, when discussing the relationship between Article 6(2) EC and Article 235 EC in Case C-295/90 *Parliament* v. *Council (Students' Rights)* it seems that the argument of institutional balance will always retain some relevance to the question of legal basis.

Summary

1   The basic conditions of legality for EU legal acts are a statement of reasons, a valid and correct legal basis, and respect for the principles of subsidiarity and proportionality and other EU legal principles. The question of the correct legal basis for an act is a question of law, resolvable on the basis of objectively ascertainable facts. There is no single law-making process under the Treaties, but in general a power of proposal is given to the Commission.

2   The old procedure, in particular as envisaged under the original treaties, is based around the basic pattern of Commission proposal, Parliament consultation, and Council unanimous decision, although with variants. This old style retains its attraction for new law-making powers attributed to the EC under the Treaty of Maastricht.

3   The cooperation procedure is an advance in terms of Parliamentary input, providing for a second reading. It enhances the accountability of the Council.

4   The introduction of co-decision for a limited range of law-making powers under the Treaty of Maastricht raises the Parliament to the status of co-legislature. Co-decision provides for a third reading, and the possibility of convening a Conciliation Committee. So far, the Parliament has experienced a good level of success in the context of the work of the Conciliation Committee.

5   CFSP and CJHA do not have 'legislative processes' in the same sense as those under the EC Treaty. Nonetheless they have frameworks under which measures such as joint actions may be adopted – in some cases by QMV.

6   The operation of EU policy-making processes can only be properly understood in the light of the many interests which are represented.

7   The Commission exercises many delegated powers under the structures of 'comitology', whereby the Council retains control through a committee framework operating within the Commission itself. Comitology may also make a contribution to the effectiveness of EU policy-making, although in its current form it is perceived by the Commission and the Parliament as bringing about excessive levels of Member State supervision.

8   The EU derives its revenue – termed 'own resources' – from customs duties, agricultural levies, a proportion of VAT collected by the Member States, and a fourth resource based on Member State GNPs. The EU budget stands at around 1.25 per cent of EU GNP.

9   The budgetary process involves the Council and Parliament as joint budgetary authorities. The budgetary process is governed by Article 201 EC and has been the subject of a number of disputes before the Court. The 1988 and 1993 interinstitutional agreements on financial perspectives and budgetary discipline is intended to reduce the level of budgetary dispute.

10   The range of EU activities is greatly increased by the availability of general law-making powers in Articles 6(2) 100, 100A and 235 EC. The latter is a genuinely residual law-making power which can be used only where another more specific power does not give the means necessary for the attainment of an objective of the EU.

11   Disputes between institutions are inevitable in an evolving EU. Litigation and interinstitutional agreements are two of the mechanisms, apart from negotiation and compromise, most commonly used for the settlement of interinstitutional disputes.

Questions

1   What impact does the lack of a single law-making process for the EU have upon the effectiveness of the institutions?

2   How have the EU legislative processes changed since the Single European Act? Has the democratic deficit effectively been corrected?

3   What is the significance of the concept of legal basis?

4 Does the Parliament have sufficient control over the collection of EU revenues and the allocation of expenditure?
5 How does comitology work, who is opposed to it, and why?
6 Why do interinstitutional disputes arise within the EU and what mechanisms are used to resolve them? Are these mechanisms effective?

Further Reading

Barents (1994), 'The Quality of Community Legislation', 1 *MJ* 101
Bieber (1984), 'The Settlement of Institutional Conflicts on the Basis of Article 4 of the EEC Treaty', 21 *CMLRev.* 505.
Bradley (1991), 'Sense and Sensibility: *Parliament* v. *Council*, continued', 16 *ELRev.* 245.
Bradley (1992). 'Comitology and the Law: Through a Glass, Darkly', 29 *CMLRev.* 693.
Commission (1995a), *Commission Report for the Reflection Group*, Luxembourg, OOPEC.
Dashwood (1994b), 'Community Legislative Procedures in the Era of the Treaty on European Union', 19 *ELRev.* 343.
Earnshaw and Judge (1995), 'Early days: the European Parliament, co-decision and the European Union legislative procedure post-Maastricht', 2 *JEPP* 624.
Emiliou (1994), 'Opening Pandora's Box: The Legal Basis of Community Measures before the Court of Justice', 19 *ELRev.* 488.
Maher (1995), 'Legislative Review by the EC Commission: Revision without Radicalism', in Shaw and More (1995).
Mazey and Richardson (1995), 'Promiscuous Policymaking: the European Policy Style?', in Rhodes and Mazey (1995).
Monar (1994), 'Interinstitutional Agreements: The Phenomenon and its New Dynamics After Maastricht', 31 *CMLRev.* 693.
Nugent (1995), 'The leadership capacity of the European Commission', 2 *JEPP* 603.
Peters (1994), 'Agenda-setting in the European Community', 1 *JEPP* 9.
Peterson (1995), 'Decision-making in the European Union: towards a framework for analysis', 2 *JEPP* 69.
Pinder (1995), Ch. 8, 'European Budget and Public Finance Union'.
Ress (1994), 'Democratic Decision-Making in the European Union and the Role of the European Parliament' in Curtin and Heukels (1994).
Ungerer (1993), 'Institutional Consequences of Broaderning and Deepening the Community: the Consequences for the Decision-making process', 30 *CMLRev.* 71.
Weiler (1989), 'Pride and Prejudice – *Parliament* v. *Council*', 14 *ELRev.* 334.

6 Sources of Law in the European Union

6.1 Introduction

We are concerned in this chapter with identifying the body of legal rules which comprise the sources of law in the European Union and, where this is not already clear from earlier discussion, the origins and authors of these rules. Sources of law are often divided into different categories; for example, there are external sources (international agreements) and internal sources (the founding treaties, EU legislation), as well as primary sources (treaties, general principles of law) and secondary sources (EU legislation). All these categories of sources of law will be considered in this chapter, which also outlines certain basic features of each type of legal rule (e.g. nature and extent of binding force). Important distinctions are made, where necessary, between the supranational 'Community' pillar, and the Second and Third Pillars of the European Union, as these determine the scope of relevant sources of *EC law*. One important aspect of the nature of EC law is not discussed in detail in this chapter, namely the relationship between EC law and national law. This is reserved for consideration in Chapters 9 and 10. To a certain extent, the material covered in this chapter repeats, but offers an alternative perspective upon, material introduced in earlier chapters, in that it systematises the different types of legal rules which together comprise the body of EC law.

6.2 The Founding Treaties

The Court of Justice has on a number of occasions referred to the founding or constitutive treaties as the Community's constitution (see 1.5). The structure of this constitution is now extremely complex. In addition to the three pillar structure introduced by the Treaty of Maastricht which was described in Chapter 1, incorporating within the Union the ECSC, Euratom and EC Treaties and the Single European Act, the founding treaties also comprise the various Acts of Accession, the Merger Treaty, and the Budgetary Treaties. All of these treaties have required conclusion and ratification by the Member States according to their respective constitutional requirements before entry into force. Once these procedures have been completed, the Member States are bound to comply with their obligations; certain of these obligations are also enforceable at the instance of individuals in national courts. The EU institutions are also bound by the contents of the EU constitution. As with any legal system, the EU's constitutional documents represent the supreme internal source of law. As such they are not challengeable before the Court of Justice.

6.3   Other International Agreements

A second primary source of EC law comprises the other international agreements by which the EU is bound (3.12). These include agreements with one or more third states or other international organisations concluded by the Community itself in exercise of its external relations powers, of both a bilateral nature (e.g. an association or cooperation agreement with a third state) and a multilateral nature (e.g. a trading arrangement regarding a particular commodity, such as the Multi-fibre Agreement). This category also contains agreements predating the foundation of the EC/EU under which it has succeeded to the rights and obligations of the Member States. An important example is the General Agreement on Tariffs and Trade (GATT), which represents the basic framework for the evolution of global free trade. Finally, there are international conventions which form part of the legal patrimony of all states and organisations which claim respect for the rule of law, including, within Europe, the European Convention on Human Rights and Fundamental Freedoms (ECHR), as well as truly international human rights instruments such as the International Covenant of Civil and Political Rights. On the other hand, the Schengen agreements on cross-border movements between the states involved cannot be regarded as a source of EC law, as they are not binding on all the Member States. The Court of Justice will enforce the EU's international legal obligations within the EU legal system, so far as those international treaties touch upon Community competence. In certain circumstances, individuals may also be able to rely on provisions of international agreements by which the EU is bound as creating rights which they may invoke in national courts.

A different status attaches to Conventions concluded by the Member States under Article K.3(2)(c) TEU, such as those governing the establishment of EUROPOL or certain questions relating to asylum and extradition. Even were the Court to be given jurisdiction within the framework of those Conventions, this would not render these Conventions part of 'EC law', as they remain outwith the scope of *Community competence*, but concern rather the third pillar of *European Union*.

6.4   General Principles of Law

The final category of primary sources are the general principles of law, a body of superordinate rules of law, for the most part unwritten and derived by the Court of Justice by reference to its general duty to ensure that the law is observed (Article 164 EC). These principles bind the EU, its institutions, and, within the sphere of Community competence, the Member States and individuals. 'General principles of law' are a familiar source of law within those Member States with 'civil law' systems based on the traditions of Roman Law. They offer a background statement of values and basic standards which courts can use to inform their interpretation of rules of written law and to fill gaps in the written law. General principles comprise above all rules which are sufficiently general, such as 'the right to equality' or 'the principle of legal certainty', to be widely accepted. It is the application of such principles to specific fact situations which is more likely to cause controversy than the principles themselves.

The International Court of Justice is explicitly called upon to apply general principles of law in its case law. Article 38(c) of its Statute provides:

'The Court . . . shall apply . . . the general principles of law recognised by civilised nations.'

In contrast, the EU treaties offer no equivalent statement, although general support for the practice of the Court in using general principles can be derived from the treaties. In addition to Article 164 EC, referred to above, Article 173 EC gives as one of the grounds for review of the legality of EU acts:

'infringement of this Treaty *or any rule of law relating to its application*' (emphasis added).

More explicit reference to general principles, albeit within a more limited remit, is to be found in Article 215(2) EC which governs the tortious liability of the EU for wrongful acts. The Court is to decide disputes:

'in accordance with the general principles common to the laws of the Member States.'

The reference to what is 'common' to the laws of the Member States highlights the comparative method which has frequently marked the Court's search for general principles. This comparative method appears most clearly in the Opinions of the Advocates General rather than the judgments of the Court itself (see for example A-G Warner in Case 17/74 *Transocean Marine Paint Association* v. *Commission* [1974] ECR 1063 – the right to a fair hearing in competition proceedings, and the excursus given by Usher, 1976: 370). For a principle to be 'common' does not necessarily mean that it must be recognised in all the Member States in precisely the same form. It is sufficient that a general trend can be discerned amongst the Member States. As an alternative to comparative methodology, the Court may find inspiration for a general principle of EC law in international instruments such as the European Convention of

Human Rights and Fundamental Freedoms and the International Covenant of Civil and Political Rights. However, whatever the source of inspiration, the Court invariably stresses the 'Community' nature of the principle once expressed. The general principles of law are principles of EC law, elaborated in the specific context of the EC/EU with its particular mission and subject to the authoritative interpretation of the Court of Justice alone.

Four main groups of general principles can be identified although a number of important general principles such as 'equality' straddle the first three categories in various guises. These are:

- certain rules and standards which operate as restrictions upon the exercise of EU administrative and legislative powers either by the EU itself or by the Member States where they are required to implement EU measures;
- the economic freedoms contained in the EC Treaty, which the Court has consistently elevated to the status of 'general principles' and given constitutional force to (3.15), and which act principally as fetters upon the Member States. For example, in Case 240/83 *Procureur de la République* v. *Association de défense des brûleurs d'huiles usagées* ([1985] ECR 520) the Court stated (at p.531):

  'It should be borne in mind that the principles of free movement of goods and freedom of competition, together with freedom of trade as a fundamental right, are general principles of Community law of which the Court ensures observance';

- a somewhat ill-defined body of fundamental rights. It could be said that fundamental rights are the most deeply entrenched and morally important value statements of a given social grouping, and as such can be encompassed within the first two categories of the general principles. In view of the general importance of fundamental rights and of the specific history of the protection of those rights within the EU it is, however, useful to analyse them as a third separate category;
- an emerging group of 'political' rights, drawing specifically on the model of subsidiarity and including in the future potentially a general principle of 'transparency' or 'openness'.

To a certain extent, these divisions are arbitrary; for example, there is little 'space' between a principle of administrative or legislative legality, and a fundamental right, as a recent paper entitled 'Administrative Justice: A Developing Human Right?' makes clear (Bradley, 1995). Moreover, it has been the Court's failure to draw a conceptual distinction between 'economic' rights guaranteed as part of the market-building process and fundamental socioeconomic or humanistic values which has given rise to some of the controversy in this field, as the discussion below of the Irish Abortion Case (*Grogan*) will show (6.8; see the criticisms of Phelan, 1992). Furthermore, the general principles of law represent a product of judicial activism and creativity which is typical of the Court. The proactive role which has been taken by the Court in this regard has been used as one basis for the claim that the Court has exceeded its judicial role and trespassed into the realm of politics (Rasmussen, 1986; 4.18).

6.5 Principles of Administrative and Legislative Legality

The comparative methodology referred to above has been particularly useful for the Court in the context of the development of those general principles which can be characterised as principles of administrative and legislative legality. A number of pointers to the development of this group of principles are to be found in the Treaty itself. For example, Article 173 EC cites 'lack of competence' and 'infringement of an essential procedural requirement' as well as infringement of the Treaty and 'any rule of law' as grounds for review. Article 190 EC also requires all regulations, directives and decisions to be accompanied by a statement of reasons (5.2). However, there are also many unwritten principles of administrative and legislative legality, and these have evolved through the case law of the Court which has drawn much of its inspiration in this field from the national administrative systems of the Member States. The most important are the principles of legal certainty and proportionality, and the rights to non-discrimination and procedural fairness.

Procedural fairness is particularly important in those areas of EC law where the EU institutions must enforce the law directly against individuals, such as competition law and anti-dumping law. The *Transocean Marine Paint* case provides an example of the development of the right to a hearing in the competition law field for those whose trading activities come under the scrutiny of the Commission on the grounds of alleged anti-competitive or monopolistic effects; Case C-49/88 *Al-Jubail Fertiliser* v. *Council* ([1991] ECR I-3187) extends this principle to companies which are required to pay anti-dumping duties imposed on allegedly subsidised imports into the EU. A rather different principle of procedural fairness was developed in Case 155/79 *A.M. & S.* v. *Commission* ([1982] ECR 1575) where the Court of Justice recognised the confidentiality of communications between lawyer and client in the context of Commission competition investigations. This right of legal professional privilege extends only to independent lawyers established within the EU; it does not apply to communications with lawyers outside the EU, or with in-house lawyers. *A.M. & S.* provided the first significant instance of the Court drawing more heavily upon the common law heritage offered by English and Irish law. Likewise in the field of competition law, the Court of First Instance has articulated a general principle of 'equality of arms' in administrative procedures, which requires the Commission to make available to those under investigation so-called 'exculpatory documents' which may assist them in their defence (Case T-30/91 *Solvay* v. *Commission* [1995] ECR II-1775).

Other procedural rights have been developed by the Court of Justice as fetters upon the investigatory activities of the Commission which are more akin to fundamental rights, such as the right to be protected against arbitrary administrative action; this will be considered below.

The principle of legal certainty has been cited by the Court in a number of diverse contexts. For example in Case 43/75 *Defrenne* v. *SABENA* ([1976] ECR 455) legal certainty was used as a justification for imposing a temporal limitation upon the effects of a preliminary ruling under Article 177 EC. In that case, the Court concluded that Article 119 EC could have direct effect; in other words, individual women and men could bring equal pay claims in national courts on the basis of Article 119 itself. The Court held that this applied only for the future, so that with the exception of claims already submitted at the date of the ruling, back pay could not be claimed in respect of periods of service at an unequal rate of pay prior to that time. The Court has made it clear that the limitation of the temporal effects of a ruling is a wholly exceptional measure imposed on grounds of legal certainty because of the seriously disruptive effects of the ruling; such reticence is desirable since the imposition of such a limitation on a Court ruling represents one of the most blatant examples of judicial legislation within the EU legal system, and wholly abandons the pretence that the Court is merely interpreting, as opposed to making, the law.

Furthermore, legal certainty has a particular role to play as EU legislation becomes ever complex, and in particular where the EU shifts from one system of regulatory control to another (as has occurred in the field of customs law, following widespread international developments). The EU lacks of a principle of implied repeal, whereby later enactments are regarded as implicitly taking precedence over contradictory earlier provisions. Instead, legal certainty may require the EU institutions to repeal provisions to ensure that individuals can know their rights, and consequently earlier and now redundant provisions should not be applied by national administrative authorities or courts (Case C-143/93 *Gebroeders van Es Douane Agenten BV* v. *Inspecteur der Invoerrechten en Accijnzen* (13.2.96)).

Legal certainty may also take the form of the protection of 'legitimate expectations'. Since the EU is actively involved in the customs and agricultural fields in the management of the market by intervening to set prices, levies and duties, it must take care not to violate the legitimate expectations of those concerned which it might previously have aroused. This is illustrated by Case 74/74 *CNTA* v. *Commission* ([1975] ECR 533). Here it was held that the Commission was not permitted to abolish without warning so-called 'monetary compensatory amounts' ('MCAs') granted to exporters of agricultural products to compensate them for fluctations in exchange rates since:

'a trader may legitimately expect that for transactions irrevocably undertaken by him because he has obtained, subject to a deposit, export licences fixing the amount of the refund in advance, no unforeseeable alteration will occur which could have the effect of causing him inevitable loss, by re-exposing him to the exchange risk' (p. 550).

There are a number of alternative scenarios on which a successful claim for breach of the principle of legitimate expectations may be based. For example, there may have been a course of conduct undertaken by the EU authorities (e.g. the construction of an EU scheme to persuade milk producers to cease production for a number of years: Case 120/86 *Mulder* v. *Minister van Landbouw en Visserij* [1988] ECR 2321). Alternatively, the structure of EU legislation may specifically require particular interests to be taken into account in future measures (e.g. a Commission power allowing it to prohibit certain imports from third countries but requiring it to take into account the specific position of those with goods in transit: Case C-152/88 *Sofrimport Sarl* v. *Commission* [1990] ECR I-2477). However, the Court of First Instance has stressed that in a field where the EU institutions have broad discretion in the framing of policy – such as agriculture – the institutions must retain the ability to modify the regulatory framework in particular markets without facing challenges based on the principle of legitimate expectations. The principle cannot, according to the Court, be extended to the point of generally preventing new rules from applying to the future effects of situations which arose under earlier rules (Case T-466/93 etc. *O'Dwyer* v. *Council* [1995] ECR II-2071).

Finally, legal certainty operates in the guise of the principle of non-retroactivity. Legislation is presumed not to take effect retrospectively unless this is expressly stated, and retroactivity will not be permitted unless it is essential for the purpose of the measure to be achieved and the legitimate expectations of the persons affected have been protected. In Case 108/81 *Amylum* v. *Council* ([1982] ECR 3107) the conditions for retroactivity were met. This concerned a Council Regulation imposing a system of quotas and levies on the production of isoglucose (a sugar substitute) intended to equalise the production conditions of the two products. Since an earlier Regulation to the same effect had been annulled on procedural grounds (failure to consult the Parliament: see 5.4), it was permissible to pass a second Regulation imposing the same system with retrospective effect. The objective of equality could not otherwise be achieved, and the isoglucose producers were presumed to be put on notice about the scheme by the earlier abortive Regulation.

Equality and non-discrimination themselves operate as important general principles governing the legality of EU action. This is expressed most clearly in Article 40(3) EC which demands that the common organisations of the market set up under the Common Agricultural Policy (CAP) must 'exclude any discrimination between producers or consumers within the Community', and there are many cases in which this principle of equality has been successfully invoked to challenge EU legislation in the agricultural field (see for example the *Skimmed Milk Powder* case – Case 114/76 *Bela Mühle Josef Bergman* v. *Grows-Farm* [1977] ECR 1211). The principle also has a wider impact as the principle that the EU legislature may not treat similar situations differently unless differentiation is objectively justified. In Case 41/84 *Pinna* v. *Caisse d'allocations familiales de la Savoie* ([1986] ECR 1) the Court held that the Council was not permitted, when legislating to determine the conditions under which migrant workers enjoy family benefits, to differentiate between those who were subject to French legislation and those who were not (a differentiation created on the insistence of France which has a particularly generous system of family benefits). This legislative intervention by the Council had the effect of accentuating the existing disparities between the national systems and was not permitted.

Proportionality is a concept which has entered EC law primarily out of German law, where it is given constitutional status. Essentially it requires a measure to be no more burdensome than is necessary to achieve its objective. Once the legitimate aim or objective of a measure is identified, a threefold test can be applied: is the measure a suitable or useful means of achieving the objective, is the measure necessary for the achievement of the objective, and is there a reasonable relationship between the measure and the objective? The latter, and most controversial limb, of the test essentially requires a measure not to have an excessive or disproportionate impact upon a person's interests (de Búrca, 1993a: 113). Where there is a choice between two effective means to achieve an obective, recourse should be had to the least onerous or intrusive.

An example of proportionality operating is offered by Case 181/84 *R* v. *Intervention Board for Agricultural Produce, ex parte Man (Sugar) Ltd* ([1985] ECR 2889) where the Court held that it was disproportionate for a Regulation to require the forfeiture of the entire security deposited by a company, where the security is intended to ensure that goods for which an export licence is to be obtained will actually be exported (the primary obligation), for failure to satisfy a secondary obligation, namely the duty to submit the licence application within a certain time period. The sanction was particularly harsh since the applicant was only four hours late in submitting the application.

On the other hand, in the field of general legislative discretion, the approach taken by the Court of Justice does not appear to involve strict scrutiny of institutional action. In Case C-331/88 *R* v. *Minister for Agriculture, Fisheries and Food, ex parte Fedesa* ([1990] ECR 4023), a challenge was mounted to a 1988 Directive prohibiting use of certain hormonal substances in livestock farming, on the grounds of a breach of the principle of proportionality. It was argued that the ban would be ineffective, that it would lead to the growth of a black market, that consumer anxieties could be allayed by means of an informational campaign, and that the effect on traders would be disproportionate. All aspects of the claim failed, although the Court reiterated the principle that proportionality can affect legislative discretion. The Court held however:

'It must be stated that in matters concerning the common agricultural policy the Community legislature has a discretionary power which corresponds to the political responsibilties given to it by Articles 40 and 43 of the Treaty. Consequently, the legality of a measure adopted in that sphere can be affected only if the measure is manifestly inappropriate having regard to the objective which the competent institution is seeking to pursue' (p. 4063).

Proportionality has become an extremely important principle in the economic law of the EU. Not only is it used to assess the legality of the measures of EC law and implementing measures of the Member States in the context of customs and agricultural law but, like the principle of equality, it has also become a vital component in assessing interferences by the Member States in the economic freedoms guaranteed under the EC Treaty which have been elevated to the status of general principles.
   The operation of these general principles of law as the basis for actions for the annulment or invalidity of EU legislation, or for actions for damages against the EU institutions, is reviewed again in Chapters 12 and 14.

6.6   The Pillars of Economic Integration as General Principles of EC Law

The Court of Justice has consistently repeated its view that the four basic economic freedoms under the Treaty (free movement of goods, persons, services and capital), along with the general right to non-discrimination on grounds of nationality contained in Article 6 EC are protected not just as written rules within the Treaty system, but also as general principles of EC law. The breadth of protection now offered by EC law is illustrated by the cases discussed in 3.6, such as *Cowan* (Case 186/87 *Cowan* v. *Le Trésor public* [1989] ECR 195). The Court of Justice held that a British tourist attacked, robbed and injured while on holiday in Paris was entitled to make a criminal injuries compensation claim under French law under the same conditions as a French national. As a recipient of services (tourism), Cowan fell within the scope of the application of the Treaty, and he was therefore entitled to the protection of what was then Article 7 EEC (Article 6 EC). The Court stated (at p. 222) that:

> '[national] legislative provisions may not discriminate against persons to whom Community law gives the right to equal treatment or restrict the fundamental freedoms guaranteed by Community law.'

Article 6 EC is an important – but residual – legal provision. It only applies in circumstances – e.g. discriminatory provisions in national copyright law (Cases C-92, 326/92 *Phil Collins* v. *Imtrat Handelsgesellschaft mbH* [1993] ECR I-5145) or discriminatory provisions of national civil procedure law (Case 398/92 *Mund & Fester* v. *Firma Hatrex International Transport* [1994] ECR I-467: Article 6 read in conjunction with Article 220 EC and the Brussels Convention).

Finally, in a number of cases the Court has stressed the importance of associated procedural rights to due process without which the exercise of the fundamental freedoms is meaningless. For example, where a public authority takes a decision which impinges upon an individual's rights under EC law, he or she has the right to be given reasons, to make it possible to challenge this decision in court. In Case 222/86 *UNECTEF* v. *Heylens* ([1987] ECR 4097), Heylens' application for the recognition in France of his Belgian diploma as a football trainer was rejected on the basis of an adverse opinion given by a special committee which gave no reasons for its decision. Without that recognition Heylens could not work in France. The Court held that reasons must be given for such a decision to enable effective judicial review, since the adverse opinion affected a fundamental right conferred by the Treaty on EU workers, namely the right of free access to employment.

EU legislation has been held to confer a right to judicial review on beneficiaries of EU rights. In the field of sex discrimination, the Court held in Case 222/84 *Johnston* v. *Chief Constable of the Royal Ulster Constabulary* ([1986] ECR 1651) that an alleged victim of sex discrimination bringing a claim for equal treatment guaranteed by the Equal Treatment Directive (76/207) could not be denied access to a judicial remedy by a ministerial order. In this context, the Court has also relied on the importance of Article 6 ECHR as conferring a right to judicial process (on the role of the ECHR see the discussion of fundamental rights below).

These cases are expressions of a general principle that individuals must be given effective remedies against the Member States, which allow them to protect or assert their rights under EC law. In Cases 6, 9/90 *Francovich* v. *Italian State (Francovich I)* ([1991] ECR I-5357) the Court held that it is for national courts to ensure the full effect of the provisions of EC law, and to protect the rights which EC law confers on individuals. This principle will be examined in more detail in Chapters 9 and 10.

6.7   Fundamental Rights

The EU Constitution lacks a clear and identifiable catalogue or charter of fundamental rights protecting the interests of those who fall under the jurisdiction of EC law. Instead, under EC law, fundamental rights are protected as general principles of law, a point articulated by the Court's case law and more recently in Article F(2) TEU (a non-justiciable provision). Some issues relating to fundamental rights – particularly those relating to the political meaning and effect of rights – have already been discussed in 3.6 and 3.11. This paragraph will examine more closely the doctrinal basis for fundamental rights protection.

The emergence of a specific category of general principles termed 'fundamental rights' is attributable to the need on the part of the Court of Justice to assert the supremacy of the EU legal order, even in the face of national constitutions, such as that of the Germany, which enshrine the protection of fundamental human rights. In effect, the Court has read into the EU legal order an unwritten Bill of Rights, drawing on both national constitutional expressions of fundamental rights and international human rights instruments (especially the European Convention on Human Rights and Fundamental Freedoms) as the sources of inspiration for EU fundamental rights. The articulation of a specific category of rights termed 'fundamental' was in part forced upon the Court by the reluctance of certain national courts, notably German and Italian courts, to acknowledge the full supremacy of EC law. In particular, these courts were reluctant to accept that the superior nature of EC law precluded them from testing provisions of EU legislation against national constitutional guarantees of fundamental rights.

The German Federal Constitutional Court held in the case of *Internationale Handelsgesellschaft* ([1974] 2 CMLR 549) that so long as an adequate standard of fundamental rights protection was not offered under EC law itself, it would not regard itself as precluded from scrutinising measures of EC law for conformity with German fundamental rights, and where necessary, invalidating or disapplying such measures within Germany. Recognising the progress made by the Court of Justice, however, the Federal Constitutional Court decisively shifted its position in the case of *Wunsche Handelsgesellschaft* ([1987] 3 CMLR 225) indicating that an effective level of protection was now generally ensured, and scrutiny by the national court was no longer required, so long as that was maintained.

The position previously taken by the German court, and still maintained by the Italian Constitutional Court (Gaja, 1990; Schermers, 1990), is in fact inconsistent with the position taken by the Court of Justice on the supremacy of EC law (9.3). However, in practice, the Court felt constrained to defend its position by developing a line of case law beginning with Case 29/69 *Stauder* v. *City of Ulm* ([1969] ECR 419) in which it has proclaimed the existence of fundamental rights enshrined within the EU legal order which are protected as general principles of law. To reassure the national courts, it was stressed in *Internationale Handelsgesellschaft* (Case 11/70 [1970] ECR 1125), that human rights in EC law are inspired by the constitutional traditions common to the Member States. That source of inspiration was extended in Case 4/73 *Nold* v. *Commission* ([1974] ECR 503) to include 'international treaties for the protection of human rights on which the Member States have collaborated or of which they are signatories'. In Case 44/79 *Hauer* v. *Land Rheinland Pfalz* ([1979] ECR 3740) the Court made an extensive examination of the right to property as protected in a number of the national constitutions, as well as Article 1 of the First Protocol to the ECHR, before concluding that there had been no human rights violation by the Community when it adopted an agricultural Regulation which prohibited the planting of new vines for three years. In 1989 the Court referred for the first time to the International Covenant of Civil and Political Rights as a potential source of EC fundamental rights (Case 374/87 *Orkem* v. *Commission* ([1989] ECR 3283). However, whatever the sources of inspiration for its case law, the Court has always stressed that EU fundamental rights, like the other general principles of law, become specifically EU rights, subject to interpretation 'within the framework of the structure and the objectives of the Community' (Case 11/70 *Internationale Handelsgesellschaft*).

This frank admission of the influence of the objectives of the EU upon the interpretation of fundamental rights, when viewed in the light of specific purpose of the Court when it first introduced the doctrine of EU fundamental rights protection, has led some commentators to doubt the real effectiveness of EU human rights protection (Coppel and O'Neill, 1992) – a claim which represents just one of several areas of criticism which the Court of Justice has encountered in relation to its fundamental rights jurisprudence (cf. the defence offered by Weiler and Lockhart, 1995a and 1995b).

The claim that adequate respect is not ensured derives some support from the paucity of cases in which the Court has in fact held that there has been a human rights violation by the EU institutions. Successful claims are largely confined to the realm of administrative law enforcement by the Commission, especially in the field of competition policy where the cases are closely linked to those on principles of administrative legality discussed in 6.5, and to staff cases. In Case 46/87 *Hoechst* v. *Commission* ([1989] ECR 2859) the Court held that undertakings which are under investigation by the Commission for alleged infringements of the competition rules have the right to be protected against arbitrary or disproportionate interventions on the part of public authorities in their sphere of activities. This means in practice that before conducting surprise searches of the premises of undertakings under investigation the Commission is obliged to observe whatever procedural formalities apply within the Member State where the undertaking is established, such as the duty to obtain a search warrant before a judge. In similar vein the Court declared in Case 374/87 *Orkem* v. *Commission* that an undertaking under investigation should not be required to answer leading questions about its activities, although it declined to recognise a formal right of protection against self-incrimination under Article 6 ECHR. One question which does arise about the case law of the Court in this context is whether it represents a sufficiently strict application of the standards contained in the ECHR which represent the essential judicial benchmark in this field. We shall return to this point below.

Staff cases – a rather *sui generis* body of EU case law – offer some of the very few examples of protection being sought successfully for *individual* civil or political rights under EC law. In Case 100/88 *Oyowe and Traore* v. *Commission* ([1989] ECR 4285) the Court held that the duty of allegiance owed by all staff to the EU institutions they are employed by cannot be interpreted and applied in such a way as to conflict with the principle of freedom of expression. The issue of the administration of HIV tests on EU officials without their effective consent was raised in Case C-404/92 P *X* v. *Commission* ([1994] ECR I-4780), and the Court of Justice, annulling the judgment of the Court of First Instance, found a violation of the applicant's right to respect for private life protected under Article 8 ECHR.

Cases such as these reinforce the point that – for whatever reason – so far the EU catalogue of fundamental rights remains relatively unsophisticated and under developed in the sense of the range of fundamental rights which it includes. Perhaps of greatest significance is that so far the Court has not so far had occasion to declare a general principle based on the right to non-discrimination on grounds of race, ethnic origin or nationality (as opposed to *EU* nationality, guaranteed by Article 6 EC) (de Búrca, 1995). A recent development of note is the conclusion by Advocate General Tesauro that the Equal Treatment Directive (76/207) should extend to cover discrimination against transsexuals (Case C-13/93 *P*. v. *S. and Cornwall County Council*, Opinion of 14 December 1995, a conclusion subsequently supported by the Court ([1996] IRLR 347). That the EU will increasingly intervene in areas where issues of civil liberties are raised is apparent, however, from the adoption by the European Parliament and Council of the Data Protection Directive (Directive 95/46 on the protection of individuals with regard to the processing of personal data and on the free movement of such data, OJ 1995 L281/31; Carlin, 1996). This makes the need for a comprehensive catalogue of rights all the more urgent.

6.8   The Scope of EU Fundamental Rights Protection

A second area of difficulty which arises in relation to fundamental rights protection is the question of the 'reach' of EC law, and the extent to which national law is subject to scrutiny by reference to EU fundamental rights (de Búrca, 1993b). Although it was thought in the early stages of the evolution of fundamental rights doctrine in the Community that the Court would apply its analysis only as a means of testing the validity of measures adopted by the EU institutions themselves, in more recent cases it has applied a fundamental rights argument across the range of Community competence, whether measures are adopted by the institutions or by the Member States. To understand the recent case law, it is important to note that the Court has frequently made reference instrumently to fundamental rights in its case law in order to enhance, in general terms, the socio-economic foundations on which the EU is constructed (e.g. the reference to the fundamental right of access to employment in *UNECTEF* v. *Heylens*; the reference to the fundamental right of sex equality as one of the general principle of EC law in Case 149/77 *Defrenne* v. *SABENA* [1978] ECR 1365). Frequent reference to fundamental rights reinforces the legitimacy which the EU can claim as a body subject to the rule of law, as the Court asserted in Case 294/83 *Parti Ecologiste 'Les Verts'* v. *Parliament* ([1986] ECR 1339).

It is in the light of these generalised assertions that the principles developed by the Court in cases such as Case 5/88 *Wachauf* v. *Federal*

Republic of Germany ([1989] ECR 2609) should be viewed. In *Wachauf* the Court reiterated the principle of fundamental rights protection in the EU legal order, applying it specifically to a case in which a tenant farmer might, under the rules of the CAP, be deprived, without compensation, of his livelihood, on expiry of his lease. Such rules would infringe fundamental rights protection, as required by the EU legal order, and

> 'since those requirements are also binding on the Member States when they implement Community rules, the Member States must, as far as possible, apply those rules in accordance with those requirements' (p. 2639).

It seems perfectly acceptable that where the Member States are acting effectively in an 'agency' situation, on behalf of the EU albeit in some cases exercising a discretion, that Member State actions should be subject to scrutiny under EU fundamental rights. Although this may mean that a form of fundamental rights protection through judicial action and interpretation enters a Member State 'by the back door' as a consequence of membership of the EU (Grief, 1991), this seems to be an incontrovertible consequence of the transfer of sovereign rights entailed by membership.

A more contentious situation arises where the Court of Justice has applied fundamental rights scrutiny to the actions of Member States taken within the realm of the derogations from the fundamental (economic) freedoms guaranteed by the Treaty. The first case where this approach was taken was Case 36/75 *Rutili* v. *Minister for the Interior* ([1975] ECR 1219) where the Court examined the limitations which bind Member States when they seek to rely upon the Article 48(3) public policy derogation which allows them to exclude migrant workers exercising their rights of free movement under Article 48. Reviewing the various limitations upon the national discretion, the Court concluded that they were all specific manifestations of a more general principle, enshrined in a number of provisions of the ECHR, that

> 'no restrictions in interests of national security or public safety shall be placed on the rights secured by [Article 48] other than such as are necesary for the protection of those interests "in a democratic society" ' (p. 1231).

In Case C-260/89 *Elliniki Radiophonia Tileorasi* v. *Dimotiki Etairia Pliroforissis (ERT)* ([1991] ECR I-2925) the Court expressed a similar principle in much broader terms, by stating when it was examining the acceptability national public policy derogations (under Articles 56 and 66 EC) from the principle of free movement of services (Article 59 EC), it was applying fundamental rights standards to national measures falling 'within the scope of Community law'. It held that the prohibition in Greece on the broadcasting of television programmes by all undertakings apart from the State Television Company, which Greece sought to justify by reference to important public policy interests protected by Articles 56 and 66, had to be assessed in the light of general principles of law, notably fundamental rights. In particular, the principle of freedom of expression, enshrined in Article 10 ECHR, could be invoked before the national court which is called upon to assess the validity of the purported justification for the derogation from the principles of EC law.

The logical corollary of this point is that EU fundamental rights protection does not extend to areas which fall within the jurisdiction of the Member States, rather than the EU (see Cases 60-1/84 *Cinéthèque* v. *Fédération nationale des cinémas français* [1985] ECR 2605). This pattern is in marked contrast to the scope of human rights protection afforded by the Supreme Court of the USA under the US Constitution, where creative judicial interpretation of the Fourteenth Amendment which guarantees the right to due process has allowed extensive federal judicial oversight over how the states manage their residual legislative and administrative competences (see Lenaerts, 1991b).

The widest formulation of EU fundamental rights protection so far proposed comes from AG Jacobs in Case 168/91 *Konstantinidis* v. *Stadt Altensteig* [1993] ECR I-1191 (3.6). The case involved the transliteration of a Greek name by the German authorities, whereby it lost its cultural and religious significance, on being transformed from 'Christos' into 'Hrestos'. Konstantinidis fell within the scope of EC law, as a self-employed migrant worker of Greek nationality working in Germany, and the Court found that any change in his name which was liable to confuse customers constituted an infringement of his *economic* rights. AG Jacobs suggested a more radical approach to the problem. An EU national who goes to work in another Member State is

'entitled to assume that, wherever he goes to earn his living in the European Community, he will be treated in accordance with a common code of fundamental values, in particular those laid down in the European Convention on Human Rights. In other words, he is entitled to say 'civis europeus sum' and to invoke that status in order to oppose any violation of his fundamental rights' (p. 1211).

As this broad approach was not accepted – or even referred to – by the Court of Justice, it must be assumed at present the 'Citizen of Europe' status remains – at least within the scope of the Treaty – a market, rather than a civic status.

The intervention of the Court of Justice into the field of fundamental rights protection has raised some very sensitive issues involving potential conflicts between different rights, where the very *economic* orientation of the EU has left the Court open to the challenge that it does not pay adequate attention to other values and princples. The potential for conflict is amply illustrated by Case C-159/90 *Society for the Protection of Unborn Children (Ireland) Ltd (SPUC)* v. *Grogan* ([1991] ECR I-4685). The applicants, SPUC, had relied upon Article 40.3.3 of the Irish Constitution which guarantees the right to life of the unborn, in order to obtain an

injunction prohibiting the distribution of information about abortion
clinics in the UK by the defendants, who were officers in a students
union. They argued that Article 59 EC precluded the application of the
Irish Constitution in such a way as to hinder the free movement of
services; EC law required the free availability of the information required
by Irish women if they were to take advantage, as recipients of services, of
abortions lawfully available in other Member States. On a reference by the
Irish High Court concerning these points the Court of Justice held that
abortion – at least where it is provided for remuneration – is a service for
the purposes of Article 59. It should follow that any measures taken by
Ireland which hinder the free movement of such services and of the
recipients of such services should be capable of scrutiny under EC law,
including fundamental rights, in this case freedom of expression protected
by Article 10 ECHR. However, the Court avoided the need to consider
the issue by holding that the distribution of abortion information by the
students union fell outside the ambit of the Treaty. Since there was no
economic link between the provider of the service (the UK clinics) and
the advertiser of the service (the students union), the situation fell
outside the scope of Article 59. No charge was made to the UK clinics
in respect of the advertisements contained in the handbooks.

This distinction is, of course, a tenuous one, and could easily be
circumvented in a future instance by the imposition of even a small charge
for the advertisements. The Court would then have to confront the issue of
the availability of information about abortion in a Member State where
abortion itself is unlawful and, consequently, the possible conflicts between the freedom of information of the service recipients and providers
and the right to life of the unborn which underlies the prohibition on
abortion in Ireland. For having classed abortion as a service, the Court
will logically be faced with the question of whether national variations in
the conditions under which abortion is available, including a constitutional prohibition, represent restrictions on the free movement of services,
in the same way that variations in product standards are categorised as
potentially restrictive of the free movement of goods (Case 120/78 *Rewe-
Zentrale* v. *Bundesmonopolverwaltung für Branntwein (Cassis de Dijon)*
[1979] ECR 649). This could lead to the undermining of what is an
important constitutional value in one Member State, and tends in general
to indicate that those Member States which assert constitutional values
which are not shared by the others may find them under attack from the
imperatives of the internal market which requires the sweeping away of
restrictions on trade. At the very least it requires Ireland to justify the
operation of its prohibition on abortion, at least in so far as that has
effects outside the Irish jurisdiction – a requirement that many might
consider beyond the limits of a body such as the EU (Phelan, 1992). It
might furthermore bring about a concrete conflict between the EU's
economic law and the guarantee of respect for national identity contained
in Article F1 TEU – one of the non-justiciable provisions of the Treaty of
Maastricht.

In reviewing the approach taken by the Court of Justice in *Grogan*, it is necessary to take into account also the decision of the European Court of Human Rights in a parallel case on abortion information which came before it through the ECHR mechanisms, where it found that a prohibition on advertising does contravene Article 10 ECHR as a disproportionate interference in freedom of expression (*Open Door and Dublin Well Woman* v. *Ireland* (1992) Series A, no 246; (1993) 15 EHRR 244). Even though the Court of Justice sidestepped the problem of conflicts between differing constitutional values by drawing an 'economic/non-economic' distinction in *Grogan*, it is clear that a future case may require application of the ECHR in circumstances where the Member States find it politically unacceptable for provisions of their constitutions to be adjudicated upon by the judges of the Court of Justice, or even judges of other national courts.

6.9   Fundamental Rights outside the European Court

This discussion has demonstrated that there may be cause for some doubt regarding both the effectiveness and the coherence of the fundamental rights protection provided by the Court. However, that institution has at least gone much further than the political institutions towards developing a framework which ensures that existing national systems of protection are not undermined by the transfer of sovereign powers to the EU. Outside the field of the EU itself, the Member States already operate a dual system of fundamental rights protection. In addition to more or less comprehensive and effective systems of protection within the domestic order, all the Member States are signatories of the ECHR and recognise the right of individual petition to the institutions of the ECHR which may pronounce upon alleged fundamental rights violations within those states. While it seems probable that those institutions would not hesitate to hold each of the fifteen Member States responsible for fundamental rights violations within their territories which stemmed from the exercise of sovereign powers transferred to the EU, this seems an indirect means of resolving the problem.

It might be more desirable if the EU itself were subject to a single written catalogue of fundamental rights which directly guaranteed the observance of basic standards (rather than the current case-based 'code'), and/or some means were instituted to ensure that the supreme arbiter of fundamental rights questions in EU remains, as it is for questions falling within the purview of national law, the European Court of Human Rights. The second solution would overcome difficulties which arise because of allegedly differing interpretations of the ECHR given by the Court of Justice and the Court of Human Rights. Some examples of this have arisen in the field of competition law (van Overbeek, 1994). The problem for the EU in adopting the first solution is that there are substantial differences between the catalogues of fundamental rights currently subscribed to by the various Member States, and so resolving on a single catalogue in the context, for example, of an IGC concerned also with many other institutional and substantive issues, is unlikely to be a realistic endeavour.

So far in the political sphere only 'soft law' (see 6.16) measures have been agreed between the institutions, comprising in particular a Joint Declaration on Fundamental Rights, adopted by the three political institutions in 1977 (OJ 1977 C103/1), and a number of joint declarations and resolutions of the institutions specifically concerned with racism and xenophobia (e.g. Resolution of the Council and the representatives of the Member States of 29 May 1990 on the fight against racism and xenophobia OJ 1990 C157/1). The fundamental rights commitment in the Treaty of Maastricht, referred to in 3.6 and 3.11, although legally binding is not justiciable since it is to be found in the section on 'common provisions'. Furthermore, it is phrased in the same terms as the Court's own case law, by reference to the concept of general principles of EC law (see 3.6). Reference to the respect for fundamental rights is also to be found in Article J.1(2) TEU and Article K.2(1) TEU, in the context of CFSP and CJHA. These likewise fall outside the 'Community' sphere. Only Article 130U(2) EC makes reference within the EC Treaty to fundamental rights, but this provision is limited to ensuring that EU policy in the area of development cooperation contributes to the objective of respecting human rights and fundamental freedoms.

On a number of occasions, the Commission and the Parliament have both suggested that a solution to the problems of identifying a catalogue of justiciable rights for those subject to EC law, and of ensuring that the ECHR and EU systems operate in tandem, could be found if the EU (or, more precisely, the Community) could accede to the Convention itself (e.g. EP Resolution on Community Accession to the ECHR, OJ 1994 C44/32). This raises a number of problems, from both the EU and the ECHR perspectives. The latter at present only provides for the accession of 'states', and it is not clear how the EU would become involved in the judicial structure (one judge or fifteen? involvement in all cases or only those involving the EU?). To endeavour to find a resolution to the problems on the EU side, the Commission submitted a request for an Opinion by the Court of Justice under Article 228(6) EC on the question of accession (Opinion 2/94 *Accession by the Community to the ECHR* (28.3.96).

The Court's Opinion will have disappointed profoundly those in favour of accession. Dealing with the questions posed in rather a technical manner, it largely declared the Opinion inadmissible. The only concrete question it considered is whether – in the absence of a Treaty amendment under Article N TEU – the Community has the *competence* to accede by means of an instrument based on Article 235 EC. Perhaps with one eye on the *Brunner* judgment of the German Federal Constitutional Court ([1994] 1 CMLR 57; 3.3) the Court was at pains to stress that the Community operates upon the basis of *conferred* and *limited* powers, supplemented where appropriate by implied powers. Reiterating likewise the importance of fundamental rights as an integral part of EC law, the Court argued that accession to the ECHR would make a difference to *institutional* (rather than the *substantive*) basis of human rights protection and enforcement. Consequently, it would fall outwith the scope of Article 235 EC to use it for accession:

> 'That provision, being an integral part of an institutional system based on the principle of conferred powers, cannot serve as a basis for widening the scope of Community powers beyond the general framework created by the provisions of the Treaty as a whole and, in particular, by those that define the tasks and activities of the Community . . . (para. 30).
>
> Accession to the Convention would, however, entail a substantial change in the present Community system for the protection for the protection of human rights in that it would entail the entry of the Community into a distinct international institutional system as well as integration of all the provisions of the Convention into the Community legal order' (para. 34).

On the other hand, having denied the present competence of the Community to accede, the Court of Justice then unfortunately did not go on to say whether the EC legal order could accommodate – in the event of the necessary Treaty amendments – its own incorporation into a superordinate system, on the grounds that the question was essentially premature. Yet this was precisely the question which the Court of Justice did address on Opinion 1/91 on the *EEA Agreement* ([1991] ECR I-6079) where the Court found that the arrangements involved would lead to a compromising of the autonomy of EC law. If states are able to submit to the jurisdiction of the ECHR and its Court, however, there seems no reason, institutionally, why the EU cannot do likewise. The question remains open, however. What the Court's Opinion did at least provide was a comprehensive review of the various positions taken by the Member States on this question, the opinions of all of them having been canvassed by the Court in the course of the proceedings. Because of the manner in which the questions were raised and dealt with by the Court it is not entirely clear as to the views taken by the Member States, but it would appear that a majority, but not all, are in favour of accession. As the judgment was handed down on the eve of the beginning of the IGC in late March 1996, the initiative to take matters forward on the basis of the Opinion immediately devolved to the governments.

6.10 Political Rights

In earlier paragraphs we have discussed the gradually emerging political status of EU citizens (3.5), but pointing out that so far neither EU court has so far declared a political principle such as 'transparency' to be a general principle of EC law (see Case T-194/94 *Carvel and Guardian Newspapers* v. *Council* [1995] 3 CMLR 359). However, such a notion was mooted by AG Tesauro in his opinion in Case 58/94 *Netherlands* v. *Council* (30.4.96), but it would be premature to suggest that the Court of Justice may take the 'general principles' route in its interpretation of the political status of EU citizens. In *Netherlands* v. *Council* it carefully eschewed this approach. A cautious approach seems also mandated by the Court of First Instance's approach to the principle of subsidiarity in Case T-29/92 *SPO* v. *Commission* ([1995] ECR II-289). Denying the retroactive application of Article 3B EC to a situation which arose before the Treaty of Maastricht came into force, the Court firmly declared that before that time the principle of subsidiarity did not 'constitute a general principle of law by reference to which the legality of Community acts should be reviewed' (p. 394). This leaves open the status of subsidiarity since the entry into force of Article 3B.

6.11   Acts of the Institutions – EU Legislative and Administrative Measures

The acts of the institutions within the framework of the EC Treaty are classified and described in brief terms in Article 189 EC which provides:

> 'In order to carry out their task and in accordance with the provisions of this Treaty, the European Parliament acting jointly with the Council, the Council and the Commission shall make regulations and issue directives, take decisions, make recommendations or deliver opinions.
>
> A regulation shall have general application. It shall be binding in its entirety and directly applicable in all Member States.
>
> A directive shall be binding, as to the result to be achieved, upon each Member State to which it is addressed, but shall leave to the national authorities the choice of form and methods.
>
> A decision shall be binding in its entirety upon those to whom it is addressed.
>
> Recommendations and opinions shall have no binding force.'

The legislative processes whereby EU measures may be adopted and the basic requirements for the lawful adoption, entry into force and publication of such measures including the duty to give reasons, and the requirement of a legal basis were considered in Chapter 5. It remains here to describe in brief terms the basic nature of each form of EU act, leaving for Chapters 9 and 10 the detailed consideration of the effects of such acts within the domestic legal systems of the Member States. As a preliminary point it should be noted that although there is a crude hierarchy of EU acts, with regulations ranking as the strongest form and non-binding recommendations and opinions as the weakest, there is no very clear logic as to where the Treaty will mandate, in a particular provision, the adoption of one or more specific forms of legislation, or where it leaves it open to the adopting institution to adopt any necessary 'measures'. Furthermore, the Court has consistently held that it is the content of a measure which is decisive as to its nature, not the form which it is given by the adopting institution. In Cases 41-44/70 *International Fruit Company* v. *Commission* ([1971] ECR 411) the Court held that a measure labelled a regulation was in truth a bundle of individual decisions. This finding was crucial as it affected the ability of the applicant company to bring a challenge to the measure in question under the EU's system of judicial control (see Chapter 12). It is therefore necessary to scrutinise in all cases both the concrete enabling provision (legal basis) to ensure that the relevant institution has acted within its power and the substance of the act adopted to ensure that it is what it purports to be.

The system used in Article 189 EC, although replicated in Article 161 Euratom, did not adopt that already used in the ECSC Treaty. Under the ECSC Treaty only three types of measure are envisaged; these are decisions, recommendations and opinions. An ECSC decision is broadly equivalent to either an EC regulation or an EC decision, depending upon whether it is general or individual in nature. An ECSC recommendation can be equated to an EC directive, and ECSC opinions, like their EC counterparts, have no binding force. The analysis throughout this book follows the EC schema. Finally, it should be noted that no detailed analysis is offered of the forms of action which can be taken under CFSP and CJHA (joint actions, common positions). Self-evidently, these fall outside the framework of *EC law*, and are not justiciable in the Court of Justice. That is not to say that they are legally entirely irrelevant since they are binding at least in international law; in so far as they operate as 'sources' of EC law they should be classified as more akin to forms of 'soft law' (6.16).

6.12 Regulations

Regulations are like EU 'Acts of Parliament'. Regulations have 'general application', are binding in all respects and 'directly applicable'. Thus they are general, non-individualised legislative measures which take effect directly in the national legal order, without need for national implementing measures. Indeed national re-enactment is not permitted, unless it is required by the terms of the regulation (Case 34/73 *Variola* v. *Italian Finance Administration* [1973] ECR 981). The Court held (at p. 990):

'the direct application of a Regulation means that its entry into force, and its application in favour of or against those subject to it are independent of any measure of reception into national law. . . . Member States are under a duty not to obstruct the direct applicability inherent in Regulations. Strict compliance with this obligation is an indispensable condition of the simultaneous and uniform application of Community Regulations throughout the Community.'

Examples can be given of regulations which are explicitly stated to be dependent upon national implementation. The Tachograph Regulation (Council Regulation 1463/70 OJ 1970 (Sp. Ed.) p. 482) provides:

> 'Member States shall, in good time and after consulting the Commission, adopt such laws, regulations and administrative provisions as may be necessary for the implementation of this Regulation.'

In crude terms, the existence of a regulation in a particular field adopted by the EU normally acts as a 'keep out' sign to the national legislature (Usher, 1981: 17). The pre-emptive effect of EU legislation will be examined further in the context of the discussion of supremacy in 9.13.

6.13   Directives

The specific character of directives lies in the type of obligation which they impose upon addressees. Directives amount only to obligations of result, not obligations of conduct. However, the implementation of directives is a positive obligation for the Member States, and the effective implementation of directives is one of the keys to the realisation of the EU's objectives in the internal market sphere. In recent years, enforcement proceedings under Article 169 EC are begun automatically by the Commission in the event of failure by a Member State to implement a directive by the time limit which it is set in each measure (usually between one and three years) (*8th Annual Report* by the Commission to the European Parliament on the Monitoring of the Application of Community Law, OJ 1991 C338/1).

The Member States have a discretion as to how they implement directives. This normally involves either adopting or changing legislation, but exceptionally nothing need be done if existing legislation is sufficient. They may also be given alternatives within the directive itself. In practice, the mis-implementation of directives is as serious a problem as the failure to implement, and the Court of Justice is frequently faced with preliminary references regarding the interpretation of particular directives where national courts are required to decide upon the adequacy of national implementing measures. Specific examples of this and related problems will be discussed in 9.10 and 9.11, where the important question is often whether the provisions of directives can themselves be invoked in national courts as giving rise to rights for individuals and, if this is not possible, the scope of the duty upon the national court to achieve a harmonious resolution of apparently conflicting provisions in the directive and the national implementing measures (9.4). An additional element in enforceability of directives emerged in the case of Cases C-6, 9/90 *Francovich I* where the Court held that a Member State could be liable for the damage which results from its failure to implement a directive (9.17, 10.6).

6.14 Decisions

These are measures of an individual nature which may be addressed either to individuals or undertakings, or to Member States. Article 115 EC, for example, gives a power to the Commission to adopt decisions addressed to the Member States authorising them to restrict imports of third country products from other Member States, in derogation from the normal principle that third country products, once they have entered the EU, may circulate freely. Decisions adopted by the Commission under Regulation 17 in application of Articles 85 and 86 EC (the competition rules) offer an example of decisions addressed to individuals or undertakings. Decisions are not normally normative, in the sense of creating generally applicable EC law; this is certainly the case with competition decisions which do not create general rules of conduct for undertakings, but merely bind those to whom they are addressed. On the other hand, decisions adopted by the Commission in pursuance of a policy objective laid down by the Treaty such as that of coordinating cooperation between the Member States in a field of social policy (Article 118 EC) are more akin to a general normative act (see Cases 281, etc./85 *Germany et al.* v. *Commission* [1987] ECR 3203).

One of the difficulties which arise with the identification and interpretation of 'decisions' is that the effect of Article 173(4) EC is to lend a special status to decisions as individual measures which are capable of challenge by so-called non-privileged applicants before the Court of Justice. By non-privileged applicants is meant the natural and legal persons whose activities are affected by the regulatory activities of the EU institutions, who have only limited standing to challenge EU measures in the Court of Justice (12.4 *et seq.*). In this sense, the concept of 'decision' has been refined in two ways. The first is in contradistinction to regulations – i.e. general measures not amenable to individual challenge. The second is in contradistinction to measures which have no legal effects at all. This is in the sense of a 'reviewable act' (see 6.15 and 12.2; see Greaves, 1996). For example, the Court has gone so far as to characterise as a 'decision' the conclusion of the Commission that it had no jurisdiction in relation to a particular merger between two airlines, made public entirely informally by the spokesman for the Commissioner responsible for competition policy (Case T-3/93 *Société Anonyme à Participation Ouvrière Nationale Air France* v. *Commission (Air France)* [1994] ECR II-121). In that context, the characterisation of a measure as a 'decision' is a policy measure intended to ensure the efficacy of judicial review (cf. Toth, 1995).

6.15 *Sui Generis* Acts

Not all binding legal acts of the institutions are readily capable of inclusion within the categories set out in Article 189 EC. The Court has recognised a further category of so-called *sui generis* acts. These include in particular internal management measures of the EU institutions, such as measures establishing committees, or allocating funds for European Parliament elections (see Case 294/83 *'Les Verts'*). This category also includes certain measures which might be thought, at first sight, to fall within the 'soft law' category of non-binding acts such as recommendations and opinions. An example of this is the 'resolution' adopted by the Council determining the format for Community participation in the negotiation of the European Road Transport Agreement. In Case 22/70 *Commission* v. *Council (ERTA)* ([1971] ECR 263), the Commission successfully established that such a measure could be challenged under Article 173 EC which provides that the 'Court of Justice shall review the legality of *acts . . . . other than recommendations or opinions*' (emphasis added). The important point in such a case is the binding nature of the act, which must in some way change the legal position of those affected by it. In contrast to the position in *Air France* described in 6.14, the applicant in *ERTA*, as a privileged applicant with no restrictions on standing, had no formal need for a characterisation of the measure as a 'decision'.

Challenges to resolutions of the Parliament have also been declared admissible: in Case 230/81 *Luxembourg* v. *Parliament* ([1983] ECR 255) Luxembourg brought the first of a number of cases in which it has challenged resolutions concerned with the geographical relocation of the Parliament. The full range of reviewable acts is considered in 9.2.

Falling outside the 'Community' system, and not susceptible to judicial review as part of EC law are measures adopted under the second and third pillars of European Union. Nonetheless, measures such as CFSP and CJHA 'common positions' and 'joint actions' must be regarded as binding, at least in the sphere of international law.

6.16   'Soft Law'

'Soft law' has been defined as 'rules of conduct which, in principle, have no legally binding force but which nevertheless may have practical effects' (Snyder, 1993b: 32) In the EU soft law takes a multitude of forms: recommendations and opinions (which are explicitly recognised by Article 189 EC), as well as 'communications', 'conclusions', 'declarations', 'action programmes' and 'communiqués'. In recent years, particularly since the advent of the subsidiarity principle, the EU has resorted to regulation through soft law, in preference to binding measures such as directives or regulations. Moreover, the role of these types of measures should be seen as part of a general shift in administrative or regulatory culture, in which the EU is by no means isolated from other regulatory authorities, such as states (Snyder, 1994).

The contents of such measures may be used as persuasive guides to interpretation of other measures adopted by the EU or the Member States, and may influence the conduct of those parties (Wellens and Borchardt, 1989). We shall see in 9.15 that the Court has held that EU soft law measures may need to be used by national courts for the purposes of interpreting national legislation (see Case C-322/88 *Grimaldi* v. *Fonds des Maladies Professionnelles* [1989] ECR 4407). On the other hand, the Court has always consistently held that soft law measures cannot prevail where they contradict other 'hard' measures. The Court has reached that conclusion twice in recent years in relation to one particular form of soft law which is distinct from the types of published measures cited above, namely 'entries' in the margins of Council minutes. This technique is often used as a way of defusing political tensions surrounding the adoption of particularly contentious measures by the Council (see 5.9) (Case C-292/89 *R* v. *Immigration Appeal Tribunal, ex parte Antonissen* [1991] ECR I-745; Case C-25/94 *Commission* v. *Council (FAO)* (19.3.96)). The case of interinstitutional agreements such as the one at issue in the *FAO* case (5.16) may indicate a type of measure which is capable of having internal binding effects but may have no impact on the national legal orders in the manner that regulations, directives and decisions, as well as Treaty provisions, will often do. In that case, the Council had inserted an entry in its minutes stating that notwithstanding the decision to allow the Member States to exercise their voting rights in the FAO Council in that particular case, it had not by that means resolved questions relating to future voting rights or issues of competence under the Agreement thereby to be concluded in the FAO. The Court held on the contrary that the decision on the exercise of the voting rights in relation to the conclusion of the Agreement did have a future 'message' to third parties about the scope of Community competence. The Council could not deny that by reference to its statement in the minutes which could not be read into the text of the decision.

Another notable feature of EU soft law has been its progressive nature. Where a policy field lies at the margins of Community competence, the evolution of a common Community policy may well shift from the soft to the hard over a period of time, with non-binding measures such as those cited above forming a useful prelude to the adoption of more rigorous measures. Such a development has taken place in the field of vocational training. Less positively, soft law can also be the refuge of the Council when it is unable to agree upon binding measures. This has occurred in particular in the social policy field, where some of the proposals put forward by the Commission under the Social Action Programme agreed in 1974 (see 2.9) were watered down from directives to recommendations.

6.17 The Case Law of the Court of Justice and the Court of First Instance

Although the task of the two EU Courts is to interpret and not to make the law, and although the Courts themselves are not bound by their own previous decisions, it is nonetheless true that in a practical sense the case law of the Courts (especially that of the Court of Justice) is an important source of law within the jurisdiction of EC law. We have seen already the unwritten general principles which the Court of Justice has distilled from national and international traditions as being 'inherent' in the EU legal order. We have referred also to the Court's occasional practice of limiting the retrospective effect of its preliminary rulings. This case law is, of course, binding upon national courts; nowhere is this clearer than in the UK where s.3(1) of the European Communities Act 1972 states:

'any question as to the meaning or effect of any of the Treaties, or as to the validity, meaning or effect of any Community instrument, shall be treated as a question of law (and, if not referred to the European Court, be for determination as such in accordance with the principles laid down by and any relevant decision of the European Court or any court attached thereto).'

Following the case law of the Court of Justice is made easier by the fact that the Court is generally consistent in its judgments, and, since 1973, has frequently referred to its earlier judgments as one, or even the sole line of argument in a subsequent judgment. The various phrases used by the Court to indicate that a case is located within an established line of case law reveal on occasion an element of impatience that a particular point is not in fact seen as established law. Thus it sometimes states '. . . as the Court has repeatedly held . . .' (Koopmans, 1991b: 504).

The element of stare decisis in EC law has now become so strong that when the Court occasionally changes its mind it makes it clear that it is doing so (e.g. Case C-70/88 *Parliament* v. *Council (Chernobyl)* [1990] ECR I-2041 in which the Court reversed its finding in Case 302/87 *Parliament* v. *Council (Comitology)* [1988] ECR 5615 that the Parliament did not have standing under Article 173 to challenge the acts of other institutions) (see Arnull, 1993).

Summary

1   The following are the main sources of EC law:
    - the constitutive treaties and other international instruments binding the EU;
    - general principles of law;
    - the acts of the institutions, including where relevant, non-binding measures (soft law);
    - the case law of the Court of Justice.
2   The important body of general principles of law can in turn be sub-divided into four groups:
    - principles of administrative legality, and due process;
    - the economic pillars of the internal market;
    - fundamental rights;
    - political rights.

3 General principles bind the EU and, in so far as their activities fall within the scope of Community competence, the Member States.
4 At present fundamental rights protection in the EU remains at an uncertain stage of development with a lack of clarity as to the scope of protection, the range of rights protected, and the interaction between important constitutional values subscribed to by the Member States and the economic pillars of the internal market.
5 Although accession of the Community to the ECHR has been suggested as a means of securing the status and protection of fundamental rights within the EU, this option is unlikely to be taken in the near future following the Court's ruling that accession will not be possible without a formal treaty amendment.
6 The main features of the acts of the institutions are described in Article 189 EC; however, the legal nature and effects of these acts have been the subject of creative interpretation by the Court of Justice.
7 The case law of the Court of Justice has been an important source of law within the EU since its inception, and is now more firmly based within an evolving system of stare decisis.

Questions

1 Why and how has the protection of fundamental rights within the EU evolved?
2 To what extent should the actions of the Member States be controlled under the framework of EU fundamental rights protection?
3 What are the challenges which the EU currently faces in achieving a satisfactory resolution of the conflicts caused by the differences in fundamental rights protection within the Member States?
4 What are the important features which distinguish regulations, directives and decisions?
5 Using the material discussed in this and earlier Chapters identify some examples of creative 'law-making' by the Court of Justice? Would you agree with the argument that the Court oversteps the limits of acceptable judicial interventionism?

Further Reading

Arnull (1993), 'Owning up to fallibility: precedent and the Court of Justice', 30 *CMLRev* 247.
de Búrca (1993a), 'The Principle of Proportionality and its Application in EC Law', 13 *YEL* 105.
de Búrca (1993b), 'Fundamental Human Rights and the Reach of EC Law', 13 *Oxford Journal of Legal Studies* 283.
de Búrca (1995), 'The Language of Rights and European Integration', in Shaw and More (1995).
Clapham (1990), 'A Human Rights Policy for the European Community', 10 *YEL*, 309.
Coppel and O'Neill (1992), 'The European Court of Justice: taking rights seriously?', 12 *LS* 227.

Grief (1991), 'The Domestic Impact of the ECHR as Mediated through Community Law', *PL* 555.

Lenaerts (1991b), 'Fundamental Rights to be included in a Community Catalogue', 16 *ELRev.* 367.

Phelan (1992), 'Right to Life of the Unborn v. Promotion of Trade in Services: The European Court of Justice and the Normative Shaping of the European Union', 55 *MLR* 670.

Schwarze (1991), 'Tendencies towards a Common Administrative Law in Europe', 16 *ELRev.* 3.

Schwarze (1995), 'Towards a Common European Public Law', 1 *Eur. Pub. L.* 227.

Snyder (1994), 'Soft Law and Institutional Practice in the European Community', in Martin (1994).

Twomey (1994), 'The European Union: three Pillars without a Human Rights Foundation', in O'Keeffe and Twomey (1994).

Usher (1976), 'The Influence of National Concepts on decisions of the European Court', 1 *ELRev.* 359.

Weiler and Lockhart (1995a), '"Taking Rights Seriously" Seriously: the European Court and its Fundamental Rights Jurisprudence – Part I', 32 *CMLRev.* 51.

Weiler and Lockhart (1995b), '"Taking Rights Seriously" Seriously: the European Court and its Fundamental Rights Jurisprudence – Part II', 32 *CMLRev.* 579.

Weiler (1995b), 'European Citizenship and Human Rights', in TMC Asser Instituut (1995).

7 The Implementation and Enforcement of EC Law

7.1 Introduction

Two of the most important factors which distinguish the EU legal order from that of other international legal orders are the complexity of the regulatory structure and associated implementation mechanisms and the relative effectiveness of the enforcement mechanisms available. It is crucial that the binding legislative measures envisaged by the Treaty should not only be passed, but also implemented and enforced. However, the EU largely lacks the means and personnel whereby it can itself implement EC law. It cannot, for example, police and enforce the external borders and collect customs duties and agricultural levies, or carry out the detailed implementation of the Common Agricultural Policy (CAP). Only exceptionally is direct implementation by the EU envisaged, although where it is, it is the Commission which is the institution charged with this task (see 4.4). The EU is therefore in large measure dependent upon the effective implementation of EC law by the national administrations, in accordance with detailed procedures laid down in individual EU measures and the general duty of 'Community' loyalty or fidelity incumbent upon the Member States by virtue of Article 5 EC. This is termed 'indirect implementation' or 'indirect administration' (Daintith, 1995a), and to a great extent the successful implementation of EC law will be intimately linked to the structures, regulatory cultures and values of national law. In recent years, the Commission has shifted its focus towards encouraging vertical (EU/Member State) and horizontal cooperation (between Member States), often concentrating on the exchange of information and the creation of 'partnership' structures (e.g. in relation to EU Structural Funds disbursing regional and other aids). A Commission Communication on the development of administrative cooperation in the implementation and enforcement of EU legislation in the internal market (COM(94) 29) led to the adoption of a Council Resolution on coordinating information exchange between the national administrations (OJ 1994 C181/1) and on developing administrative cooperation between the national administrations (OJ 1994 C179/1). Inevitably, the involvement of the EU will at times be intrusive, and will entail changes in the way national regulatory structures are organised (Daintith, 1995a; Weatherill, 1995b).

Beyond the facilitation of cooperation, with the internal consequences which this will entail, the Commission's role will principally be that of supervising the Member States in order to ensure the effective enforcement of EC law (see 4.6). To this end, the Treaty provides a mechanism in Article 169 EC which permits the Commission to bring alleged Treaty violations by the Member States before the Court of Justice for a declaratory judgment. A similar procedure is also available to Member States in Article 170 EC, which can themselves pursue the interests of the EU by taking defaulting states before the Court of Justice. This can be termed the 'direct' enforcement of EC law, in contradistinction to its 'indirect' enforcement through the medium of actions in the national courts, at the instance of aggrieved individuals (see Chapter 9).

This chapter examines the effective implementation and enforcement of EC law by reference, in particular, to Articles 5 and 169–171 EC. It also reviews other means of enforcement provided by the Treaty – as Articles 169–171, although the most important, are by no means the only enforcement mechanisms available to the Commission – and assesses the problem of enforcement as a challenge to the EU institutions in ensuring the 'effectiveness' of EC law.

7.2   The Role of Article 5 EC in the Implementation and Enforcement of EC Law

Article 5 EC provides:

> 'Member States shall take all appropriate measures, whether general or particular, to ensure fulfilment of the obligations arising out of this Treaty or resulting from action taken by the institutions of the Community. They shall facilitate the achievement of the Community's tasks.
> They shall abstain from any measure which could jeopardize the attainment of the objectives of this Treaty.'

The role of Article 5 in the system of the Treaty has grown over the years. It is a general statement of the duties of Member States in relation to the achievement of the tasks of the EU which are in any case implicit in the binding force of the Treaties, and in the obligation under international law upon the Contracting Parties not to hinder the operation of the Treaties. Until recently it was thought that Article 5 took effect only when read in conjunction with the objectives of the Treaty, and other provisions of EC law which set out the EU's policies (Temple Lang, 1990). However, in recent years, the Court of Justice has shown a markedly increased tendency to refer to Article 5 as a separate source of Member State obligations within the Treaty system (e.g. Case C-374/89 *Commission* v. *Belgium* [1991] ECR I-367). It is therefore appropriate to analyse it as a distinct feature of the EU's constitutional structure, emphasising here its particular importance in the context of implementation (see Chapter 9 for the role of Article 5 in the context of the relationship between EC law and national law;).

In Cases 205–215/82 *Deutsche Milchkontor GmbH* v. *Germany* ([1983] ECR 2633 at p. 2665) the Court stated:

> 'According to the general principles on which the institutional system of the Community is based and which govern the relations between the Community and the Member States, it is for the Member States, by virtue of Article 5 of the Treaty, to ensure that Community regulations, in particular those concerning the common agricultural policy, are implemented within their territory.'

Thus Article 5 imposes the obligation on the Member States to adapt their national provisions and practices to the requirements of EC law. The Court has held that the obligations under EC law fall upon all organs of the state, including the legislature, executive and judiciary, and apply at all levels of authority. It amplified this point in Case C-8/88 *Germany* v. *Commission* ([1990] ECR I-2321) when stressing that, while all state authorities must ensure observance of the rules of EC law within their sphere of competence, the Commission was not empowered to rule upon the division of competences made by national rules (e.g. between federal and regional levels), but could merely verify whether internal supervisory and inspection procedures were effective to ensure that EC law is applied. The duty of national courts is to ensure the effective application of EC law for individuals (Case 14/83 *Von Colson and Kamann* v. *Land Nordrhein Westfalen* [1984] ECR 1891). This point will be addressed in Chapter 9.

Individual/administrative authority relationships at national level can also be structured by the operation of Article 5. This occurs most frequently in relation to the instrumentalisation of the fundamental freedoms. In Case 222/86 *UNECTEF* v. *Heylens* ([1987] ECR 4097), the Court held that an individual who was exercising his right of free movement as a worker had a right to a judicial remedy to challenge an administrative determination denying him recognition of a foreign diploma. Building on this, the Court held in Case C-340/89 *Vlassopoulou* v. *Bundesministerium für Justiz, Baden-Württemberg* ([1991] ECR I-2357) that Article 5 required the German authorities to set up some form of system whereby they could assess the individual elements of the applicant's Greek legal training, such that she could be given recognition for those elements which were relevant to the practice of law in Germany.

Finally, Article 5 contains a duty of cooperation; the Member States have the duty to facilitate the achievement of the Commission's tasks under Article 155, and this includes, where necessary, providing information which is requested. The Commission has a general right to obtain information from the Member States about their implementation of EC law, quite apart from any specific reporting requirement contained in EU legislation (Case C-33/90 *Commission* v. *Italy* [1991] ECR I-5987). Where

Member States persist in refusing provide information, even to the Court of Justice itself, this constitutes a 'serious impediment to the administration of justice' (Case 272/86 *Commission* v. *Greece* [1988] ECR 4875 at p. 4903).

The duty of loyalty is mutual, and applies also to the EU institutions. In Case C-2/88 Imm *Zwartveld* ([1990] ECR I-3365) the Court used Article 5 as the basis for a duty on the Commission to respond to a request for mutual assistance made by a Dutch examining magistrate in which he asked for information regarding fisheries inspections carried by Commission inspectors, which he required to pursue an investigation into alleged violations of EU fish marketing Decisions. It has since applied these principles in the context of Article 85 EC; it held in Case C-234/89 *Delimitis* v. *Henninger Bräu AG* ([1991] ECR I-935) that the Commission must, where requested, assist the national courts in their task of applying EC competition law. It must not only supply information about the state of any relevant proceedings before the Commission itself, but also make available any information of a legal and economic nature which might assist the national court in resolving the case before it.

7.3   Enforcement Proceedings under Articles 169–171 EC

It is in pursuit of the Commission's obligation under Article 155 EC to 'ensure that the provisions of this Treaty and the measures taken by the institutions pursuant thereto are applied' that the primary obligation of direct enforcement of Member State obligations falls upon that institution. The principal instrument of enforcement is Article 169 which provides:

> 'If the Commission considers that a Member State has failed to fulfil an obligation under this Treaty, it shall deliver a reasoned opinion on the matter after giving the State concerned the opportunity to submit its observations.
>
> If the State concerned does not comply with the opinion within the period laid down by the Commission, the latter may bring the matter before the Court of Justice.'

Article 170 EC gives a similarly framed power to the Member States which they may use against each other. It has been rarely used. The successful challenge by France to the UK's unilateral fishery conservation measures (Case 141/78 *France* v. *United Kingdom* [1979] ECR 2923) is one of the few examples of the invocation of this procedure. The use of the Article 170 procedure will always increase the tension and conflict between two states which are in dispute. The Member States prefer to leave the enforcement role primarily to the Commission, although in appropriate cases they are prepared to intervene in support of the Commission before the Court.

Remedies under the enforcement procedures of Articles 169 and 170 are set out in Article 171 EC. Prior to the Treaty of Maastricht, the Court of

Justice was limited to a 'finding' of breach of the Treaty and the obligation which fell upon the Member State in breach was merely to take the necessary measures to comply with the judgment of the Court. However, although failure to comply with Court judgments has never been as serious a problem as non-compliance in general, a new paragraph was inserted in Article 171 by the Treaty of Maastricht which provides as follows (7.15):

> 'If the Commission considers that the Member State concerned has not taken such measures [i.e. to comply with a judgment of the Court] it shall, after giving that State the opportunity to submit its observations, issue a reasoned opinion specifying the points on which the Member State concerned has not complied with the judgment of the Court of Justice.
>
> If the Member State concerned fails to take the necessary measures to comply with the Court's judgment within the time-limit laid down by the Commission, the latter may bring the case before the Court of Justice. In so doing it shall specify the amount of the lump sum or penalty payment to be paid by the Member State concerned which it considers appropriate in the circumstances.
>
> If the Court of Justice finds that the Member State concerned has not complied with its judgment it may impose a lump sum or penalty payment on it.'

A number of preliminary points can be made about the enforcement procedures of Articles 169–171. First, Articles 169 and 170 both divide the enforcement process into an administrative and a judicial phase. Opportunities for settlement exist throughout the administrative phase, but once the Commission has brought the matter before the Court at the conclusion of the period for compliance laid down in the reasoned opinion, it may continue with the proceedings, notwithstanding compliance by the Member State during the course of the proceedings (Case 240/86 *Commission* v. *Greece* [1988] ECR 1835), for the purposes of obtaining a clarification of the law by the Court. The Court indicated that such a declaratory judgment would still be useful, since it would clarify the possible liability of the Member State at national level for breach of the Treaty, and make it unnecessary for a national court to make a subsequent reference under Article 177 EC. This point may be increasingly important in view of the decision of the Court in Cases C-6, 9/90 *Francovich* v. *Italian State (Francovich I)* ([1991] ECR I-5357) regarding the award of damages against Member States for loss stemming from the failure to implement a directive.

Secondly, the Commission cannot take binding measures under Article 169 to order the compliance of the Member State, or to state the nature of the infringement. In this context, Article 169 should be contrasted with the enforcement of the competition rules against individuals under Articles 85 and 86 EC and Regulation 17. In that context, the Commission may issue binding decisions which are enforceable against individuals unless successfully challenged in the Court. The Commission also has similar powers under Article 90(3) EC which enables it to address decisions or directives to the Member States in order to enforce the provisions of Article 90 on the application of the competition rules to public undertakings (4.3; 7.12). General enforcement proceedings under Article 88 ECSC also consist of a decision taken by the High Authority, which may be challenged before the Court.

The basic elements of a successful action by the Commission are the following:

(a)   The Commission takes the view that a Member State is in breach of its obligations; the relevant obligations include those flowing from the constitutive treaties and any other international instruments which impose obligations upon the Member States, and from secondary acts of a binding nature. Failure to apply a general principle of law in the interpretation of provisions of EC law would probably also engage Member State responsibility under Article 5 and give rise to an Article 169 action, although the Court has not stated this explicitly (Temple Lang, 1990: 655).

(b)   The Commission informs the state of its view and gives it an opportunity to answer the allegation or to end the offending practice or to repeal the offending law.

(c)   The Commision delivers a reasoned opinion demonstrating the existence of the infringement.

(d)   The state fails to comply with its Treaty obligation within the time limit laid down by the Commission. [*End of the administrative phase.*]

(e)   [*Beginning of the judicial phase.*] The Commission brings the matter before the Court.

(f)   The Court finds a violation.

(g)   In the event of failure to comply, the procedure in Article 171 may be engaged.

7.4   The Range of National Conduct Capable of Engaging State Responsibility

The defendant in an enforcement action is the state, not the government, although it is conventionally the government which conducts the defence on behalf of the state. It is 'state conduct' which engages state responsibility, and the Court has defined this category broadly. It includes the following:

–   acts or omissions on the part of the legislature, including the maintenance in force of an infringing statute, even if it is not applied (Case 167/73 *Commission v. France (French Merchant Seamen)* [1974] ECR 359);

- acts or omissions on the part of the executive, including the maintenance in force of an infringing administrative measure, even if it is not applied;
- even a single incident can form the basis for an enforcement action: in Case C-431/92 *Commission* v. *Germany (Environmental Impact Assessment)* ([1995] ECR I-2189) the Court held that proceedings under Article 169 do not need to be brought in respect of failure to implement a particular directive in general; they may instead concentrate on a failure in a specific case to apply a directive which has not yet been implemented;
- actions of constitutionally independent public authorities, such as local or regional authorities (Case 1/86 *Commission* v. *Belgium (Water Pollution)* [1987] ECR 2797) or the constituent states within a federation (Case 9/74 *Casagrande* v. *Landeshauptstadt München* [1974] ECR 773);
- decisions of national courts, which are subject to the duty of Community loyalty under Article 5. It was suggested by AG Warner in Case 30/77 *R.* v. *Bouchereau* ([1977] ECR 1999) that mere judicial error should not engage state responsibility, but only the deliberate flouting of EC law by a national court. In fact, the Commission has been extremely hesitant to take proceedings in respect of judicial conduct citing 'the universal principle of the independence of the judiciary' as the reason (*6th Annual Report* by the Commission to the European Parliament on the Monitoring of the Application of Community Law, COM(89) 411, p.95). Such proceedings have been started by the Commission, but have never actually been brought before the Court.

More contentiously, the Court has extended state responsibility to cover the acts of a private party under the control of the state. In Case 249/81 *Commission* v. *Ireland (Buy Irish)* ([1982] ECR 4005), Ireland was held responsible for the actions of the Irish Goods Council, a private limited company funded by the government, with a management appointed by and policies determined by the government, which was charged with the running of a 'buy Irish' campaign which contravened EU rules on the free movement of goods.

7.5   The Administrative Phase

The administrative phase is more than just a necessary precondition for the engagement of an action before the Court of Justice. From the perspective of the Commission, it is probably the most important phase, as it engages in the vital process of negotiation with Member States, seeking to achieve compliance without recourse to law, and establishing practices with which it hopes in the future Member States will comply. Snyder describes its role as in part 'playing for rules' (Snyder, 1993b: 30), in a context where 'the main form of dispute settlement used by the Commission is negotiation, and litigation is simply a part, sometimes inevitable but nevertheless generally a minor part, of this process.' (Snyder, 1993b: 30)

In similar terms, Mendrinou argues against viewing enforcement in isolation from the Commission's other roles:

'through its monitoring function, the Commission may reinforce policy priorities while taking into account general balances, sensitivities and issues in the policy environment. In this way, the Commission itself and the handling of its monitoring role become critical factors in determining the impact of non-compliance on integration . . . . Not only is the Commision's role central in understanding the impact of non-compliance on integration, but the analysis of the Court's role would have to take into account the Commission's strategies.'

The administrative phase is itself subdivided into an informal and a formal phase. In the informal phase, the Commission investigates the possibility of a breach, and attempts to settle matters informally. In the formal phase, the Commission requests the Member State to submit its observations, stating the alleged infringement and laying down a time limit for the submission of observations (the formal letter of notice); if it is not satisfied by the replies it receives it may deliver a reasoned opinion. Article 169 EC incorporates the principle of *audi alteram partem* (the right to a fair hearing). Consequently, it is incumbent upon the Commission to ensure that the Member State is told in clear terms exactly what constitutes the alleged violation in order that it may submit its observations (Case 211/81 *Commission* v. *Denmark* [1982] ECR 4547).

The alleged violations must be defined by the reasoned opinion; the Commission cannot subsequently raise matters before the Court which were not contained in the reasoned opinion (Case 31/69 *Commission* v. *Italy (Export Rebates)* [1970] ECR 25). It gives a time limit for the Member State to comply with EC law, which must be reasonable. This may vary according to the circumstances of the case. In Case 85/85 *Commission* v. *Belgium* ([1986] ECR 1149), the Commission required Belgium to remove a property tax imposed on EU officials resident in Belgium within two weeks of the reasoned opinion. The Court held that the time limit was reasonable because the Belgian Government knew of (and had not contested) the Commission's position long before the Article 169 procedure was initiated. However, in Case 293/85 *Commission* v. *Belgium* ([1988] ECR 305) two weeks was considered an unreasonably short time limit for Belgium to remove discriminatory fees imposed on foreign nationals studying within the Belgian higher education system. In Case 74/82 *Commission* v. *Ireland (Imports of poultry)* ([1984] ECR 317) the Court even accepted a five-day time limit.

The reasoned opinion cannot be challenged by an aggrieved private party (or a Member State) by way of Article 173 EC annulment proceedings, as it is not an act which produces legal effects; it is merely a step in the proceedings (Case 48/65 *Lütticke* v. *Commission* [1966] ECR 19) (see 9.2). However, a Member State which is subject to proceedings will have an opportunity in the context of the judicial phase to raise irregularities in the reasoned opinion, such as the failure to state reasons, as it can any other procedural irregularities which have occurred during the course of the administrative phase. No party can force the Commission to take enforcement proceedings; failure to act is not actionable under Article 175 EC (Case 247/87 *Star Fruit* v. *Commission* [1989] ECR 291). The Commission's discretion is likewise unfettered as to when it may wish to bring enforcement proceedings. In Case 7/71 *Commission* v. *France (Euratom Supply Agency)* ([1971] ECR 1003) – an action brought under the materially identical Article 141 Euratom – the Court held:

'The action for a declaration that a state has failed to fulfil an obligation . . . does not have to be brought within a predetermined period, since, by reason of its nature and purpose, this procedure involves a power on the part of the Commission to consider the most appropriate means and time-limits for the purposes of putting an end to any contraventions of the Treaty.'

Of course, Member States can have recourse to Article 170 if they are dissatisfied with the conduct of the Commission, but an aggrieved private party can only seek to bring proceedings in the national court which have the effect of enforcing EC law against the national authorities (for further discussion of the status of complainants, see 7.16).

The Commission's discretion is also not restricted by any form of 'estoppel' whereby it is deemed to have consented by previous informal or even formal approval of the Member State's conduct. It may at any point revise its view and take infringement proceedings (Case 288/83 *Commission* v. *Ireland (Potatoes)* [1985] ECR 1761). Nor will the Commission's action be 'time-barred' by delay in bringing proceedings. This is well illustrated by a rather strange enforcement action brought by the Commission against Germany in respect of failures to implement certain EU directives on waste more than six years after the entry into force of the basic German legislation on the shipment of waste, and at a time when the EU had in fact changed its policy in that field along the same lines as those followed by that legislation. The Court expressed the view that the Commission's decision to institute and pursue the action was 'surprising'. However, it went on to conclude that:

'It is settled law that the rules of Article 169 of the Treaty must be applied and the Commission is not obliged to act within a specified period. The Commission is thus entitled to decide, in its discretion, on what date it may be appropriate to bring an action and it is not for the Court to review the exercise of that discretion' (Case C-422/92 *Commission* v. *Germany (Waste Directives)* [1995] ECR I-1097 at p. 1131).

7.6   The Judicial Phase

In the judicial phase, the Court will examine both the procedural propriety of the action as so far conducted by the Commission, as an issue of the admissibility of the action, and the substance of the alleged violations. Although the Commission has an extensive discretion in relation to the decision *whether* to bring an action, it is strictly bound by the procedural formalities of Article 169. This has often been the most fruitful area for Member States when searching for a defence (for a recent example, see Case C-266/94 *Commission* v. *Spain* [1995] ECR I-1975, where the Court declared the Commission's action inadmissible because of its failure to take into account the observations made by Spain in response to the Commission's letter). In contrast, the following paragraphs set out the arguments put forward by the Member States which have consistently been judged by the Court to be ineffective defences to enforcement actions.

7.7   Questions of National Law in General

No matter pertaining to the status of the national measure in question can hinder a finding of infringement by the Court. In Case 48/71 *Commission* v. *Italy (Art Treasures II)* ([1972] ECR 527) Italy cited as a defence the difficulties of parliamentary procedure it had experienced in abolishing a tax on the export of artistic and historical treasures to other Member States, owing to the need to observe the relevant constitutional requirements. Attributing the obligation to comply to the supremacy of EC law, the Court stated that:

> 'the attainment of the objectives of the Community requires that the rules of Community law established by the Treaty itself or arising from procedures which it has instituted are fully applicable at the same time and with identical effects over the whole territory of the Community without the Member States being able to place any obstacles in the way.
>
> The grant made by Member States to the Community of rights and powers in accordance with the provisions of the Treaty involves a definitive limitation on their sovereign rights and no provisions whatsoever of national law may be invoked to override this limitation.'

7.8   Legislative Paralysis and Change of Government

The ineffectiveness, permanent or temporary, of the national political system cannot be used as a defence. There is no element of fault contained in a finding of infringement of the Treaty under Article 169; the finding is a simple objective statement of fact concerning the failure of the Member State to fulfil its obligations, and it is irrelevant whether the failure stems from inertia or opposition (see Case 322/82 *Commission* v. *France* [1983]

ECR 3705, per AG Rozès). In Case 77/69 *Commission* v. *Belgium (Pressed Wood)* ([1970] ECR 237) the Belgian government was unable to secure the passage through the legislature of a bill revising a law which imposed a discriminatory tax upon imported pressed wood. The constitutional separation between the legislature and the executive did not preclude the responsibility of Belgium for infringement. In Italy, frequent changes of government have often hampered the effective implementation of EU directives, but this has not been accepted as a defence by the Court (e.g. Case 136/81 *Commission* v. *Italy* [1982] ECR 3547 – failure to implement directive harmonising provisions of company law).

7.9 Defences Related to the Nature of the Relevant Provision of EC Law

The obligation upon Member States under Article 5 and more specific provisions of the Treaty is to implement EC law in full and proper form. Thus it is insufficient and no defence to adopt a circular binding only upon the administration but with an uncertain effect *vis-à-vis* third parties in order to implement a directive on atmospheric pollution (Case C-361/88 *Commission* v. *Germany* ([1991] ECR I-2567). Similarly the Member State may not rely upon the direct effect of a directive as a substitute for implementation. It was held to be no defence in proceedings against the Netherlands for failure to implement a Council Directive on the quality of drinking water that regional and local authorities were in any case directly bound by the Directive, provisions of which were justiciable before national courts, and that the authorities had in fact implemented the Directive in the practical management of water quality (Case 96/81 *Commission* v. *Netherlands* [1982] ECR 1791).

It is not clear whether the alleged unlawfulness of the EU measure with which non-compliance is alleged is an effective defence. Case 156/77 *Commission* v. *Belgium* ([1978] ECR 1881) and Case 3/59 *Germany* v. *High Authority* ([1960] ECR 53) are usually cited as demonstrating that if a Member State has failed to challenge a EU measure directly under the relevant provisions of the EC or ECSC Treaties, it cannot raise the unlawfulness of the measure in enforcement proceedings brought against it. The two sets of provisions are separate, with different objectives. However, there may be an exception for measures which contain such serious and manifest defects that they can be regarded as 'non-existent' (Case 226/87 *Commission* v. *Greece* [1988] ECR 3611) (see 12.2).

7.10 The Principle of Reciprocity

The EU legal order differs sharply from the general public international legal order in that there is no defence of reciprocity. A Member State cannot escape a finding of infringement by claiming that another Member State is also failing to comply (Case 232/78 *Commission* v. *France (Lamb Wars)* [1979] ECR 2729). The same principle applies to the claim that the EU institutions are in breach of their obligations. In Cases 90 and 91/63 *Commission* v. *Luxembourg and Belgium (Dairy Products)* ([1964] ECR 625) the Court declared:

> 'except where otherwise expressly provided, the basic concept of the Treaty requires that the Member States shall not take the law into their own hands. Therefore the fact that the Council failed to carry out its obligations cannot relieve the defendants from carrying out theirs.'

7.11   Expedited Proceedings

Expedited proceedings, which allow the Commission to bring an alleged infringement before the Court without observing the procedural requirements laid down in Article 169, are provided for *inter alia* in Articles 93, 100A(4) (see 7.12), 100B and 225 EC. Articles 92 and 93 charge the Commission with the task of reviewing state aids, and where necessary, with issuing decisions requiring Member States to abolish, to alter or not to bring into force aids which are incompatible with the common market. A Member State which fails to comply with such a decision may be brought directly before the Court by the Commission, without prejudice to Articles 169 and 170.

Article 225 EC allows the Commission to bring before the Court a Member State which it considers is abusing the powers it is given under Article 224 to derogate from the Treaty rules in event of a threat to internal or external security (after consulting with the other Member States). If it considers that the derogation from the rules of the Treaty applied by the Member State is having the effect of distorting competition in the common market, the Commission (or a Member State) may bring matter before the Court of Justice, which will give its ruling *in camera*. The Commission made its first use of this provision in 1994, when it brought an action against Greece for applying unilateral sanctions against the former Yugoslav Republic of Macedonia (FYROM). Greece alleges that Macedonia has territorial ambitions in relation to the creation of a 'greater Macedonia' which threaten Greek territorial integrity. The Court dismissed the Commission's application for interim measures (7.14; Case C-120/94R *Commission* v. *Greece (FYROM)* [1994] ECR I-3037).

7.12   Enforcement and the Internal Market

Although actions brought under Article 169 EC remain numerically by far the most important, it is interesting to note the development of a greater variety of means of enforcement specifically concerned with the evolution of the internal market. In particular, there has been a marked shift in this area away from the use of individualised litigation as the basis for the enforcement strategy. Evidence for this comes from the use of Article 90(3) EC which allows the Commission to issue directives or decisions aimed specifically at the deregulation or restructuring of highly regulated markets, such as the telecommunications market (4.3; Flynn, 1995: 224–27); according to Emiliou (1993: 314) this 'is a provision of a hybrid nature where the supervisory and administrative functions of the Commission merge'. Clearly it may be more efficient for the Commission to make use of its own powers of decision, rather than relying on either a negotiation or litigation strategy based around Article 169.

Then there is the Commission's role in relation to the operation of Article 100A(4) EC, which represents potentially a very significant element of variability in the operation of the internal market. Member States may continue to apply, after the adoption of harmonisation measures by QMV under Article 100A, national provisions justified by reference to a 'major need' such as health and safety or protection of the environment. The Commission must verify that the national provisions are not excessive or arbitrary, and must then confirm them. It may also bring the offending Member State before the Court of Justice through expedited proceedings (7.11). The Commission's own activities here are, however, subject to challenge in a way which its discretionary role in relation to Article 169 is not. In Case C-41/93 *France* v. *Commission (PCP)* ([1994] ECR I-1829), the Court accepted a challenge by France to a Commission Decision confirming German rules on pentachlorophenol which were more restrictive than the relevant EU harmonisation measures. The Court ruled that the reasoning given by the Commission was inadequate (5.2), in particular because it had not done sufficient to state what reasons of health and safety justified the preservation of the German rules.

Finally, internal market measures themselves may construct mechanisms for their own supervision and enforcement. This was the case with the Product Safety Directive (Directive 92/59 OJ 1992 L228/24), which was based on Article 100A. Germany mounted an unsuccessful challenge to the legal basis of this measure, focusing its attention specifically on Article 9 of the directive which establishes a process whereby the Commission can, after following a specified procedure, take temporary measures to ensure the free movement of a product against which one or more Member States have taken restrictive measures. Such measures can take the form of decisions addressed to the Member States. The Court rejected an argument that such individual measures cannot be regarded as a form of harmonisation, and therefore could not be validly adopted on the basis of Article 100A (Case C-359/92 *Germany* v. *Council (Product Safety Directive)* [1994] ECR I-3681). The case demonstrates an elision of the policy-making and enforcement functions which operates to enhance the effectiveness of the work of the Commission.

7.13   Enforcement and Economic and Monetary Union

In an amendment to the scope of the jurisdiction of the Court introduced by the Treaty of Maastricht, Article 180(d) EC give the Court jurisdiction in disputes concerning

> 'the fulfilment by national central banks of obligations under this Treaty and the Statute of the ESCB. In this connection the powers of the Council of the ECB in respect of national central banks shall be the same as those conferred upon the Commission in respect of Member States by Article 169. If the Court of Justice finds that a national central bank has failed to fulfil an obligation under this Treaty, that bank shall be required to take the necessay measures to comply with the judgment of the Court of Justice.'

While this provision is presently largely of academic interest, as the level of monetary integration becomes greater – at least as between certain Member States – and the stringent duties on national central banks under Articles 102A–109M EC start to apply, it may become a great deal more important.

7.14   Interim Measures

Article 186 EC states:

> 'The Court of Justice may in any cases before it prescribe any necessary interim measures.'

This possibility applies both to Article 169 proceedings (e.g. Case 61/77R *Commission* v. *Ireland (Fisheries)* [1977] ECR 937) and to expedited proceedings, such as those brought under Article 93 (e.g. Cases 31 and 53/77R *Commission* v. *United Kingdom (Pig Producers)* [1977] ECR 921). An application for interim relief may be made at any time once the administrative stage has been completed. Applications for interim measures are heard generally by the President sitting alone, without the assistançe of an Advocate General. Interim measures may be awarded if two conditions are satisfied; the Commission must show:

- a *prima-facie* case (i.e. the case must not be manifestly ill-founded);
- urgency, which is assessed in relation to the necessity for interim measures in order to prevent serious and irreparable damage to the interests of the EU.

At first sight it might appear that the powers of the Court are greater in interim proceedings than they are in the main proceedings. This is because the Court's judgments are framed in more trenchant terms (e.g. the order to suspend the application of the Merchant Shipping Act 1988 in Case C-246/89R *Commission* v. *United Kingdom* [1989] ECR 3125); however, the judgment remains declaratory in effect.

In a departure from the usual practice, the dismissal of the Commission's application for interim measures in the *FYROM* case (Case C-120/94R *Commission* v. *Greece*) was given in a judgment handed by a full Court of 13 judges. The Court concluded that the Commission had failed to show that Greece had committed a 'manifest' breach of EC law (although it was prepared to accept that it had shown a *prima-facie* case). More serious was the Commission's failure to show that there would be 'serious and irreparable' damage to the interests of the EU. It was not sufficient to show that there was damage to FYROM.

7.15 Sanctions

The declaratory nature of the Court's judgment under Article 169 means that the Court does not have the power to declare national measures void. On the other hand, it would be inconsistent with the principle of the supremacy of EC law for a national court which was aware of such a finding on the part of the Court to apply an infringing national rule; national law is thus in effect rendered 'inapplicable' (Case 106/77 *Amministrazione delle Finanze dello Stato* v. *Simmenthal (Simmenthal II)* [1978] ECR 629; see 9.13).

The declaratory judgment under Article 171 is binding, and thus failure to comply with a Court judgment is itself a Treaty obligation and can therefore be the subject of further enforcement proceedings. In Case C-291/93 *Commission* v. *Italy* ([1994] ECR I-859) the Court held that although Article 171 does not specify the period within wich a judgment must be complied with, compliance as soon as possible is required in the interests of the immediate and uniform application of EC law.

For a number of years, the Commission argued that there was a need for more effective sanctions, and it put before the Intergovernmental Conference (IGC) on Political Union convened in 1990 proposals for the imposition of financial penalties for failure to give effect to a judgment. These proposals attracted the support in particular of the UK, and consequently, amendments to Article 171 were introduced by the Treaty of Maastricht. The initial proposal to impose a penalty comes from the Commission, but the discretion to fine lies with the Court. Members of the Court of Justice were known to be reluctant to be given the entire responsibility for fining Member States. The question remains open whether fines will need to be high to bring about compliance and to deter recidivism, or whether the simple fact of the imposition of a fine, however small, and the associated political opprobrium, will be sufficient. The Article 171 procedure has yet to be used by the Commission – at least

222 The European Union at Work

before the Court. Its existence may, of course, have been made use of in the context of the negotiation process before formal proceedings are begun. What evidence there is, from the Commission's own annual reports to the Parliament on the application of EC law (e.g. *11th Annual Report* OJ 1994 C154/1) would seem to indicate that the Commission is most enthusiastic about integrating the fining element firmly into its own incentive and negotiation practices.

There were other proposals to enhance the sanctions system put before the IGC, including the suggestion that the Court should be given the power to strike down infringing (i.e. unconstitutional) national legislation, a power held by the constitutional courts of many federal states. An alternative suggestion was that the Court should have the power to award compensation to the victims of an infringement in the context of enforcement proceedings, but the Court has come closer to giving effect to this suggestion by articulating the responsibility of Member States for damage caused by failure to implement a Directive in *Francovich I*, and subsequent cases applying the principle of State liability (9.17, 10.6).

Under Article 93(2) the Commission has a policy of requiring Member States to reclaim monies paid to the beneficiaries of state aids which are found to be incompatible with the Common Market (OJ 1983 C318/3). However, the Commission has to take care to observe the procedural rights of the interested parties. This is illustrated by the Rover/British Aerospace 'sweetener'. In 1988 the Commission issued a decision authorising certain capital aids by the UK to Rover in connection with its acquisition by British Aerospace. It later came to the conclusion that certain financial concessions had been made which were not authorised by the decision, and it issued a further decision ordering the UK to reclaim the payments. This was successfully challenged by British Aerospace and Rover (Case C-294/90 *British Aerospace and Rover Group Holdings plc* v. *Commission* [1992] ECR I-493). The Court held that if the Commission objected to the granting of a new aid, it was obliged to follow the procedures laid down in Article 93 once more in order to respect the rights of the defence of interested parties, in particular the right to be heard. It could not short-circuit these procedures by simply requiring the aid to be reclaimed.

7.16 The Individual and the Commission's Enforcement Powers

The 'direct' and 'indirect' enforcement processes for EC law should exist and function in a manner which is complementary and cooperative. One point which has been notable about EC law has been its construction of the individual as a subject of law – particularly in the context of actions before the national courts. In one field, that of public procurement, a

Remedies Directive has been adopted precisely for the purposes of enhancing the enforcement possibilities of individuals in national courts. In contrast, the individual has a much more vestigial position in relation to the Commission's own direct enforcement powers, a point already referred to in the context of Article 169 proceedings (Case 247/87 *Star Fruit* v. *Commission* [1989] ECR 291; 7.5), but equally relevant in the context of other enforcement mechanisms.

The point was discussed in some detail by the Court of First Instance in Case T-84/94 *Bundesverband der Bilanzbuchhalter eV* v. *Commission* ([1995] ECR II-101), when it dismissed an action for annulment of a Commission Decision rejecting the applicant association's complaint seeking a declaration by the Commission that German legislation on tax advisors infringes Articles 59 and 86 EC (free movement of services; abuse of a dominant position by an undertaking). The Court repeated the well-established principle that the Commission has full discretion in relation to Article 169 proceedings, and then applied this principle to Article 90(3), which might have offered an alternative means of proceeding in such a (competition policy) case for the Commission. It concluded that this provision too implies 'a wide margin of discretion' for the Commission in deciding whether to take action (p. 112).

Only in the areas of competition policy, merger control and state aid control is a different pattern of treatment of the individual visible (see also Chapter 12). Under Article 93(2) EC, which provides for the Commission to take decisions applying in specific cases the substantive standard of legality of state aid contained in Article 92 EC ('incompatibility with the common market'), interested parties – which may include individuals or undertakings – do have consultation rights. If they disagree with the final decision taken by the Commission, they do have a right to challenge it before the Court of First Instance under Article 173 EC (Case C-198/91 *William Cook plc* v. *Commission* [1993] ECR I-2486). Likewise, those who submit complaints to the Commission about alleged violations of Articles 85 and 86 EC, under Article 3 of Regulation 17, are entitled to a basic investigation of the issues of fact and law raised by their complaint, followed – it would appear – by a determination on the part of the Commission which they can challenge before the Court of First Instance (Case T-24/90 *Automec* v. *Commission (Automec II)* [1992] ECR II-2223). They are not entitled to force the Commission to undertake a full investigation of their complaint, or to begin proceedings under Articles 85 and 86. Total inaction on the part of the Commission in relation to the complaint, however, can be sanctioned by an action for failure to act under Article 175 EC (Shaw, 1995; Vesterdorp, 1994). Complainants may also challenge substantive determinations by the Commission (Case 26/76 *Metro-SB-Großmärkte* v. *Commission* [1977] ECR 1875), as can complainants under the Merger Control Regulation (Case T-3/93 *Société Anonyme à Participation Ouvrière Nationale Air France* v. *Commission (Air France)* [1994] ECR II-121).

7.17   The Problem of Non-Compliance

Enforcement of the law is taken very seriously within the EU legal order. The pursuit and prosecution of violations of the Treaty is viewed as one aspect of the application of the rule of law. Non-compliance is therefore a challenge to the fabric of the legal order, as well as a failure to give effect to the intentions of the drafters of the Treaty and of the framers of legislation. The Commission has responded to this challenge by monitoring national compliance and it submits Annual Reports on the Application of Community Law to the Parliament (see most recently the *12th Annual Report for 1994* OJ 1995 C254/1; COM(95) 500). It has adopted measures to improve the effectiveness of the enforcement procedures. For example, it has created two categories of enforcement proceedings: actions for failure to implement directives and actions in respect of other breaches of the Treaty. Proceedings for failure to implement directives – a serious concern given the degree to which the success of the Internal Market Programme rests upon the adoption and implementation of directives – are now begun routinely and mechanically whenever Member States fail to notify the Commission of the measures taken to notify a particular directive. The latest figures indicate much higher implementation rates: of the directives due to be transposed by 31 December 1994, implementation rates at the end of 1994 varied between 86.7 per cent (Greece) and 97.6 per cent (Denmark). The average is now 91.89 per cent, with the figures indicating much smaller disparities in the rate of *numerical* (as opposed to *qualitative*) compliance between the Member States. Difficulties in one of the main trouble spots, Italy (88.4 per cent), have been alleviated by the adoption of a new procedure in 1988 whereby an annual EC law is passed implementing en bloc all applicable EU legislation. The UK, which has traditionally prided itself in on a high level of compliance – whatever its political difficulties with the obligations of membership. This is not borne out by the 1994 figures, which put the UK at below the EU average, with only 89.4 per cent notification to the Commission of measures transposing directives which are due for transposition.

Each year the Commission opens between up to 1,200 new proceedings by issuing formal letters of notice. Its procedures in relation to directives have led to a sharp rise in the number of reasoned opinions delivered (up from 279 in 1990 to 546 in 1994). However, there has been little or no corresponding increase in the number of actions actually reaching the Court (from 78 in 1990 to 89 in 1994), with a sharp dip to 44 in 1993, suggesting that earlier compliance is becoming the norm now that it is clear just how restricted a range of excuses the Court is prepared to accept. Even so, Article 169 actions do occupy a good proportion of the Court of Justice's available time. In 1995 it decided over 30 such actions brought by the Commission. However, apart from monitoring the implementation of directives, the Commission is very greatly indebted to the vigilance of the public to enable it to uncover infringements of the Treaty. It receives more than 1,000 complaints per year from private parties, and has produced a standard complaint form (OJ 1989 C26/7; [1989] 1 CMLR 617) to facilitate the process of making a complaint. It also receives information about alleged infringements via Parliamentary questions, and petitions sent to the Parliament by aggrieved citizens. The Commission's conclusion from its 1994 report was that there was a higher rate of formal compliance with directives, but that it needed to remain vigilant about the quality of national measures transposing directives which are notified to it. It is particularly concerned about a *drop* in the transposition rate in the field of the environment (1.1 per cent in 1994), the environment being one of three main areas (with agriculture and the internal market) where significant transposition duties fall on the Member States.

There are a multitude of reasons for non-compliance; only rarely is it outright opposition to a particular measure or the protection of national sovereignty which lies behind a failure to comply. Of course, being outvoted in the adoption process is one reason why a Member State might very well drag its heels over the implementation process, but it may equally be the fact that a EU measure is badly drafted and subject to misinterpretation or that representatives of the Member States were not fully and properly involved in preliminary negotiations within the Commission. Reasons which are internal to the Member States themselves are often significant; legislative paralysis has been a particular problem where there are coalition governments or frequent changes of government. Executive inefficiency with no clear line of authority determining who is responsible for ensuring the implementation of EC law, and the particularities of the national division of power within each state can also be contributing factors. The alleged infringement may also result from a measure which previously the Commission has shown no particular inclination to enforce, but for which compliance is now required following a change in policy.

The enhancement of sanctions for non-compliance with a Court judgment is just one mechanism aimed at solving a more general problem. It may be that in addition to its perennial need for more resources, the Commission also needs a clear order of priority for the pursuit of cases of non-compliance. Perhaps, for example, complaints brought by entire sectors of industry should be given a higher status. Finally, it has often been suggested that the task of bringing about compliance could be hived off to a separate service, thus separating the enforcement role from the policy-making role. In view of the comments made in 7.5 about the relationship between policy-making and enforcement this seems an undesirable development from the point of view of the Commission.

The enforcement proceedings contained in the Treaty need to be viewed in the context of the alternative mechanisms available for the enforcement of EC law against the authorities of the Member States in the form of proceedings brought before the national courts. Direct and indirect enforcement need to be seen as two aspects of one overall structure; indeed, frequently they will run side by side, with the same issue coming before the Court for decision in the context of different proceedings. This occurred with the litigation surrounding the restrictions on non-national fishing boats introduced by the Merchant Shipping Act 1988, which has still not reached a final culmination in the UK courts. In Case C-246/89R *Commission* v. *United Kingdom*, the Court awarded interim measures against the UK at the behest of the Commission, who had received complaints from Spanish fishing boat owners based in the UK; just a few months later, in Case C-213/89 *R* v. *Secretary of State for Transport, ex parte Factortame Ltd (Factortame I)* ([1990] ECR I-2433) the Court gave a judgment making it clear that the House of Lords should give an interim remedy in the national proceedings concerned with the same dispute. Most recently, in Cases C-46, 48/93 *Brasserie du Pêcheur and Factortame III* [1996] I CMLR 889, the Court concluded that the UK Government could in principle be liable for damages suffered by the private individuals in such circumstances.

Private or indirect enforcement is efficient in the sense that it does not use EU administrative resources. It also emphasises the relationship between the EU citizen and the EU legal system. The disadvantage is that such an approach depends upon the vagaries of individual decisions to litigate and upon the varying attitudes of national courts to EC law. Part III will examine the grounds for bringing actions based on EC law in national courts, addressing the status of EC law within the national legal order and the range of sanctions for non-compliance which courts must make available for failure to observe the Treaty. First, however, the organic connection in the form of Article 177 EC between the national courts and the Court of Justice will be examined.

Summary

1 EC law and EU policies are principally implemented by the Member States, rather than by the Commission. Article 5 EC imposes a duty of loyalty upon the Member States in the implementation of EC law, breach of which may give rise to an enforcement action under Article 169 EC by the Commission.
2 Enforcement proceedings may be brought by the Commission or by a Member State under Articles 169 and 170 EC. They comprise an administrative and judicial phase. It is during the administrative phase that the Commission is often able to achieve compliance by the Member States, without recourse to the Court.
3 Failure to comply with any obligation arising under EC law, by any organ of the state, may engage the responsibility of the Member State.
4 The Court of Justice will not accept defences to enforcement proceedings based on national law.
5 The sanctions available under Article 171 EC prior to the adoption of the Treaty of Maastricht were solely declaratory. Article 171 has now been amended to provide for the possibility of financial penalties being imposed upon Member States which fail to comply with a declaratory

judgment of the Court which states that they are in breach of their EU obligations.

6   The availability of stiffer sanctions is one means by which the problem of non-compliance with EC law can be dealt with. The procedures for enforcement can also be made more effective. The Commission rigorously monitors the application of EC law and produces regular reports. These indicate that the level of compliance is gradually improving.

Questions

1   What obligations does Article 5 EC impose upon Member States in relation to the implementation and enforcement of EC law?
2   What is meant by the direct and indirect administration of EC law?
3   How could the system of enforcement mechanisms available under the EC Treaty be made more effective?
4   Why is the administrative phase of the enforcement process so important to the Commission?
5   Identify the key differences between the direct and indirect enforcement of EC law.

Workshop

In June 1995 the Council adopted a directive which required, on grounds of the protection of the consumer, that all milk sold in the European Union should be packaged in cylindrical 1.5 litre cartons. Measures were to be brought into force by the Member States to give effect to the directive before 31 December 1995. The measure was adopted by a qualified majority with the states of Ajax and Zeno voting against. The Parliament, when consulted, had been unhappy about the measure, but the Council ignored its objections. In July 1995, the Parliament brought an action for annulment against the measure arguing that the directive should be declared void because it was adopted using the wrong legal basis; Article 100A should have been used instead of Article 43. This action is still pending. Zeno agrees with the proceedings brought by the Parliament, but has neither joined the Parliament as a co-applicant, nor intervened in the case.

In Zeno, instead of implementing the directive in the Parliament, the Minister of Agriculture and Consumer Protection issued an instruction to all Trading Standards Officers ordering them not to enforce the directive. Cowcrop, a company which already sells its milk in cylindrical cartons, challenges the validity of these instructions in the Zeno administrative courts, arguing that they give a competitive advantage to companies which are not adopting the EU standard and are in breach of EC law. The matter proceeds quickly to the Zeno Supreme Administrative Court, which refuses to refer the matter to the Court of Justice on the grounds that directives cannot give rise to rights which individuals may enforce. It also doubts whether the directive is lawful, on the grounds that it has been adopted on an incorrect legal basis.

Cowcrop has also complained to the Commission. After a period of informal consultation in which Zeno has shown itself unwilling to compromise or accept the Commission's objections, the Commission issued a reasoned opinion on 4 February 1996, stating as the basis of Zeno's violation the instructions issued to Trading Standards Officers. It gave Zeno fourteen days in which to bring its conduct into line with the Treaty, and then on 19 February, brought the matter before the Court of Justice, citing as an additional ground of objection the refusal of the Zeno Supreme Administrative Court to refer the matter to the Court of Justice. It is now seeking the award of interim measures by the Court.

Zeno objects that Ajax is also not enforcing the directive, and that the Commission has not brought proceedings against Ajax. In addition it points out that another Member State (Kenjo) has unilaterally stopped all imports of milk from Ajax and Zeno on the grounds that the latter two Member States are in flagrant breach of EC law. Zeno argues that while there is a clearly a political issue which needs to be settled in the Council of the EU, this is not an appropriate matter for the Court of Justice.

Discuss

[**Note**: It would be useful to review again this Workshop after you have completed work on Chapters 8–10]

Further Reading

Dashwood and White (1989), 'Enforcement Actions and Article 169 and 170', 14 *ELRev.* 388.

Everling (1984), 'The Member States of the European Community before their Court of Justice', 9 *ELRev.* 315.

Mendrinou (1996), 'Non-compliance and the European Commission's role in integration', 3 *JEPP* 1.

Snyder (1993b) 'The Effectiveness of European Community Law: Institutions, Processes, Tools and Techniques', 56 *MLR* 19, pp.19-40.

Temple Lang (1990), 'Community Constitutional Law: Article 5 EEC Treaty', 27 *CMLRev.* 645.

Weatherill (1995b), 'Implementation as a Constitutional Issue', in Daintith (1995b).

Weiler (1988), 'The White Paper and the Application of Community Law', in Bieber *et al.* (1988).

Part III

The EU Legal Order and the National Legal Orders

8 Article 177 EC – The Organic Connection Between National Courts and the Court of Justice

8.1 Introduction

An American political scientist looking at the European Union legal order has commented recently:

'an exclusive focus on the ECJ's case law gives us an incomplete, and at times erroneous, picture of the dynamics of constitutionalization. The construction of a constitutional, rule of law Community has been a participatory process, a set of constitutional dialogues between supranational and national judges.' (Stone Sweet, 1995: 1)

Since the decision of the German Federal Constitutional Court in the *Brunner* case (3.3), as well as the popular discontent with the Treaty of Maastricht, it is more true than ever that the Court of Justice must be aware that it operates within a series of dialogues. Within the constraints of this book, it is impossible to stray far from the framework for the EU legal order set up by the Treaties and elaborated by the Court of Justice. However, as we examine the principal organic link between national courts and the Court of Justice, which has provided the mechanism for these dialogues to occur, it is important to remember these cautionary words.

Article 177 EC makes provision for national courts to ascertain from the Court of Justice its views on the status and meaning of EC law. After amendment by the Treaty of Maastricht to incorporate the institutions of EMU, it now provides:

'The Court of Justice shall have jurisdiction to give preliminary rulings concerning:

(a) the interpretation of this Treaty;
(b) the validity and interpretation of acts of the institutions of the Community and of the ECB;
(c) the interpretation of the statutes of bodies established by an act of the Council, where those statutes so provide.

Where such a question is raised before any court or tribunal of a Member State, that court or tribunal may, if it considers that a decision on the question is necessary to enable it to give judgment, request the Court of Justice to give a ruling thereon.

Where any such question is raised in a case pending before a court or tribunal of a Member State, against whose decisions there is no judicial remedy under national law, that court or tribunal shall bring the matter before the Court of Justice.'

The grand objectives of the EU legal order, which include the inter-meshing of EC law and national law, could not be achieved without some organic mechanism for ensuring the uniform application of EC law, in which the Court of Justice can give authoritative rulings on the meaning of EC law. The Court of Justice frequently reminds us that it is the purpose of Article 177 to provide such a mechanism:

'Article 177 is essential for the preservation of the Community character of the law established by the Treaty and has the object of ensuring that in all circumstances the law is the same in all States of the Community' (Case 166/73 *Rheinmühlen-Düsseldorf* v. *Einfuhr- und Vorratstelle für Getreide und Futtermittel* [1974] ECR 33 at p. 43).

With this purpose in mind, the Court has been able to use Article 177 preliminary rulings as the centrepieces for the construction of a legal edifice in which EC law can be uniformly interpreted and enforced within the national courts of the Member States in the same terms as it is within the Court of Justice itself. To this end, of course, Article 177 references have given the Court the opportunity to articulate the principles on which it is possible for individuals to enforce EC law against infringing Member States and, where this is permitted under EC law, against infringing individuals. In addition, however, Article 177 is a key element in the system of judicial control within the EU, and its role in this context will be reconsidered in Part IV. For Article 177 provides a mechanism for indirect challenges to the validity of EU legal acts in national courts, using the medium of direct challenges to national implementing acts based on an allegedly invalid 'parent' EU acts.

As Article 177 provides a 'reference procedure' in the hands of the referring court and not an 'appeals procedure' in the hands of parties who consider their rights under EC law to be infringed or feel themselves to be the victims of an invalid EU act, its success has always rested on the willingness of national courts to collaborate by making references and by accepting the subsequent judgments of the Court. The Court has based its approach on a philosophy of the separate functions of national court and 'Community' court, a philosophy which can be derived from the views of AG Lagrange in the first case submitted under Article 177. In Case 13/61 *Bosch* v. *de Geus* ([1962] ECR 45 at p. 56) he asserted that:

'applied judiciously – one is tempted to say loyally – the provisions of Article 177 lead to a real and fruitful collaboration between the municipal courts and the Court of Justice of the Communities with mutual regard for their respective jurisdictions. It is in this spirit that each side must solve the sometimes delicate problems which may arise in all systems of preliminary procedure, and which are necessarily made more difficult in this case by the differences in the legal systems of the Member States as regards this type of procedure.'

A similar view emerges from the ruling of the Court itself in Case 16/65 *Firma Schwarze* v. *Einfuhr- und Vorratstelle für Getreide und Futtermittel* ([1965] ECR 877 at p. 886):

'[Article 177 establishes] a special field of judicial cooperation which requires the national court and the Court of Justice, both keeping within their respective jurisdiction, and with the aim of ensuring that Community law is applied in a unified manner, to make direct and complementary contributions to the working out of a decision.'

The 'separate functions' conception gives the national court a broad discretion to formulate the questions which it believes to be appropriate. However, as the Court put it in the early case of *Costa* v. *ENEL* (Case 6/64 [1964] ECR 585), the fact that a question is 'imperfectly formulated' does not deprive the Court of the power to extract from that question those matters which are relevant to the interpretation of the Treaty. It will pull in provisions of EC law which it considers pertinent, even though these were not raised by the national court (see Case 78/70 *Deutsche Grammophon* v. *Metro-SB-Großmärkte* [1971] ECR 487). In fact, the Court rarely hesitates to rephrase questions posed by national courts where it deems this necessary. On the other hand, it has frequently used the separation of functions argument in order to evade the argument that it is overstretching its remit as the EU's court, stressing that it has no jurisdiction to interfere with the discretion of the national court as to what to refer, or indeed when to refer. When challenged about the nature of its case law, the Court insists on the fine line between the interpretation and application of EC law, maintaining it is restricted in the Article 177 context only to the former. It frequently insists on the right of the national court to judge the relevance of the questions which it poses to the litigation before it when it determines the issue of 'necessity' in Article 177 (e.g. Case C-186/90 *Durighello* v. *INPS* ([1991] ECR I-5773)). In that case it held:

'A request from a national court may be rejected only if it quite obvious that the interpretation of the Community law or the examination of the validity of a rule of Community law sought bears no relation to the actual nature of the case or to the subject-matter of the main action' (p. 5795).

In Case C-343/90 *Lourenço Dias* v. *Director da Alfândega do Porto*
[1992] ECR I-4673 the Court put it slightly differently:

> 'the national court, which is alone in having a direct knowledge of the
> facts of the case, is in the best position to appreciate the necessity for a
> preliminary ruling, having regard to the particular features of the case,
> so as to enable it to give judgment' (p. 4708).

The only requirements which the Court places upon the questions which it
receives are that they arise out of a 'genuine dispute' before the national
court, that they are not purely hypothetical questions, and that the
national court should furnish sufficient factual and legal context to permit
the Court to address the questions put to it.

8.2   Court Controls on the Preliminary Reference Procedure

In the two *Foglia* v. *Novello* cases, the Court articulated and applied the
requirement of a genuine dispute. In Case 104/79 *Foglia* v. *Novello (No. 1)*
([1980] ECR 745) the Court was asked by the Italian court before which
the case had come to assess the compatibility with EC law of a French tax
imposed on imported wine. It appeared that the parties were in agreement
that the tax was in breach of EC law, and that they had artificially
constructed the litigation before the Italian courts, involving an action by
Foglia (a dealer) to force Novello (an importer) to pay the French tax,
knowing that an Italian court was more likely than a French court to
expose the tax to the scrutiny of the Court of Justice by making a
reference. The Court unexpectedly refused to answer the questions,
sending the case back to the Italian court in the following terms (at p. 759):

> 'It thus appears that the parties to the main action are concerned to
> obtain a ruling that the French tax system is invalid for liqueur wines by
> the expedient of proceedings before an Italian court between two
> private individuals who are in agreement as to the result to be attained
> and who have inserted a clause in their contract in order to induce the
> Italian court to give a ruling on the point . . .
>   The duty of the Court of Justice under Article 177 of the EEC Treaty
> is to supply all courts in the Community with the information on the
> interpretation of Community law which is necessary to enable them to
> settle genuine disputes which are brought before them. A situation in
> which the Court was obliged by the expedient of arrangements like
> those described above to give rulings would jeopardise the whole system
> of legal remedies available to private individuals to enable them to
> protect themselves against tax provisions which are contrary to the
> Treaty.'

Quite why the Court chose to argue that such allegedly apocalyptic consequences would result from the 'misuse' of the Article 177 reference procedure in these circumstances is not clear. The expedient of friendly litigation is practised and tolerated in many countries including the UK. It would seem bizarre – and excessively intrusive – if the result of EC law were that non-hostile litigation involving, for example, a test case, could not result in a reference to the Court of Justice (see the comments of AG Jacobs in Case C-412/93 *Leclerc-Siplec* v. *TFI Publicité* [1995] ECR I-179 at pp. 183–4). What is more, judges in many of the Member States find themselves subject to a prohibition on refusing to give judgment. In keeping with the view that the judge's role is to interpret the law, not to judge the appropriateness of litigation or to interfere in the political sphere, the so-called *déni de justice* (refusal to judge) is a violation of the judge's duty and a criminal offence in France (Article 4 of the code civil). On the other hand, the Court's position is not the same as the conventional national judge. It has claimed a unique and highly political position within the EU legal order, and it is arguable that fictitious litigation (as opposed to friendly litigation, if a distinction can be drawn) is damaging to the gradual evolution of the supranational system in that it may unnecessarily bring into conflict the courts and governments of different states. In that case, it may be legitimate to argue that the rights of the defence of states which find their laws impugned before the courts of other Member States will be undermined. The Court may well have been concerned to avoid handing down a decision which the French Government would be unwilling to execute, and thereby to endanger the system of enforcement of EC law. The decision in Case 104/79, and its follow-up in Case 244/80 *Foglia* v. *Novello (No. 2)* ([1981] ECR 3045) where the Court reproduced the substance of its views when re-questioned by the Italian court and reinforced the point that it is not subject to a duty to give advisory opinions at the request of national courts, have divided academic commentators and the arguments for and against can be found in Barav (1980), Wyatt (1982) and Bebr (1982).

However, while the *Foglia* v. *Novello* case law was never formally overruled by the Court of Justice, for a number of years it did not in practice show a great readiness to apply it. For example, it has accepted implicit challenges to the validity of legislation in the court of another Member State, such as the challenge to an Italian law in the German courts in Case C-150/88 *Eau de Cologne* v. *Provide* ([1989] ECR 3891). In that case it stated that there was a genuine dispute and that the Court is under a duty to provide the national court with the answers to questions of interpretation which it needs to settle the dispute. It made it clear that it did not by any means intend to exclude the possibility that the courts of one Member State may determine the compatibility of the laws of another Member State with EC law, and that it will participate by providing any necessary interpretations of EC law.

The Court has since moved onto a slightly different tack with a new approach to certain types of preliminary references. In a series of cases since 1992 it has started to subject some of the references it receives to the following enquiries before concluding whether or not they are admissible:

- are the questions purely 'hypothetical'? and
- has the national court supplied the Court of Justice with sufficient information of a factual and legal nature to enable it to answer the questions which the former has posed?

It is not hard to see these questions as an expression of the Court's exasperation with its ever growing workload, and its perceived need to place some sort of control on the numbers of references which are now reaching it from national courts (8.9).

In Case C-83/91 *Meilicke* v. *ADV/ORGA* ([1992] ECR I-4871) the Court refused to answer certain questions regarding the interpretation of the Second Company Law Directive, and the compatibility with this Directive of certain German case law The Court characterised the questions referred by the German court as 'hypothetical', and, with a passing reference to *Foglia* v. *Novello* and other cases on the cooperative structure of the Article 177 procedure, reached the conclusion that it could not answer the questions as it would be exceeding its proper function under Article 177 if it did so. One of the difficulties which the Court faced when assessing the relationship between the litigation in the German court and the questions referred to it by that court, was that if the Court of Justice had given the interpretation of EC law which the plaintiff sought, he would in fact have lost his case in the national court. He would, however, have succeeded in his ulterior goal, which was to establish the incompatibility of the German case law which he had challenged in the domestic litigation with EC law. Unlike the Court itself, AG Teasuro did not decline to answer the rather convoluted questions referred by the national court, but rather found a way to reformulate them so they could be answered. The Court has given similar reasons in two further cases: in Case C-343/90 *Lourenço Dias* it refused to answer six out of the eight questions which were put to it, commenting that they bore no relation to the case as set out in the order for a reference; in Case C-428/93 *Monin Automobiles* v. *France (Monin II)* ([1994] ECR I-1707) it denied that an interpretation of EC law was objectively necessary in the case.

Subsequently, the Court has gone a step further and demanded a certain level of information from national courts. In Cases C-320-322/90 *Telemarsicabruzzo* v. *Circostel* ([1993] ECR I-393) it declined to answer questions on the EC competition rules posed by an Italian court in the context of proceedings brought to prohibit a group of television broadcasters from using certain broadcasting frequencies, on the grounds that it was essential to have precise details of the situation at issue before the national court before the Court of Justice was able to give a useful interpretation of EC law. Strangely it took the Court of Justice more than two years after the reference was lodged to reach this conclusion, and it did so despite the availability of full information – if not in the order for a reference itself, at least in Report for the Hearing and the Opinion of the Advocate General (Tesauro, 1993: 14). A similar line of reasoning has been employed since by the Court in Case C157/92 *Pretore di Genova* v. *Banchero* ([1993] ECR I-1085), Case C-386/92 *Monin Automobiles* v. *France (Monin I)* ([1993] ECR I-2049), and Case C-167/94 *Grau Gomis* ([1995] ECR I-1023). In other words, neither the *Meilicke* nor the *Telemarsicabruzzo* approaches represent isolated cases in the way that the *Foglia* v. *Novello* cases appear to have been, and may be interpreted as one response by the Court of Justice to its burgeoning workload problem and as a possible attempt to impose a quality control on national courts (8.9).

8.3 Provisions of EC Law which may be the Subject of Reference

Article 177 itself defines those provisions which may be the subject of a reference. These are provisions of the Treaty, acts of EU institutions (including the ECB) and the statutes of bodies established by an act of the Council (for an example of the latter category see Case 44/84 *Hurd* v. *Jones* [1986] ECR 29). Acts of the EU institutions which can be the subject of a reference include non-binding acts such as recommendations and opinions; in Case C-322/88 *Grimaldi* v. *Fonds des Maladies Professionelles* ([1989] ECR I-4407) the provisions referred were contained in Commission Recommendations on the adoption of a European schedule of occupational diseases, and on the conditions for the granting of compensation to those suffering from such diseases. The fact that agreements with third countries are concluded by the Council has provided a convenient justification for the acceptance of references on the interpretation of such agreements (e.g. Case 12/86 *Demirel* v. *Stadt Schwäbisch Gmund* [1987] ECR 3719 – a reference on the Association Agreement between the European Community and Turkey). More tenuous is the decision of the Court to accept references on international agreements to which the European Community has never formally adhered, but where it has succeeded to the rights and obligations of the Member States, such as the [old] GATT (Cases 267–269/81 *SPI* [1983] ECR 801). The best justification for this practice is the fact that such agreements are binding upon the EU, and the Court regards the provisions of these agreements as penetrating the EU legal order and as giving rise, where appropriate to rights upon which individuals may rely in national courts.

General principles of law alone do not appear to be capable of forming the basis of a reference, although in practice a national court may request a ruling from the Court of Justice on how other provisions of EC law should be interpreted in the light of general principles of law recognised in the EU legal order (Case 44/79 *Hauer* v. *Land Rheinland Pfalz* [1979] ECR 3740).

8.4   Courts and Tribunals of the Member States Capable of Making a Reference

References may be made by the whole range of bodies which embody the judicial power of the state, regardless of what title they are given. For example, in Case 61/65 *Vaassen* ([1966] ECR 261) the Court accepted a reference from a Dutch arbitral tribunal or *Scheidsgericht*, pointing to those features which it displayed which brought it within the ambit of Article 177. It was a permanent body instituted by the law, with members appointed by a Minister; it was given compulsory jurisdiction over the cases assigned to it by law, used a form of adversarial procedure, and applied the law in its decisions. A Dutch general practitioners' registration appeal committee was also held to fall within Article 177 in Case 246/80 *Broeckmeulen* ([1981] ECR 2311). The Court stated that:

> 'in the absence, in practice, of any right of appeal to the ordinary courts, the Appeals Committee, which operates with the consent of the public authorities and with their cooperation, and which, after an adversarial procedure, delivers decisions which are in fact recognized as final, must, in a matter involving the application of Community law, be considered as a court or tribunal of a Member State within the meaning of Article 177 of the Treaty' (at p. 2328).

A judicial body exercising investigatory functions within an inquisitorial system of criminal law is likewise capable of making a reference, even at a preliminary stage of the investigations where the potential defendants have not yet been identified. In Case 14/86 *Pretore di Salò* v. *X.* ([1987] ECR 2545) the Court accepted a reference from the Italian *pretore* or examining magistrate, which requested an interpretation of EU pollution legislation precisely with a view to identifying the potential defendants in criminal pollution proceedings. However, in Case C-24/92 *Corbiau* ([1993] ECR I-1277), the Court found that the *Directeur des Contributions* who exercised an appellate function within the Luxembourg taxation authorities was not a 'court or tribunal' because the Director did not have an independent 'third party' relationship with both parties to the proceedings.

Commercial arbitration is also excluded from the scope of Article 177. This was decided by the Court in Case 102/81 *Nordsee* v. *Reederei Mond* ([1982] ECR 1095). Although the decision of an arbitrator has force of law between the parties, and although the arbitrator must apply the law, it is more significant that the jurisdiction is contractual and therefore not compulsory and that, as a private arrangement, does not involve the public authorities. The Court therefore concluded that the link between the arbitration procedure and the organisation of legal remedies through the court structure was insufficiently close for the arbitrator to be deemed a 'court or tribunal'. The importance in practice of avoiding incorrect applications of EC law in national arbitration proceedings is emphasised by the indication given by the English Court of Appeal in *Bulk Oil* v. *Sun*

International ([1984] 1 WLR 147) that the existence of a point of EC law for decision before an arbitrator should become a ground for giving leave to appeal to the court against the decision of an arbitrator.

8.5 The Discretion to Refer: Article 177(2)

Article 177 is concerned with two separate scenarios for national courts. The first is the discretion to refer, which is held by all courts faced with questions of EC law. The second is the obligation to refer, imposed only on courts of last resort.

The discretion to refer given to lower courts is entirely unfettered – subject to the principles set out in 8.2. References are not precluded by, for example, the existence of a prior ruling by the Court of Justice on a similar question (Cases 28–30/62 *Da Costa en Schaake NV* [1963] ECR 31). Nor may internal rules governing the hierarchy of the court structure limit the discretion of inferior courts. An inferior court which regards itself as internally bound by a rule of law stated by a superior court either in the same case or in an earlier case (e.g. the common law system of binding judicial precedent) is not prevented from making a reference to the Court of Justice if it believes applying the internal rule would lead it to a violation of EC law (Case 166/73 *Rheinmühlen*).

In the light of this conclusion in *Rheinmühlen*, it was therefore somewhat surprising that in the same case the Court went on to hold that as a matter of EC law nothing precluded an internal appeal against the decision of an inferior court to refer, and that such appeals were to be regulated by national rules on procedure. However, where a reference has been made but is under appeal, the Court will proceed to the hearing of the reference which will be regarded as valid and effective until such time as it has actually been revoked. In this decision the Court went against the view of AG Warner who argued that appeals against orders to refer should not be available as a matter of EC law, and this is the view which has been espoused by the Irish Supreme Court in *Campus Oil* v. *Ministry for Industry and Energy* ([1984] 1 CMLR 479). It held that appeals against orders to refer are precluded within Ireland by the terms of Article 177 which it held to be part of Irish law.

The discretion to refer also extends to a discretion as to when to refer. We have noted already the early reference made by an Italian *pretore* (Case 14/86), and the Court will not reject a reference on the grounds that it is too 'early'. However, the Court has suggested that it might be convenient for the national court to decide the facts and issues of purely national law before making the reference, in order to enable the Court itself to take fuller cognisance of the relevant circumstances of the case (Cases 36, 71/80 *Irish Creamery Milk Suppliers Association* v. *Ireland* [1981] ECR 735). This is presumably in order to increase the effectiveness of the reference procedure from the perspective of the Court of Justice.

Finally, although the question of EC law must be necessary in the sense of being relevant to the resolution of the dispute, the Court has not placed any restrictions on the meaning of such a question. In Cases C-297/88 and C-197/89 *Dzodzi* v. *Belgium* ([1990] ECR I-3763) the Court asserted the primary importance of the uniform interpretation and application of EC law when it held that it had jurisdiction to give a ruling on a preliminary reference made by a national court in circumstances where national law had extended the ambit and application of certain EC law provisions beyond the scope required by EC law itself. In other words, the Court gave a ruling in an area which was beyond the scope of Community competence, because the national law made reference to the content of EC law. The overwhelming need to ensure uniformity required the Court to be able to interpret EC law for the purposes of the interpretation of national law. In contrast, AG Darmon did advise that the Court had no jurisdiction in that case, or in one raising similar questions which was decided shortly thereafter (Case C-231/89 *Gmurzynska-Bscher* v. *Oberfinanzdirektion Köln* [1990] ECR I-4003).

Although the English inferior courts remain free to exercise their discretion to refer, subject to appeals (under Rules of the Supreme Court, Order 114, r.6 in the case of the High Court and above), in fact Lord Denning MR purported in the early stages of UK membership of the European Community to give some guidance on the question of references. In *Bulmer* v. *Bollinger* ([1974] Ch. 401; [1974] 2 All ER 1226) he argued that before a reference is made the judge must be certain that the point is conclusive of the case and that there is no previous ruling of the Court of Justice or no grounds for applying the doctrine of *acte clair* (see below 8.6, although this point is not strictly relevant to the exercise of the discretion to refer). Finally, he or she should decide the facts first, and should bear in mind the delay caused by a reference and the workload of the Court of Justice. These guidelines have been criticised as encouraging courts too strongly not to refer (Arnull, 1990b: 382).

A much more positive attitude towards the Court is displayed by Bingham J in *Commissioners of Customs and Excise* v. *Samex ApS* ([1983] 3 CMLR 194) who pointed out that the Court of Justice is much better equipped than an English court to decide matters of EC law, as a consequence of the linguistic advantages it enjoys in the scrutiny of the various different language texts, the oversight it has over the whole field of EC law, and its particular understanding of the highly purposive methods interpretation which it is necessary to apply to EC law.

Subsequently, in *R* v. *International Stock Exchange of the United Kingdom and the Republic of Ireland, ex parte Else* ([1993] 1 All ER 420) the guidelines were further refined by the same judge, this time in the first case in which the Court of Appeal overturned the decision of a lower court to make a reference to the Court of Justice. Three factors must be present: the facts must be clarified; the judge must be satisfied that the provision of EC law is critical to the final determination of the case; and the judge must consider whether she can herself resolve the question of EC law, with complete confidence. Once these factors have been addressed, it will 'ordinarily' be appropriate for a lower court to make a reference (for further details see Dwyer, 1994).

8.6 The Obligation to Refer: Article 177(3)

The obligation to refer falls upon a court against whose decisions there is no judicial remedy under national law. This formulation has led to the development of two different theories of the scope of the obligation. First there is the abstract or organic theory whereby the court of last resort within the judicial hierarchy against which there is never a judicial appeal carries the obligation to refer. This would cover the House of Lords, the Irish Supreme Court and other comparable courts. Support for this theory can be obtained from the wording of Article 177(3) which refers in plural to the 'decisions' of such courts. The opposing theory is the concrete or specific case theory which considers the case in question, not the court in abstract. This would obviously, in appropriate cases, cover the English Court of Appeal, or even inferior courts where the right of appeal is restricted by the nature of the case. Support for this view comes from Case 6/64 *Costa* v. *ENEL* ([1964] ECR 585) which involved a reference from an Italian *guidice conciliatore*, a magistrate who is the judicial authority of last resort for certain minor cases; the Court stated (at p. 592) that:

> 'by the terms of [Article 177], however, national courts against whose decisions, as *in the present case*, there is no judicial remedy, must refer the matter to the Court of Justice' (emphasis added).

The adoption of this position, however, still leaves the English Court of Appeal in a rather ambiguous position, since it is not clear until the end of any particular case – i.e. after the decision not to refer to the Court has been taken – whether an appeal to the House of Lords will be possible. In *R.* v. *Henn and Darby* ([1978] 3 All ER 1190 (CA); [1980] 2 All ER 166 (HL)) the question was not discussed in the Court of Appeal, which refused to refer and refused leave to appeal. The House of Lords granted leave to appeal, and made a reference to the Court of Justice. The matter was addressed again in what has been described as the 'peripatetic' case of *Chiron* v. *Murex* ([1994] FSR 187 (CA); [1995] All ER (EC) 88 (HL)) (Demetriou, 1995: 628). In that case, the applicants failed on two occasions to persuade the Court of Appeal to refer or to give leave to appeal to the House of Lords; it also failed to persuade the House of Lords to give leave to appeal. It is not surprising that the applicants' attempts, in effect, to have the Court of Appeal override the House of Lords failed, but it is perhaps regrettable that the House of Lords failed to refer this difficult question to the Court of Justice for resolution subject to the principles of EC law. It is all the more disappointing because the House has in the past used its ability (and indeed obligation) to refer in order 'to protect its neutrality and impartiality' within the UK's complex constitutional framework (Maher, 1995: 312).

There are three sets of circumstances in which there is no obligation to refer on a court of last resort (although, of course, there remains a discretion to refer). First, there is no duty to refer a question of interpretation in interlocutory proceedings providing that the findings of law are subject to review in main proceedings. In Case 107/76 *Hoffmann-La-Roche* v. *Centrafarm* ([1977] ECR 957 at p. 973) the Court held that Article 177(3)

> 'must be interpreted as meaning that a national court or tribunal is not required to refer to the Court a question of interpretation . . . mentioned in that Article when the question is raised in interlocutory proceedings for an interim order, even where no judicial remedy is available against the decision to be taken in the context of those proceedings, provided that each of the parties is entitled to institute proceedings or to require proceedings to be instituted on the substance of the case and that during such proceedings the question provisionally decided in the summary proceedings may be re-examined and may be the subject of a reference to the Court under Article 177.'

Interlocutory proceedings involving challenges to the validity of EU legislation are discussed in 8.7.

The second category of cases in which the obligation to refer lapses is where the Court has previously answered a materially identical question. This point emerges from Cases 28–30/62 *Da Costa en Schaake* where the Court referred to the authority of a previous ruling which it had given on a materially identical question as in effect depriving a subsequent preliminary reference of its *raison d'être*. A similar situation arises where the Court has already declared an act of one of the EU institutions void; this is sufficient reason for a court in another Member State to treat that act as void and to be exonerated from the duty to refer (Case 66/80 *International Chemical Corporation* v. *Amministrazione delle Finanze dello Stato* [1981] ECR 1191).

Finally, it is argued that the doctrine of *acte clair* can override the obligation to refer. This doctrine, espoused in particular by certain French courts in the early stages of development of the EU legal order, holds that a sufficiently clear legal provision does not require interpretation, but only application. Since the matter of 'application' falls within the remit of the national court under the principle of the separation of functions, it should follow that there is no question of interpretation to be referred. This doctrine was eventually accepted by the Court in Case 283/81 *CILFIT* ([1982] ECR 3415), but in such a qualified and watered-down form that it is questionable whether the Court was not also seeking simultaneously to destroy its substance. In its judgment the Court referred to *Da Costa*, and indicated that further circumstances in which references might be meaningless included those where the previous rulings of the Court effectively decided a point of law even though the questions at issue were not materially identical, and where the correct application of EC law is so obvious as to leave no scope for any reasonable doubt as to how the question raised is to be resolved.

However, the Court went on to say (at p. 3430) that

> 'before it comes to the conclusion that such is the case, the national court or tribunal must be convinced that the matter is equally obvious to the courts of the other Member States and to the Court of Justice. Only if those conditions are satisfied may the national court or tribunal refrain from submitting the question to the Court of Justice and take upon itself the responsibility for resolving it.'

The Court then indicated the factors to be taken into account by the national court in deciding this point. These include the characteristic features of EC law, and the particular difficulties to which its interpretation gives rise, the fact that EC law is drafted in several languages and that the different language versions are all equally authentic; the existence of difficulties relating to terminology and legal concepts, the meanings of which may vary significantly between Member States and between national and EC law; and finally the fact that EC law must be interpreted in its context, having regard to its purpose and object. It would be rare that a provision of EC law would satisfy these requirements of simplicity and clarity, or indeed that a national court would feel itself equipped with the resources for the comparative analysis which ought to underlie a faithful application of the *CILFIT* criteria. Notwithstanding this ruling, there have been subsequent instances of the application of acte clair by national courts, including examples from case law in the UK (see *SA Magnavision NV* v. *General Optical Council* [1987] 1 CMLR 887 and [1987] 2 CMLR 262 (Div. Court). Even more worrying, perhaps, is the decision of the House of Lords in *R* v. *London Boroughs' Transport Committee, ex parte Freight Transport Association* ([1991] 3 All ER 915) in which it declined to make a reference in circumstances of uncertainty over the precise interpretation of certain EU Directives (which the Court of Appeal and the House of Lords interpreted quite differently), without referring to what other judges have called the 'cautionary comments' in the Court of Justice in *CILFIT* (see for a contrast *R* v. *Secretary of State for Transport, ex parte Factortame Ltd* [1989] 2 CMLR 353 (HL)) (for a general discussion see Weatherill, 1992). However, the complexities of faithfully applying the *CILFIT* criteria may be such that the ruling must be regarded as 'unrealistic and unworkable in practice' (Bebr, 1988: 355).

Failure by a court of last resort to make a preliminary reference where unresolved issues of EC law remain crucial to the resolution of a case is, of course, a breach of a Treaty obligation by the judicial arm of the state which could potentially form the subject matter of an action under Article 169 EC. There is no individual redress available against the failure to refer.

8.7   Rulings on Validity

Only the Court of Justice has the power to declare an act of an EU institution invalid. In Case 314/85 *Firma Foto-Frost* v. *Hauptzollamt Lübeck* ([1987] ECR 4199) the Court acknowledged that this point was not definitively settled by the Treaty itself, but concluded that while national courts have the power to decide that there are no serious grounds for impugning the validity of EU legislation without recourse to the Court of Justice, it would be contrary to the objective of ensuring the uniform application of EC law by national courts, which underlies Article 177, to allow them to decide on the invalidity of an EU act. In this context, divergences in national interpretation would be intolerable from the perspective of the unity of the EU legal order, the cohesion of the system of remedies under the Treaty and the imperatives of legal certainty. It follows from this decision that there is in effect an obligation on all courts to refer issues of validity to the Court of Justice.

In *Foto-Frost* the Court explicitly left open the question of how national courts should deal with the problem of the alleged invalidity of an EU act in the context of interim proceedings, where the urgency of matters would tend to render a reference to the Court meaningless. In Cases C-143/88 and C-92/89 *Zuckerfabrik Süderithmarschen & Zuckerfabrik Soest* ([1991] ECR I-415), the Court was confronted directly with this issue, but again it refused to allow the national court the power to declare EU measures invalid. Instead it stated that the national court should, in interim proceedings, invalidate the national implementing measures which are based on the impugned EU act, if there are factual and legal matters brought by the applicants before the national court which suggest that there are serious doubts about the validity of the EU measure (in that case, a regulation). There must also be evidence that the matter is urgent and that the applicant is threatened by grave and irreparable harm if no action is taken by the national court, and the national court must not act before it has taken into account the interests of the EU. With respect to the latter point, the Court indicated that some form of guarantee could be required from the applicant against loss which might be suffered by the EU if the national measure is suspended in these circumstances.

The matter was taken a step further by the Court in Case C-465/93 *Atlanta Fruchthandelsgesellschaft mbH* v. *Bundesamt für Ernährung und Forstwirtschaft* ([1995] ECR I-3761) where the Court concluded that a national court may also under the same conditions issue a positive order granting interim relief. The Court stressed the importance of the parallelism between interim relief in respect of allegedly unlawful EU measures, and interim relief in respect of national legal provisions alleged to be in breach of EC law (Case C-213/89 *R* v. *Secretary of State for Transport, ex parte Factortame Ltd (Factortame I)* [1990] ECR I-2433) (10.3). It also referred to a close link to the Court's own power to issue interim relief under Article 186 EC, in proceedings brought under Article 173 (12.12).

Interim relief should be available under the same conditions, and the national court was reminded that it must take into account the interest of the EU in such questions and that it could no longer grant or maintain in place interim relief in circumstances where there remained no real doubt that the EU measure in question was in fact valid.

We shall review the role of Article 177 in the system of judicial review of EU acts in Chapter 12.

8.8 The Authority and Effects of Rulings of the Court of Justice

No provision in the Treaties prescribes the effects or authority of rulings of the Court of Justice within the national legal orders. However, the Court has evolved an extensive case law on the effects of Article 177 rulings *vis-à-vis* the parties to the case, third parties and national courts.

A ruling of the Court of Justice in proceedings in which a reference has been made is binding on the national court, at least in so far as it chooses to resolve the case on the basis of EC law (Case 29/68 *Milch- Fett- und Eierkontor* v. *HZA Saarbrücken* [1969] ECR 165). On the other hand, a ruling on the interpretation of EC law does not have the effect of *res judicata* (decided issue) in other proceedings raising similar or identical questions (Cases 28–30/62 *Da Costa*). This means that the Court will not dismiss as inadmissible references made on points which it has already decided although, of course, the referring court may choose to withdraw the questions. The key question is whether a national court is bound to follow the rulings of the Court of Justice, or, where it disagrees with the ruling given by that Court, to ask it to reconsider its case law. This happened in Case 28/67 *Molkerei Zentrale Westfalen* v. *HZA Paderborn* ([1968] ECR 143) when the referring court asked the Court to review its interpretation of Article 95 EC in Case 57/65 *Lütticke* v. *HZA Saarlouis* ([1966] ECR 205). Although the point is not made explicitly, however, it must follow from Article 5 EC that all national courts are bound to decide cases in accordance with the case law of the Court of Justice. In the UK, section 3(1) of the European Communities Act 1972 removes all remaining doubts, in that it provides that questions of EC law, if not referred to the Court of Justice for a ruling, must be decided in accordance with the principles laid down by any relevant decision of the Court. In other words, the Court is inserted at the apex of the system of binding judicial precedent in the UK.

The position *vis-à-vis* other courts has been articulated more clearly by the Court in relation to the effects of rulings on invalidity. Although such a ruling is not strictly binding *erga omnes*, it is nonetheless 'sufficient reason for any other national court to regard that act as void' (Case 66/80 *International Chemical Corporation* v. *Amministrazione delle Finanze dello*

Stato [1981] ECR 1191 at p. 1216). It follows from a finding of invalidity that a national court must not apply any national provisions based on the invalid EU act (Case 162/82 *Cousin* [1983] ECR 1101).

Using Article 174(2) EC as a starting point, the Court of Justice has shown itself prepared to modulate the effects of a preliminary ruling according to the circumstances. Article 174(2) provides, in the context of the annulment of acts by means of direct actions under Article 173, that:

> 'In the case of a regulation . . . the Court of Justice shall, if it considers this necessary, state which of the effects of the regulation which it has declared void shall be considered as definitive.'

The Court has implicitly claimed a similar power in the context of preliminary rulings, holding in Case 4/79 *Providence Agricole de la Champagne* ([1980] ECR 2823) that it may rule that an act is valid for the past but invalid for the future. It has likewise asserted the power to place a temporal limitation upon the effects of an interpretative ruling under Article 177 (Case 43/75 *Defrenne* v. *SABENA* [1976] ECR 455 – the direct effect of Article 119; see more recently Case C-262/88 *Barber* v. *Guardian Royal Exchange* [1990] ECR I-1889 – the application of Article 119 to occupational pensions, where the ruling on limited temporal effects itself required further clarification: Case C-109/91 *Ten Oever* v. *Stichting Bedrijfspensioenfonds* [1993] ECR I-4879). However, it is clear that only the Court itself may place a temporal limitation upon the effects of a ruling, and that it must place that restriction in the context of the actual judgment in which it rules upon the interpretation or validity of the relevant provision (Case 61/79 *Denkavit Italiana* [1980] ECR 1205).

8.9   The Assessment of the Preliminary Reference Procedure

The Article 177 reference procedure has been described as a specific expression of the duty of mutual cooperation between the EU and its Member States contained in Article 5 EC, creating a system of judicial cooperation which has worked remarkably well and in which the Court has delivered numerous judgments of constitutional significance for the EU legal order (Slynn, 1992: 9–10). This is in part attributable to the manner in which the Court has chosen to frame its interpretative role, breaking down the barrier between interpretation and application, and phrasing its judgments on some occasions in terms which leave little doubt to the national court as to how it should apply the ruling. Equally important it has construed the task of giving interpretations of provisions of EC law as allowing it also to determine the effect of those provisions. This can be seen, for example, in the many rulings delivered by the Court since the groundbreaking case of Case 26/62 *Van Gend en Loos* v. *Nederlandse Administratie der Belastingen* ([1963] ECR 1) in which it has held that in certain circumstances provisions of EC law give rise to individual rights which national courts must protect.

The most important factor has, however, been the willingness of national courts to refer questions to the Court. Although 'reference rates' vary considerably between the Member States with, for example, German, Dutch, and Belgian courts showing themselves amongst the most ready to refer, and UK judges closer to the bottom of any reference 'league table' (particularly by head of population), the success of Article 177 in terms of volume of cases which have been generated cannot be denied. The Court now receives over 250 references each year from national courts, and decides rather over 100. Although this disparity can in part be accounted for by cases dealt with other than by the rendering of a judgment (e.g. withdrawal of the reference by the national court, order other than a full judgment), it inevitably means that the average length of proceedings has risen and now hovers around twenty months for preliminary references. Thus in many ways, the Court has become a victim of its own success, since by interpreting Article 177 in such a way as to expand its jurisdiction and to encourage national courts to refer it has a created a flood of cases with which it is barely equipped to deal, even after the transfers of jurisdiction in other areas to the Court of First Instance. Yet in principle the reference procedure should be a relatively light procedure for the Court. It does not decide cases, but merely answers questions. It does not decide the facts, or take a position (at least in principle) on matters of national law. In the context of its report to the Reflection Group preparing the IGC agenda (see 4.18), the Court commented upon the need for further procedural simplifications in relation to 'cases of lesser importance', and proposed, to give it greater flexibility, a change to Article 188(3) EC which requires its Rules of Procedure to be approved by the Council (it took until December 1994 for the Court's revised Rules of Procedure following the entry into force of the Treaty of Maastricht to be approved). However, the Court continued to express its opposition to any suggestion that all or part of the preliminary ruling jurisdiction should be given in the first instance to the Court of First Instance. A preliminary ruling procedure is not apt for resolution under a two-tier judicial structure.

Extensive work has been done on proposals to reform Article 177, both structurally and procedurally (Schermers *et al.*, 1987; Watson, 1986). Procedural proposals to reduce delays have included making the Article 177 procedure entirely written, with no oral argument. Structural reforms have concentrated on considering the reconciliation of two objectives: that the Court of Justice should continue to hear and to decide the important cases which develop the law and that national courts should increasingly decide the less important cases without recourse to the Court itself. Judicial education is widely recognised as a vital component in such a strategy. The efficiency of the Court's own work might also be increased by encouraging specialization amongst its own judiciary – a move which has been resisted in the past, which appears increasingly attractive as the areas covered by EC law range across ever wider fields of public and private law, calling for a 'multifunctional' court (Weatherill, 1995a: 282–4). Other suggested measures include 'docket control' (the Court chooses the cases it wishes to take) and a simplified procedure under which the Court can give a 'green light' to an interpretation proposed by the national court. While it may be that the Court is moving towards a stricter control of the question of admissibility (8.2), as yet no firm proposals have been tendered on docket control. Commentators have always stressed that docket control cannot be cost-free, at the very least in terms of tampering with sacrosanct principles such as the right to a judicial hearing. An additional method of reinforcing the level of cooperation between the national courts and the Court of Justice may be to institute lines of communication to seek to ensure that the Court does not receive multiple essentially similar but slightly different sets of questions which all require separate resolution.

Lawyers and political scientists agree about the significance of the Article 177 reference procedure: it has contributed greatly to the widespread acceptance of the authority of EC law and of the Court of Justice's rulings in particular. Exactly how this has occurred is not so clear (Alter, 1995; 1996; Wincott, 1995b). After all, there is a slight paradox in the suggestion that involving more courts in the judicial hierarchy by, in effect, making national courts into 'Community courts' (Maher, 1994) will have this effect. It seems equally probable that this could lead to a watering down of the authority of EC law, through a loss of uniformity, not to its strengthening. Amongst the 'political' explanations which have been tendered include the use by the Court of its 'mask of law' (Burley and Mattli, 1993), or 'legal formalism', behind which it has brought about a startling political agenda; and the effect of 'intercourt competition', both vertically between courts within the same state and between the courts of different Member States, which has enhanced the status of EC law, as national courts 'compete' to achieve compliance. Equally, lawyers would point to the Court's astute harnessing of the resources of national law to achieve compliance: just as the EU lacks powers of direct implementation in the administrative sphere, but can effect through other means considerable changes in regulatory culture in the Member States (7.1), so it lacks the powers of national courts to issue and enforce injunctions, and to make and enforce compensation orders. As the next two chapters will show, building on the opportunities provided by the Article 177 reference procedure, the Court has ensured that the rules of EC law now shape to an astonishing extent, from inception to conclusion, from issues of constitutional principle to procedural minutiae, any action before the national courts in which EU rights and duties are at issue.

Summary

1   Article 177 EC provides an organic connection between national courts and the Court of Justice, enabling national courts to obtain authoritative rulings on the interpretation and validity of provisions of EC law.

2   The preliminary rulings procedure is based on a separation of functions between the national court and the Court of Justice, and its effectiveness depends upon the cooperative application of this distinction by all courts.

3   In general the Court of Justice does not interfere with the discretion of the national court in referring questions. However, it will not answer abstract or hypothetical questions, and has imposed the requirement that there be a genuine dispute in the national court. The national court must supply the Court of Justice with sufficient information of a factual and legal nature to enable it to answer the questions.

4   Article 177 provides for references on questions of the interpretation (and, implicitly, the effect) of:

– provisions of the Treaty and other international agreements binding the EU;

– provisions of EU legislation, including non-binding acts.

References on validity can be made in respect of binding legal acts of the EU.

5   The concept of a 'court or tribunal' of a Member State is interpreted broadly as any body representing the judicial power of the state.

6   Inferior courts have a discretion to refer; orders for references may be appealed within the national juridical structure. The obligation to refer is imposed on courts of last resort, and is qualified in only three cases:

– in interlocutory proceedings, where the issues of EC law can be reconsidered at trial;

– where the Court has already answered materially identical questions;

– where the limited doctrine of *acte clair* as laid down by the Court in *CILFIT* applies.

7   Only the Court of Justice may rule upon the validity of EU acts. The Court has indicated that in cases of urgency a national court should invalidate the national measures implementing an EU act which is allegedly invalid, or adopt other appropriate interim measures, making a reference on the validity of the EU act.

8   The authority of rulings of the Court of Justice is such that in general no national court should depart from a position taken by the Court of Justice. The Court has asserted the power in limited circumstances to restrict the temporal effects of its rulings.

9   The preliminary rulings procedure has been effective in generating a flow of cases to the Court of Justice in which it has laid down many of the central constitutional precepts of the EU legal order. In some ways, Article 177 has proved too successful, with increasingly long delays before the Court is now able to give judgment on references for preliminary rulings. It has been suggested that the Court's increased rigour in examining the admissibility of some references for preliminary rulings is the first signs of a new policy of 'docket' control.

Questions

1   What purposes does Article 177 serve within the EU legal order?
2   What is meant by the 'separation of functions' in the context of Article 177?
3   Which bodies may refer questions to the Court of Justice?
4   Why did the Court refuse to answer the questions posed by the Italian court in *Foglia* v. *Novello*?
5   Was the Court correct to refuse to answer the questions posed by the German court in *Meilicke*?
6   In what circumstances is a national court obliged to make a preliminary reference to the Court of Justice?
7   Why does the Court maintain that it has sole authority to declare invalid provisions of EC law?

Workshops

1   'In providing for references on questions of the interpretation and validity of EC law from national courts to the Court of Justice, the authors of the Treaty settled on a compromise solution to the problem of developing a uniform application of EC law within the EU under the control of a single supranational court.'
     Discuss in the light of the detailed provisions and conditions which govern the operation of Article 177.
2   Refer back to the text of the workshop in Chapter 7. What would be the appropriate action for the Supreme Administrative Court of Zeno to take if it believes that the EU Directive is unlawful?

Further Reading

Anderson (1994), 'The Admissibility of Preliminary References', 14 *YEL* 179.
Arnull (1990b), 'References to the European Court', 15 *ELRev.* 375.
Barav (1980), 'Preliminary Censorship? The Judgment of the European Court in *Foglia* v. *Novello'*, 5 *ELRev.* 443.
Bebr (1988), 'The Reinforcement of the Constitutional Review of Community Acts under Article 177 EEC', 25 *CMLRev.* 684.
Lenaerts (1994), 'Form and Substance of the Preliminary Rulings Procedure', in Curtin and Heukels (1994).
Mancini and Keeling (1991), 'From *CILFIT* to *ERT*: the Constitutional Challenge facing the European Court', 11 *YEL* 1.
Schermers *et al.* (eds.) (1987), esp. Bebr, 'The Preliminary Proceedings of Article 177 EEC – Problems and Suggestions for Improvement', p. 345.
Tesauro (1993), 'The Effectiveness of Judicial Protection and Co-operation between the Court of Justice and the National Courts', 13 *YEL* 1.
Watson (1986), 'Asser Institute Colloquium on European Law 1985: Experience and Problems in applying Article 177 EEC', 23 *CMLRev.* 207.

9 EC Law and the Legal Systems of the Member States

9.1 The Nature of the EU Legal Order and its Impact upon the National Legal Orders

The problem we shall consider in this chapter is how the evolving EU legal order has established itself as a superior legal order operating within, but nonetheless independently of the national legal systems. It demonstrates how the Court of Justice has used the organic connection offered by Article 177 EC both to assert its own ability to give authoritative interpretations of the meaning and effect of EC law, and to emphasise that where EC law applies, national courts themselves must act as 'Community courts' (Maher, 1994), interpreting and applying EC law subject to the authority of the Court of Justice. Once the general principles have been identified in this chapter, Chapter 10 will focus on certain key aspects of the way in which they have been instrumentalised, with a particular focus, as necessary, upon the Member States, and especially the UK.

The edifice of rules and principles set out in this chapter has been built out of relatively unpromising material. The constitutive treaties themselves contain little indication of the precise nature of the relationship between EC law and national law or of the extent to which, if at all, the legal order created by the Treaties of Paris and Rome should be regarded as differing from the system of international law in general. Reference can be made, of course, to Article 5 EC (the duty of Community loyalty applying to Member States and institutions alike) and Article 164 EC (the duty of the Court of Justice to ensure that 'the law is observed'). With the exception of these provisions, the principles of a unique supranational legal order have evolved entirely through judicial action.

A cautionary note about the role of the Court is sounded in a recent 'political science' analysis of the 'constitutionalisation' process, which it would be useful to bear in mind here:

'On reading some of legal literature it would be easy to come to the conclusion that this process of constitutionalization inevitably followed on once the initial steps had been taken. As . . . political scientists come to take the Court of Justice seriously in the analysis of European integration, there is a danger that this sense of a teleological legal process of ever closer union will be swallowed whole. The fact that the Court has often acted as a protagonist for integration, and that its interpretation of Community law often sought to bring about the ever closer union of Europe, should not be allowed to cover over the fact that even these foundational doctrines of Community law had to be constructed' (Wincott, 1995b: 590).

This chapter will describe the essential features of an effective supranational legal order, in which the law and the institutions entrusted with the tasks of enforcing and applying the law have indeed claimed a central role as motors of the integration project. The key features have commonly been termed the direct effect and supremacy of EC law, and these concepts have been referred to already in earlier chapters. They will be considered in greater detail here, within a constitutional framework which identifies the different levels at which EC law impacts upon the national legal orders. They will also be located within the broader notion of the 'effectiveness' or '*effet utile*' of EC law. In a classic exposition of the doctrine of direct effect, Pescatore (1983) argued that it is fundamental to any legal system that the institutions responsible for its stewardship should seek always to render the law operative. In keeping with this pragmatic philosophy, the approach taken in this chapter of describing the important legal concepts and principles is buttressed by the attempt, in Chapter 10, to identify the practical mechanisms evolved by the Court of Justice in order to make the EU legal order fully and uniformly effective throughout the Member States, and to do this in the context of the type of fundamental constitutional dialogue between the different legal orders highlighted as important by Stone Sweet (1995) (8.1).

In two early statements of principle, the Court laid down the markers for establishing the parameters of the EU legal order. In Case 26/62 *Van Gend en Loos* v. *Nederlandse Administratie der Belastingen* ([1963] ECR 1 at p. 12) it asserted that:

'the Community constitutes a new legal order of international law, for the benefit of which states have limited their sovereign rights, albeit within limited fields, and the subjects of which comprise not only member states but also their nationals.'

It continued in similar vein the following year in Case 6/64 *Costa* v. *ENEL* ([1964] ECR 585 at p. 593):

'By contrast with ordinary international treaties, the EEC Treaty has created its own legal system which, on the entry into force of the Treaty, became an integral part of the legal system of the member states and which their courts are bound to apply.'

These remarkable statements by the Court of Justice are now accepted as commonplace – although they were radical at the time. Rather than being mere descriptions of what the EU legal order then was, they constituted at the time normative assertions by the Court about what it wished that order to resemble. It is remarkable not only that the Court expressed itself in those terms in the early 1960s in cases of first impression on the relationship between EC law and the national legal orders, but also that it has experienced astonishing success in fashioning a legal order after the model put forward in those cases – even though the progress of the case law does not always follow a linear model. From these statements can be extrapolated four elements which are often taken to provide a full explanation of the EC law/national law interface:

(a) the EU legal order is a separate and autonomous system distinct from the general order of public international law; the Court has therefore been able to claim a free hand in evolving the substance of that legal order;

(b) EC law is part of national law, which means that national courts can and must apply it in accordance with the authoritative rulings of the Court of Justice;

(c) the EU legal order is based on a transfer of sovereign powers by the Member States to the EU; Member States can no longer exercise those powers which have been transferred to the EU, and must abstain from any acts which hinder the EU in its exercise of these powers;

(d) Member States and EU citizens are the subjects of EC law, and as subjects have rights and obligations flowing from and under the Treaties.

On closer examination, however, these explanations cannot be regarded as adequate on their own. What they do not provide is a framework for distinguishing between four different aspects of the EC law/national law interface:

1. The 'policies' which structure the overall approach of the Court, and which result from its understanding of what the role of the law and of the judicial apparatus should be within the EU.

2. The constitutional qualities which distinguish EC law as a species of 'federal law', within a federal-type legal order.

3. The techniques – of a more or less novel nature – which the Court of Justice has devised and developed to give effect to those constitutional qualities.

4. The principles which the Court has developed to ensure a degree of supervision over national courts when they give effect to the techniques when faced by individual cases arising within the national legal orders which raise issues of EC law.

This chapter characterises points 2–4 as different levels of *impact* of EC law upon national law, which are structured by the three policy objectives identified under point 1 which the Court of Justice pursues more or less consistently:

- ensuring the '*effectiveness*' of EC law; this has not only occurred in relation to the EC law/national law interface, but also, as Chapter 7 has shown, in relation to administrative processes for the EC enforcement of EC law; it is a consistent underlying theme of the case law which is examined throughout Part III, as will already be apparent from Chapter 8;
- pursuing the *uniform application* of EC law, already discussed in relation to Article 177 references, but equally apparent in the degree of precision regarding the duties of national courts which emerges in many of the cases discussed here;
- constructing the *individual* within a framework of legal protection; this is not just a question of ensuring that individuals can rely upon (economic) EC rights, but also of reinforcing the symbolism of an EU legal order 'close to the citizen'.

Looking in more detail at the three levels of impact, it is perhaps important to note that this scheme differs somewhat from the approach conventionally adopted in much of the literature on these questions. In particular it will be seen that it places 'supremacy' and 'direct effect' at different levels, although many have characterised these notions as twin 'pillars' of the EU legal order. The following discussion will show why they should be regarded as essentially quite different notions. Some commentators have used a similar frame of analysis when they talk of 'second' and 'third' generation EC rights. These correspond broadly to the second and third levels identified here (e.g. Docksey, 1995).

1. EC law has certain distinctive *constitutional* qualities, as a *superior* source of law (the supremacy of EC law), and as a source of law which penetrates into the national legal orders notwithstanding its 'international' origins or the particularities of the various national constitutional orders (the *direct applicability* of EC law).
2. In order to guarantee these constitutional qualities, in the spirit of the policy objectives already identified, the Court of Justice has developed a number of *techniques* for ensuring that EC law can be enforced; some will already be familiar from earlier chapters; others will be introduced and explained in this chapter:
- EC law can in certain circumstances be relied upon directly in national courts as giving rise to rights and duties which those courts must protect ('*direct effect*', or the '*justiciable*' quality of EC law);
- a closely related idea is that EC law generates *responsibilities* which are imposed on national public authorities (and, in certain circumstances, individuals), leading, in particular to the notion that Member States are subject to compensatory obligations where they fail to give effect to EC law, operating for the benefit of individuals (often termed the principle of State liability);
- as a superior source of law, EC law has a *pre-emptive* effect on national law and national legislative competence;

- as EC law is part of national law, in any event national courts are subject to an *interpretative* obligation to give effect to EC law.
3. However, the EU lacks a complete 'federal' order, comprising judicial, remedial and procedural structures to give effect to these principles of EC law. Hence it must borrow from national law, requiring national courts to give effect to EC rights using the techniques of national law, and upholding in that context a principle of *national procedural autonomy*, but subject to two overriding principles:
- national remedies must be no less favourable than those available for the enforcement of equivalent national rights (the principle of non-discrimination);
- national remedies must not operate in such a way as to render the enforcement of EC rights impossible in practice (the principle of effective remedies). Clearly the articulation of this principle by the Court of Justice is very closely related to its overall policy objective of ensuring the effectiveness of EC law.

Figure 9.1 sets out these concepts in the form of a figure. The main objective of this figure is to show the different levels of analysis along a *horizontal* plane. However, it does hint at certain vertical links between the constitutional qualities of EC law, and the techniques for the enforcement of EC law which derive in main from those two qualities. Justiciability and responsibility owe perhaps more to the direct applicability of EC law; pre-emption and interpretation can more easily be seen as deriving from the superior nature of EC law. However, each of the four techniques is ultimately dependent upon the existence and respect for the *twin* constitutional qualities of EC law.

The review of the case law in these chapters will make clear that the emphasis of legal development at present lies in a number of specific fields:

- the refinement of a number of *detailed questions* relating to the scope of *direct effect*, the principle itself having been already long settled;
- settlement of the *scope* and *nature* of the *pre-emptive* effect of EC law, responding in particular to certain changes in the regulatory pattern of EC law;
- *continued development* of the notion of 'responsibility', and of the *conditions* under which it can apply;
- *more detailed articulation* of the contours of the non-discrimination and (especially) the effective remedies principles, as the Court's attention is drawn to an ever wider range of potential national fetters upon the effective enjoyment of EC rights, and as the Court examines the detailed implications for national legal orders of giving effect to the principle of responsibility.

To return to the point about the difference between supremacy and direct effect, it will now be seen that supremacy is a constitutional quality

Figure 9.1 Framework for analysing the different levels at which EC law impacts upon national law

Policy objectives of the Court of Justice	Ensuring the effectiveness of EC law	Uniformity of EC law		The legal protection of individuals as legal subjects	
Constitutional qualities of EC law (level one)	EC law penetrates into the national legal orders		EC law is a superior source of law within the national legal orders		
Techniques for individual protection (level two)	Justiciability (direct effect)	Responsibility (State liability)	Interpretation (indirect effect)		Pre-emption
Principles governing (*prima facie* autonomous) national remedies (level three)	National remedies must be made available on a non-discriminatory basis		National remedies must be sufficiently effective to ensure protection of EC rights		

of EC law, whereas direct effect is now increasingly seen as one of a number of techniques for giving effect to those constitutional qualities (albeit in the early years probably the most important).

9.2 The Penetration of EC Law into the National Legal Orders

The first constitutional quality of EC law which we shall examine is that it becomes part of the national legal order. From the perspective of the Court, this follows simply from the nature of EC law combined with the fact of accession. The strict logic of the transfer of sovereign powers thesis is that the Treaties themselves and any legal acts adopted by the EU institutions within the scope of their competence take their place within the domestic legal order and form part of the sources of law which the national judge must apply. Within the sphere of Community competence, EC law must take precedence. Moreover, as the Court emphasised in Opinion 1/91 *Re the Draft Agreement on a European Economic Area* ([1991] ECR I-6079), the transfer of competence has occurred 'in ever wider fields' (para. 21 of the judgment).

The structure is akin to a federal legal system, with the federal and state authorities acting within their respective spheres of competence, and with courts adjudicating over the boundaries between those spheres. In this chapter we shall refer to this quality of EC law as its 'direct applicability'. For the avoidance of terminological confusion, two points of explanation must be made.

First, the use of 'direct applicability' in this sense accords well with the terminological usage of the Court, which has referred to this concept as meaning

> 'that the rules of Community law must be fully and uniformly applied in all the Member States from the date of their entry into force and for so long as they continue in force' (Case 106/77 *Amministrazione delle Finanze dello Stato* v. *Simmenthal SpA (Simmenthal II)* [1978] ECR 629 at p. 643).

It is to be distinguished in this context from the justiciability of provisions of EC law, that is, from the question of whether a particular provision is capable of giving rise to rights and obligations enforceable by a court of law. This is the concept of 'direct effect', and is one which, in the framework set out in this chapter, operates at a 'lower' level of the EC law/national interface.

Second, confusion need not arise from the fact that Article 189 EC refers to regulations, and apparently only regulations, as being 'directly applicable in all the Member States'. The Court has made it plain on numerous occasions that it is not only regulations which are directly applicable in the sense of being part of the national legal system. Directives are undoubtedly also part of the national legal system. However, this does not detract from the fact that regulations do have certain special qualities, amounting in the view of Usher (1981) to a 'stop sign' to national legislatures which make them particularly useful instruments for the EU law-maker in fields where absolute uniformity of the rules applied is of paramount importance (e.g. customs, agriculture, social security of migrant workers) (see also 5.10). Direct applicability in this sense is a matter of legislative technique. In this chapter we use a broader notion which includes but also transcends the 'stop sign' argument, and extends to cover also the wider 'pre-emptive' qualities of EU rules of law generally (see 9.13).

9.3 EC law as a Superior Source of Law

Nowhere in the constitutive Treaties is it stated that EC law takes precedence over national law, although such a position can be derived from the duty of Community loyalty contained in Article 5 EC). Nonetheless, the supremacy of EC law has been broadly accepted since the early 1960s. Like the penetration of EC law into national law, this constitutional quality is drawn by the Court of Justice from the 'transfer of sovereign powers' thesis which makes it

> 'impossible for states, as a corollary, to accord precedence to a unilateral and subsequent measure over a legal system accepted by them on the basis of reciprocity' (Case 6/64 *Costa* v. *ENEL* [1964] ECR 585 at p. 593).

In Case 11/70 *Internationale Handelsgesellschaft* ([1970] ECR 1125), the Court held that EC law prevails over all forms of national law, including national constitutions and fundamental rights enshrined in those constitutions: EU measures derive their validity solely from EC law, and thus the validity of an EU measure or its effect within a Member State cannot be affected by objections that it runs counter to either fundamental rights as guaranteed by the constitution of that State or the principles of a national constitutional structure. The Court made the point very strongly:

> 'The law stemming from the Treaty, an independent source of law, cannot because of its very nature be overridden by rules of national law, however framed, without being deprived of its character as Community law and without the legal basis of the Community itself being called into question' (p. 1134).

In order to counter the objection that it is not reasonable to replace the sovereignty of nation states which offer citizens constitutional guarantees of fundamental rights with an EU which does not, and in order to head off possible rebellions by the German and Italian Constitutional Courts, the Court has evolved the doctrine of EU fundamental rights (see 6.7). So it would seem that the justification for supremacy in this form is that it is inherent in the ideal of creating a new 'federal-type' legal order which lies at the heart of the project of economic integration in Europe, which has always had as its ultimate objective a 'union of peoples' (see the Preamble to the EC Treaty). The process of economic integration would be much less effective if Member States were able to hinder the attainment of EU goals by denying the superiority of EC norms.

9.4   National Constitutions and the Reception of EC Law

The attraction of basing the penetration of EC law within the domestic legal systems upon its own inherent qualities, rather than upon some constitutional mechanism for giving effect to EC law is that it prevents the effectiveness of EC law being contingent upon the vagaries of national constitutional and judicial attitudes to incorporating the provisions of a 'foreign' legal system. In other words, it should enhance the uniform application of EC law. In reality, of course, as the Treaty itself recognises in its references to national mechanisms for ratification of international instruments (e.g. Article N TEU which provides for amendments to the Treaties to enter into force after ratification), the incorporation of EC law into the domestic legal system usually depends upon the creation of the appropriate 'gateway'. In the UK, where courts will refuse to take account of Treaties until they have been translated into domestic law by Act of Parliament, that gateway is to be found in the European Communities Act 1972, in particular sections 2 and 3. This will be examined in 10.8. Moreover, the point has already been made (8.1), that the constitutionalisation of the Treaties has not been an entirely unilateral endeavour on the part of the Court of Justice. It has also been the result of a number of constitutional dialogues, in which it continues to be involved. It is therefore appropriate to look briefly at the constitutional reception which Member States have given to EC law.

The written constitutions of some of the other Member States create models for the transfer or delegation of sovereign powers to international organisations which are more or less perfectly in accordance with the simplicity of the Court's own transfer thesis. For example, Article 92 of the Dutch constitution and Article 25*bis* of the Belgian constitution provide for the possibility of the transfer or attribution of sovereign powers to international organisations. Article 28(3) of the Greek constitution is rather more detailed. It provides that:

'Greece may freely proceed, by virtue of an Act passed by the votes of the absolute majority of the total number of members of Parliament, to limitations on the exercise of national sovereignty, provided that this is dictated by an important national interest, does not affect human rights and the foundations of democratic government and is effected in conformity with the principles of equality, and on condition of reciprocity.'

As we shall see, it is not possible for the domestic constitution to place riders such as these upon its transfer of powers to the EU, although in practice national judges may be unwilling for a variety of reasons to recognise the full force of EC law in the domestic system. Such provisions may also be important in a wider political context, in so far as they may express particular national aspirations in relation to the EU, or may reflect the experiences of a country relatively recently emerged from dictatorship.

Since the introduction of changes in connection with the ratification of the Treaty of Maastricht, Germany now has a detailed constitutional provision specifically concerned with the problems of German involvement, as a democratic and federal state under the rule of law, in the autonomous legal order of the EU (Article 23 of the Basic Law). Of particular interest is the fact that special provision is made for the political participation of the *Länder*, and of the *Bundestag*, the Upper Chamber of the Parliament where the *Länder* are represented.

9.5 Conceptions of International Law in the Member States

The second factor conditioning the reception of EC law is the conception of the relationship between public international law and national law. Classically, there are two conceptions: monism and dualism (Jackson, 1992). Under monism, international law and municipal law are conceived of as part of one single legal system, with international law taking precedence. A dualist conception views international law and municipal law as two separate systems, each supreme within its own sphere. For example, since Parliament in the UK is sovereign, a dualist position on international law must necessarily be adopted by the UK courts which can recognise international obligations only once, and to the extent that, they have been incorporated into national law by Parliament in the form of a statute (*British Airways* v. *Laker Airways* [1984] 3 All ER 39). No account was taken of the EEC Treaty after agreement by the Crown on behalf of the UK but before the passing of the European Communities Act 1972 (*Blackburn* v. *Attorney General* [1971] 1 All ER 1380). In contrast, both the Dutch constitution (Articles 91–94) and the French constitution (Article 55) provide that duly ratified international obligations take precedence over municipal law. The Belgian courts have also achieved the same constitutional position in the absence of an explicit provision by proclaiming that international obligations have an effect superior to domestic law in the Belgian legal system (*Fromagerie Le Ski* [1972] CMLR 330).

Ostensibly since the ratification such as that referred to in the Dutch and French constitutions will often require some form of parliamentary approval, there is little difference between the monist and dualist positions in terms of the formalities required before international law can be recognised domestically. Where a difference does remain is in judicial attitudes subsequent to incorporation. The UK judges consistently betray their dualist heritage, either because they treat the application and enforcement of EC law principally as a matter of construction of the European Communities Act 1972 (see, for example, *Duke* v. *GEC Reliance* [1988] 1 All ER 626 discussed in Chapter 10), or because they treat the rules of EC law which they do apply as if they were statutes, interpreting them accordingly (see for example the interpretation of breach of Articles 85 and 86 EC as if it were a breach of statutory duty in *Garden Cottage Foods* v. *Milk Marketing Board* [1984] AC 130). In contrast, even the French *Conseil d'Etat* (Supreme Administrative Court) – long resistant to the claims of EC law – has now begun to refer to the basis for the authority of EC law in France as being the transfer of sovereign powers (*Boisdet* [1991] 1 CMLR 3).

9.6   EC Law and the Sovereignty of Parliament

There remain substantial obstacles to the successful reconciliation of the implications of membership of the EU with the classic Diceyian thesis of the sovereignty of Parliament. The sovereignty of Parliament is to be distinguished from the sovereignty of the UK as a nation state. The sovereignty of all the Member States is limited, or perhaps better 'pooled' or 'shared' by accession to the EU. However, the existence of a set of rules governing the conduct of the UK courts in relation to Parliament, under which the latter is recognised as the supreme law-making body, does present particular difficulties for the reception of EC law in the UK. Of most significance are the rule that Parliament may do anything except bind its successors and the universally accepted principle that courts may not call into question the validity of Acts of Parliament. From the first principle, it would appear that future Parliaments could not be restrained from legislating expressly in a manner which is inconsistent with the UK's Community obligations. If this principle is coupled with the doctrine of the implied repeal of Acts of Parliament, it is arguable that the European Communities Act 1972 would be vulnerable to change as a result of subsequent inconsistent enactments, regardless of whether a repudiation was intended or not. Upholding the sovereignty of Parliament thus comes into conflict with the loss of national sovereignty inherent in accession to the EU. This is expressed most clearly by the Court of Justice in Case 6/64 *Costa* v. *ENEL* (at p. 594):

'The transfer by the States from their domestic legal systems to the Community legal system of the rights and obligations arising under the Treaty carries with it a permanent limitation of their sovereign rights, against which a subsequent unilateral act incompatible with the concept of the Community cannot prevail.'

The transfer of sovereign powers thesis denies the effectiveness of uni-lateral repudiations of EU obligations. Such repudiations would be seen merely as violations of the Treaty system. In the absence of a negotiated return of the powers originally transferred, a state will not be released from its obligations under the Treaties. Such a position is also in conformity with the international law principle of *pacta sunt servanda.*

At the time of the accession of the UK to what was then the European Communities, a position emerged on the sovereignty of Parliament which contrasted somewhat with Diceyian absolutism. Authors such as Mitchell (Mitchell, Kuipers and Gall, 1972; Mitchell, 1979) argued that British constitutional history has always demonstrated a capacity for constitu-tional change, in recognition of changes in political circumstances. It is precisely out of political circumstances that a convention of Parliamentary sovereignty has arisen. Now that the UK has acceded to a political entity within which absolute Parliamentary sovereignty is no longer tenable, it must be regarded as abrogated, with legislative and judicial sovereignty passing to the European Community, within its spheres of competence. However, the majority of British constitutional lawyers still adhere to the orthodox position that the binding effect of EC law in the UK flows only from the European Communities Act 1972, an Act which Parliament remains as free to repeal as any other Act, although for the time being it chooses not to (e.g. Munro, 1987).

Not surprisingly, the courts have for the most part declined to pass comment on theoretical conflicts between Parliamentary sovereignty and EU obligations. The essential problem is, of course, whether the UK judges now owe their allegiance to the EU authorities in respect of matters falling within the competence of those authorities, just as they undoubt-edly owe allegiance to the Westminster Parliament in respect of matters falling within the jurisdiction of that body. According to Lord Denning MR in *Macarthys* v. *Smith* ([1979] 3 All ER 325 at p. 329):

'If the time should come when Parliament deliberately passes an Act with the intention of repudiating the Treaty or any provision of it or intentionally of acting inconsistently with it and says so in express terms then I should have thought it would be the duty of our courts to follow the statute of our Parliament. I do not envisage any such situation. . . . Unless there is such an intentional and express repudiation of the Treaty, it is our duty to give priority to the Treaty.'

For the most part, however, the judges have contented themselves with resolving, in generally satisfactory terms, the specific practical problems thrown up by the penetration of EC law into the UK legal system. These problems will be examined, using examples, in Chapter 10.

9.7   The Instrumentalisation of the Constitutional Qualities of EC Law

The next level of detailed analysis involves the four techniques developed by the Court of Justice for the purposes of giving effect to these two principal constitutional qualities. They have not all been accorded equal attention. By far the largest proportion of cases have been concerned with the question whether provisions of EC law can give rise to rights in national courts which individuals may rely upon, the conditions in which this can occur, the range of provisions which are so covered, and the duties which they cast. Pescatore described 'direct effect' as an 'infant disease' of EC law (Pescatore, 1983). The justiciability of provisions of EC law was an instrument devised at an early stage in the history of the EU legal order for maximising the effectiveness of EC law. Historically, it has proved most important in those Member States such as the Netherlands and the UK where, as a matter of national law, EC law appears capable of overriding national law only where it generates rights enforceable by individuals (see Chapter 10). Partly as a consequence of some of the tensions which have been thrown up by the Court's own case law on direct effect, it has increasingly emerged not as an isolated centrepiece of the EC law/national law interface, but as one of several techniques each deserving of separate and equal attention.

9.8   The Justiciability of EC Law in National Courts

The principle that provisions of EC law may be justiciable in national courts provided they satisfy certain conditions has been recognised since the landmark case of *Van Gend en Loos*. In that case, the Court held that an importer could rely upon the standstill clause in Article 12 EC, prohibiting any increases in customs duties between the Member States after the coming into force of the Treaty, in order to challenge such an increase by the Dutch authorities in the Dutch courts. The self-executing nature of Treaty provision is a phenomenon not entirely unknown in international law generally (Jackson, 1992; Wyatt, 1982) and flows from the principle of direct applicability as enunciated in this chapter. The most powerful justification for the doctrine of direct effect, as it is known, is that it enhances the effectiveness or '*effet utile*' of binding norms of EC law. As a doctrine which principally protects the individual, and often gives individuals rights which they can rely upon as against Member States, it sets up a mechanism for the individual or indirect enforcement of EC law. In practical terms, this relies upon the operation of the preliminary rulings procedure examined in Chapter 8. The existence of a centralised enforcement procedure in the hands of the Commission under Article 169 EC has never been considered an argument for preventing the decentralised enforcement of EC law.

However, the doctrine of direct effect is not simply limited to the Member State/EU citizen interface. Although the principle that states should not be able to rely upon their own failure or inefficiency in implementing EC law in order to deny to individuals the rights which flow from EU provisions – the so-called 'estoppel argument' (Curtin, 1990b) – is a powerful argument for direct effect, it is not the only one. The need to ensure the effectiveness of EC law in some circumstances applies to relations between private parties. In appropriate cases, EC law is also justiciable in disputes between individuals. In other words, certain provisions of EC law may be horizontally as well as vertically directly effective.

9.9 Prerequisites of Direct Effect

To be directly effective, a provision of EC law must constitute a complete legal obligation capable of enforcement as such by a court. This means that it must be sufficiently precise and unconditional (Cases C-6, 9/90 *Francovich* v. *Italian Republic (Francovich I)* [1991] ECR I-5357). In its early case law the Court appeared to limit direct effect to negative obligations, such as that contained in Article 12 EC, which prohibited Member States from raising their customs duties or introducing any new customs duties after the coming into force of the Treaty. It was held in *Van Gend en Loos* (at p. 13) that

'the wording of Article 12 contains a clear and unconditional prohibition which is not a positive but a negative obligation. This obligation, moreover, is not qualified by any reservation on the part of States which would make its implementation conditional upon a positive measure enacted under national law. The very nature of this prohibition makes it ideally adapted to produce direct effects in the legal relationship between Member States and their subjects.'

That limitation has since been dropped, and the Court has subsequently held that numerous provisions of the EC Treaty are capable of judicial enforcement, including Article 30 (prohibiting non-tariff barriers to inter-state trade in goods erected by Member States), Article 48 (guaranteeing free movement of workers), Articles 52 and 59 (guaranteeing freedom of establishment and freedom to provide services), Articles 85 and 86 (prohibiting anti-competitive conduct by undertakings) and Article 95 (prohibiting taxation by the Member States which discriminates against imported products) (for a fuller list of the directly effective Treaty provisions, see Collins, 1990: 122 *et seq.*). Articles 85 and 86 provide a perfect example of Treaty provisions which are horizontally directly effective. The prohibitions on anti-competitive agreements and the abuse of a dominant position enacted in these provisions are by their very nature aimed at economically active individuals, defined as 'undertakings'. The obligations inherent in the provisions can be enforced against infringing undertakings, at the instance of other individuals injured by anti-competitive conduct, in national courts. Some provisions, such as Article 6 EC (the general prohibition on discrimination on grounds of nationality) are judicially enforceable in combination with another provision of the Treaty. For example, Article 128 EEC, as it was drafted prior to the Treaty of Maastricht, established an outline competence on the part of the Community in relation to the creation of a Community vocational training policy. Article 128 read in conjunction with what was then Article 7 EEC created a right to non-discrimination on grounds of nationality for vocational training students who move to study in another Member State, at least as regards matters of educational access (Case 293/83 *Gravier* v. *City of Liège* [1985] ECR 593 – e.g. they cannot be charged fees when domestic students are not).

Those Treaty provisions which have been held not to be capable of judicial enforcement are those which are worded in conditional or contingent terms. The pre-1994 formulation of the provisions on the free movement of capital provided a good example. For example, Article 71 EC provided that:

'Member States shall endeavour to avoid introducing within the Community any new exchange restrictions on the movement of capital and current payments connected with such movements, and shall endeavour not to make existing rules more restrictive.'

In Case 203/80 *Casati* ([1981] ECR 2595 at p. 2616) the Court noted that

'by using the term "shall endeavour", the wording of that provision departs noticeably from the more imperative forms of wording employed in other similiar provisions concerning restrictions on the free movement of goods, persons and services. It is apparent from the wording that, in any event, the first paragraph of Article 71 does not impose on the Member States an unconditional obligation capable of being relied upon by individuals.'

Since 1 January 1994, this provision has been superceded by stricter obligations in relation to the free movement of capital (Articles 73A–73C), linked to the move towards Economic and Monetary Union. Even before that date, one of the key directives of the 1992 programme had largely given unconditional force to this aspect of the internal market (Directive 88/361). In two cases in 1995 concerned with exports of banknotes out of Spain, the Court held that the relevant provisions of both the Directive and the Treaty were capable of giving rise to rights which individuals may enforce in national courts (Cases C-358, 416/93 *Bordessa* [1995] ECR I-361; Cases C-163/94, etc. *Sanz de Lera* [1996] 1 CMLR 631 [1995] ECR I-4821).

Similarly there are certain provisions of the Treaty which grant a discretion to Member States which make it impossible to identify a particular obligation to which they are subject. An example is Article 97 EC, which states that:

'Member States which levy a turnover tax calculated on a cumulative multi-stage tax system may, in the case of internal taxation imposed by them on imported products or of repayments allowed by them on exported products, establish average rates for products or groups of products' (see Case 28/67 *Molkerei Zentrale Westfalen* v. *HZA Paderborn* [1968] ECR 143).

9.10 Provisions of EC Law Capable of Judicial Enforcement

All provisions of EC law containing a binding obligation of conduct or of result are capable of direct judicial enforcement, providing they are sufficiently precise and unconditional. No category of legal acts is *a priori* excluded. Thus in addition to Treaty provisions, the Court has held that provisions of regulations (Case 43/71 *Politi* v. *Italian Minister of Finance* [1971] ECR 1039), directives (Case 41/74 *Van Duyn* v. *Home Office* [1974] ECR 1337), decisions (Case 9/70 *Grad* [1970] ECR 825) and agreements with third countries (Case 104/81 *Kupferberg* [1982] ECR 3641) are all capable of giving rise to rights which individuals can enforce in national courts. Notably, in the latter category, the Court has ascribed direct effect only to certain types of international agreements. It has, in particular, refused to accept that the GATT (at least in its old pre-WTO form) can have direct effect, even though it does 'bind the Community' (Cases 2–4/72 *International Fruit Company NV* v. *Produktschap voor Groenten en Fruit* [1972] ECR 1219; Cheyne, 1994). This has rendered the internal impact of GATT within the EU somewhat 'ineffectual' (Scott, 1995b: 149).

In the case of regulations there was little doubt that they should be capable of enforcement in national courts, since they are expressed to be 'directly applicable', which, according to the Court in *Politi* (at p. 1048), means that 'by reason of their nature and their function in the system of the sources of Community law, regulations have direct effect and are as such capable of creating individual rights which national courts must protect.'

Occasionally, however, regulations will not be capable of judicial enforcement, because of the nature of the obligations which they contain (e.g. they are too vague, or are contingent upon action by a third party). This point was recognised by AG Warner in Case 131/79 *R* v. *Secretary of State for Home Affairs, ex parte Santillo* ([1980] ECR 1585). An analogy can be drawn with Acts of Parliament in the UK, not all provisions of which are enforceable by the courts. For example, section 23 of the British Telecommunications Act 1981 expressly provides that no action in tort shall lie against British Telecom in respect of failure to provide or delay in providing a telecommunications services. If this line of argument is pursued it is clearly possible to maintain a conceptual distinction between direct applicability and direct effect, as suggested by Winter (1972) and as argued in this chapter, even though the terminology used by the Court has had a tendency to confuse the two concepts.

An extended controversy surrounding the direct effect of directives was finally resolved by the Court in *Van Duyn*. It had been argued that since directives contain obligations of result, and not of conduct (see 6.13), and since only regulations are expressed to be 'directly applicable' in Article 189 EC, they could not be capable of judicial enforcement. The Court refuted these arguments in the following terms (at p. 1348):

'If . . . by virtue of the provisions of Article 189 regulations are directly applicable and, consequently, may by their very nature have direct effects, it does not follow from this that other categories of acts mentioned in that article can never have similar effects. It would be incompatible with the binding effect attributed to a directive by Article 189 to exclude, in principle, the possibility that the obligation which it imposes may be invoked by those concerned.'

The Court showed itself prepared, therefore, to overlook the fact that the binding obligation in a directive is principally an obligation to implement, not a substantive obligation; while that may originally have represented a slender foundation for arguing the direct effect of directives, it cannot be denied that subsequent developments have rendered this doctrinal shift irreversible. In *Van Duyn* the Court held that the applicant, who was threatened with exclusion from the UK on the grounds of her membership of the Church of Scientology – an organisation which attracted official disapproval in the UK, but was not actually proscribed – could rely upon the provisions of Directive 64/221 in order to claim certain procedural rights which limited the exercise of the UK's discretion to exclude Member State nationals on public policy grounds.

Consequently, as with other provisions of EC law, the question is one of construction. The fact that the directive gives a choice to Member States as between alternative methods of attaining a given result does not necessarily mean that the provisions in question are not capable of judicial enforcement. In Case C-271/91 *Marshall* v. *Southampton and South West Hampshire AHA (Marshall II)* ([1993] ECR I-4367), the Court was faced with a request for the interpretation of Article 6 of the Equal Treatment Directive (76/207), which guarantees an effective judicial remedy to those who suffer discrimination in the employment context. In an earlier case (Case 14/83 *Von Colson and Kamann* v. *Land Nordrhein Westfalen* [1984] ECR 1891; see 9.14), the Court had held that this provision was insufficiently precise to give rise to a specific obligation on Member States to choose a particular method of sanctioning discrimination (damages or (re)instatement by the employer). It had however held in Case 222/84 *Johnston* v. *Chief Constable of the Royal Ulster Constabulary* ([1986] ECR 1651) that this provision could be relied upon at least to the extent of giving rise to a right a *judicial remedy* (in that case purportedly denied under the UK system by a ministerial certificate). Building on this conclusion, the Court held in *Marshall II* that once a state had chosen pecuniary compensation as the means by which it would instrumentalise this provision, it was then bound to provide an *effective* compensatory remedy (i.e. compensation matching the loss suffered, and not limited by law to some arbitrarily low amount). It had 'no discretion in applying the chosen solution' (para. 36). To reach this conclusion, the Court stretched the doctrine of direct effect, and combined it with the doctrine of effective remedies (10.4).

The time limit given for the implementation of a directive is, however, crucial. Before the time limit has expired, the provisions cannot be regarded as containing perfect legal obligations (Case 148/78 *Ratti* [1979] ECR 1629).

9.11   Horizontal and Vertical Direct Effect

Having held that directives can have direct effect, the Court was then faced with a subsidiary question of scope, namely whether directives could be horizontally directly effective. This matter was initially decided in Case 152/84 *Marshall* v. *Southampton and South West Hampshire AHA (Marshall I)* ([1986] ECR 723). The Court held (at p. 749):

'With regard to the argument that directives may not be relied upon against an individual, it must be emphasised that according to Article 189 of the EEC Treaty the binding nature of a directive, which constitutes the basis for the possibility of relying on the directive before a national court, exists only in relation to "each Member State to which it is addressed". It follows that a directive may not of itself impose obligations on an individual and that a provision of a directive may not be relied upon as such as against such a person.'

In relation to the direct effect of directives, therefore, it appears that the so-called 'estoppel' justification has prevailed. The objective sought by allowing individuals to rely upon directives is to deny to Member States the benefits which they might derive from their failure to implement directives. This being so, it would be inconsistent to allow horizontal as well as vertical enforcement. Since *Marshall I* never fully silenced those holding the opposing view (and taking a formalist view, the position taken by the Court was strictly *obiter dicta*, since the plaintiff in that case was relying on the Directive *vis-à-vis* a public authority), the Court took the precaution in a subsequent case of explicitly revisiting the issue. In deciding once more against the horizontal direct effect of directives in Case C-91/92 *Faccini Dori* ([1994] ECR I-3325), the Court stood out against the strongly held views of at least three of its own Advocates General (AG van Gerven in Case C-271/91 *Marshall II*; AG Jacobs in Case C-316/93 *Vaneetveld* v. *SA Le Foyer* [1994] ECR I-763; AG Lenz in *Faccini Dori*), and numerous academic commentators. However, it went with the views of the majority of Member States – whose opinions it had taken the precaution of canvassing in a series of questions submitted to national governments in *Faccini Dori*. The caution displayed by the Court in *Faccini Dori* is notable:

> 'The effect of extending [the case law on the direct effect of directives] to the sphere of relations between individuals would be to recognize a power in the Community to enact obligations for individuals with immediate effect, whereas it has competence to do so only where it is empowered to adopt regulations' (at p. 3356).

Consequently, the plaintiff in *Faccini Dori* could not take the benefit of Directive 85/577 on the protection of the consumer in respect of contracts negotiated away from the business premises. The plaintiff was approached in Milan railway station, and prevailed upon to purchase an English language correspondence course. She changed her mind about the purchase, and sought the right to cancel the contract within seven days, which is guaranteed by the Directive in such a case. However, at that point the Directive had not been implemented in Italian law, and there was no such right in Italian law. Nor, in the absence of the horizontal direct effect of directives, could Dori rely directly upon the Directive as against the seller (another private party). In basing its decision on a formalist distinction between directives and regulations, drawing on the wording of Article 189 EC, the Court now appears to be distancing itself slightly from the 'estoppel' theory, which has been heavily criticised particularly as the Court has given an increasingly broad view of what can constitute 'the state' against which a directive may be relied upon (9.12). Regarding entities such as health authorities (as in *Marshall I*) as the state may be convincing at one level, but they cannot in any real sense be held responsible for a failure to implement the directive. But given that the Court has previously done much to undermine the validity of a formalist reading of Article 189, for example, by recognising the direct effect of directives, it seems odd that it should now retreat behind that same provision. Consequently, the Court's judgment in *Faccini Dori* has failed to convince all. In the view of Tridimas:

'Where it comes to relations between individuals, the reason why directives should be able to produce horizontal effect is not that a Member State must not be allowed to derive an advantage from its own failure to implement Community law but that the effective protection of Community rights must be guaranteed unless overriding principles (for example, legal certainty, non-retroactive application of criminal laws) require otherwise' (Tridimas, 1994: 633).

9.12 The Notion of an 'Emanation of the State'

The effect of the restriction on the direct effect of directives is, of course, to create an important borderline which is not based upon the nature of the provision to be enforced, but upon the actual nature of the dispute between the parties. In fields where EC law frequently takes the form of directives, and where it is aimed ultimately at altering the conduct of individuals as well as states (e.g. environmental law, labour law and social law) the potential for injustice is clear. For example, a public sector employee may rely upon the guarantee of equal treatment as regards sex in employment matters contained in the Equal Treatment Directive (76/207) in order to challenge alleged sex discrimination on the part of his or her employer, whereas a private sector employee may not. Injustices could also emerge as between the Member States given that the numbers and types of public sector jobs do vary greatly between the different states. Three mechanisms have consequently emerged which soften the harshness of this distinction. The first is concerned with the interpretation of the notion of the 'state' and constitutes a further extrapolation of the scope of direct effect; the latter two (indirect effect and State liability) go beyond the scope of direct effect, and reinforce the point made in 9.1, and by Figure 9.1, that direct effect is just one mechanism of several aimed at ensuring the effective enforcement of EC law. So, in *Faccini Dori*, the Court of Justice reminded the national court of the availability of the principle of interpretation or 'indirect effect' (9.14), and the principle of State liability for failure to implement a directive (9.17), as alternatives to relying on direct effect.

The Court has developed a broad interpretation of precisely what is this 'state' which is not allowed to benefit from its own wrong in failing to implement the directive. In *Marshall I* itself the Court held that the state includes the state as employer as well as the state as public authority. In Case C-188/89 *Foster* v. *British Gas plc* ([1990] ECR I-3313) the Court provided general guidance on the concept of the 'emanation of the state', holding that the definition of this concept is a matter of EC law, not national law. It is, nonetheless, for the national court to decide whether a given body falls within the criteria offered by the Court of Justice. *Foster* involved the question of whether certain women employees made redundant by (pre-privatisation) British Gas in circumstances in which they would not have been made redundant had they been men, could rely upon the Equal Treatment Directive as against their employer. The Court summarised the bodies previously held to be emanations of the State: tax authorities (Case 8/81 *Becker* [1982] ECR 53); local or regional authorities (Case C-221/88 *ECSC* v. *Acciaierie e ferriere Busseni* ([1990] ECR I-495; see also Case 103/88 *Fratelli Costanzo* v. *Milano* [1989] ECR 1839); the police (Case 222/84 *Johnston* v. *Royal Ulster Constabulary*; and bodies responsible for state-funded health care (*Marshall*). It then went on to say (at p. 3348) that

> 'a body, whatever its legal form, which has been made responsible pursuant to a measure adopted by the State, for providing a public service under the control of the State and has for that purpose special powers beyond those which result from the normal rules applicable in relations between individuals is included in any event among the bodies against which the provisions of a directive capable of having direct effect may be relied upon.'

The categories of 'emanation of the state' are clearly, therefore, not yet closed. Moreover, on this interpretation it is not clear that a post-privatisation utility would necessarily be held not to be an emanation of the state if it retains sufficient special statutory powers. Since *Foster*, the Court has had occasion to treat an Italian university as an emanation of the state, but that leaves open the question as to universities in other Member States which may be funded and organised along different lines should be treated (Case C-419/92 *Scholz* v. *Opera Universitaria di Cagliari* [1994] ECR I-505).

9.13   The Effect of EC Law on National Law and National Legislative Competence

Just as the 'penetrative' quality of EC law has direct and intrusive consequences for the national legal order in the form of the judicial enforceability of provisions of EC law in national courts, so its superiority as a source of law has an impact upon the validity of national law and the exercise of national legislative competence.

In Case 106/77 *Simmenthal II* the Court deduced from the principles established in Case 6/64 *Costa* v. *ENEL* that the supremacy of EC law logically must limit national law-making powers. It held ([1978] ECR 629 at p. 643):

'Furthermore, in accordance with the principle of the precedence of Community law, the relationship between provisions of the Treaty and directly applicable measures of the institutions on the one hand and national law of the Member States on the other is such that those provisions and measures not only by their entry into force render automatically inapplicable any conflicting provision of current national law but – in so far as they are an integral part of, and take precedence in, the legal order applicable in the territory of each of the Member States – also preclude the valid adoption of new national legislative measures to the extent to which they would be incompatible with Community provisions.

Indeed any recognition that national legislative measures which encroach upon the field within which the Community exercises its legislative power or which are otherwise incompatible with the provisions of Community law had any legal effect would amount to a corresponding denial of the effectiveness of the obligations undertaken unconditionally and irrevocably by Member States pursuant to the Treaty and would thus imperil the very foundations of the Community.'

In practice, of course, these principles can be put into effect only by the domestic institutions themselves. The Court has no power to invalidate national legislation, although it may state in a preliminary ruling that national legislation of the type at issue in a given case is inconsistent with EC law, or make a declaration under Article 171 in proceedings brought under Articles 169 or 170 EC that a given provision of national law is incompatible with EC law. Consequently, as C-213/89 *R.* v. *Secretary of State for Transport, ex parte Factortame Ltd (Factortame I)* ([1990] ECR I-2433) makes clear, the coupling of these principles with the principle of effective national remedies may mean that national courts need to set aside a national rule – such as a procedural limitation upon their ability to award interim relief – in order to make an appropriate ruling (10.3).

The pre-emptive effect of EC law is particularly apparent in those areas where EU legislature has exhaustively regulated the field, in particular using legislation in the form of regulations. This is so, in particular, under the rules governing the Common Agricultural Policy (CAP). In Case 16/83 *Prantl* ([1984] ECR 1299 at p. 1324) the Court stated that:

'once rules on the common organisation of the market [in wine] may be regarded as forming a complete system, the Member States no longer have competence in that field unless Community law expressly provides otherwise.'

However, in areas of 'shared competence' the position is not always so clear-cut (Weatherill, 1994). It depends upon the Court's interpretation of the type of EU measures – such as harmonisation directives – which have been adopted. One example of the loss of national regulatory competence is offered by Case 60/86 *Commission* v. *UK (Dim-dip headlights)* ([1988]

ECR 3921) which was concerned with whether the UK could validly require motor vehicles sold in the UK to be fitted with 'dim dip' devices for their headlights. In view of the effect of the relevant Directive which contained an exhaustive list of permissible lighting devices, the Court concluded that the UK

> 'cannot unilaterally require manufacturers who have complied with the harmonised technical requirements . . . to comply with a requirement which is not imposed by that directive' (at p. 3935).

In sharp contrast, in Case C-479/93 *Francovich* v. *Italian Republic (Francovich II)* ([1995] ECR I-3843) the Court reached quite a different conclusion about the effect of the Insolvency Directive. It concluded that the Directive in question constituted only a partial harmonisation of the issues raised by the protection of the employee in the event of the insolvency of the employer. It found in this instance that previously existing differences in national insolvency regimes – which had the result of making any protection offered by the directive exceedingly uneven in coverage – were not affected by the provisions of the Directive. Ironically, therefore, it would seem that the applicant Francovich – to whose endeavours in the courts we owe the doctrine of State liability for failure to implement a directive (9.17) – is unlikely to receive compensation precisely because of the effect of Italian insolvency law is to place his employer in a category of insolvency which does not fall within the scope of Article 2(1) of the Directive (proceedings 'to satisfy collectively the claims of creditors'). No principle of direct effect, indirect effect or State liability will assist an applicant whose situation is ultimately regulated by national law.

9.14   The Development of the Interpretative Obligation

The second way in which the Court has sought to alleviate the consequences of the limitation which it has placed upon the direct effect of directives has been through its promotion of the principle of construction which requires national courts, in conformity with their duty under Article 5 EC to give full effect to EC law, to interpret all national law in the light of relevant EC law, regardless of whether it has direct effect. Although this principle of construction is sometimes called *Von Colson* effect, following the case in which it was first discussed (Case 14/83 *Von Colson and Kamann* v. *Land Nordrhein Westfalen*; see 9.10), it is now more generally termed 'indirect effect' (Fitzpatrick, 1989) (and occasionally the 'duty of sympathetic interpretation' or the doctrine of 'substantive effectiveness' (Meads, 1991)).

It flows in general terms from the duty on Member States to enforce EC law, inherent in the constitutional principles articulated at the beginning of this chapter, and clearly stated in Cases 314/81, etc. *Procureur de la République* v. *Waterkeyn* ([1982] ECR 4337 at p. 4360) that:

> 'all the institutions of the Member States concerned must . . . ensure within the fields covered by their respective powers, that judgments of the Court are complied with.'

For example, contravention of national legislation which breaches EC law may not be prosecuted by the domestic authorities as a criminal offence (Case 269/80 *R* v. *Tymen* [1981] ECR 3079). Conversely, Member States have a duty to prosecute breaches of EC law using national criminal legislation as diligently as they would in purely domestic circumstances (Case 68/88 *Commission* v. *Greece* [1989] ECR 2965). This duty also comprises the duty on national courts to interpret national law in the light of EC law and the duties on national courts to give effective remedies in respect of breaches of EC law.

The duty on the national court to apply the law in such a way as to facilitate the achievement of the EU's objectives flows directly from the penetration of EC law into the national legal system, and is expressed most clearly in Article 5 EC. It is not limited to giving effect to EU rules which are judicially enforceable as such, but also extends to the development of a range of interpretative devices which derive their force from EC law. In other words, EC law does not have to be directly effective in order for it to benefit from the general doctrine of supremacy.

In *Von Colson*, where the doctrine first emerged, the Court found itself unable to hold that a particular provision of the Equal Treatment Directive was sufficiently precise and unconditional to support the implication alleged by the plaintiff (9.10). It nonetheless held that (at p. 1909):

> 'the Member States' obligation arising from a directive to achieve the result envisaged by the directive and their duty under Article 5 of the Treaty to take all appropriate measures, whether general or particular, to ensure the fulfilment of that obligation, is binding on all the authorities of Member States including, for matters within their jurisdiction, the courts. It follows that, in applying the national law specifically introduced in order to implement Directive No. 76/207, national courts are required to interpret their national law in the light of the wording and purpose of the directive in order to achieve the result referred to in the third paragraph of Article 189.'

The Court held that Article 6 of the Equal Treatment Directive, which guarantees the victims of sex discrimination in employment matters the right to a judicial remedy, is not sufficiently precise to support the implication that a particular sanction (in that case the obligation on the discriminating employer to conclude a contract of employment with the victim) must be applied by the national court. In general terms, however, it does include the right to a sufficient remedy, which constitutes an adequate deterrent against future acts of discrimination. It is in the light of this general interpretation that the national court was required to intepret the German Equal Treatment Act, passed to implement the Directive.

As Fitzpatrick (1989) pointed out, *Von Colson* left two matters undecided. First, it was not clear what categories of national law had to be interpreted in the light of EC law. *Von Colson* itself contained an ambiguity, with the Court appearing to refer at some points (such as the paragraph cited) only to national legislation specifically introduced to implement an EU obligation, but at other points to cast the net wider to include potentially all national law. On this point of doubt, the Court repeated, but had no need to apply, the wider formula in Case 222/84 *Johnston* v. *Chief Constable of the Royal Ulster Constabulary*. The same formula also found strong words of support from AG van Gerven in Case C-262/88 *Barber* v. *Guardian Royal Exchange* ([1990] ECR I-1889).

The second uncertainty concerned the scope of the rule of construction: how far, precisely, were national courts required to go in order to ensure conformity between national law and EC law? Was there in truth any difference between giving effect to EC law through the direct effect doctrine, which would mean where necessary overriding conflicting national legislation (9.13), and construing it in conformity with EC law (including, if necessary, reading words into a statute or reconstructing the intention of the legislature)? If not, that would appear to reduce greatly the consequences of the rules on the justiciability of EC law.

Both difficulties appeared to have been resolved by the Court in favour of the widest possible ambit of the indirect effect principle. In Case C-106/89 *Marleasing SA* v. *La Comercial Internacional de Alimentación* ([1990] ECR I-4135) the Court repeated its formulation from *Von Colson* on the responsibilities of national courts, going on to say (at p. 4159) that:

'in applying national law, whether the provisions in question were adopted before or after the directive, the national court called upon to interpret it is required to do so, as far as possible, in the light of the wording and the purpose of the directive in order to achieve the result pursued by the latter and thereby comply with the third paragraph of Article 189 of the Treaty.'

There seems to be no limitation in this judgment that the national provisions subject to interpretation in the light of EC law should be those intended or deemed to implement EC law. Potentially, therefore, UK courts could be required to reconsider the rules of the common law in the light of EU obligations. Second, courts must seek 'as far as possible' to achieve a resolution of EC law and national law. Does this mean that national courts must depart from national canons of construction when performing their interpretative duties under Article 5? Must UK courts abandon their preference for the literal rule of statutory interpretation and their adherence to the convention of *stare decisis* when applying EC law? Certainly, the methods of interpretation used by national courts must match those preferred by the Court of Justice, looking for the purpose of a measure, and going beyond its literal meaning (Millett, 1989; Kutscher, 1976). Overall, it must be possible to discern a difference in practice between the obligation to achieve conformity 'as far as possible' with a Directive, and the approach of the Court in *Simmenthal II* to a Regulation which required the national court to do all that was 'necessary' to achieve enforcement of EC law, including the disapplication of national law.

The evidence from the Court of Justice since *Marleasing* is that there are clear limits to the interpretative obligation on national courts. In *Marleasing*, the Court itself reached the conclusion that the Spanish court in question was precluded from interpreting national law other than in a way which achieved conformity with the company law Directive at issue. In Case 334/92 *Wagner Miret* v. *Fondo de Garantía Salarial* ([1993] ECR I-6911), it reached the opposite conclusion, this time in relation to the interpretation of Directive 80/987 on the protection of employees in the event of the insolvency of their employer. The Court found that the terms of the Spanish provisions intended to implement that Directive were not in conformity, as they excluded company directors from making a claim for unpaid salary against the guarantee fund set up to protect employees. Although the Court explicitly recognised the existence of the indirect effect principle, stating that it was particularly relevant to the situation where a Member State deemed its pre-existing legislation to be an adequate implementation for a subsequent directive, it acknowledged and accepted the conclusion of the national court that an interpretation in conformity with the Directive, as interpreted, could not here be achieved by applying the interpretative obligation – an apparent change from formulation used in *Marleasing* (Bettlem, 1995: 17–18). Instead of insisting on the national court's duty to achieve a 'conforming interpretation', the Court instead reminded the court of the possibility of applying the State liability principle, introduced in Cases 6, 9/90 *Francovich I*, which had concerned Italy's failure to implement the same Directive. In the view of Tridimas (1994: 533), in *Wagner Miret* the Court revealed the weakness of the indirect effect principle.

9.15 The Scope of the Indirect Effect Principle

The interpretative duties of national courts apply also in relation to certain non-binding measures of EC law. In Case C-322/88 *Grimaldi* v. *Fonds des Maladies Professionnelles* ([1989] ECR I-4407) the Court applied the indirect effect principle to the Commission Recommendations on the adoption of a European schedule of occupational diseases and on the conditions for granting compensation to persons suffering from occupational diseases. Such (non-binding) Recommendations had to be taken into consideration by a national court in order to enable it to decide disputes, in particular where they are capable of clarifying other provisions of national or EC law.

However, the application of the indirect effect principle by national courts is limited by reference to other general principles of the EU legal order, such as the prohibition on retroactivity and the principle of legal certainty. This point is made by AG van Gerven in *Marleasing* and is illustrated by the judgment of the Court in Case 80/86 *Kolpinghuis Nijmegen* ([1987] ECR 3969) where the use of the principle of indirect effect would have come into conflict with the principle of *nulla poena sine lege*. A national judicial authority could not rely upon an unimplemented directive in order to 'sharpen' existing domestic sanctions on the marketing of unfit goods. The Court stated (at p. 3986):

> 'A directive cannot, of itself and independently of a national law adopted by a Member State for its implementation, have the effect of determining or aggravating the liability of persons who act in contravention of the provisions of that directive.'

In other words, the state could not in such circumstances benefit from the operation of the principle of indirect effect.

9.16   The Relationship between Direct Effect and Indirect Effect

In Case 222/84 *Johnston* v. *Chief Constable of the Royal Ulster Constabulary* the Court appeared to link the two concepts of direct effect and indirect effect together, indicating that it was the first duty of national courts to seek to interpret national law in conformity with EC law, and only if this was not possible, to enforce EC law itself in preference to national law through the doctrine of direct effect. To formulate the duty of the national court thus matches the attempts by Pescatore (1983) to de-emphasise the significance of direct effect. It is also consistent with the evolution of a wider array of mechanisms concerned with increasing the effectiveness of EC law within the domesic legal system, through a focus on sanctions for breach of EC law rather than on the precise nature of the provision which is alleged to have been breached. It has the advantage of maintaining national procedural autonomy in determining the precise form of the remedy given, without undermining the crucial uniformity of EC law.

9.17   The Responsibility of the State in Respect of Breaches of EC law

The possibility of the *responsibility* of the State in respect of breaches of EC law giving rise to a compensatory obligation has long been envisaged, but for many years the issues were not taken forward by the Court of Justice. For example, in Case 199/82 *Amministrazione delle Finanze dello Stato* v. *San Giorgio* ([1983] ECR 3595), the Court held, as a matter of EC law, that unlawfully levied charges and taxes must be reimbursed to aggrieved importers and exporters, subject to principles of national procedural autonomy, non-discrimination and effective remedies (Figure 9.1). Furthermore, in Case 60/75 *Russo* v. *AIMA* ([1976] ECR 45 at p. 56) the Court held that:

'if . . . damage has been caused through an infringement of Community law the state is liable to the injured party of the consequences in the context of the provisions of national law on the liability of the state.'

Since Cases C-6, 9/90 *Francovich I*, the possibilities raised by this principle have come under detailed scrutiny. The claims in *Francovich I* were brought by workers in Italy made redundant when their employers became insolvent, who received no compensation or redundancy payments. No funds were available from the employers themselves, and Italy had failed to implement Directive 80/987 which requires Member States to set up guarantee funds to cover the compensation claims of employees made redundant in the event of their employers' insolvency. The employees claimed that the Italian State was responsible for payment of the compensation, either by virtue of the direct effect of the Directive, or on grounds of liability for a failure to act.

Having considered the provisions of Directive 80/987, the Court reached the conclusion that those provisions concerned with the creation of a minimum guarantee were not sufficiently precise in themselves to support a claim for the lost wages against the Italian State. In particular, the failure to implement the Directive meant that the state had not chosen what form the guarantee would take, and how it would be funded. The argument that the relevant provisions of the Directive were directly effective therefore failed since the Directive gave a discretion in the implementation process to the Member States. The only remaining remedy, therefore, was a right to damages for non-implementation.

In its judgment the Court offered two alternative bases for the right to damages. First it returned to basics in deriving the right to damages from the specific nature of EC law, its justiciability and superior nature, going on to hold:

'that the full effectiveness of Community rules would be impaired and the protection of the rights which they grant would be weakened if individuals were unable to obtain compensation when their rights are infringed by a breach of Community law for which a Member State can be held responsible' (p. 5414).

This repeats, in similar terms, the position already reached in *Russo* v. *AIMA*, and highlights the availability of damages for breach of a substantive EU obligation by a Member State. It then continued:

'The possibility of obtaining redress from the Member State is particularly indispensable where, as in this case, the full effectiveness of Community rules is subject to prior action on the part of the State and, consequently, in the absence of such action, individuals cannot enforce before the national courts the rights conferred upon them by Community law' (p. 5414).

The alternative basis for the damages obligation given by the Court is Article 5, and in that context the Court drew support from an early ECSC case concerned with an analogous provision of that Treaty (Case 6/60 *Humblet* v. *Belgium* [1960] ECR 559).

The Court was equally brief on the subject of the conditions for State liability: the right to damages was subjected to a test based on the nature of the provisions, which was similar, but not identical, to the test applied to determine the direct effect of a provision. Three conditions must be satisfied: the result prescribed by the provision must involve the conferring of rights on individuals; the content of the rights must be capable of definition on the basis of the directive; and there must be a causal link between the violation of the Treaty obligation by the Member States and the loss suffered by the individual. In applying these conditions the national court is bound to apply national procedural rules which are no less favourable than those governing similar actions. The provisions of Directive 80/987 would appear to satisfy these tests, since the beneficiary of the rights and the nature of the rights were defined; the Directive failed only to define the subject of the obligation, namely the precise nature of the guarantee fund.

The *Francovich* or 'State liability' action quickly received a warm welcome from observers of the Court's case law (e.g. Steiner, 1993; Curtin, 1992). It presents numerous advantages. It avoids the need to make the provisions of the directive themselves justiciable before the national courts using direct effect, or to achieve an uncomfortable resolution between irreconcilable provisions of EC law and national law through strained constructions under the doctrine of indirect effect. It also avoids the possibility that either increasingly marginal 'emanations of the state' (through the *Foster* doctrine) or even private parties (through the medium of indirect effect) will be asked to carry the principal burden of giving effect to the substantive rights for individuals contained in directives. Instead it concentrates on what has always been the primary obligation of the Member State under a directive, namely the obligation to implement, and attaches a rigorous sanction to failure to fulfil that obligation. It is arguable that this mechanism may be a much more effective way of securing compliance on the part of Member States in the implementation of EC law than either direct effect or indirect effect. Certainly it represents a very neat coupling of the principle of 'responsibility' conceived of as one way of instrumentalising the constitutional qualities of EC law, and the principle of 'effective national remedies'.

On the other hand, just as quickly new questions were raised (e.g. Bebr, 1992; Ross, 1993; Craig, 1993), both about the basis of the action itself and about its practical instrumentalisation in the national legal orders. The Court of Justice had simply given insufficient detail in *Francovich I* itself, and it was inevitable that further references would follow. Four questions have preoccupied commentators in particular:

- what are the limits of the State liability principle? what provisions of EC law does it apply to? can the principle of responsibility extend to subjects of EC law other than States?
- what, if any, should be the relationship between the State liability imposed on the Member States and any similar 'non-contractual' liability falling upon the EU itself by virtue of the principles contained in Article 215 EC (Chapter 14)?
- following that question, it is pertinent to enquire what standard of liability should be imposed; should it be the same standard of liability which governs the liability of the EU institutions under Article 215 EC?
- finally, the principal difficulty with the *Francovich* action would appear to be that it drives a coach and horses through the formulations of national procedural autonomy which govern the impact of EC law on national law at the third level of analysis identified in Figure 9.1. A number of Member States simply do not recognise actions against the State for loss caused by legislative action or inaction; it is difficult, therefore, to imagine how analogies can be drawn between the *Francovich* action and the national procedural rules governing non-existent similar actions. The national courts may be required to invent *de novo* a cause of action against the State.

Moreover, the welcome was not universal, with the judgment in *Francovich I* attracting the label of being overactivist from some of the Court's more 'conservative' critics. Sir Patrick Neill described it as being 'novel', and a surprising conclusion for the Court to reach that there was indeed an *EC law* principle of State liability, since it had previously argued for such a principle to be included in the Treaties by means of *formal amendment* (Neill, 1995: 230).

9.18 The Clarification of *Francovich I*

Two further judgments clarifying the principle of State liability were given in March 1996 (Cases 46, 48/93 *Brasserie du Pêcheur* v. *Germany, R* v. *Secretary of State for Transport, ex parte Factortame Ltd (Factortame III)* [1996] I CMLR 889; Case C-392/93 *R* v. *HM Treasury, ex parte British Telecom* (26.3.96)), and numerous references for preliminary rulings requesting clarification in many areas have been forwarded to the Court of Justice. In *Factortame III*, the Court dealt with two separate references which it had put together for the sake of convenience. The first case was brought by a French brewery which claimed damages for loss of profits for the period 1981–87 from the German authorities, allegedly caused by the German authorities' unlawful *failure* to revise the Beer Purity laws which were held by the Court in 1987 to constitute a restriction on the free movement of goods, contrary to Article 30 EC (Case 178/84 *Commission v. Germany* [1987] ECR 1227) (i.e an omission on the part of the German legislature). During the period covered by the claim it had been forced to discontinue exports of beer to Germany. The second case was the continuation of the litigation brought about by the adoption by the UK of the Merchant Shipping Act 1988, which prevented a number of Spanish fishing boats from fishing out of the UK until a new registration system was introduced which no longer restricted Spanish-owned vessels (see 7.16, 9.13, 10.3) (i.e an act of the UK legislature). The applicants now claimed damages from the UK government in respect of the documented breach of Article 52 EC (right of establishment).

The Court began by clarifying the scope of the principle of State liability and delimiting its relationship to direct effect. It firmly claimed jurisdiction over the right to create through judicial action a right to reparation, in the absence of express Treaty or legislative provisions, reiterating that the right of reparation is 'inherent in the system of the Treaty' (para. 31). It also rejected an argument that State liability can only occur in circumstances where the relevant EC provisions are not directly effective. In other words, it is not a residual, but a complementary, technique of protection:

'The Court has consistently held that the right of individuals to rely on the directly effective provisions of the Treaty before national courts is only a minimum guarantee and is not sufficient in itself to ensure the full and complete implementation of the Treaty. The purpose of that right is to ensure that provisions of Community law prevail over national provisions. It cannot, in every sense, secure for individuals the benefit of the rights conferred on them by Community law and, in particular, avoid their sustaining damage as a result of breach of Community law attributable to a Member State . . . [T]he full effectiveness of Community law would be impaired if individuals were unable to obtain redress when their rights were infringed by a breach of Community law' (para. 20).

It then concluded that State liability could attach not only to a failure to transpose a directive, as in *Francovich I*, but also to a breach by a Member State – by action or inaction – of

'a right directly conferred by a Community provision upon which individuals are entitled to rely before the national courts. In that event, the right to reparation is the necessary corollary of the direct effect of the Community provision whose breach caused the damage sustained' (para. 22).

In these cases, that meant two EC Treaty provisions – Article 30 and Article 52. State liability can attach to any organ of the state, and no exclusion can be claimed on the basis of domestic rules as the division of powers between constitutional authorities. In particular, the Court stressed that national legislatures are responsible under the State liability principle.

It then went on to address the circumstances in which national legislatures could be liable for acts or omissions in breach of EC law, here drawing heavily upon its own case law on the 'non-contractual' liability of the EU legislature governed by Article 215 EC. In that context, the Court went on to reformulate and slightly revise the three conditions for liability set out in *Francovich I*, bearing in mind that the circumstances of the two cases were rather different to that case, and did not involve the tightly constrained duty of implementation which Articles 5 and 189 EC impose on Member States in respect of directives, but broader questions of legislative policy and discretion. We shall discuss these aspects of the judgment in 10.6 as they concern primarily the interaction of the EU and national legal orders within the framework of the effective national remedies principle, and the extent to which EC law fetters national procedural autonomy. Similarly, in Case C-392/93 *R* v. *HM Treasury, ex parte British Telecom*, the Court of Justice provided a small reformulation of the conditions of liability in respect of the implementation of directives (here a 'mis-implementation' of a public procurement directive by the UK government), in the light of the detailed discussion of *Francovich I*, in *Factortame III*.

The judgment in *Factortame III* concluded with a refusal by the Court to impose a temporal limitation upon its effects, despite a request from the German government. The Court pointed out that the principle of legal certainty which underlies the possibility of imposing a temporal limitation would be built in to the national substantive and procedural conditions which would govern the precise availability of damages in cases like *Factortame III* (6.5). Hence, there was no need for a temporal limitation. In *Francovich I*, it had likewise ignored without comment the plea of AG Mischo for a temporal limitation in the event that it decided in favour of a principle State liability.

One question of principle remains unresolved, and that is whether the notion of 'responsibility' identified in this chapter as one of four principal means for giving effect is limited to 'State liability', or whether it extends in appropriate cases to cover individuals as well, where they are directly subject to duties imposed by EC law. This arises particularly – but not solely – in relation to the application of Articles 85 and 86 EC. The Court of Justice has never had occasion to determine whether or not there exists a right to damages for aggrieved individuals harmed by private action in breach of those provisions, *as a matter of EC law*. Clearly such an action may exist at national law, as one of range of sanctions made available to give effect to the direct effect of those provisions, but there is an arguable case – made out in detail by AG van Gerven in his opinion in Case

C-238/92 *Banks & Co. Ltd.* v. *British Coal Corporation* ([1994] ECR I-1209), and extra-judicially in van Gerven (1994b) – for an *EC right* to damages in appropriate cases, subject to the procedural conditions of national law (see Shaw, 1995: 138–45). In the event, the Court of Justice did not find it necessary to consider this question, as it concluded that the relevant competition law provision (Article 65 ECSC) was not capable of giving rise to rights which national courts must enforce, in the absence of a Commission decision finding an infringement. In this respect the ECSC Treaty differs sharply from the EC Treaty. Since the only means by which EC law can impose *duties* on individuals (as opposed to the State which is bound by the general provisions of the Treaty, including Article 5) is through the medium of direct effect, it seems difficult to argue with the conclusion that direct effect must be a prerequisite of 'individual responsibility', in contradistinction to State liability. However, in view of the Court's finding in late 1995 in the *Bosman* case that Article 48 EC (free movement of workers) can in certain circumstances impose obligations on individuals (football clubs and football associations) not to impose restrictions on free movement of footballers (Case C-415/93 *Union Royale belge des Sociétés de football association ASBL* v. *Bosman* ([1996] 1 CMLR 645; [1995] ECR I-4921), it may soon be faced with this question. It seems likely that Bosman will continue his well publicised action in the form of a claim for compensation against the Belgian football authorities.

Summary

1 The impact of the EU legal order on the national legal orders is mediated principally through three main policy objectives of the Court of Justice:
   – ensuring the effectiveness of EC law;
   – ensuring the uniformity of EC law;
   – ensuring the legal protection of individuals as legal subjects.
2 These policy objectives, and the implications for the national legal orders, were made clear by the Court of Justice in a number of early pronouncements about the nature of the future EU legal order.
3 EC law has two principal constitutional qualities:
   – it is a superior source of law;
   – it penetrates into the national legal orders.

   It bases these on a thesis of the transfer of sovereign powers by the Member States to the EU, on accession.
4 Four main techniques are available for the ensuring that these constitutional qualities are given effect to by national courts:
   – direct effect;
   – the 'pre-emptive' qualities of EC law;
   – indirect effect;
   – the responsibility of the Member States in respect of violations of EC law.

5 These developments have occurred not as a result solely of unilateral action by the Court of Justice, but through a continuing constitutional dialogue between the EU and national legal orders, at the constitutional level.

6 There are particular theoretical difficulties with reconciling membership of the EU with a strict view of the sovereignty of the Westminster Parliament, but for the most part the European Communities Act 1972 offers the UK courts the means whereby they can resolve any practical difficulties which arise.

7 The justiciability, or direct effect, of EC law in national courts is well-established, and depends on a construction of the individual provision at issue. Provisions of EC law which are sufficiently precise and unconditional may be enforced in national courts at the instance of individuals to whom they grant rights. Directives are not capable of giving rise to horizontal direct effect, and so do not bind individuals.

8 As EC law prevails over all national law, including national constitutions, it also limits the law-making powers of the Member States and imposes duties to enforce EC law on the authorities of the Member States, including the courts.

9 The interpretative duties of national courts in relation to EC law are extensive, and extend to interpreting all national law in the light of the text and spirit of relevant EC law, and to do everything possible to achieve a resolution of the two.

10 The principle of State liability for breaches of EC law is still evolving. Since *Francovich I* and *Factortame III*, the principle now seems firmly established, although some details of its application remain to be worked out. It rests partly on Article 5 EC, and partly on the notion that the responsibility of the Member States is 'inherent' to the system of the Treaty.

Questions

1 In what ways do the statements of principle by the Court of Justice in *Van Gend en Loos* and *Costa* v. *ENEL* define the fundamental relationship between EC law and national law?

2 Why is it important to distinguish the different levels at which EC law and national law interact?

3 Do you agree with the argument that the relationship between EC law and national law is based on a dialogue, rather than on the unilateral statements of the Court of Justice?

4 How can the right of individuals to rely upon potentially any provisions of EC law which can give rise to justiciable rights in national courts be justified?

5 Why might direct effect be said to be an 'infant disease' of the EU? What other mechanisms exist to give effect to the constitutional qualities of EC law?

6 Why is indirect effect a difficult principle for national courts to give effect to?

7 What advantages and disadvantages are offered by the principle of State liability?

8   In 2.1 it was suggested that there was often a time lag between significant developments in the political arena led by the Member States, and the achievement of comparably important legal goals. Assess this assertion, by reference to the historical survey in Chapter 2 and the pattern of judicial development of the EU legal order which emerges in this chapter.

Workshop (for Chapters 9 and 10)

In July 1993, the Council of Ministers adopted (fictitious) Directive 93/8000 requiring Member States to introduce a principle of strict liability for personal injury and property damage on the part of occupiers for the escape of toxic substances from their premises. It also requires Member States to establish a guarantee fund out of which compensation is to be paid to victims of accidents resulting from the escape of toxic substances where the occupier is unable, because of inadequate insurance, to satisfy a judgment debt. The directive does not determine the details of the operation and funding of the guarantee fund. The Directive was to be implemented by 31 December 1995.

Consider the following sets of circumstances:

1   The UK has not implemented the directive by the due date. On 2 January 1996, Anna is injured by the escape of a toxic chemical from a Government Research Institute situated near to her house. Discuss the nature of her claim for damages under EC law.
    Would your answer be any different if the toxic chemical escaped from (a) a University or (b) a pharmaceutical company?

2   The UK believes that the directive is fully implemented by the existing (fictitious) Toxic Substances (Occupiers Liability) Act 1970, under which occupiers are subject to a reversal of the burden of proof requiring them to prove that any escapes of toxic substances from their premises are not the result of any lack of reasonably care on their part. Bert claims that his garden has been contaminated by the escape of contaminated substances during a flood from the premises of Rip Off plc, a manufacturer of chemicals. Assess the likelihood that Bert will succeed with his claim.
    Would your answer be any different if Rip Off plc has gone into liquidation, and it is discovered that it had no insurance to cover the loss such as that caused to Bert?

3   The UK is fundamentally opposed to the directive, believing it to be inconsistent with the principle of subsidiarity. Parliament adopts the (fictitious) Toxic Substances (Derogation) Act 1993 under which it specifically prohibits the UK courts from giving effect to the directive. Advise the Community Rights Group, a pressure group concerned with the proper enforcement and implementation of EC law, of the likelihood of a successful challenge to the Act in the UK courts.
    In the event that you conclude that a challenge would be possible in principle, consider whether the Community Rights Group could properly be denied standing to challenge the Act on the grounds that it has suffered no damage.

Further Reading

de Búrca (1992), 'Giving Effect to European Community Directives', 55 *MLR* 215.

Docksey and Fitzpatrick (1991), 'The Duty of National Courts to Interpret Provisions of National Law in Accordance with Community Law', 20 *ILJ* 113.

van Gerven (1994a), 'The Horizontal Effect of Directive Provisions Revisited: The Reality of Catchwords', in Curtin and Heukels (1994).

Maltby (1993), 'Marleasing: What is All the Fuss About?' 109 *LQR* 301.

Pescatore (1983), 'The Doctrine of 'Direct Effect': An Infant Disease of Community Law', 8 *ELRev*. 155.

Plaza Martin (1994), 'Furthering the Effectiveness of EC Directives and the Judicial Protection of Individual Rights Thereunder', 43 *ICLQ* 26.

Prechal (1995), *Directives in European Community Law*, Oxford University Press.

Ross (1993), 'Beyond Francovich', 56 *MLR* 55.

Snyder (1993), 'The Effectiveness of European Community Law: Institutions, Processes, Tools and Techniques', 56 *MLR* 19.

Szyszczak (1992), 'European Community Law: New Remedies, New Directions?', 55 *MLR* 690.

Tridimas (1994), 'Horizontal effect of directives: a missed opportunity?', 19 *ELRev*. 621.

Wyatt (1982), 'New Legal Order or Old?', 7 *ELRev*. 147.

10 The National Dimension: Domestic Remedies for Breach of EC Law and National Reactions to the Challenge

10.1 Introduction

This chapter draws directly on the notion that the relationship between EC law and national law is bi-dimensional (8.1), and looks at two key facets of the 'national dimension': it examines first the third level of analysis identified in Figure 9.1 (the availability of national remedies within the constraints of the principles of non-discrimination and effectiveness articulated by the Court of Justice), and then turns briefly to the responses of some national courts to some of the principal conceptual and practical challenges posed by EC law.

10.2 National Remedies and Breach of EC Law

National courts are under a duty to give comprehensive remedies to individuals seeking redress against national law in conflict with EC law, or seeking to enforce EC rights (Case 811/79 *Amministrazione delle Finanze dello Stato* v. *Ariete SpA* [1980] ECR 2545). Rights granted to individuals by directives or other EU provisions must be capable of protection by judicial process (Case 222/84 *Johnston* v. *Chief Constable of the Royal Ulster Constabulary* [1986] ECR 1651; Case 222/86 *UNEC-TEF* v. *Heylens* [1987] ECR 4097). These points have already emerged earlier in the discussion of general principles of EC law (6.6).

The nature of the remedies granted are a matter for national courts and the national legal order, under the principle of national procedural autonomy; but they must be no less favourable than those accorded by the court in respect of violations of similar rights arising under national law (the principle of non-discrimination). Moreover, the procedural conditions, such as limitation periods or *locus standi* rules, which govern actions for the enforcement of EC law are a matter for national law and are not subject to the control of EC law (at least until they have been harmonised by the EU legislature), unless such 'conditions and time limits made it impossible in practice to exercise the rights which the national courts are obliged to protect' (Case 33/76 *Rewe-Zentralfinanz* v. *Landwirtschaftskammer für das Saarland* [1976] ECR 1989 at 1998) (see also to the same effect Case 45/76 *Comet* v. *Produktschap* [1976] ECR 2043).

In many cases since then, the Court has referred to these principles, stating them to be an articulation of the principle of cooperation contained in Article 5 EC. In Cases 46, 48/93 *Brasserie du Pêcheur and Factortame III* [1996] I CMLR 889, the Court reiterated the point once more, stating that

'the conditions for reparation of loss and damage laid down by national law must not be less favourable than those relating to similar domestic claims and must not be such as in practice to make it impossible or excessively difficult to obtain reparation' (para. 67).

It will be apparent that two extra words have crept in over the years: 'excessively difficult'. Craig and de Búrca (1995: 236) argue that the increasingly interventionist case law on national remedies which the Court has handed down in recent years (and which we shall examine below) has

'demonstrated what was perhaps an increasing impatience on the part of the Court with the pace and weakness of national enforcement of Community law, and the inadequacies of existing national remedies for this purpose.'

Perhaps the additional words are attributable to this impatience. Certainly, just as the formula on national procedural autonomy has changed, so the Court can be shown to have changed its position on another fundamental principle of national autonomy: that the effect of EC law within the national legal order is not to require the creation of new legal remedies to those which exist already, although every type of action available under national law must be available also for the protection of EC rights (Case 158/80 *Rewe-Handelsgesellschaft Nord mbH* v. *Hauptzollamt Kiel* [1981] ECR 1805).

10.3   National Remedies and the Disapplication of National Law

Case 106/77 *Amministrazione delle Finanze dello Stato* v. *Simmenthal SpA (Simmenthal II)* ([1978] ECR 629) tells national courts that they are responsible for 'disapplying' national law which comes into conflict with

EC law (Gravells, 1989, 1991; Barav, 1989) (9.13). The idea of disapplying an Act of Parliament is a novel concept for a UK judge, accustomed to occupying a subordinate position in relation to the legislature. However, as the Court made clear in its ruling on the reference from the House of Lords in Case C-213/89 *R* v. *Secretary of State for Transport, ex parte Factortame Ltd (Factortame I)* ([1990] ECR I-2433), it is inherent to the system of EC law that national courts must be able, in either final or interim proceedings, to issue appropriate orders to give effect to EC law. It held (at p. 2473):

> 'In accordance with the case law of the Court, it is for the national courts, in application of the principle of co-operation laid down in Article 5 of the EEC Treaty, to ensure the legal protection which persons derive from the direct effect of provisions of Community law . . .
>
> The Court has also held that any provision of a national legal system and any legislative, administrative or judicial practice which might impair the effectiveness of Community law by withholding from the national court having jurisdiction to apply such law the power to do everything necessary at the moment of its application to set aside national legislative provisions which might prevent, even temporarily, Community rules from having full force and effect are incompatible with those requirements, which are the very essence of Community law . . .
>
> It must be added that the full effectiveness of Community law would be just as much impaired if a rule of national law could prevent a court seised of a dispute governed by Community law from granting interim relief in order to ensure the full effectiveness of the judgment to be given on the existence of the rights claimed under Community law. It follows that a court which in those circumstances would grant interim relief, if it were not for a rule of national law, is obliged to set aside that rule.'

On these grounds the House of Lords was obliged to abrogate, at least as regards matters of Community competence, the rule prohibiting the granting of interim injunctions against the Crown, as it had indicated in its judgment prior to ordering a reference that it would be prepared to do if required by the Court (*R* v. *Secretary of State for Transport, ex parte Factortame Ltd* [1990] 2 AC 85; [1989] 3 CMLR 1; award of interim relief: [1991] 1 All ER 70; [1990] 3 CMLR 375). The Court also held that a national court must be prepared to grant such a remedy even in advance of an authoritative ruling by the Court on the existence of an infringement of EC law. Consequently, the House of Lords was required to contemplate two novelties: first, removing a procedural bar on interim relief against the Crown, and second, giving interim relief which effectively disapplied an Act of Parliament. The effect of the ruling must be regarded as coming very close to requiring the creation of new remedies (Ross, 1990).

10.4   Adequate Sanctions and EC Law

One of the most important aspects of the 'effective remedies' principle has been the Court's approach to the issue of the adequacy of sanctions. This point was initially addressed in Case 14/83 *Von Colson and Kamann* v. *Land Nordrhein-Westfalen* ([1984] ECR 1891) (see 9.10 and 9.14). In the context of a provision of the Equal Treatment Directive which the Court had found allowed Member States to choose from a range of sanctions, the Court concluded

> 'if a Member State chooses to penalize breaches of that prohibition by the award of compensation, then in order to ensure that it is effective and that it has a deterrent effect, that compensation must in any event be adequate in relation to the damage sustained and must therefore amount to more than purely nominal compensation. . .' (p. 1909).

This conclusion led easily to a challenge in Case C-271/91 *Marshall* v. *Southampton and South West Hampshire AHA (Marshall II)* ([1993] ECR I-4367) to the UK's then applicable compensation limits on sex discrimination claims, which limited the maximum amount to £6,250 and appeared to deny a right to interest on compensation awarded (9.10). The Court concluded that 'full' compensation was the only appropriate remedy where the Member State had chosen compensation as the means of sanctioning the discriminatory act, and that this included also a right to interest; this was necessary to ensure 'real and effective judicial protection' and to 'have a real deterrent effect on the employer' (p. 4407). Only then could 'real equality of opportunity' be ensured through adequate reparation (p. 4409).

10.5   Effective Remedies and the Procedural and Jurisdictional Conditions Applying to National Remedies

The general trend in the case law on national remedies and procedural and jurisdictional conditions in recent years has been for the Court to take an increasingly interventionist line. For example, it has held that the rights granted by EC law may not be limited by the application of additional substantive conditions. For example, in Case C-177/88 *Dekker* v. *Stichting Vormingscentrum voor Jong Volwassenen* ([1990] ECR I-3941) the Court held that national provisions may not subject liability for sex discrimination in employment matters arising under the Equal Treatment Directive to the requirement that the victim show fault on the part of the employer since all that is required under the Directive is proof of the objective fact of discrimination. In similar vein, in Case C-377/89 *Cotter and McDermott* v. *Minister for Social Welfare (No. 2)* ([1991] ECR I-1155), the Court held that the state may not defeat a claim to a social benefit based on the right to non-discrimination on grounds of sex based on the EC Social Security Directive (Directive 79/7), by claiming that the applicant would be unjustly enriched by the receipt of the benefit because she had received an equivalent benefit via her husband. Unjust enrichment may not, therefore, be a valid defence to a claim based on EC rights – an argument reminiscent, not of the effective national remedies principle, but of the 'estoppel' argument often put forward to justify the direct effect of directives (9.11).

In a further case also concerned with rights under the same Directive, the 'estoppel' argument once more came to the fore: in Case C-208/90 *Emmott* v. *Minister for Social Welfare* ([1991] ECR I-4269) the Court held that the application of time limits which preclude the applicant from bringing a claim can only occur as from date when the provision of EC law in question had been transparently implemented by that state. Only from that date could the applicant be in a position to know what her EC rights were; hence time should not begin to run until that date. Until then the national authorities were precluded from relying upon the ordinary national time limits relating to the bringing of proceedings in the national courts. In recent cases, however, the Court does appear to have resiled somewhat from that approach to Directive 79/7; the application of this measure for the benefit of women has proved to be exceedingly problematic in the context of widespread welfare benefit cuts across many Member States. In a series of rulings, the Court has found itself forced to accept arguments from the Member States effectively bringing about levelling down, in the name of equality, rather than levelling up.

In both Case C-338/91 *Steenhorst-Neerings* v. *Bestuur van de Bedrijfsvereniging voor Detailhandel* ([1993] ECR I-5475) and Case C-410/92 *Johnson* v. *Chief Adjudication Officer* ([1994] ECR I-5483) the Court refused to apply the *Emmott* principle to national provisions which limited not the right to bring an action, but the length of time for which a claim could be backdated. The Court applied the two limb national remedies test, and concluded that the national conditions were not discriminatory and did not make it 'virtually impossible' for an action to be brought on the basis of EC law (*Johnson*, p. 5510). The tenor of the judgments was that *Emmott* should be very much regarded as an exceptional case.

Finally, in two judgments decided on the same day (Case C-312/93 *Peterbroeck* v. *Belgian State* [1996] 1 CMLR 793; [1995] ECR I-4599 and Cases 430, 431/93 *van Schijndel* v. *Stichting Pensioenfonds voor Fysiotherapeuten* [1996] 1 CMLR 801; [1995] ECR I-4705), the Court was asked to consider the status of national procedural rules which limit the ability of national courts to raise of their own motion questions of EC law which the parties have failed to raise themselves within the relevant national time limits. *Peterbroeck* was a taxation action, brought against a state authority, and the Court concluded that such a national procedural provision would contravene the 'effective remedies' principle by making the application of EC law virtually impossible or excessively difficult. The Court offered some further guidance on judging national procedural provisions:

'Each case . . . must be analysed by reference to the role of that provision in the procedure, its progress and special features, viewed as a whole, before the various national instances. In the light of that analysis the basic principles of the domestic judicial system, such as the protection of the rights of the defence, the principle of legal certainty and the proper conduct of procedure, must, where appropriate, be taken into consideration' (para. 14).

In that case, a 60-day time limit after which new points of law could not be raised by the parties or by the court was objectionable because it had expired before the referring court (which was the first court capable of making a reference under the applicable domestic appeals system: see Case C-24/92 *Corbiau* [1993] ECR I-1277 (8.4)) had even held its hearing, and no other national court further up the judicial hierarchy could of its own motion raise the point of EC law.

In contrast, in *van Schijndel*, although a substantial part of the judgment was identical to that in *Peterbroeck*, the Court applied different reasoning to a general principle of the Dutch legal system that a court in civil proceedings should normally take a passive role, leaving the conduct of litigation to the parties, and should take the initative only in exceptional circumstances. Whatever EC principle there is that national courts should be *able* to raise points of EC law of their own motion, it does not override such a fundamental national principle of procedural economy such as to generate an *obligation* to raise points of EC law in cases involving the resolution of rights and obligations in private law.

10.6   The Conditions Governing the Principle of State Liability

It is difficult to argue against the proposition that the development of a principle of State liability, based on a uniform EC principle of reparation, represents a rupture in the distinction drawn hitherto – and highlighted in Figure 9.1 – between the ways in which the fundamental constitutional qualities of EC law are given effect within the EU legal order, and the practical enforcement of those techniques at national level. This point is particularly clear because, having articulated the general principle in a judgment (Cases 6, 9/90 *Francovich I*) described by one commentator as 'extremely brief and sweeping' and 'terse and laconic' (Bebr, 1992: 568, 575), the Court has been forced by the demand for clarification from below to look in much more detail at the precise conditions under which this particular remedy should be available in the national legal orders. In other words, although the Court refers at several points in its judgment in Cases 46, 48/93 *Brasserie du Pêcheur and Factortame III* to national procedural autonomy, it has in effect laid out in some detail the terms under which liability will arise. In so doing, it has effectively slightly reformulated the original three conditions which it articulated in *Francovich I* which were the only guidance it offered on implementing this remarkable new principle (9.17), drawing heavily, in response to comments and suggestions made by observers including the Commission, a number of Member States and many academic commentators, on its own case law on the non-contractual liability of the EU institutions for unlawful acts in order to create a parallelism between State liability and EU liability. This paragraph will discuss these revised formulations; the facts of *Brasserie du Pêcheur and Factortame III* (hereinafter '*Factortame III*') are set out in 9.18.

In *Factortame III* the Court identified four factors which affect the conditions under which liability will arise:

– the nature of the breach of EC law giving rise to the damage;
– the principle of the full effectiveness of EC rules and the effective protection of EC rights;
– the obligation of cooperation imposed on Member States under Article 5 EC; and
– the relevance of the Court's own case law on Article 215 EC, acknowledging that without particular justification there cannot be a difference between the conditions under which the EU institutions and the Member State governments are liable.

The Court then went on to apply the principles that it applies to actions for damages in respect of loss arising as a result of the legislative acts of the EU institutions, where it takes into account factors such as the complexity of the situation, difficulties in the interpretation or application of legal texts, and particularly the margin of discretion given to legislative actors. This leads to a test under which the EU institutions (and now the Member States) can only be held liable for an act taken in a legislative context characterised by the exercise of wide discretion where they have 'manifestly and gravely disregarded the limits' on the exercise of their powers (para. 45) (14.9). It was that consideration which led it to conclude in Case C-392/93 *R* v. *HM Treasury, ex parte British Telecom* (26.3.96) that the UK government could not be liable in damages in respect of loss allegedly caused by its good faith (if incorrect) interpretation and misimplementation of a provision in a public procurement Directive. Such an act was not a sufficiently serious breach of EC law.

On the other hand, in many circumstances Member States do not have a wide discretion when they act 'in a field governed by Community law' (para. 46). EC law imposes many obligations of conduct or result on Member States which reduce their margin of discretion – in particular the obligation to implement a directive (note that the Directive in *British Telecom* had been *mis*implemented; this formulation leaves a question mark over the incorrect 'deeming' of existing national law to be a sufficient implementation, as occured in Case 334/92 *Wagner Miret* v. *Fondo de Garantía Salarial* ([1993] ECR I-6911) (9.14) where the Court specifically referred the national court to the *Francovich I* case). In contrast, the German and UK legislatures in the two cases at issue in *Factortame III* were in a situation comparable to the EU legislature, faced with a wide range of choices in fields lacking harmonisation measures or an exhaustive set EU regulations (beer contents, and implementation of the common fisheries policy). On the basis of this the Court concluded that the three conditions for liability should now be reformulated for such cases as follows:

- the rule of law infringed must be intended to confer rights on individuals;
- the breach must be sufficiently serious; and
- there must be a direct causal link between the breach of the obligation resting on the State and the damage sustained by the injured parties.

The Court felt easily able to conclude for itself that the first condition was satisfied in respect of both Articles 30 and 52. On the second condition, the Court concluded that this was a matter for the national court, but offered some guidance to the national courts on its reading of seriousness of the breaches manifested by the legislative measures in question. The circumstances to be considered by the national court include the degree of clarity and precision of the rule breached, the measure of discretion which it provides for, the intentional or involuntary nature of the infringement, the excusable or inexcusable nature of any actual error of law by the Member State, the contributory role of any positions taken by the Community institutions, and the adoption of national measures or practices especially where these contravene settled case law of the Court of Justice.

In the case of the Merchant Shipping Act 1988, the Court offered the view that the introduction of provisions making registration of trawlers subject to a nationality condition constituted 'direct discrimination manifestly contrary to Community law' (para. 61). Other provisions on residence and domicile, while *prima facie* contrary to Article 52 were arguably justifiable by reference to the objectives of the common fisheries policy, although the Court rejected that argument in Case C-221/89 *Factortame II* [1991] ECR I-3905 (the judgment on the substance of the case on Article 52, referred by the Divisional Court). Furthermore in assessing the seriousness of a breach, it is important to take into account the promptness of any national reaction to a finding of a violation of EC law by the Court of Justice. Failure to observe such a finding would be determinative of the question of the seriousness of the breach; this is a matter of fact to be determined by the national court. A number of other points arose for consideration in *Factortame III*. The Court concluded – unsurprisingly in view of its decision in Case C-177/88 *Dekker* (10.5) – that beyond the concept of a 'serious' breach, the national court could not demand an additional element of 'fault' in the action under national law. It referred to the fact that the national legal systems have very different concepts of 'fault'. Finally, it held that the principle of 'full' compensation should apply, subject to the duty to mitigate with due diligence – incumbent also on plaintiffs in actions under Article 215. Nonetheless a number of questions relating to compensation remain inconclusive, especially the possibility of exemplary damages.

10.7   The Alternative: Legislative Action

The parallels drawn between Article 215 and the principle of State liability may, in the view of some, presage the emergence of a 'Common Law' of Europe in the field of legal remedies (e.g. van Gerven, 1994b; 1995; Caranta, 1995). The Court has been eager, as in *Factortame III*, to refer to both Article 215 and State liability as

> 'simply an expression of the general principle familiar to the legal systems of the Member States that an unlawful act or omission gives rise to an obligation to make good the damage caused' (para. 29).

In view of that conclusion, there may be arguments in favour of moving fairly rapidly towards a harmonisation of the conditions on the basis of which that general principle is given effect, in the interests of improving individual legal protection and reducing the complexity of the systems which EU citizens currently face. Back in 1976, in Case 33/76 *Rewe-Zentralfinanz* (10.2) the Court seemed to indicate that the EU had competence – on the basis of Articles 100–102 and 235 EC – to adopt harmonisation measures in the procedural field in order to

> 'remedy differences between the provisions laid down by law, regulation or administrative action in Member States if they are likely to distort or harm the functioning of the Common Market' (p. 1998).

There are three pieces of evidence which indicate a gradual movement towards harmonisation. The first is the Remedies Directive operating in the field of public procurement (Directive 89/665 OJ 1989 L395/33), which specifically recognised in its preamble that in some Member States the absence or inadequacy of existing remedies, at least in that field, might deter undertakings from submitting tenders for public procurement contracts. It would not be so difficult to extrapolate outwards from that argument in favour of harmonisation of remedies in other fields, or across the board. Second, there are a series of measures taken to protect the financial interests of the EU, which aim specifically at the creation of adequate penalties in the criminal field to deter and punish those involved in fraud against the EU (5.12). Again this is a sectoral measure, but it is an indication of a willingness to intervene with binding measures in fields which appear at first sight to within the sphere of national sovereignty in order to achieve an important EU objective. Finally, in mid-1995 the Council did adopt a general measure on effective uniform application of EC law and on remedies, but it took the form of a non-binding resolution (OJ 1995 C188/1). The Resolution refers throughout to the importance of Article 5, the need for effective remedies, and the essential element of cooperation. The Council concludes by agreeing to examine 'openly and constructively' proposals on effective penalties put forward by the Commission in the future.

10.8   Domestic Responses to the Challenges of EC Law

Details were given in 9.4 and 9.5 regarding the differing constitutional responses which the national legal systems have made to the demands of EC law. These were in effect the responses to the first level of analysis identified in Figure 9.1. In the spirit of the dialogue which underlies the constitututionalisation of the EU legal order, we shall now concentrate principally on the progress made towards a complete acceptance of the approaches taken by the Court of Justice at the second and third levels in national courts. Ideally the Court should always seek to balance its approach between the need to promote dynamism within the EU legal order, and the need to avoid accelerating beyond the bounds of what national courts consider acceptable. It is from the reactions of the national courts that it is possible to discern whether the Court has achieved that balance.

For example, some courts such as the French *Conseil d'Etat* (Supreme Administrative Court) and the German Federal Finance Court have been unwilling to accept that Directives could give rise to rights justiciable at the instance of individuals. The views of the two courts in *Minister of the Interior* v. *Cohn-Bendit* ([1980] 1 CMLR 543) and *Kloppenburg* v. *Finanzamt Leer* ([1989] 1 CMLR 873) were founded on an analysis of Article 189 which focused on the differences between regulations and directives, and which has found support amongst academic commentators also (e.g. Hamson, 1976). It is ironic how the Court itself has turned to a similar analysis in Case C-91/92 *Faccini Dori* ([1994] ECR I-3325) (9.11).

The *Conseil d'Etat* has also experienced difficulties accepting the full consequences of the superior nature of EC law. However, in recent cases such as *Boisdet* ([1991] 1 CMLR 3) it has accepted an interpretation of the Article 55 of the French Constitution which allows EC law to take precedence over subsequent French laws, an interpretation which accords with the position already long-adopted by the highest French court in the private law field, the Cour de Cassation (*Café Jacques Vabre* ([1975] 2 CMLR 336).

In the UK debate has centred around key provisions of the European Communities Act 1972. These should ensure the effective application and enforcement of EC law in the UK.

Section 2(1) enshrines the concept of direct effect:

'All such rights, powers, liability, obligations and restrictions from time to time created or arising by or under the Treaties, and all such remedies and procedures from time to time provided for by or under the Treaties, as in accordance with the Treaties are without further enactment to be given legal effect or used in the United Kingdom shall be recognised and available in law, and be enforced, allowed and followed accordingly.'

The supremacy of EC law appears to be guaranteed by the rather obscurely worded section 2(4) which contains the text:

'any enactment passed or to be passed, other than one contained in this Part of this Act, shall be construed and have effect subject to the foregoing provisions of this section.'

The best view of section 2(4) is as a rule of construction for national law aimed at avoiding conflicts with EC law. According to Lord Bridge in *Factortame* ([1989] 2 All ER 692 at p. 701) section 2(4):

'has precisely the same effect as if a section were incorporated in [Part II of the Merchant Shipping Act 1988] which in terms enacted that the provisions with regard to registration of British fishing vessels were to be without prejudice to the directly enforceable rights of nationals of any Member States of the EEC.'

At the practical level, the House of Lords in *Factortame* complied fully with the requirements of EC law as laid down by the Court, with Lord Bridge remarking on the rehearing of the case following the judgment of the Court ([1990] 3 CMLR 375) on the misconceived comments of those who regarded the requirement that the courts override national legislation in violation of EC law as a novel and dangerous invasion of the sovereignty of the UK. He regarded the approach taken by the Court as mandated by the supremacy of EC law, a concept well entrenched in the EU legal order before even the UK acceded to the Treaties.

However, achieving the enforcement of EC law through the medium of interpretation rather than through simple acceptance of the direct applicability principle (9.2) has caused a number of difficulties for the UK courts, particularly when they have been asked to apply the *EU* interpretative obligation – the principle of indirect effect. The judges have generally shown themselves willing to give sympathetic interpretations of national provisions introduced with the specific purpose of implementing EU legislation. In *Pickstone* v. *Freemans plc* ([1988] 2 All ER 813) the House of Lords interpreted section 1(2)(c) of the Equal Pay Act 1970, which was introduced by the Equal Value Regulations 1983 in order to bring UK law into conformity with the requirements of Article 119 EC on equal pay, in order to give effect to what it saw as the purpose of Parliament. This meant that it was permissible to give an interpretation of the words in the light of the purpose of the equal value principle and to allow it to function effectively to deal with the 'mischief' which it was introduced to counter. In an equal value claim, one group of workers is compared against another group of workers in order to assess the respective value of the work done by each group of workers. Sec. 1(2)(c) should not be rendered inoperative by the employment of one token man amongst what is normally a disadvantaged group of female workers; it should be sufficient that the group of workers disadvantaged was predominantly female (or, exceptionally, male).

A similar approach was taken in *Litster* v. *Forth Dry Dock and Engineering Co Ltd* ([1989] 1 All ER 1134) to the Transfer of Undertakings Regulations 1981, passed to implement the Acquired Rights Directive 77/187.

However, in a case where there was at the time when the facts arose no specific implementing legislation, the House of Lords found itself unable to adopt the same approach. In *Duke* v. *GEC Reliance* ([1988] 1 All ER 626) the House was asked to interpret the provisions of the Sex Discrimination Act 1975 on retirement ages in accordance with the provisions of the Equal Treatment Directive 76/207, in order to give a remedy to a woman working in the private sector who was made redundant earlier than a man in the same position, on grounds of having reached a (discriminatory) retirement age. This would have equalised the position of private and public sector workers, since the latter had a remedy based on the direct effect of the Directive as interpreted by the Court of Justice in Case 152/84 *Marshall* v. *Southampton and South West Hampshire AHA (Marshall I)* ([1986] ECR 723) (9.11). The House of Lords used the European Communities Act 1972 in order to draw a much stronger distinction between EC law which is and is not justiciable than is probably tenable in the light of the case law of the Court of Justice on indirect effect, holding that section 2(4) only applies the supremacy principle to directly effective EC law, and that no other principle of EC law required it to give what it considered to be a strained interpretation of the Sex Discrimination Act in order to achieve a reconciliation with the terms of the Equal Treatment Directive. In the absence of specific implementing legislation the House regarded itself as outside the duty of sympathetic interpretation which it was fulfilling in *Pickstone* and *Litster*. It is difficult to reconcile the position in *Duke* with the subsequent judgment of the Court of Justice in Case C-106/89 *Marleasing* (9.14).

Although *Duke* has not been formally overruled, there is evidence that some of its harshest effects have been quietly dropped by the House of Lords in subsequent cases. In its judgment in *Webb* v. *EMO Cargo Ltd* ([1993] 1 WLR 49), ordering a reference on the question of pregnancy discrimination to the Court of Justice, the House of Lords appeared no longer to see a difficulty in applying an interpretative obligation to national legislation (again the Sex Discrimination Act 1975) which preceded an EU Directive (Equal Treatment Directive). It did not refer a question to the Court of Justice on the interpretative obligation, perhaps somewhat to the surprise of the Court of Appeal which had found itself in the same case unable to find an interpetation of the Sex Discrimination Act which did not distort its meaning ([1992] 2 All ER 43). When the case returned to the House of Lords following the Court of Justice judgment (Case C-32/93 *Webb* v. *EMO Cargo Ltd* [1994] ECR I-3567) which was wholly concerned with the question of what constitutes 'pregnancy discrimination', the House of Lords did find a way to fit the ruling of the Court of Justice into the Sex Discrimination Act – without discussing exactly how it was achieving that within the framework offered by either the European Communities Act or the principle of indirect effect – albeit one which commentators may find a little narrow in scope ([1995] 4 All ER 577; see Szyszczak, 1996).

This line of case law reveals most clearly the difficulties which flow in the UK from the dualist inheritance under which the authority of EC law is seen as deriving its force from the European Communities Act 1972, rather than from its inherent qualities as interpreted by the Court of Justice using the theory of the transfer of sovereign powers.

Perhaps the most notable 'success story' in terms of the enforcement of EC law in the UK has been the *Factortame* litigation, which continues to proceed through the courts which are now dealing with the compensation issue. A further indirect consequence of that litigation has been the resolution of a difficult *locus standi* issue relating to the powers of the Equal Opportunities Commission to enforce sex discrimination law. In *R* v. *Secretary of State for Employment, ex parte EOC* ([1994] 1 All ER 910), the House of Lords relied upon *Factortame* to assist in holding that the EOC can bring judicial review proceedings in a matter of public importance and in relation to which it was given a role under public law, notwithstanding that it had no direct personal interest in the outcome of the proceedings that there was no 'decision' which it wished to challenged but merely a legislative policy (which discriminated against part-time workers). This ruling opens up the possibilities of 'public interest' actions in the UK courts not only by the EOC, but also potentially by a range of interested groups concerned with the effective enformcent of EC law. On the issue of substance, it is useful to note that the House of Lords felt able to decide for itself that there had been a breach of EC law, without recourse to an Article 177 reference; this is an indication, perhaps, that UK judges are becoming more adept at handling the substantive law of the EU, albeit that they remain still a little wary of some of its procedural and remedial implications.

Indeed, in the field of damages actions, the development of the law in the UK has been notably slow. There is only rather oblique authority for the proposition that Articles 85 and 86 EC should give rise to an action in damages by a person injured by anti-competitive or monopolistic conduct (*Garden Cottage Foods* v. *Milk Marketing Board* 1984] AC 130) and in *Bourgoin* v. *MAFF* ([1986] QB 716) the Court of Appeal gave a restrictive interpretation of the right to damages in respect of conduct of the State in violation of Article 30 EC which will need reconsideration in the light of

Francovich I and *Factortame III* (a point accepted *obiter* by Lord Goff in *Kirklees BC* v. *Wickes Building Supplies Ltd* ([1992] 3 All ER 717 at p. 734).

Caution with regard to remedies has undoubtedly led in part to the references in *Factortame III* and *British Telecommunications.* In contrast, in a number of other Member States including France and the Netherlands, courts have shown a willingness to apply the *Francovich I* ruling in order to find State liability, even before the additional clarification now offered. On the other hand, as the number of references requesting clarification of *Francovich I* (more than ten) are showing, the UK is by no means alone. In particular, in Germany *Francovich I* encountered a fairly negative reaction, especially from public lawyers (as opposed to EU lawyers), reflecting a considerable sensitivity in the Germany/EU legal interface, which is even greater since the Federal Constitutional Court decision in *Brunner* ([1994] 1 CMLR 57; 3.3) (Uecker, 1994).

Summary

1   National courts must give comprehensive remedies for breach of EC law, and although subject to national procedural conditions, these must be at least as generous as those applicable in equivalent national actions and not such as to render rights under EC law incapable of enforcement in practice.
2   Although in principle there is no obligation on the part of national courts or national legal orders to create new remedies for the enforcement of EC law, in reality the effect of the Court's case law, particularly in *Factortame I* and *Francovich I/Factortame III* comes close to requiring this.
3   Where compensatory sanctions are chosen by the national legislature as the means to ensure that rights arising under EC law are effectively enforced, the sanction of damages must be adequate.
4   The application of the effective remedies principle has resulted in EC law effectively determining most aspects of the conditions under which remedies are granted in practice in national courts.
5   Damages for State liability for breach of EC law will be available – subject to national procedural rules – if the following conditions are satisfied:
    – the rule of law infringed must be intended to confer rights on individuals;
    – the breach must be sufficiently serious; and
    – there must be a direct causal link between the breach of the obligation resting on the State and the damage sustained by the injured parties.
6   The Court has introduced a parallelism between the liability of the Member States and the non-contractual liability of the EU institutions under Article 215 EC.
7   The record of national legal systems in giving effect to the case law of the Court of Justice is mixed. In the UK particular difficulties centre around the right to damages, and the willingness of the courts to make

use of the indirect effect principle, the latter problem resulting from the interpretation of the European Communities Act 1972, and the continued insistence of the courts upon that Act as the foundation for the enforcement in the UK of EC law, rather than its inherent qualities, as interpreted by the Court of Justice.

Questions

1   Has EC law gone too far in policing the 'effective' and 'non-discriminatory' national remedies principles?
2   How does *Factortame III* differ from *Francovich I*, both as regards the facts of the case, and the principles of State liability as determined by the Court of Justice? Has the Court of Justice now given sufficiently clear advice to the national courts so that they will be able to apply the principle in future?
3   Is the record of the higher English courts in the application of EC law satisfactory?

Further Reading

Craig (1993), '*Francovich*, Remedies and the Scope of Damages Liability', 109 *LQR* 595.

van Gerven (1994b), 'Non-contractual Liability of Member States, Community Institutions and Individuals for Breaches of Community Law with a View to a Common Law for Europe', 1 *MJ* 6.

van Gerven (1995), 'Bridging the Gap Between Community and National Laws: Towards a Principle of Homogeneity in the field of Legal Remedies?', 32 *CMLRev.* 579.

Gravells (1989), 'Disapplying an Act of Parliament pending a Preliminary Ruling: Constitutional Enormity or Community Law Right?', *PL* 568.

Gravells (1991), 'Effective Protection of Community Law Rights: Temporary Disapplication of an Act of Parliament', *PL* 180.

Lewis and Moore (1993), 'Duties, Directives and Damage in European Community Law', *PL* 151.

Maher (1994), 'National Courts as European Community Courts', 14 *LS* 226.

Maher (1995), 'A Question of Conflict: the Higher English Courts and the Implementation of European Community Law', in Daintith (1995b).

Meads (1991), 'The obligation to apply European law: is *Duke* dead?', 16 *ELRev.* 490.

Szyszczak (1990), 'Sovereignty: Crisis, Compliance, Confusion, Complacency', 15 *ELRev.* 480.

Ward (1995), 'Effective Sanctions in EC Law: A Moving Boundary in the Division of Competence', 1 *ELJ* 204.

Wincott (1995b), 'The role of law or the rule of the Court of Justice? An 'institutional' account of judicial politics in the European Community', 2 *JEPP* 583.

de Witte (1991), 'Community Law and National Constitutional Values', *LIEI*, Issue no. 2, p. 4.

Part IV

The Judicial Control of the EU Institutions

11 Introduction to the Judicial Control of the EU Institutions

11.1 Introduction

Every developed legal system needs a system of judicial control which places fetters upon the exercise of state power. In the EU the clear mandate for such a system lies in the task of the Court under Article 164 EC to ensure that the law is observed. This was elaborated by the Court in Case 294/83 *Parti Ecologiste 'Les Verts'* v. *Parliament* ([1986] ECR 1339) in the following terms (at p. 1365):

'It must first be emphasised in this regard that the European Economic Community is a Community based on the rule of law, in as much as neither its Member States nor its institutions can avoid a review of the question whether the measures adopted by them are in conformity with the basic constitutional charter, the Treaty. In particular, in Articles 173 and 184, on the one hand, and in Article 177, on the other, the Treaty established a complete system of legal remedies and procedures designed to permit the Court of Justice to review the legality of measures adopted by the institutions. Natural and legal persons are thus protected against the application to them of general measures which they cannot contest directly before the Court by reason of the special conditions of admissibility laid down in the second paragraph of Article 173 of the Treaty. Where the Community institutions are responsible for the administrative implementation of such measures, natural or legal persons may bring a direct action before the Court against implementing measures which are addressed to them or which are of direct and individual concern to them and, in support of such an action, plead the illegality of the general measure on which they are based. Where implementation is a matter for the national authorities, such persons may plead the invalidity of general measures before the national courts and cause the latter to request the Court of Justice for a preliminary ruling.'

The system of judicial control extends also to a system of reparation for tortious acts (what the Treaty terms 'non-contractual' liability); according to the Court in Cases 46, 48/93 *Brasserie du Pêcheur and Factortame III* [1996] I CMLR 889,

'The principle of the non-contractual liability of the Community expressly laid down in Article 215 of the Treaty is simply an expression of the general principle familiar to the legal systems of the Member States that an unlawful act or omission gives rise to an obligation to make good the damage caused. That provision also reflects the obligation on public authorities to make good damage caused in the performance of their duties' (para. 29).

In the last part of this book we will show how these principles have been put into effect, with separate chapters on the judicial review of EU action, on the review of wrongful omissions by the institutions, and on the availability of compensation for loss caused by the EU institutions. It will assess the extent to which the 'state' authorities (i.e. EU institutions and, where appropriate, the national authorities acting under EC law) are bound by the rule of law in their enforcement of EC law *vis-à-vis* individual subjects. It will also provide some assessment of how the balance between the requirements of administrative efficiency and protection of the individual is achieved by the Court of Justice.

This introductory chapter puts in place some essential background for the understanding of this field of EC law, by laying out the key Treaty provisions, and explaining the many functions which these provisions have to fulfil. As will be apparent, the variety of functions fulfilled by Articles 173 and 177 EC in particular are such that aside from vague generalities such as 'the protection of the rule of law' it is hard sometimes to see what these functions share in common with each within the framework of the EU legal order. It is this 'multifunctionalism' which makes this field of EC law sometimes difficult to understand. In this chapter and the ones which follow, the terms 'Court of Justice' and 'Court' should be understood to include both EU courts, as the 'Community judicature', until a distinction is explicitly drawn between the different functions which they now fulfil, by virtue of the current division of jurisdiction.

11.2   The Framework of Treaty Provisions

It should be recalled that the Court of Justice is a court of limited jurisdiction, exercising only the powers conferred upon under the Treaties. Occasionally, it has moved to fill small *lacunae* in the system of judicial protection offered by the Treaty (notably by introducing the *locus standi* of the Parliament under Article 173, and an extended possibility for imposing temporal restrictions on the impact of its rulings under Article 177). However, in general terms, any actions brought before the Court must come under one of the heads of claim contained in the Treaty.

For the purposes of the judicial review of unlawful EU action, the Treaty offers both *direct* and *indirect* means of challenge. The main means of *direct* challenge is Article 173, which we have discussed already in many contexts in this book (e.g. interinstitutional litigation: 5.17; individual complainants and the Commission's enforcement powers: 7.16)

Article 173 provides:

'The Court of Justice shall review the legality of acts adopted jointly by the European Parliament and the Council, of acts of the Council, of the Commission and of the ECB, other than recommendations and opinions, and of acts of the European Parliament intended to produce legal effects *vis-à-vis* third parties.

It shall for this purpose have jurisdiction in actions brought by a Member State, the Council or the Commission on grounds of lack of competence, infringement of an essential procedural requirement, infringement of this Treaty or of any rule of law relating to its application, or misuse of powers.

The Court shall have jurisdiction under the same conditions in actions brought by the European Parliament and by the ECB for the purpose of protecting their prerogatives.

Any natural or legal person may, under the same conditions, institute proceedings against a decision addressed to that person or against a decision which, although in the form of a regulation or a decision addressed to another person, is of direct and individual concern to the former.

The proceedings provided for in this Article shall be instituted within two months of the publication of the measure, or of its notification to the plaintiff, or, in the absence thereof, of the day on which it came to the knowledge of the latter, as the case may be.'

In the event of a finding by the Court of Justice that these principles of legality have been breached, the consequence is annulment. Article 174 EC provides:

'If the action is well founded, the Court of Justice shall declare the act concerned to be void.

In the case of a regulation, however, the Court of Justice shall, if it considers this necessary, state which of the effects of the regulation which it has declared void shall be considered as definitive.'

Article 175 provides a direct complement to Article 173: it covers unlawful inaction, and makes provision for challenges to unlawful omissions:

'Should the European Parliament, the Council or the Commission, in infringement of this Treaty, fail to act, the Member States and the other institutions of the Community may bring an action before the Court of Justice to have the infringement established.

The action shall be admissible only if the institution concerned has first been called upon to act. If, within two months of being so called upon, the institution concerned has not defined its position, the action may be brought within a further period of two months.

Any natural or legal person may, under the conditions laid down in the preceding paragraphs, complain to the Court of Justice that an institution of the Community has failed to address to that person any act other than a recommendation or an opinion.

The Court of Justice shall have jurisdiction, under the same conditions, in actions or proceedings brought by the ECB in the areas falling within the latter's competence and in actions or proceedings brought against the latter.'

The consequences of a successful action under Articles 173 or 175 are dealt with in Article 176 EC which provides:

'The institution (or institutions) whose act has been declared void or whose failure to act has been declared contrary to this Treaty shall be required to take the necessary measures to comply with the judgment of the Court of Justice.

This obligation shall not affect any obligation which may result from the application of the second paragraph of Article 215 [the obligation to pay compensation for wrongful acts causing loss].

This Article shall also apply to the ECB.'

On the basis of these provisions, the following summary can be given: a successful *direct* action to challenge an unlawful act or omission presupposes three basic requirements:

(a)   a reviewable act or omission;
(b)   *locus standi* on the part of the applicant;
(c)   illegality on the part of the defendant (i.e. the presence of the grounds for review in Article 173 or the violation of a duty to act in the context of Article 175).

In the event that a general measure of the EU is at issue, Article 184 EC makes provision for *indirect* challenge in the context of other proceedings:

'Notwithstanding the expiry of the period laid down in the fifth paragraph of Article 173, any party may, in proceedings in which a regulation adopted jointly by the European Parliament and the Council, or a regulation of the Council, of the Commission, or of the ECB is at issue, plead the grounds specified in the second paragraph of Article 173, in order to invoke before the Court of Justice the inapplicability of that regulation.'

The possibility also exists for mounting indirect challenges to EU measures through the medium of an action in the national court which raises a question about the validity of an EU measure. In that context, the national court is under an obligation to make a reference on the question of validity, if it has reason to doubt the validity of the EU measure. It cannot itself in any circumstances invalidate an EU measure (8.7). Of course, neither Article 184 nor Article 177 in themselves constitutes a separate 'cause of action' against unlawful EU action, but mechanisms whereby the Court of Justice can, in the context of other proceedings, review the legality of underlying EU acts, particularly those of a general legislative nature.

The jurisdiction in relation to *compensation* actions follows from Article 178 which provides that 'in disputes relating to the compensation of damage provided for in the second paragraph of Article 215'. The latter provision sets out the conditions governing non-contractual liability:

'In the case of non-contractual liability, the Community shall, in accordance with the general principles common to the laws of the Member States, make good any damage caused by its institutions or by its servants in the performance of their duties.'

Again, as we shall see, actions in national courts have a role to play in this context. Frequently, where the issue raised is one of the return of monies unlawfully levied or unlawfully denied, the correct action for an applicant to bring will be one in the national court against the national implementing authority, which so often is the body which has direct contact with those who are being 'administered'. On the other hand, as the EU institutions – particularly, of course, the Commission – become increasingly directly involved in certain fields of redistributive social policy, through the disbursement of aids and subsidies for example through the various funds, then the proper will be through the medium of an action in the Court of Justice.

Two further provisions should be cited to complete the basic framework for judicial offered by the Treaty. Article 185 provides:

'Actions brought before the Court of Justice shall not have suspensory effect. The Court of Justice may, however, if it considers the circumstances so require, order that application of the contested act be suspended.'

Consequently, one category of actions before the Court will be applications for suspension of contested measures. Likewise, the Court will hear applications for interim measures – under the same jurisdiction which covers interim measures in the case of Article 169 enforcement actions (7.14). Article 186 provides:

'The Court of Justice may in any cases before it prescribe any necessary interim measures.'

11.3   The Many Functions of the System of Judicial Protection

Article 173 in particular conceals behind its text a whole multitude of different functions, which highlight the many different ways in which various actors – institutions, Member States, 'individuals' (all natural or legal persons, including any potential applicants such as pressure groups, trade or other types of associations, sub-national governments) – interact with the EU legal order. The different types of interactions are expressed according to the various conditions which Article 173 imposes upon each actor, in particular:

- the extent of *locus standi* (limited or unlimited);
- the range of EU measures which can be challenged (all acts having legal effects, or only certain categories of 'decisions';
- finally, we shall see that in some cases Article 173 interacts with other provisions of the Treaty, in particular the Article 177 preliminary reference provisions.

It would be useful to summarise the numerous usages of the action for annulment:

- The action brought by one institution against another for annulment of any legal act, ranging from general legislative measures, through administrative acts, to even the most informal act which can be characterised as having legal effects. Only the Parliament and the ECB have limited *locus standi* (to protect their prerogatives). The Council and Commission are in contrast presumed always to have an interest in taking action – doubtless because they represent most directly the 'supranational' and 'intergovernmental' elements in the EU. As we saw in the examination of interinstitutional litigation in 5.17, these types of actions could properly be termed *constitutional* in so far as they raise fundamental questions about the division of competence, interinstitutional balance, and principles such as democracy, and institutional accountability and legitimacy.
- Also *constitutional* in nature are many actions brought by Member States against the institutions. In the example of legal basis litigation, here too the preoccupation is very much with questions of competence and interinstitutional balance. The same could be said of the various actions which Luxembourg has taken against the Parliament in order to enforce its right to host the seat of that institution and to prevent it moving wholesale to Strasbourg or elsewhere. Alternatively, a Member State may be arguing that an EU measure was taken in violation of general principles of law, or even fundamental rights. This situation is more likely to arise with increased use of QMV, perhaps as an alternative to the veto which unanimity gives each Member States. A good example would be the attempt by Germany, which had already

expressed its bitter opposition within the political forum, to obtain annulment of the EU's banana regime, established in 1993 by means of Council Regulation (Case C-280/93 *Germany* v. *Council* [1994] ECR I-4873; 3.12). Germany argued vehemently, but unsuccessfully, that the regulation breached both international trade law (the GATT), and fundamental rights of economic actors involved (banana traders). As with the Council and the Commission, there are no problems of *locus standi* for the Member States.

• From time to time, however, the Member States may become involved in litigation – particularly with the Commission – which is *administrative* rather than constitutional in character. That is, it contests the use of executive power by the Commission, rather than fundamental constitutional principles of the legal order. It would normally arise in instances where the Commission has the power, by decision, to apply the Treaty rules to an individual situation (4.4; 7.12). Examples arise commonly in relation to the management of the CAP, especially the disbursement of monies under the European Agricultural Guidance and Guarantee Fund and to the management of other structural funds (Social Fund, Regional Development Fund, etc.). The Commission also has direct executive powers in many fields of customs law, especially the use of Article 115 EC to prevent distortions in the internal market, Article 90(3) on the application of the competition rules to highly regulated markets, and under Article 100A(4) in relation to the management of national derogations from harmonisation measures. All of these provisions have given rise to actions based on Article 173 EC, but provided there are no difficulties for the applicant in identifying the reviewable act, and provided the action is brought within the correct time limits, there will be no problems of admissibility as Member States have unlimited *locus standi*. Moreover, many such actions deal with small questions of technical detail on the powers of the Commission, rather than large issues of principle.

• Then there are a number of categories of *administrative* cases which arise because of the involvement of 'individuals' (i.e. anyone who is not an institution or a Member State) in the Commission's executive processes. Outside a narrow range of circumstances, as we shall see in Chapter 12, such individuals will have great difficulty satisfying the *locus standi* requirement. Essentially, the system of the Treaty sees these types of actions as protecting an individual, 'private' (and normally economic) interest, and not as operating for the broader public interest:

  • in the fields of customs law and agricultural law, difficulties tend to arise either because the measure challenged does not have a sufficiently individuated impact upon the applicant, or because the Commission's procedures do not directly affect the applicant (e.g. in a case of indirect administration, involving the national authorities: 7.1); the rules preclude individuals in such circumstances challenging by means of actions under Article 173 allegedly unlawful legislative measures which form the framework for the executive rules;

- in cases of 'direct administration', e.g. in relation to the structural funds, individual applicants are more likely to be able to establish *locus standi*, providing, that is, that they are not trying to challenge the general legislative framework;
- the cases of competition law, anti-dumping law and state aid law are *sui generis*, as they both involve the Commission in a 'quasi-judicial' role which impacts directly on individuals, investigating alleged instances of breaches of the EU rules by individual or groups of undertakings. Rights of 'due process' arise in these areas, both for those subject to investigation and those who make complaints, which can be protected by means of direct actions for annulment. In the case of competition law where the Commission also takes all of the relevant decisions, the Court explicitly has 'unlimited jurisdiction' (Article 172) in relation to the fines and penalties which the Commission can impose.

- However, Article 173 does *not* normally offer the basis for the judicial review of *unconstitutional* legislation at the instance of individual applicants (that is legislation which was adopted *ultra vires*, or in breach of some general principle or fundamental right upheld under the Treaty). Even so, the system of EC law does recognise the principle of constitutional supremacy, under which the Court of Justice (but not national courts), can invalidate unconstitutional EU legislation. Challenges by individual applicants to general legislative measures should be brought against the implementing measures of the national authorities in the national courts (or brought about by resisting the application of such rules at national level, again in the national court), and the challenge to the underlying EU measure effected indirectly via a reference on validity under Article 177. This system has been heavily criticised as 'letting individuals down' by making them 'explore the highways and byways of national procedural law' (Mancini and Keeling, 1994: 189). A certain level of illogicality is introduced into the system because the Court will hear claims by individuals for damages under Article 215 in respect of loss suffered, even as the result of general legislative measures where the relevant measures cannot be challenged by means of a direct action under Article 173. However, such actions will only very rarely succeed. One of the main focus of discussion in these chapters on the judicial control of the institutions, therefore, will be the question of the access of individual applicants to the Court of Justice.

In comparison to Article 173, Article 175 does not have so many functions to perform. The relative lack of complexity reflects partly the fact that it is not used as the basis for actions anywhere near as often. Even less often are actions actually successful, as Article 175 will only apply where an institution is under a duty to act. For non-privileged applicants, the utility of Article 175 has been clearest in the field of competition law (where it is especially useful for complainants (7.16)). In the interinstitutional sphere it is the Parliament which has been able to make greatest use of the provision, with a successful claim against the Council in respect of failure to adopt a number of measures relating to the Common Transport Policy (Case 13/83 *Parliament* v. *Council* ([1985] ECR 1513).

For each of the situations identified above there will be a different set of policy factors operating; these will underlie the view which the Court takes of the actions of the EU institutions, determining very often the 'intensity' of the review to which it will subject these actions. In other words, policy factors may influence how closely the Court enquires into the actions of the institution under challenge. As a final point about the complexity and difficulty of this field of EC law, a note should be made of the highly technical and often impenetrable frameworks of EU legislation which are the subject of claims in fields such as agriculture and customs. These will frequently make it more difficult for the reader to identify readily the precise policy point which is emerging from any given case, and reduce the sense of a coherent body of law controlling the exercise of public power in the EU.

11.4   Articles 173 and 175 and Public Interest Litigation

A notable feature of many modern legal systems has been the development of public interest litigation, where either one litigant takes action on behalf of a number of others, or a representative association takes action on behalf of its members, or of some 'abstract' interest which it represents (e.g. the environment) (Harlow and Rawlings, 1992). Public interest litigation has proved to be particularly useful as a strategy to be followed in relation to some areas of EC law, notably the private enforcement of sex discrimination law and environmental law (Harlow, 1992a), and some 'repeat players' such as the UK Equal Opportunities Commission have achieved some important successes (Barnard, 1995). These successes have occurred, however, in the national courts, using the medium of Article 177 references in order to secure an authoritative pronouncement by the Court of Justice.

In contrast, because of the restrictive standing rules in the Court of Justice itself, public interest litigation has had almost no impact in relation to direct actions brought by individuals. There have been some attempts to bring cases which have sought to raise some 'public interest' which was more than the aggregate of the 'private interests' of those directly involved. Few have succeeded. Virtually the sole success outside the field of competition law has been Case T-194/94 *Carvel and Guardian Newspapers* v. *Council* ([1995] 3 CMLR 359; 3.5) brought by a journalist and his newspaper as an attack upon the Council's so-called 'transparency arrangements' for allowing public access to documents.

Competition law has brought some successes, notably for consumer groups; this is due to the very specific participatory rights which many of the actors in the process have under the EU rules, and the ease with which a non-participant can become a participant through the presentation of a complaint. The role of BEUC (the *Bureau Européen des Consommateurs*, an umbrella group partly funded by the Commission) has been particularly important. In Cases 228, 229/82 *Ford of Europe Inc* v. *Commission* ([1984] ECR 1129) two groups – BEUC and the UK Consumers' Association – were granted the right by the Court of Justice to intervene in an appeal by Ford against an unfavourable decision of the Commission under the competition rules. However, in Case C-170/89 *BEUC* v. *Commission* ([1991] ECR I-5709) the Court rejected an attempt by BEUC to gain access to confidential documentation in an anti-dumping case concerning the importation of audio cassettes from the Far East. Significantly, the Court did not dispose of the action by holding that BEUC had no standing to challenge a Commission ruling denying the access to documentation, but dismissed the arguments on their merits, observing in its conclusions that it was for the EU legislature to consider the introduction of the types of procedural rights which BEUC was claiming. In Case T-37/92 *BEUC* v. *Commission* ([1994] ECR II-285), BEUC took action again, this time before the Court of First Instance, and successfully challenged a decision of the Commission not to pursue a complaint which BEUC had lodged regarding certain restrictive practices between British and Japanese car manufacturers relating to the British car market.

The possibility of an amendment to Article 173 has been raised, either to extend *locus standi* for private parties, or possibly to allow a specific right of action to certain types of representative associations. The need for amendment will be discussed in greater detail below, as the weaknesses of the standing rules emerge clearly only from a full discussion of how they operate.

11.5   The Division of Jurisdiction and the Appellate Role of the Court of Justice

Since its establishment, the Court of First Instance has acquired a particularly important role in relation to EC 'administrative' law, as it now hears all direct actions brought by non-privileged applicants (i.e. under Articles 173, 175 and 215 EC). It will from time to time decline jurisdiction in circumstances where the same measure has been challenged in proceedings before the Court of Justice. This has occurred in the fields of merger control (Case T-88/94 *Société Commerciale des Potasses et de l'Azote* v. *Commission* [1995] ECR II-222) and state aid (Case T-490/93 *Bremer Vulkan Verbund AG* v. *Commission* [1995] ECR II-477). To ensure the protection of the interests of the individuals concerned, they will exceptionally be permitted leave to intervene in the proceedings before the

Court of Justice where the same measures are challenged (see Case C-329/93 *Germany* v. *Commission* pending in which the Commission Decision at issue in Case T-490/93 has been challenged by the Member State concerned).

As we shall see, the continuing refusal of the Court of First Instance to loosen the standing rules means that it rejects as inadmissible all actions brought against general EU acts. It therefore has very little role to play in respect of the 'constitutional' aspects of the judicial protection scheme identified above (but cf. its role in relation to Article 215). In the first years of its operation, the Court of First Instance was widely acknowledged to be underemployed, as it took only staff cases and competition cases. It now has a heavy workload – comparable with that of the Court of Justice itself – and that may change the way in which, so far, it has been able to deal with cases by handing down rather fuller and more detailed reviews of the facts and law in the cases it decides. These have compared favourably with the judgments of the Court of Justice itself, whose pronouncements are notably delphic. Obviously a widening of the standing rules would have as dramatic an impact upon the Court of First Instance as the transfer of additional categories of case, although the latter seems unlikely to occur in the very near future. The Court of Justice is likely to continue to have responsibility for most *constitutional* aspects of the system of judicial control, as well as for overall review of the system through the exercise of its appellate jurisdiction.

The exercise of that jurisdiction is governed by the the Statute of the Court of Justice and the Rules of Procedure of the Court of Justice. Article 51 provides:

'An appeal to the Court of Justice shall be limited to points of law. It shall lie on the grounds of lack of competence of the Court of First Instance, a breach of procedure before it which adversely affects the interests of the appellant as well as the infringement of Community law by the Court of First Instance.'

If the appeal is well founded, the Court of Justice can either quash the judgment and remit it to the Court of First Instance for decision, or, where the state of the proceedings so permits, it may decide the case itself (as it did in Case C-137/92 P *Commission* v. *BASF* [1994] ECR I-2555, which concerned Commission procedures for taking decisions in competition cases; 4.2). So long as much of the work of the Court of First Instance consisted of staff cases, the level of appeals was bound to remain low, as there are financial disincentives in staff cases against appealing. This will undoubtedly change as the Court of First Instance now deals with a much wider range of cases, and a number of the cases discussed in the chapters which follow are under appeal. However, as it takes nearly two years for the Court of Justice to decide appeals, it would appear that there are disincentives other than mere questions of money.

Summary

1   The Court of Justice attaches great importance to the system of remedies for judicial control of the actions of the EU institutions under the Treaties, aiming to ensure that the European Community is a Community based on the rule of law.
2   The system of remedies is principally based on Articles 173, 175, 177, 184 and 215 EC. Many of these provisions fulfil a number of different constitutional and administrative functions, depending upon the nature of the litigants before the Court, the type of provision under challenge, and whether the litigation began in the national court, the Court of First Instance or the Court of Justice.
3   For the EU institutions and the Member States, Article 173 offers a mechanism for maintaining the constitutional checks and balances offered by the separation of powers and functions within the EU, and between the EU and its Member States.
4   Individuals wishing to challenge general EU measures must normally begin their challenge in the national court, and seek a reference on validity from the national court under Article 177. Compensation claims rarely succeed.
5   The Court of Justice exercises an important appellate jurisdiction in relation to the judgments of the Court of First Instance.

Questions

See Chapters 12–14.

Workshop (for Chapters 11–13)

What changes (if any) would you introduce in the text of Articles 173 and 175 EC to increase the level of individual access to the Court of First Instance and the Court of Justice?

Further Reading

See Chapters 12–14.

12 Judicial Review of the Acts of the Institutions

12.1 Introduction

This chapter examines the main elements of annulment actions brought under Article 173, concentrating on the concept of the 'reviewable act', the difficulties of establishing *locus standi*, and the basic approach which the Court of Justice takes to the grounds for review. All of these elements are essential to a successful action for annulment. The text of Article 173 is set out in 11.2. The chapter also examines the conditions governing the availability of indirect review, through the medium of a national court reference on the validity of an EU measure under Article 177, as well as on the basis of Article 184. The different approaches which the Court takes to the cases it encounters, in particular the types of policy factors which it applies, have to be viewed in the light of the typology of cases outlined in 11.3. Perhaps the most important variable concerns the parties to the litigation: EU institutions, Member States or 'private' parties.

12.2 The Notion of a Reviewable Act

Article 173 provides for the Court of Justice to review the legality of certain 'acts' of the institutions. The exclusion in the original Treaty of acts of the Parliament did cause problems in the context of the increased role and powers of the Parliament. Judicial recognition of these changes was gradually given by the Court. The terms of Article 173, as amended by the Treaty of Maastricht, are now clear: certain acts of the Parliament are explicitly included, along with those of the Council and the Commission, and of the Council and the Parliament acting jointly as legislator using the co-decision procedure.

In Case 230/81 *Luxembourg* v. *Parliament* ([1983] ECR 255) the Court had already annulled a resolution of the Parliament concerning the moving of its seat from Luxembourg to Strasbourg and Brussels which obviously affected the Parliament's role under all three founding Treaties. However, the annulment was effected under Article 38 ECSC alone, which explicitly recognises the power to annul acts of the Parliament. The Court went one stage further in Case 294/83 *Parti Ecologiste 'Les Verts'* v. *Parliament* ([1986] ECR 1339) annulling the decision of the Bureau of the Parliament allocating money to parties for campaigning in the 1984 direct elections. It stated (p. 1365):

'It is true that, unlike Article 177 of the Treaty, which refers to acts of the institutions without further qualification, Article 173 refers only to acts of the Council and the Commission. However, the general scheme of the Treaty is to make a direct action available against "all measures adopted by the institutions . . . which are intended to have legal effects", as the Court has already had occasion to emphasize in [Case 22/70 *Commission* v. *Council (ERTA)*] . . . The European Parliament is not expressly mentioned among the institutions whose measures may be contested because, in its original version, the EEC Treaty merely granted it powers of consultation and political control rather than the power to adopt measures intended to have legal effects *vis-à-vis* third parties.'

After a comparison with the system of judicial control under the ECSC Treaty, the Court went on:

'An interpretation of Article 173 of the Treaty which excluded measures adopted by the European Parliament from those which could be contested would lead to a result contrary both to the spirit of the Treaty as expressed in Article 164 and to its system. Measures adopted by the European Parliament in the context of the EEC Treaty could encroach on the powers of the Member States or of the other institutions, or exceed the limits which have been set to the Parliament's powers, without its being possible to refer them for review by the Court. It must therefore be concluded that an action for annulment may lie against measures adopted by the European Parliament intended to have legal effects *vis-à-vis* third parties.'

In application of these principles, and in recognition of the role of the European Parliament in relation to the budget, the Court also held that the Order of the President of the Parliament adopting the 1986 budget could be annulled in Case 34/86 *Council* v. *Parliament* ([1986] ECR 2155). The inclusion of the words of the Court *verbatim* in the revised third paragraph of Article 173 is testimony to the role of the Court as the originating force of many of the institutional developments contained in the Treaty of Maastricht.

The most important element of a reviewable act has already been referred to in the quotations from '*Les Verts*', and that is the requirement that it be one which produces 'legal effects'. Although Article 173 refers to this as a requirement only in relation to acts of the Parliament, it applies likewise to both the Council and the Commission, and was read into Article 173 by the Court in recognition that it has been faced with annulment proceedings concerned with acts of the institutions which do not fit neatly into the typology of legal acts offered by Article 189. An early example of such a *sui generis* act is provided by the challenge to the minutes of the Council incorporating a resolution which determined the negotiation procedures for the European Road Transport Agreement brought by the Commission in Case 22/70 *Commission* v. *Council (ERTA)* ([1971] ECR 263). The reason the Commission sought the annulment was in order to demonstrate that these negotiations were matters falling within Community rather than national competence. The Court held that it was not an obstacle to judicial review that a legal act does not formally fall within the system set up by Article 189, but that there is a category of *sui generis* legal acts. The only question is whether the act has legal effects. *Sui generis* acts are very much an open category, as the cases which follow will show.

There is an obvious case for the application of these principles to the many internal management measures of the institutions:

–   staffing decisions (Case 15/63 *Lassalle* v. *Parliament* [1964] ECR 31);
–   the decision of the Parliament Bureau in *'Les Verts'* concerning the allocation of electoral campaign funds'.

In two cases, the Court has construed internal Commission measures as reviewable acts, even though they were essentially non-binding in nature. France was succesful in challenges both to instructions on the management of the EAGGF (Case C-366/88 *France* v. *Commission* ([1990] ECR I-3571) and to a Code of Conduct concerning the management of the structural funds issued by the Commission (Case C-303/90 *France* v. *Commission* [1991] ECR I-5315). What was notable was that in each case the Commission precisely lacked the competence to adopt the type of measures which purported to have legal effects; the cases therefore illustrate the interaction between the basic structural requirements for a successful action and the grounds for review which the Court must apply.

Finally, the concept of a 'reviewable act' has proved particularly important in the context of the control of the legality of competition proceedings, where the Court has found it important to identify the stages at which undertakings may legitimately challenge preliminary decisions taken during the course of such proceedings, without waiting for the final decision. The Court decided in Cases 8-11/66 *Cimenteries* v. *Commission (Noordwijks Cement Accoord)* ([1967] ECR 75) that a decision under Article 15(6) of Regulation 17 whereby the Commission removes from an undertaking, after a preliminary investigation, the protection from fines accorded to them if they notify their agreement to the Commission, could be challenged under Article 173. The Court held (at p. 91):

'this measure deprived them of the advantages of a legal situation which Article 15(5) attached to the notification of the agreement, and exposed them to a grave financial risk. Thus the said measure affected the interests of the undertakings by bringing about a distinct change in their legal position. It is unequivocally a measure which produces legal effects touching the interests of the undertakings concerned and which is binding on them. It constitutes not a mere opinion but a decision.'

The Court repeated substantially the same arguments in holding in Case 60/81 *IBM* v. *Commission* ([1981] ECR 2639) that a letter informing IBM that the Commission was of the opinion that it had abused a dominant position in breach of Article 86 and a 'statement of objections' containing the Commission's allegations were not reviewable acts. A reviewable act must be one which definitively lays down the position of the institution in question on the conclusion of a procedure, and is not merely a provisional or preparatory measure which itself could be challenged if the final decision was challenged.

In the context of complaints, the procedural equivalent of a statement of objections is the 'Article 6' letter, named after the provision which requires the Commission to inform a complainant if it intends to reject their complaint, and to give them an opportunity to make known their views. An Article 6 letter is not a reviewable act (Case T-64/89 *Automec* v. *Commission (Automec I)* [1990] ECR II-367). The letter rejecting a complaint, and informing the complainant that the Commission believes there are no grounds for the application of Articles 85 and 86 is reviewable (Case T-186/94 *Guérin Automobiles* v. *Commission* [1995] ECR II-1753), and even if the letter from the Commission is not couched in particularly formal terms the Court will not hesitate to construe it as a reviewable act, in order to protect the complainant's right to a judicial review (Case C-39/93 P *SFEI* v. *Commission* [1994] ECR I-2681).

The field of merger control also offers an example of just how informal an act can be (or at least its means of public communication), while still being construed as reviewable on the 'legal effects' test. In Case T-3/93 *Société Anonyme à Participation Ouvrière Nationale Air France* v. *Commission (Air France)* ([1994] ECR II-121) the Court of First Instance held that an oral statement by the spokesman for the competition Commissioner could be the basis of an annulment action. The Court found that there was a definitive 'act' which had been made public.

The act must nonetheless be one of the institutions. Two cases involving the Parliament illustrate this point. In Case C-316/91 *Parliament* v. *Council (Lomé Convention)* ([1994] ECR I-6250) the Parliament brought an action against the Council for annulment of a financial regulation granting development aid under the Fourth ACP-EEC Convention. The basis of the development aid was an 'internal agreement' relating to the financing and administration of EU aid, adopted by the representatives of the Governments of the Member States, 'meeting in Council'. It wished to establish the principle that such aid ought to be provided as Community expenditure under Article 209 EC, with the Parliament involved in the legislative process. It failed on this point, but succeeded in establishing that it could at least bring a challenge against a financial regulation adopted by the Council acting under 'intergovernmental' powers. In contrast, the action in Cases C-181, 248/91 *Parliament* v. *Council and Commission (Aid to Bangladesh)* ([1993] ECR I-3685) was declared inadmissible, because the act in question was one involving the Member States acting not as the Council, but simply as the representatives of their governments. It involved an agreement amongst the Member States to pay special aid to Bangladesh after the 1991 cyclone, aid which was paid by every Member State but Greece directly, rather than through a special bank account opened by the Commission for that purpose. It was construed as an independent decision of the Member States who happened to be meeting in the Council. In addition, as they are not 'institutions', 'acts' of the European Council and of COREPER cannot be annulled (Case T-584/93 *Roujansky* v. *European Council* [1994] ECR II-585; Case C-25/94 *Commission* v. *Council (FAO)* (19.3.96)).

In certain exceptional circumstances an act may be so vitiated by defects that it is 'non-existent' (4.2), and therefore incapable of annulment by the Court. Such an act is not reviewable; neither, however, does it have legal effects. The definition of a non-existent act has not been extensively discussed in the Court, but in Cases 1, 14/57 *Société des Usines à Tubes de la Sarre* v. *High Authority* ([1957] ECR 105) the Court held that the absence of reasons renders an act non-existent. In a more recent application of this doctrine (4.2), the Court of First Instance held a Commission Decision imposing heavy fines on a number of chemical companies in respect of an alleged cartel to be so vitiated by defects of form and procedure as to be non-existent (Cases T-79, etc./89 *BASF AG et al.* v. *Commission* [1992] ECR II-315). The judgment was overturned by the Court of Justice which did not consider the defects, on the facts, to be sufficiently serious to merit the application of this exceptional doctrine, which operates as an exception to the principle that acts of the EU institutions are presumed to be lawful and accordingly to produce legal effects, even if tainted with irregularities, until such time as they are annulled or withdrawn (Case C-137/92 P *Commission* v. *BASF* [1994] ECR I-2555). In so doing the Court suggested the following definition of acts which would be 'inexistent', and therefore having no legal effect, even provisional:

> 'acts tainted by an irregularity whose gravity is so obvious that it cannot be tolerated by the Community legal order' (at p. 2647).

12.3   *Locus Standi*

Applicants under Article 173 now fall into three categories. There are privileged applicants (Commission, Council and Member States) who may challenge any measures adopted by any of the institutions. They need prove no specific interest in the act challenged, but must be presumed to have a general interest to act. At the opposite end of the scale are the non-privileged applicants – any natural or legal person – who are subject to restrictive rules on standing. An intermediate category was created by judicial evolution of the standing of the Parliament, and has since been confirmed by the terms of the Treaty of Maastricht, which allows two bodies – the Parliament and the ECB – to take action against the other institutions only for the purpose of protecting their prerogatives.

This is, therefore, another example of institutional developments in the Treaty of Maastricht directly shadowing the developments promoted by the Court. However, the position now confirmed by the Treaty was not reached without a change of heart by the Court (see also 5.17). The Court initially denied the standing of the Parliament in Case 302/87 *Parliament* v. *Council (Comitology)* ([1988] ECR 5615), refusing to draw parallels with either Article 175 which has always recognised the right of the Parliament to bring actions for failure to act, or with its decision in *'Les Verts'* in which it confirmed that the Parliament was capable of being a defendant in Article 173 proceedings. It asserted that the Parliament was adequately protected by Commission's general right to take action on behalf of the 'Community' interest, working on the assumption that the Commission would always have an interest and desire to take action to protect the interests of the Parliament. The Parliament had to be contented with this and the right to intervene in Article 173 proceedings brought by other parties (Article 37 of the Statute of the Court) (see Case 138/79 *Roquette Frères* v. *Council* [1980] ECR 3333 – failure to consult the Parliament before the adoption of a Regulation). Less than two years later the Court reviewed its position, and adopted the halfway house offered by Advocate General Darmon in *Comitology*, and since incorporated in the Treaty of Maastricht, namely that the Parliament is treated as a special case able to take action only in order to protect its own prerogatives (Case C-70/88 *Parliament* v. *Council (Chernobyl)* [1990] ECR I-2041).

12.4   *Locus Standi*: Non-Privileged Applicants

The rules governing the *locus standi* of non-privileged applicants are to be found in the fourth paragraph of Article 173, and are designed to restrict access to judicial review in the Court of Justice to measures which are in essence individual rather than general, and in which the applicant has a personal interest. Consequently, the reference in Article 173 to 'decision' means a decision in the material sense of an individual measure having legal effects, regardless of its formal designation or the formalities which have necessarily attended its adoption. Challenge is restricted to:

- decisions addressed to the applicant;
- decisions (a) addressed to third parties or (b) 'in the form of' regulations, which are of 'direct and individual concern' to the applicant.

In general, the provisions have been narrowly interpreted by the Court, but there have been inconsistencies in its approach such that it is not possible to identify a single line of authority. In particular, there are special rules governing standing to challenge measures adopted by the Council and the Commission which are the result of quasi-judicial procedures, such as anti-dumping regulations, and competition and state aid decisions. There are also a number of anomalous cases which will be highlighted in this discussion, where the result achieved by the Court has been clearly determined by policy considerations. Where judicial review is not possible within the Court itself, an alternative route can normally be taken via the national court and the indirect review of the measure in question using Article 177. There are a number of cases where the Court has rejected the standing of the applicant in an Article 173 case only to examine the validity of the offending measure in the context of an Article 177 ruling. An example is offered by the 'Berlin butter' cases: in Case 97/85 *Union Deutsche Lebensmittelwerke* v. *Commission* ([1987] ECR 2265) an Article 173 challenge was unsuccessfully brought against a Commission scheme based for the sale of cheap butter in Berlin. The scheme was adopted in the form of a Decision addressed to Germany which the applicant had no standing to challenge. However, in Case 133–6/85 *Walter Rau* v. *BALM* ([1987] ECR 2289), in the context of a challenge in the German courts to the German implementing measures, which was based on the argument that the originating Commission measure was invalid, the Court was prepared to review the legality of the underlying act in the context of an Article 177 reference. It held the measure valid.

The simplest case is that of the decision addressed to the applicant. Decisions of the Commission adopted under the procedures laid down in Regulation 17 are frequently challenged by their addressees – the alleged infringers of the competition rules. In this context, the Court also has the power to review the fines imposed by the Commission (Article 172 EC).

Decisions addressed to third parties can only be challenged by those who are directly and individually concerned. Proving direct and individual concern involves more than simply showing some sort of legal interest in the measure. These criteria must be examined separately.

12.5 Direct Concern

A measure will be of direct concern provided that there is a relationship of cause and effect between the act and its impact on the applicant. The question must be asked whether there is any intervening discretion between the decision and the applicant, for example, on the part of a Member State.

In Case 69/69 *Alcan* v. *Commission* ([1970] ECR 385) the applicant importers were held to be not directly concerned by a Commission Decision refusing a request from the Belgian government for a quota of unwrought aluminium imports at a reduced rate of duty. The Belgian government could have declined to use the quota once it had received it, or could have granted it to other importers. In contrast, the applicant in Case 62/70 *Bock* v. *Commission* ([1971] ECR 897) was held to be directly concerned. Bock had applied to the German authorities for a permit to import Chinese mushrooms and was told that the request would be refused as soon as the authorisation had been obtained from the Commission. When the Commission took a Decision addressed to the German government authorising the refusal of the application, Bock was able to challenge the decision. The Court held that there was direct concern because the German government had already made it clear what it would do with the authorisation once received. A further example of direct concern is Case 11/82 *Piraiki-Patraiki* v. *Commission* ([1985] ECR 207), a case which is notable for its generous interpretation of the rules on individual concern, where the possibility that the French government would not take advantage of a Commission authorisation to impose restrictions on imports of cotton yarn from Greece was held to be 'purely theoretical' when the measures were challenged by Greek manufacturers.

The criterion of direct concern precludes challenges to measures adopted by the EU which grant discretionary powers to the Member States, such as the Commission Decision authorising Luxembourg to grant aids to steel firms which undertook reductions in capacity, which was unsuccessfully challenged in Case 222/83 *Municipality of Differdange* v. *Commission* ([1984] ECR 2889).

Two recent decisions of the Court of First Instance on the Merger Regulation seem to have added a new layer to the test of direct concern. In Case T-96/92 *Comité central d'entreprise de la Société générale des grande sources* v. *Commission* ([1995] ECR II-1213) and Case T-12/93 *Comité central d'entreprise de la Société anonyme Vittel* v. *Commission* ([1995] ECR II-1247) the Court was faced with a challenge to a Commission Decision declaring the takeover of Perrier by Nestlé compatible with the common market, subject to compliance by Nestlé with certain conditions such as the sale of Perrier's Vittel subsidiary. Actions were brought by the Works Councils of Perrier and Vittel, who were both held to be individually concerned by the decision (see below). However, they were not directly concerned by the decision: as representatives of the employees, their 'own rights' were not prejudiced by the Decision approving the merger. The Court denied that a reduction in the workforce, or indeed the closure of plant would adversely affect the rights of the Works Councils. According to the Court in Case T-12/93, the fact that the closure of one plant leading, by virtue of the operation of French law, to the end of the central enterprise Works Council did not mean that the applicants were directly concerned by the decision as

> 'the central works council has not demonstrated an interest in the preservation of its functions where by reason of a change in the structure of the undertaking concerned the conditions under which the applicable national law provides for it to be set up are no longer met' ([1995] ECR I-1247 at p. 1271).

The Court also refused to base direct concern on an argument that the merger Decision would directly prejudice the interests of Perrier employees, including the loss of jobs and collective benefits, pointing, perhaps overoptimistically, to the existence of legislation, including legislation at EU level, intended to safeguard the rights of employees in the event of a transfer of undertaking (including a takeover). That would appear to break the causal link between the Decision of the Commission and any adverse employment consequences for employees and their representatives. Effectively, therefore, the Court is denying any responsibility on the part of the Commission for the employment consequences of the merger.

12.6   Individual Concern

In Case 25/62 *Plaumann* v. *Commission* ([1963] ECR 95), an early case which set the tone of restrictive interpretation for the entire system of direct judicial review in the Court of Justice, a German importer of clementines sought to challenge a Commission Decision addressed to Germany refusing it an authorisation to levy only 10 per cent duty on imports of clementines into the European Community from third countries, in place of the full duty of 13 per cent. On the question of admissibility the Court held that (at p. 107):

'Persons other than those to whom a decision is addressed may only claim to be individually concerned if that decision affects them by reason of certain attributes which are peculiar to them or by reason of circumstances in which they are differentiated from all other persons and by virtue of these factors distinguishes them individually just as in the case of the person addressed. In the present case the applicant is affected by the disputed decision as an importer of clementines, that is to say, by reason of a commercial activity which may at any time be practised by any person and is not therefore such as to distinguish the applicant in relation to the contested decision as in the case of the addressee.'

In practice, in the course of an extensive case law in which many cases have been declared inadmissible on the grounds of no individual concern, it has emerged that the Court requires the applicant to be part of a closed class, membership of which is fixed and ascertainable at the date of the adoption of the contested measure. An example is provided by Cases 106–107/63 *Toepfer* v. *Commission* ([1965] ECR 405) where the applicant was held to be individually concerned by a Commission Decision confirming the decision of the German government to refuse licences for imports of cereals from France, since the measure applied only to a closed class of importers who had applied for an import licence on a particular day. This test can also explain the distinction between cases such as Case 62/70 *Bock*, where the applicant was held to be individually concerned by a Commission Decision adopted in response to its request to the German government for an import licence and authorising the refusal of that licence, and Case 231/82 *Spijker Kwasten* v. *Commission* ([1983] ECR 2559), where the action failed. In *Spijker Kwasten*, the applicant sought annulment of a Commission Decision addressed to the Dutch government authorising it to ban imports of Chinese brushes for six months following the applicant's submission of a request for a licence. The applicant's difficulty was that although there was some evidence that the Decision was passed specifically to deal with its position, and indeed it was the only importer of Chinese brushes into the Benelux countries at that time, the ban was imposed for a period subsequent to the application for a licence, a period during which, hypothetically, other persons could have made an application for an import licence. Consequently, the action was held inadmissible on grounds of no individual concern.

It will be seen from these cases that there is a clear focus in terms of subject-matter on areas like customs and agriculture, reflecting particularly strongly the nature of the Commission's involvement in administering these fields – in conjunction with the Member States as appropriate. The nature of the subject matter of the cases may, it is argued, perhaps best explain the Court's reluctance to give a broader interpretation of the concept of individual concern. It has protected the Commission's scope for discretionary determinations, particularly under the CAP (Craig, 1994).

Even as the EU has extended the range of its activities, however, the general thrust of the approach to Article 173 taken by first the Court of Justice and, more recently, the Court of First Instance has not changed. This is well illustrated by a number of recent cases. From the field of merger control comes Case T-83/92 *Zunis Holdings SA* v. *Commission* ([1993] ECR II-1169) in which the Court of First Instance rejected as inadmissible for lack of individual concern an action brought by shareholders in a company against a Decision by the Commission, using discretionary powers under the Merger Control Regulation, that the acquisition of a shareholding of 12 per cent did not constitute a merger under the terms of the Regulation. In Case T-117/94 *Associazione Agricoltori della Provincia di Rovigo et al.* v. *Commission (Po Delta)* ([1995] ECR II-455), the applicant associations and agriculturalists objected to a Commission Decision approving an Italian government plan for actions related to the protection of the environment in the Po Delta funded by an EU financial instrument. They argued that they had been disregarded in the process of drawing up the plan, and the Commission had therefore disregarded their interests in approving it. The Court rejected the applications as inadmissible on the grounds that those of the applicants who were agriculturalists were not affected in any way other than all other residents of the Po Delta by the Decision. None of the rules governing the disbursement of monies put the Commission under a duty to take acccount of the particular situation of either the agriculturalists or indeed the associations representing them. No special rules apply to the situation of representative associations – in contrast to the situation under Italian law where the associations were recognised as having a special status. The Court stated (at p. 466):

'It cannot be accepted as a principle that an association, in its capacity as the representative of a category of traders, is individually concerned by a measure affecting the general interests of that category.'

Consequently, the associations must prove individual concern in the same way as the individual agriculturalists, and, like them, failed at that hurdle.

Case T-585/93 *Stichting Greenpeace Council* v. *Commission* ([1995] ECR II-2205) also concerned the disbursement of aid from the EU under the structural policies. Greenpeace challenged a Commission Decision addressed to Spain granting aid under the regional development programme for the building of two power stations in the Canary Islands. The concerns raised by Greenpeace were whether the aid was being disbursed to projects which were in keeping with the EU's other policies, particularly its environmental policies, as required by the relevant Regulations. There was some question as to whether the Spanish government had carried out the proper environmental impact assessment measures. The actions were held inadmissible, on the grounds that none of the applicants – who included residents of the Canaries, Greenpeace International, and a number of local environmental organisations – had shown individual concern. Notably the Court of First Instance refused to take any particular cognisance of the fact that the interests involved were *environmental*, not economic, so that the principles of *Plaumann* which are principally predicated on a particular perception of economic interest should not apply in their full rigour. As in the *Po Delta* case the Court also refused to draw any distinction between the interests of individual applicants and those of representative associations.

One final example will demonstrate that the EU courts represent exceedingly stony ground for public interest litigation. In Case T-219/95R *Danielsson* v. *Commission* (22.12.95) the President of the Court of First Instance rejected an application for interim measures brought by residents of Tahiti. They were concerned about the Commission's refusal to apply Article 34 Euratom to the programme of underground nuclear tests then being undertaken by France in the Pacific Ocean. The application of Article 34 could have given the Commission grounds even for ordering the suspension of the tests on health and safety grounds. In the event, the Commission concluded that the tests did not constitute 'particularly dangerous experiments', and so Article 34 did not apply. The application for interim measures was rejected on the grounds that the applicants had not established the *prima facie* admissibility of their case. Demonstrating the possibility or even likelihood of (physical or economic) harm or serious detriment was in itself insufficient to show individual concern, because the applicants were not affected in any way which differed from other residents of Tahiti. Nor were they protected because they were part of the 'general public' in whose interests additional health and safety precautions might be sought by the Commission under Article 34 Euratom.

More 'generous' interpretations of the rules tend to be explicable on special grounds, or because they belong to a number of specific categories identified below (12.9). In Case 11/82 *Piraiki-Patraiki*, certain Greek yarn manufacturers who had already entered into contracts to export cotton to France were held to be individually concerned by the Commission Decision permitting France to impose restrictions on imports. This was because Article 130 of the Greek Act of Accession, which empowered the Commission to adopt such a measure, required it to take into account the interests specifically of those who were bound by contractual arrangements. It could be argued that the evidence derived from the Act of Accession distinguished the applicants from a wider group of persons who might suffer prejudice as a consequence of the measure in question.

Finally, Case 294/83 *'Les Verts'* must be taken as an exceptional application of the rules on individual concern. On the face of it, the French Green Party was affected by the decision of the Bureau of the Parliament concerning the allocation of electoral funds only as a member of an indeterminate class, namely parties which might stand in the elections and were not already represented in the Parliament. On policy grounds the Court granted standing, since the applicants had a good case on the merits, and there was no obvious alternative route whereby the applicants could enforce the principle of equality in the context of the Parliament's organisation of its own business.

12.7   Challenges to Regulations

The effect of the standing rules in Article 173 is that individuals may only challenge regulations which are in essence decisions. It is very difficult in practice to prove that what is in form a general normative measure is in truth a bundle of individual measures although the applicants in Cases 41-44/70 *International Fruit Co* v. *Commission* ([1971] ECR 411) succeeded in precisely this task when they challenged a Commission Regulation laying down the rules for granting or refusing licences for the importation of apples from non-Member States. At that time, the national authorities received the applications for licences and passed them on to the Commission. The Court held that the Regulation establishing the rules for licences to be granted in a particular week, which was framed directly in response to the number of applications received by the Member States, was in truth a bundle of individual decisions and held the actions by the applicants who had requested licences to be admissible. The Court of First Instance has explained this aspect of Article 173 in the following terms:

'the objective of [Article 173(4)] is in particular to prevent the Community institutions from being able, merely by choosing the form of a regulation, to preclude an individual from bringing an action against a decision which concerns him directly and individually' (Case T-476/93 *FRSEA and FNSEA* v. *Council* [1993] ECR II-1187 at p. 1195).

In practice, however, applicants have generally found it extremely
difficult to establish that measures based on the exercise of discretion in
the economic policy context are in truth individual measures, since the
Court has consistently held that individuals should not be able to use
Article 173 to challenge 'true' regulations, that is abstract, normative
measures. It defined such measures in Cases 16 and 17/62 *Confédération
Nationale des Producteurs des Fruits et Légumes* v. *Council* ([1962] ECR
471) as being 'essentially of a legislative nature, . . . applicable not to a
limited number of persons, defined or identifiable, but to categories of
persons viewed abstractly and in their entirety'. The Court then went on
apparently to conflate the question of whether a measure is individual or
general with the question of individual concern, as discussed in the
previous paragraph; however, in reality, the Court has not always consistently applied this test, and in some cases has additionally imposed a
test which looks at the terminology of the measure rather than the persons
affected by it.

For example in Cases 789-790/79 *Calpak SpA* v. *Commission* ([1980]
ECR 1949) the Court held inadmissible a challenge to a Regulation
governing the grant of production aid in respect of certain pears in the
following terms (at p. 1961):

'A provision which limits the granting of production aid for all
producers in respect of a particular product to a uniform percentage
of the quantity produced by them during a uniform preceding period is
by nature a measure of general application within the meaning of
Article 189 of the Treaty. In fact the measure applies to objectively
determined situations and produces legal effects with regard to categories of persons described in a generalised and abstract manner. The
nature of the measure as a regulation is not called in question by the
mere fact that it is possible to determine the number or even the identity
of the producers to be granted the aid which is limited thereby.'

Thus even where they have been able to establish that the measures affect
only small and easily identifiable groups (e.g. the isoglucose regulations
affecting only isoglucose producers, a small class unlikely to grow because
of the major investment required – Case 101/76 *KSH* v. *Commission* [1977]
ECR 797) or indeed a closed category of persons (e.g. Cases 103-9/78
Beauport v. *Council and Commission* [1979] ECR 17 – a measure affecting
only sugar refineries which had previously been granted a sugar quota),
direct actions to challenge regulations implementing the policies of the EU
have been unsuccessful, although some of the policies pursued have
appeared manifestly unfair to particular groups and have proved vulnerable to indirect challenge (e.g. Cases 103, 145/77 *Royal Scholten Honig
Holdings Ltd* v. *Intervention Board for Agricultural Produce* [1978] ECR
2037 – isoglucose regulation held invalid for breach of the principle
of equality in the context of Article 177 reference). It is in this type of
situation which Mancini and Keeling (1994: 188–89) see the Court

of Justice as failing the individual, describing its construction of 'what is in any event a restrictive provision' as 'bizarre and paradoxical, if not downright perverse'.

The exceptions to this approach have tended once more to be special cases, either where the Commission is involved more directly in the administration of EC law as in the *International Fruit Company* case, or where the applicant is in some way specifically identified by the measure. In Case 138/79 *Roquette Frères* v. *Council* the applicant was one of a number of producers named in an annex to a Regulation. The action in Case C-152/88 *Sofrimport Sarl* v. *Commission* ([1990] ECR I-2477) was to challenge a Commission Regulation imposing protective measures which restricted the import of Chilean apples into the Community. Applying only the test of individual concern, and ignoring the abstract terminology test elaborated in *Calpak*, the Court held the actions by importers whose apples were in transit when the measure was adopted admissible on the grounds that the enabling Council Regulation which permitted it to control the imports of fruit into the European Community required it to have special regard to the interests of importers whose products were in transit. The Court held that since the enabling Regulation gave specific protection to such importers, they must be able to enforce observance of that protection and bring legal proceedings for that purpose. Thus there was a direct link between the substance of the applicants' case and the admissibility of their action. There is a parallel between *Sofrimport* and *Piraiki-Patraiki*, since in both cases specific features in the enabling measures distinguished the applicants from other affected persons.

We are concerned here with a type of case which has relatively recently be transferred into the jurisdiction of the Court of First Instance. Some commentators had already expressed the hope that the Court of First Instance whose specific task is that of hearing actions brought by individual applicants might be able to development more flexible criteria on *locus standi* (Mancini and Keeling, 1994: 189). The chance of this occurring appeared to have been considerably enhanced by the approach taken by the Court of Justice to the one of last cases on the question of general/individual measures which it had to decide before the transfer of jurisdiction. For this reason, Case C-309/89 *Codorniu* v. *Council* ([1994] ECR I-1853) attracted a high level of interest and comment (e.g. Usher, 1994; Waelbroeck and Fosselard, 1995). It has been regarded as particularly important because it concerns general policy on the regulation of agricultural trade, rather than agricultural licences or anti-dumping policy (see 12.9).

The action brought by Codorniu was against a Council Regulation reserving the word '*crémant*' as a designation for certain quality sparkling wines produced in specified regions of France and Luxembourg. The reservation of a designation in that way is intended to protect traditional descriptions. The applicant also produced quality sparkling wines, but in Spain not France or Luxembourg, and since 1924 had designated one of its wines '*Gran Crémant de Codorniu*'. It was also the holder of a Spanish graphic trade mark in the same terms. It was the largest producer in the EU of sparkling wines described as *'crémant'*, but a number of other Spanish producers also used the term 'Gran Cremant' to designate certain quality sparkling wines. Consequently, there was no question of the applicant being the only producer, or even only Spanish producer, affected by the Regulation. Holding that the applicant had *locus standi*, the Court held that the fact that the measure was of a general legislative nature in that it applied to the traders concerned in a general way, did not prevent it being of individual concern to the applicants (a form of reasoning which it has drawn from the field of anti-dumping: see Cases 239, 275/82 *Allied Corporation* v. *Commission* [1984] ECR 1005). The Court concluded that the applicant was affected by reference to certain specific attributes because it had registered the trade mark in 1924 and traditionally used that mark before and after registration. In consequence, therefore, the reservation to French and Luxembourg producers brought about by the Council Regulation interfered with the applicant's *property rights*. It may well be, therefore, that the Court's judgment was directly influenced by Article 222 EC which provides that the Treaty should operate without prejudice to the rights of the Member States to regulate property rights. It is not clear that the Court would have found the application admissible simply on the grounds of the impact upon the applicant's competitive situation (which was undoubtedly severe, but probably no more severe than in some of the other cases where the Court has denied standing to challenge Regulations). Even so, it was the case that *Codorniu* went beyond previous approaches to the standing question, since it was not suggested that the contested Regulation was adopted in view of the situation of the applicants, a requirement which the Court had previously imposed in such cases.

As the 'torch' was passed to the Court of First Instance, it was suggested that there might be a significant general relaxation of standing under Article 173. As we saw in 12.6 this has not occurred in relation to 'decisions addressed to another person'. Nor, in the event, has it occurred in relation to challenges to regulations. In Case T-107/94 *Kik* v. *Council and Commission* ([1995] ECR II-1717) the Court rejected a challenge to the language regime instituted by the Council Regulation establishing the Community trade mark and the Community trade mark office, which excluded the applicant's language (Dutch). The Court refused to accept the application of Article 6 ECHR which guarantees a right to judicial process and which has been cited by the Court in a number of other cases notably involving the exclusion of judicial process by the Member States (e.g. Case 222/84 *Johnston* v. *Chief Constable of the Royal Ulster Constabulary* [1986] ECR 1651; 6.6). According to the Court of First Instance this provision, although part of the body of EU general principles, does not preclude the application of standing rules in provisions such as Article 173. What is unsatisfactory about this judgment is the failure of the Court to indicate the alternative remedies available to the plaintiff, and to offer a convincing justification why such a potentially serious infringement of fundamental rights should not be dealt with directly at the level of the courts of the EU itself.

More pertinent to the scenario which arose in *Codorniu* was Case T-472/93 *Campo Ebro Industrial* v. *Council* ([1995] ECR II-421). In this case the applicants challenged a Council Regulation concerned with the alignment of sugar prices in Spain with those within the Single Market, following the arrangements laid down in the Spanish Act of Accession. Adjustment aid was made available under the Regulation to aid the restructuring in the Spanish sugar industry to assist the process of reducing the Spanish sugar price to the single market level. The applicants, who were the only producers of isoglucose in Spain and who held all the Spanish quotas for isoglucose production, were not granted adjustment aid when the Regulation entered into force, unlike a number of traders producing sugar from beet and cane. The case therefore concerns the continuing disputes concerning the competitive balance between beet and cane sugar and isoglucose. The Court held the action inadmissible on the grounds that:

> 'even if, following the introduction of the quota system, the present applicants are now the only producers of isoglucose in Spain and even assuming, further, that they are affected by the contested regulation in so far as it applies to future situations, they are in any event affected only in their objective capacity as isoglucose producers in the same way as any other trader in the sugar sector who, actually or potentially, is in an identical situation' (p. 435).

The Court further denied a claim that standing could be based on the impact upon the applicants' particularly disadvantageous competitive situation. As *Campo Ebro* represents an explicit continuation of the Court of Justice's earlier case law on the regulation of markets, it may be that *Codorniu* will turn out to the an exceptional case to be confined to its facts, rather than a new dawn in the approach to *locus standi*.

12.8   Can Individuals Challenge Directives?

There is no reason, in principle, why individuals could not challenge directives using Article 173, although they will undoubtedly face formidable hurdles regarding standing. In Case C-298/89 *Government of Gibraltar* v. *Council* ([1993] ECR I-3605), the Court dismissed the application – in which the applicants were treated as 'private' individuals for the purposes of *locus standi* – on the grounds of admissibility, but did not appear to claim that directives as such could not be challenged. This suggests a reworking of Article 173, similar to that undertaken in relation to Article 184 which is likewise phrased in terms of indirect challenges to regulations only (12.16), towards allowing the annulment of potentially any general legislation, irrespective of its form.

12.9   Quasi-Judicial Determinations

Special features characterise the Court's interpretation of the standing rules under Article 173 in the context of the involvement of the applicants in procedures before or within the EU institutions which are quasi-judicial in nature. These features concern the treatment not only of those who are directly involved in the procedures, e.g. as alleged infringers, and those involved as complainants (cf. 7.16).

In the context of competition proceedings, a disappointed complainant may bring an action challenging a decision granting an exemption or giving negative clearance (Case 26/76 *Metro* v. *Commission* [1977] ECR 1875). Under Regulation 17, provision is made for the participation of complainants with a legitimate grievance in the proceedings; for example, they have a right to be heard which they are entitled to have protected by the Court. Similarly, the applicants in Case T-96/92 *Comité central d'entreprise de la Société générale des grande sources* v. *Commission* and Case T-12/93 *Comité central d'entreprise de la Société anonyme Vittel* v. *Commission* were able to establish individual concern, even though not all of them had actually participated in the administrative process. According to the Court of First Instance

> 'in a case more specifically concerning the recognised representatives of the employees of the undertakings concerned, the number and identity of which are likely to be known when the decision is adopted, the mere fact that [the Merger Control Regulation] mentions them expressly and specifically among the third persons showing a 'sufficient interest' to submit their observations to the Commission is enough to differentiate them from all other persons and neough for it to be considered that the decision adopted under that regulation is of individual concern to them, whether or not they have made use of their rights during the administrative procedure.' ([1995] ECR I-1213 at p. 1232)

The position of complainants is often made considerably easier because, as a result of their involvement in the process, they will normally be contesting decisions addressed to them by the Commission (cf. Case C-39/93 P *SFEI* v. *Commission* and Case T-3/93 *Air France*, discussed in 12.2).

Similar considerations apply in the context of state aid. French fertiliser producers who had complained to the Commission about an alleged state aid given to their Dutch competitors by the Dutch Government were held to be individually concerned by a Commission Decision addressed to the Dutch Government terminating the proceedings when the Commission concluded that there was no aid involved (Case 169/84 *COFAZ* v. *Commission* [1986] ECR 391). In this case, the applicants had been exercising participation rights granted to them under Article 93(2) EC. The Court took the protection of complainants one step further in Case C-198/91 *William Cook plc* v. *Commission* ([1993] ECR I-2486), holding that a potential participant in Article 93(2) proceedings has standing to challenge a Decision taken by the Commission under Article 93(3) following a preliminary examination to the effect that a particular aid was compatible with the Common Market. The Court held that the participation rights under Article 93(2) could only be properly protected by allowing a challenge to such a Decision. Even stronger policy considerations speak in favour of the right of action of the beneficiaries of an aid held to be incompatible with the Common Market, and the standing of a beneficiary to challenge a Commission Decision addressed to the Dutch government and requesting it to refrain from granting the aid in question was confirmed by the Court in Case 730/79 *Philip Morris Holland BV* v. *Commission* ([1980] ECR 2671). Finally, in the field of state aid it would appear that representative bodies are given particular consideration: in Case C-313/90 *CIRFS* v. *Commission* ([1993] ECR I-1125) the Court held that the applicant association had standing to challenge a decision – addressed to a third party – which adversely affected the interests of its members. The *locus standi* was based on the fact that it had been in close contact with the Commission.

The case of anti-dumping proceedings is slightly different since in that context the enabling powers provide for the adoption of regulations by the Council imposing countervailing duties intended to offset the effects of subsidies granted in third countries to imports into the EU. These regulations are obviously not 'addressed' to particular persons, although clearly some categories of economic actors may be more seriously affected than others. An unqualified application of the principles set out in 12.7 would doubtless lead to unfairness to those affected by anti-dumping duties by excessively restricting the possibility of judicial review of the procedures in question. The Court has proceeded in this context generally by distinguishing between provisions of anti-dumping regulations which in effect operate as decisions *vis-à-vis* certain categories of interested parties, and those which preserve a general normative nature. In other words, a regulation may be of individual concern to certain applicants, whilst still retaining its general normative character.

So far the following categories of applicant have been held to be individually concerned by anti-dumping regulations:

- producers named in a regulation (Case 113/77 *NTN Toyo Bearing Co.* v. *Council and Commission* [1979] ECR 1185);
- producers who have been involved in the preliminary investigations (Cases 239, 275/82 *Allied Corporation* v. *Commission*);
- complainants (Case 264/82 *Timex* v. *Council and Commission* [1985] ECR 849).

Generally importers were refused standing, unless they were in some way linked to the manufacturer or exporter, or if their resale prices had been used by the Commission to construct export prices as the basis for the duty imposed (Case C-157/87 *Electroimpex* v. *Council* [1990] ECR I-3021). An attempt by the applicants in Case 307/81 *Alusuisse* v. *Council and*

Commission ([1982] ECR 3463) to establish standing by challenging the general nature of anti-dumping regulations was firmly rejected by the Court.

However, in Case C-358/89 *Extramet Industrie SA* v. *Council* ([1991] ECR I-2501) the Court appeared to move towards a more generous approach to the standing of importers. It held that without losing its normative character an anti-dumping regulation may individually concern importers. The applicant was able to establish standing by reference to its specific characteristics as not only the major importer of the product subject to the anti-dumping duty, but also its end-user. It was held to be relevant that Extramet's operations were heavily dependent on the imports and were seriously affected by the disputed Regulation, in view of the very small number of manufacturers of the product in question and the difficulty of obtaining supplies from the only EU producer, which was, moreover, Extramet's main competitor in relation to the end product. It would therefore appear that standing to challenge an anti-dumping regulation can be established if the importer can show that the regulation has an impact on its vital economic interests. In his Opinion in *Extramet*, AG Jacobs made very clear that he considered that the EU system of judicial review needed to be able to offer a substantive investigation of this type of case; if not, it would be seriously deficient and inconsistent with the principle of the rule of law.

12.10   *Locus Standi* of Non-Privileged Applicants: Conclusions and Critique

The restrictive interpretation of the standing rules under Article 173 has long been a subject for debate (e.g. Rasmussen, 1980; Harding, 1980; Greaves, 1986; from a comparative perspective Stein and Vining, 1976). The types of arguments put forward to explain the Court's approach have included:

- a perceived need (at least in the early days) to protect a nascent Community against challenges to its activities;
- the restrictive terms of Article 173 itself, in which 'individuals' are marginal;
- the need to draw distinctions between the different types of cases, an argument apparently vindicated by the differences between 'discretionary' and 'quasi-judicial' cases highlighted above;
- the availability of indirect review through the medium of the national court and the Article 177 reference (12.17).

More recent work critiquing the approach taken by the Court has placed it within the framework of the broad based challenge which standing poses for modern administrative law (Harlow, 1992a; Craig, 1994; Arnull,

1995a). For Harlow, the question of standing cannot be separated from the question of the EU's democratic deficit, and the role for the Court within the institutional structure which this consequently leaves. Standing is intimately linked to broader questions of participation (see also Craig and de Búrca, 1995: 479–81). Arnull suggests a change in EC law to adopt a halfway house for the standing question. He propoes abandoning the restrictive approach involving the search for a concrete interference with a legal right, and the adoption of an approach which looks for an adverse effect on the applicant's interests. He does not yet consider the EU ready for the broadest approach – the so-called *actio popularis* or citizen's action based on the assumption that the citizen has an interest in any action of a public body. Arnull, like Neuwahl (1996), looked for an attempt to resolve these difficult questions within the framework of the 1996 IGC.

12.11   Time Limits

Actions under Article 173 must observe the time limit of two months from 'the publication of the measure, or of its notification to the plaintiff, or, in the absence thereof, of the day on which it came to the knowledge of the latter, as the case may be'. Details of the application in practice of the time limits can be derived from the Rules of Procedure of the Court of Justice.

12.12   Interim Measures

In appropriate cases, the Court may award interim measures in the context of Article 173 actions under its general power in Article 186 EC. The same conditions of a *prima facie* case and urgency which are applied in the context of Article 169 EC (see 7.14) govern the award of interim measures under Article 173. These have been awarded in a number of cases involving anti-dumping regulations (Case 113/77R *NTN Toyo Bearing Co* v. *Commission* [1977] ECR 1721) and decisions taken by the Commission under Article 115 EC authorising Member States to exclude imports from the other Member States of third country goods in free circulation (Case 1/84R *Ilford* v. *Commission* [1984] ECR 423). The field of competition law also offers a number of example of successful applications for interim measures. In Case T-56/89 R *Publishers Association* v. *Commission* ([1989] ECR 1693) the Court awarded interim measures in relation to the operation of a Commission Decision declaring the UK Net Book Agreement to be in breach of the competition rules, and requiring its termination. The interim measures brought about the suspension of the Commission's Decision pending the final resolution of the action on the merits.

12.13   Grounds for Review

There is considerable overlap between the four grounds for review set out in Article 173 (lack of competence, infringement of an essential procedural requirement, infringement of the Treaty or of any rule of law relating to its application, and misuse of powers). Indeed it could be argued that infringement of the Treaty and of any rule of law relating to its application is potentially a catch-all phrase which encompasses not only the written rules of the Treaty and the various provisions adopted thereunder, but also the body of unwritten general principles of law and fundamental rights, which were discussed as a source of law in Chapter 6 and must now be applied in practice here.

Lack of competence has rarely been successfully invoked although one example is provided by Case C-303/90 *France* v. *Commission*, in which France successfully established that the Commission did not have the power to adopt a legally binding implementation measure (albeit one characterised as a 'Code of Conduct') under the legal regime governing the application of the structural funds (Article 130A EC *et seq.*). The cases on procedural requirements are more common – especially, but not only, in the field of competition law, and the Court has held the following requirements to be essential:

- the requirement to consult the Parliament where required during the legislative process (Case 138/79 *Roquette Frères* v. *Council*);
- a sufficiently full statement of reasons under Article 190 EC (Case 24/62 *Commission* v. *Germany* [1963] ECR 63);
- the requirement of a specific legal basis which is an additional feature of the duty to give reasons (Case 45/86 *Commission* v. *Council (Generalised Tariff Preferences)* [1987] ECR 1493).

In contrast, use of the wrong legal basis constitutes an infringement of the Treaty. For further examples of those general principles of law which have been used as the bases for challenges to the legality of EU acts, reference should be made to the discussion in 6.4 *et seq.*

The most infrequently applied ground is the misuse of powers, which constitutes the use of a power for purposes other than that for which it was granted, and is based on the French administrative law concept of *détournement de pouvoir*. In Case 8/55 *Fédéchar* v. *High Authority* ([1956] ECR 292) the ECSC equivalent provision was considered by the Court. It held that a measure will not be annulled simply because one of the reasons for its adoption was improper, if the others are legitimate. Nor will a measure be annulled if the improper purpose had no effect upon the substance of the measure.

The essential question, from the perspective of the development of the judicial control of the EU institutions, is the nature and intensity of the review which the Court of Justice and Court of First Instance apply to their actions. The precise approach taken will depend upon the type of power under which the particular institution is operating. There will be a good deal of difference in the degree of scrutiny applied to the exercise of discretionary legislative powers in a field such as the agriculture, compared with the fairly precise procedural requirements which structure the work of the Commission in the field of competition law. In a sense the exercise of the review can become a dialogue between the institutions concerned with legislation, and the Court of Justice – as the series of cases on the evaluation of the milk quota system in the light of general principles of EC law shows very clearly. Although these cases were decided by means of Article 177 references on validity, and not as direct actions, the principles are the same as they are under Article 173.

In Case 120/86 *Mulder* v. *Minister van Landbouw en Visserij* ([1988] ECR 2321), the Court held that a legislative framework which effectively penalised those who had ceased production of milk – in response to incentives put in place to reduce the surplus production of dairy products – infringed the principle of legitimate expectations (at p. 2352):

'A producer who has voluntarily ceased production for a certain period cannot legitimately expect to be able to resume production under the same conditions as those which previously applied and not to be subject to any rules of market or structural policy adopted in the mean time.

The fact remains that where such a producer, as in the present case, has been encouraged by a Community measure to suspend marketing for a limited period in the general interest and against payment of a premium he may legitimately expect not to be subject, upon the expiry of his undertaking, to restrictions which specifically affect him precisely because he availed himself of the possibilities offered by the Community provisions.'

The Council tried again. The problem was that those who had ceased production had not delivered any milk during what is termed the 'reference year', that is the year chosen by the Netherlands as the basis for calculating milk quotas. Hence on return to production, those who had ceased production lost out. In the revised rules the Council instituted a system whereby this group of producers would receive a special reference quantity equal to 60 per cent of the quantity of milk delivered or sold during the 12 months preceding the month in which the producer applied for the incentive scheme for ceasing production. Again that restriction was challenged on the grounds that it breached legitimate expectations, and the applicants were successful once more (Case C-189/89 *Spagl* [1990] ECR I-4539). The Court again held that the reduction of 40 per cent was a restriction which specifically affected the group of producers who had ceased production precisely because they had undertaken to do just that. The Council was forced to revise the arrangements for a second time, introducing a higher special reference quantity (for a discussion of the compensation claims which resulted from these cases see 14.8).

12.14   The Consequences of Annulment

The consequence of a successful action under Article 173 is a declaration by the Court under Article 174 that a measure is void. A measure may be declared void in part only, provided the offending part can be effectively severed from the rest. In Case 17/74 *Transocean Marine Paint Association* v. *Commission* ([1974] ECR 1063) an onerous condition in an exemption from the prohibition under Article 85 issued by the Commission was annulled on the grounds that the Commission had failed to give the applicant a sufficient hearing on the matter. The Court used Article 176, which requires the institution whose act has been declared void to take the necessary measures to comply with the judgment of the Court, to refer the measure back to the Commission for consideration. The alternative – entire annulment of the Commission's Decision which would have left an earlier exemption standing – might have been too favourable to the applicant.

12.15   Indirect Challenge

The availability of indirect challenge to unlawful acts of the EU institutions completes the system of judicial review as described by the Court in *'Les Verts'* (Case 294/83). The objective is to ensure that illegal 'parent' EU acts can be attacked through the medium of implementing EU or national measures. The availability of two avenues for indirect challenge in EC law – Articles 177 and 184 – was emphasised in 11.2. Although, where Article 177 is used, the proceedings will begin in the national court, in practice indirect challenge is an instrument of judicial control which lies principally in the hands of the Court of Justice, since it has claimed the exclusive right to decide on the invalidity of EU acts (Case 314/85 *Firma Foto-Frost* v. *HZA Lübeck-Ost* [1987] ECR 4199).

The types of case in which an indirect challenge may occur obviously include actions for annulment, where the basis for the action is the illegality of a 'parent' EU act; in particular, Article 184 provides the opportunity in proceedings brought by an individual against an administrative act in the Court of Justice to challenge a normative act on which the administrative act is based and which is not susceptible itself to challenge by individuals. In the national courts, the alleged illegality of an EU act may form the basis of either the cause of action or the defence in the full range of civil, criminal and administrative proceedings (e.g. action for the recovery of money claimed by the authorities on the basis of an unlawful EU act; defence to criminal proceedings where the national criminal provisions are based on an unlawful EU act).

The Court has sought to keep the two remedies separate. In Cases 31, 33/62 *Wöhrmann* v. *Commission* ([1962] ECR 501) it held that Article 184 may only be raised in proceedings before the Court in which the allegedly illegal act is relevant. It cannot be invoked in Article 177 proceedings.

However, in Case 216/82 *Universität Hamburg* v. *HZA Hamburg-Kehr-wieder* ([1983] ECR 2771), the Court explicitly drew a parallel between Article 184 and Article 177 holding that:

'According to a general principle of law which finds its expression in Article 184 of the EEC Treaty, in proceedings brought under national law against the rejection of his application [for duty-free admission of scientific apparatus from the USA into Germany] the applicant must be able to plead the illegality of the Commission's Decision on which the national decision adopted in his regard is based.'

12.16   Article 184: The Plea of Illegality (for text see 11.2)

According to the Court of Justice in Case 92/78 *Simmenthal SpA* v. *Commission* ([1979] ECR 777 at p. 778):

'Article 184 of the EEC Treaty gives expression to a general principle conferring upon any party to proceedings the right to challenge, for the purpose of obtaining the annulment of a decision of direct and individual concern to that party, the validity of previous acts of the institutions which form the legal basis of the decision which is being attacked, if that party was not entitled under Article 173 of the Treaty to bring a direct action challenging those acts by which it was thus affected without having been in a position to ask that they be declared void.'

In view of these conclusions, the Court interpreted the term 'regulation' as used in Article 184 broadly in order to include within the scope of indirect challenge any normative acts which produce similar effects to regulations and which are therefore on those grounds not subject to direct challenge. On the other hand, the raising of a plea of illegality does not in any way exonerate the applicant from satisfying the basic conditions – *locus standi*, observance of time limits, reviewable act – which govern the proceedings in which the plea is raised.

Since it would appear that an Article 184 plea is available first and foremost for the purpose of allowing challenges to measures which the applicant could not have challenged by way of an Article 173 action, it follows that Article 184 cannot be used by applicants to challenge individual acts addressed to them in the context of other proceedings; this would in effect do away with the time limits for challenging such acts and would destroy the coherence and certainty of the remedies system under the Treaty (Case 21/64 *Dalmas* v. *High Authority* [1965] ECR 175). There have been no clear statements from the Court on whether or not Article 184 can be used to challenge measures which the applicant might have had standing to challenge, for example, by application of the rules of direct and individual concern. Nor has the Court decided the extent to which privileged applicants can rely upon Article 184; the logical extension of its views in *Simmenthal* would appear to be that since privileged applicants have unlimited standing to challenge all reviewable EU acts they should not be allowed the second chance of an Article 184 plea once the time limit for direct challenge has expired. In Case 32/65 *Italy* v. *Commission* ([1966] ECR 389), although the Court did not decide the point, AG Roemer inclined to the view that privileged applicants should be allowed to rely upon Article 184 since at the time when the act was adopted they might not have thought it was unlawful. There are certainly restrictions on the use of Article 184 as a defence in enforcement proceedings. In Case 156/77 *Commission* v. *Belgium* ([1978] ECR 1881) the Commission had brought proceedings under Article 95(2) for failure by Belgium to comply with a Commission Decision of May 1976 which Belgium had failed to challenge directly. The Court refused to allow Belgium to raise Article 184 as a defence. However, there are some differences between the specific nature of enforcement proceedings in the context of state aids which are based in part on the Commission taking enforcement decisions which the Member State must challenge by annulment proceedings if it objects, and general enforcement proceedings under Article 169, where the onus lies on the Commission to issue a statement of objections and to bring the Member State before the Court. In that context, it might remain possible for the Member State to argue that the policy measure which the Commission is seeking to enforce is in fact unlawful.

The grounds for review under Article 184 are the same as those in Article 173, which is specifically referred to in the terms of Article 184. The effects of a successful indirect challenge are not formally annulment, but for all practical purposes the act must be seen as invalidated and without legal effect.

12.17   The Scope of Indirect Challenge under Article 177

Section 8.7 outlined the powers of the Court of Justice in relation to rulings on validity, and indicated that there is an implicit obligation on national courts to make a reference in any proceedings where there is a doubt about the validity of an EU measure. The scope of judicial review via the national court is, as we have seen, much more generous to the individual applicant. This is an important aspect of ensuring that the EU is a 'Community subject to the rule of law', in accordance with the statements of the Court in Case 294/83 *'Les Verts'*.

It was thought that the ability of bring an indirect challenge operated entirely independently to the issue of an action for annulment under Article 173. In Cases 133–6/85 *Walter Rau* v. *BALM* the Court held that a national court faced with proceedings in which a national act implementing a Commission Decision is being challenged does not need to ascertain before hearing the case whether an action could have been brought against the Decision under Article 173. It is sufficient that the national conditions for the bringing of annulment proceedings are satisfied. There are two reasons for the Court to take this approach: first, the applicant in the national proceedings is unlikely to have been notified of the measure in question, and thus, secondly, it might not have been aware of the expiry of the time limit under Article 173.

There are, however, a range of cases where this principle will not apply. In Case C-188/92 *TWD Textilwerke Deggendorf GmbH* v. *Germany* ([1994] ECR I-833) the question before the Court was whether a national court was bound by a 1986 Commission Decision, addressed to the German government, declaring certain state aids paid to a producer of synthetic yarns situated in Deggendorf (i.e. TWD) to be incompatible with the Common Market. The Commission required the German government to recover the aid, using its enforcement powers. The German government informed TWD of the Decision, and indicated that it would be challengeable under Article 173 (12.9). TWD took no action under Article 173, but challenged the German measure requiring repayment of the aid in the German courts, relying on the alleged unlawfulness of the Commission Decision. In these circumstances, the Court declared that legal certainty required that there should be no further opening up of the question whether the Commission Decision was valid in the context of Article 177 proceedings. Because of the potential for application of these principles outside the narrow field of state aids, Ross argues that 'the *TWD* reasoning only works if the generally messy case law on *locus standi* is itself made more intelligible' (Ross, 1994: 644). In the light of the discussion in this chapter, it must be concluded that this happy state of affairs remains some way off.

The effects of findings of invalidity under Article 177 have already been discussed in 8.8 above.

Summary

1   A successful Article 173 action requires:

   - a reviewable act;
   - *locus standi* on the part of the applicant;
   - an application within the time limits;
   - substantive or procedural illegality on the part of the adopting institution.

2   A reviewable act is any act with legal effects which brings about a change in the legal position of the applicant.

3   For individual applicants, the need to demonstrate *locus standi* will often be an unassailable hurdle. In particular, the requirement that a decision addressed to another person must 'individually concern' the applicant has often prevented individuals showing standing. Individuals

can only very rarely bring actions under Article 173 to challenge regulations. The Court's case law has been criticised as unnecessarily restricting the access of individuals.

4 In a number of areas involving quasi-judicial determinations by the Commision (competition law, state aids, anti-dumping) the Court of Justice has taken a more liberal approach, in the interests of ensuring effective protection of individual rights.

5 The Court applies its case law on general principles of law when assessing whether there are grounds for reviewing an EU act. The intensity of review applied depends upon the circumstances of the case.

6 Indirect challenge occurs under Articles 177 and 184. Article 184 permits challenges to general EU measures in the context of challenges to administrative measures brought under Article 173. Under Article 177, the Court claims the exclusive right to declare the invalidity of EU measures the legality of which is impugned before the national court.

7 An indirect challenge via the national court and Article 177 will be excluded for an individual applicant who clearly had standing to challenge the relevant measure under Article 173.

Questions

1 What is a reviewable act?

2 In what way has the Court influenced the present text of the judicial review provisions (as amended by the Treaty of Maastricht)?

3 How and why has the Court of Justice interpreted the *locus standi* provisions of Articles 173 in such a way as to restrict the direct access of individuals to remedies in that Court?

4 Why is the Court's interpretation of the *locus standi* provisions more generous in cases involving quasi-judicial determinations by the EU institutions?

5 How does the system of indirect challenge to the legality of EU acts complement the system of direct challenge?

Further Reading

Arnull (1995a), 'Private Applicants and the Action for Annulment under Article 173 of the EC Treaty', 32 *CMLRev.* 7.

Bradley (1988), 'The variable evolution of the standing of the European Parliament in proceedings before the Court of Justice', 8 *YEL* 27.

Bradley (1991), 'Sense and Sensibility: *Parliament* v. *Council* Continued', 16 *ELRev.* 245.

Craig (1994), 'Legality, Standing and Substantive Review in Community Law', 14 *OJLS* 507.

Greaves (1986), 'Locus Standi under Article 173 EEC when seeking annulment of a Regulation', 11 *ELRev.* 119.

Greaves (1996), 'The Nature and Binding Effect of Decisions under Article 189 EC', 21 *ELRev.* 3.

Harlow (1992a), 'Towards a Theory of Access for the European Court of Justice', 12 *YEL* 213.
Hartley (1994), Ch. 14, 'Indirect Challenge'.
Neuwahl (1996), 'Article 173 Paragraph 4 EC: Past, Present and Possible Future', 21 *ELRev.* 17.
Rasmussen (1980), 'Why is Article 173 interpreted against Private Plaintiffs?', 5 *ELRev.* 112.

13 Judicial Control of Failure to Act

13.1 Introduction: Article 175 and Article 173

Articles 173 and 175 (for the text of these provisions see 11.2) are intended to provide complementary remedies; acting illegally and illegally failing to act should be two sides of the same coin. Non-privileged applicants with limited standing under Article 173 should be unable to sue in respect of a failure to adopt a legislative act which they would be unable to challenge if it were in fact adopted. In contrast, privileged applicants, who are entitled to challenge any reviewable acts should be able to challenge the refusal or failure to adopt any acts which the authority is under a legal obligation to adopt. In the context of such actions, therefore, the latter condition will be the crucial determinant of what constitutes a reviewable omission.

The Court's position on the linkage between the two provisions has been slightly inconsistent. In Case 15/70 *Chevalley* v. *Commission* ([1970] ECR 975), given the applicant's uncertainty as to whether the action in question should be under Article 175 or Article 173, for the purposes of a preliminary investigation of admissibility, the Court held that it was unnecessary to distinguish between the two remedies, since they 'merely prescribe one and the same method of recourse'. However, since then the Court has stated that where proceedings are begun under both Articles the applicant must identify the act which it intends to challenge by means of an annulment action (Case 247/87 *Star Fruit Co* v. *Commission* ([1989] ECR 291). In Case 302/87 *Parliament* v. *Council (Comitology)* ([1988] ECR 5615) when initially rejecting the Parliament's standing to sue under Article 173, the Court also denied the linkage between Articles 173 and 175. The fact that the Parliament has a right of action under Article 175 had 'no necessary link to any right of action under Article 173'.

Article 175 applies to 'pure omissions', not to refusals to act, which are characterised as negative decisions and actionable under Article 173, if at all. The interplay between the two is illustrated by Case 42/71 *Nordgetreide* v. *Commission* ([1972] ECR 105). The Commission refused to amend a Regulation when requested to do so by Nordgetreide. Article 175 proceedings were barred because the Commission's refusal was held to be a definition of its position, and Article 173 proceedings failed because although the refusal to amend the regulation was in one sense a 'decision', Nordgetreide would have no standing to challenge the Regulation which was a pure normative act and could not therefore challenge the negative act refusing to amend it. In other words, the link between the two provisions will be operated in such a way as to prevent one provision being used to evade the restrictive conditions applying to the other provision.

This was stated expressly by the Court in Cases 10, 18/68 *Eridania* v. *Commission* ([1969] ECR 459). The applicants had requested the Commission to revoke a certain measure, and when it failed to do so, they started proceedings for failure to act under Article 175. They also started an action for annulment against the act which failed because they did not have *locus standi* to challenge the act. The Court held that Article 175 cannot be used to circumvent Article 173 in this way (at p. 483):

'To admit, as the applicants wish to do, that the parties concerned could ask the institution from which the measure came to revoke it and, in the event of the Commission's failing to act, refer such a failure to the Court as an illegal omission to deal with the matter would amount to providing them with a method of recourse parallel to that of Article 173, which would not be subject to the conditions laid down by the Treaty.'

Like Article 173, Article 175 was amended by the Treaty of Maastricht to bring the Parliament fully within its terms. This is particularly important in respect of its budgetary, as well as its legislative activities. Paragraph 4 brings the ECB into the scope of Article 175, as a potential plaintiff or defendant.

13.2   Procedure

The procedure must begin with a formal request to the defendant to take action. It must state clearly what action is required, that it is made within the terms of Article 175, and that the applicant considers the defendant legally obliged to take the action required (Case 25/85 *Nuovo Campsider* v. *Commission* [1986] ECR 1531). The defendant has a period of two months to comply. If that period expires without response or action by the defendant, the applicant may take the matter to the Court within a further two months. This procedure puts the defendant formally in default, and also gives it the opportunity to comply. In a case decided under Article 35 ECSC (the equivalent to Article 175 EC) the Court has held that the preliminary procedure must be initiated within a reasonable time. In Case 59/70 *Netherlands* v. *Commission* ([1971] ECR 639) the action was held inadmissible because of a lapse of 18 months between a statement by the Commission to which the Netherlands objected, and the Netherlands submitting a formal request for action.

A definition of position by the authority terminates the Article 175 action. For example, Case 377/87 *Parliament* v. *Council* ([1988] ECR 4017) concerned an alleged failure by the Council to comply with the budget timetable. The Council acted after the action was brought before the Court, but before the judgment of the Court was delivered. The Court held that once an institution has defined its position, the action cannot continue, as its subject-matter has ceased to exist. In that sense, the Article 175 action can be contrasted with the Article 169 enforcement action, which the Commission may continue to prosecute notwithstanding compliance by the Member State (7.3). The position is the same for a non-privileged applicant (Cases C-15, 108/91 *Buckl* v. *Commission* [1992] ECR I-6061). If the act refusing the request of the applicant has been adopted by the defendant institution after the application has been submitted to the Court, there will be no need to give a judgment. Moreover, if the institution defines its position by adopting an act other than that requested by the applicant before the application has been submitted to the Court, the application will be rejected as inadmissible (Case C-25/91 *Pesqueras Echebastar* v. *Commission* [1993] ECR I-1719).

In theory, a definition of position which blocks an Article 175 action where the applicant had standing should, according to the unity principle, always be reviewable under Article 173. In fact, that is not the case, as the Court of First Instance reiterated in Case T-186/94 *Guérin Automobiles* v. *Commission* ([1995] ECR II-1753). In the field of competition law, in which Article 175 has proved to be a particularly useful tool for complainants in pushing the Commission to take a position on the complaint, what is termed an 'Article 6' letter in which the Commission expresses its provisional view that it will not take up the complaint, while not a reviewable act (12.2), will nonetheless be a classed as a 'definition of position' because it constitutes a necessary preliminary step in a procedure which will eventually lead to a reviewable act (the definitive refusal to take up the complaint).

Morover, distinguishing exactly what constitutes a definition of position is not easy, and consequently proceedings may have to be initiated under both Articles. In the most prominent successful case involving Article 175 which was concerned with the failure of the Council to enact a number of measures under the common transport policy (Case 13/83 *Parliament* v. *Council (Common Transport Policy)* [1985] ECR 1513), the case was able to continue under Article 175 as the Council's definition of position was deemed to be inadequate. For the Parliament, which still does not have full status as a privileged applicant under Article 173 even after the amendments introduced by the Treaty of Maastricht, but whose position under Article 175 is identical to the other institutions and the Member States, the difference between what is and what is not a definition of position – a question of fact, not law – could be crucial. In that case the Council failed either to confirm or to deny the alleged failure to act, and failed also to state what measures it proposed to adopt.

In the event of a finding of failure to act, there is no unlawful act for the Court to annul. The Court will make an order under Article 175 with which the institution in default must comply, but there are no further sanctions for non-compliance. For example, although the Court declined to decide the point expressly in Case 13/83 *Parliament* v. *Council*, it is clear that a legislative failure on the part of the Council does not result in the legislative power reverting to another institution which is willing to act. While changes to Article 171 EC introduced by the Treaty of Maastricht institute the possibility of imposing financial sanctions for non-compliance on the Member States, similar changes to the obligations of the EU institutions were not contemplated. However, the institutions remain under an obligation to compensate individuals in respect of unlawful conduct which causes damage, and there are a few, although so far unsuccessful, examples of actions against the institutions in respect of unlawful omissions (e.g. Cases 326/86 and 66/88 *Francesconi* v. *Commission* [1989] ECR 2087 (14.6) and Case C-63/89 *Les Assurances du Crédit SA* v. *Council and Commission* ([1991] ECR I-1799 (14.9)).

13.3   Failure to Act: Privileged Applicants

The terms of Article 175 draw a clear distinction – as do those of Article 173 – between actions brought by privileged and non-privileged applicants. The first paragraph refers simply to a 'failure to act', without being specific as the nature of that act. That raises the question of the range of *reviewable omissions* which privileged applicants can challenge. One of the few instances of success is Case 13/83 *Parliament* v. *Council* in which the Parliament challenged the Council's failure to introduce a common policy for transport and its failure to reach a decision on sixteen specified proposals submitted by the Commission in relation to transport, which were required in order to secure freedom to provide transport services. The Parliament failed on the first rather more general allegation: there was no legally complete obligation under Article 74 to introduce a common transport policy. However, it succeeded on the second ground, since the Council was legally required to implement these freedoms, as guaranteed by Articles 75, 59, 50 and 61 EC, within the transitional period. The actions sought 'must be sufficiently defined to allow the Court to determine whether . . . the failure to adopt them is lawful' (para. 36). This is the mirror image of the requirement in all Article 173 EC actions that there should be a reviewable act which produces legal effects.

It would appear that privileged applicants can seek a review of the failure to adopt certain preparatory or preliminary acts. In Case 377/87 *Parliament* v. *Council*, the Parliament's action was brought to challenge the failure of the Council to present a draft budget under Article 203(4). The action failed because the Court found that the Council had presented a draft budget. However, somewhat strangely the Court commented in a later case (Case 302/87 *Parliament* v. *Council (Comitology)* [1988] ECR 5615) that Case 377/87 'showed' that the Parliament *could* challenge the failure by the Council to present a draft budget. The position taken is justifiable in the sense that the Parliament is under a legal obligation under the Treaty to adopt the budget, and without a Council draft budget it cannot act. However, the approach taken breaks the unity of Articles 173 and 175, since the draft budget is not a challengeable act itself, under the principles set out in 12.2.

13.4 Failure to Act: Non-Privileged Applicants

The terms of the third paragraph of Article 175 restrict the action for failure to act to circumstances where a natural or legal person can claim that 'an institution of the Community has failed to address to that person any act other a recommendation or an opinion.' This would seem to indicate that only legally binding measures are covered by the provision, and that the same standing restrictions apply as do under Article 173.

So, for example, in Case 246/81 *Bethell* v. *Commission* ([1982] ECR 2277) the plaintiff found himself wholly without a remedy. At the time of the action brought by Lord Bethell, who was seeking to force stricter application of the competition rules in the air transport sector, air transport was not covered by Regulation 17 which provides enforcement procedures for Articles 85 and 86, or any other similar provisions. As such, he had no protected status as a complainant, and could not therefore lay claim even to the basic investigation of a complaint to which a complainant would otherwise be entitled (7.16). A complainant under the competition, anti-dumping or state aid provisions should be entitled to force the EU authorities adopt a position *vis-à-vis* them which would be reviewable under Article 173, or to obtain the review of a failure to act under Article 175, in particular where the action is brought in order to enforce observance of the complainant's procedural rights. In Case 191/82 *FEDIOL* v. *Commission* ([1983] ECR 2913) a challenge brought by the EU seed crushers and oil processors federation to ensure judicial review of the extent to which their procedural rights, as complainants, to be involved in anti-dumping proceedings had been observed, was held admissible. Although the position of complainants in competition proceedings long remained uncertain, in Case T-24/90 *Automec* v. *Commission (Automec II)* ([1992] ECR II-2223), the Court of First Instance finally resolved that such a complainant is entitled to the adoption of a reviewable act by the Commission. Consequently, Article 175 can be used by the complainant to force the Commission to undertake a basic investigation. On the other hand, complainants cannot force the Commission to take a final decision on the application of the competition rules, provided their procedural rights have been observed (Case 125/78 *GEMA* v. *Commission* [1979] ECR 3173).

In these types of circumstances, involving complainants, the applicant is the would-be addressee. The question which has arisen is whether the same formulation of the standing rules under Article 175 should be used as for Article 173 (i.e. direct and individual concern). Should the '*de facto* addressee' (Hartley, 1994: 413) be able to bring an action. The point appears to have been decided in favour of a parallelism in the standing rules in Case C-107/91 *ENU* v. *Commission* ([1993] ECR I-599), a case brought under Article 148 Euratom (which is materially identical to Article 175 EC). ENU was a Portuguese company producing a form of uranium, which found itself in financial difficulties as a result of a price fall on the market and a lack of demand for its product. It wished the Euratom Supply Agency to make use of its option under Article 57 Euratom to purchase some of its supplies and so relieve its difficulties. Not receiving any satisfactory response from the Agency, ENU turned to the Commission, asking it to use its powers under Article 53 to bring about a resolution of the problem. The Court held that the action was admissible, since any decision addressed by the Commission to the Agency under Article 53 would have concerned the applicant directly and individually, and this was sufficient as a basis for an action for failure to act. In the event, the Court also found that the Commission was guilty of an unlawful failure to act, and made an order accordingly.

A failure by the Commission to put a proposal for legislation has been found to be not reviewable, since it is only a preliminary act. Similar reasoning can be used to explain the decisions in Case 48/65 *Lütticke* v. *Commission* ([1966] ECR 19) and Case 247/87 *Star Fruit Co* v. *Commission* in which the Court held that individuals could not force the Commission to take enforcement proceedings against Member States. Nothing in the enforcement procedure constitutes a binding reviewable act.

It is possible that there may be certain special circumstances in which a broader approach is necessary. These are illustrated by the facts, if not the decision, in Case C-41/92 *The Liberal Democrats* v. *Parliament* ([1993] ECR I-3153), which represents a neat parallel with Case 294/83 *Parti Ecologiste 'Les Verts'* v. *Parliament* ([1986] ECR 1339). In that case, it will be recalled, the Court adopted a generous interpretation of the standing rules in the interests, it may be contended, of protecting and enhancing the democratic basis of the EU (12.6). *The Liberal Democrats* involved an action brought by the UK Liberal Democratic Party against the Parliament in respect of its failure to put forward proposals for a uniform electoral procedure under Article 138(3) EC. It was struck out as inadmissible because the Parliament, after the initiation of the legal proceedings, adopted a resolution on a uniform electoral procedure, proposing a form of proportional representation, but with a formula which would allow states such as the UK to maintain two thirds of its seats as single member constituencies. AG Darmon suggested that the failure to produce a preparatory act without which another institution cannot produce a definitive act itself has legal effects and justifies an action for failure to act. The question which this does not answer is whether the Liberal Democrats would have had standing to challenge that failure, given the nature of their 'interest' in the eventual legislation (which would considerably enhance their chances of electoral success in the UK, in comparison to the present 'first-past-the-post' system which privileges the two main parties of the left and right).

Summary

1 Article 175 provides a complementary remedy to that available under Article 173, covering failure to act. It has only very rarely been used successfully.
2 A successful Article 175 action requires:

   – *locus standi* on the part of the applicant;
   – a request by the applicant to the defendant to define its position, and a failure by the defendant to define its position;
   – a failure to adopt an act on the part of the defendant institution which it is under a duty to adopt.

Questions

1 What is the unity principle?
2 What is the relationship between a reviewable omission and a reviewable act?
3 Can you explain why Article 175 has proved to be particularly useful to two very different types of applicant: the Parliament, and complainants in the field of competition law?

Further Reading

Hartley (1994), Ch. 13, 'Failure to Act'.

14 Non-Contractual Liability and Compensation for Loss Caused by the EU

14.1 Introduction

The framework of rules governing the non-contractual (i.e. tortious) liability of the EU for the acts of its institutions and servants shares both many of the complexities and the policy-oriented nature of the rules governing judicial review. The text of the key provisions (Articles 178 and 215(2) EC) is set out in 11.2.

In principle, therefore, the EU must compensate for the damage it causes. Damage may be caused either by an institution (e.g. through a legislative measure, an administrative act or some other action or statement which inflicts loss), or by its servants, in which case the institution will be subject to a form of vicarious liability (e.g. an EU official reveals confidential information about an undertaking to a third party). The nature of the liability (i.e. fault-based or strict liability; nature of the causal link required; scope of damage recoverable) is determined according to principles common to the laws of the Member States, and has been subject to judicial evolution in the hands of the Court of Justice (and now, the Court of First Instance, which is responsible for such actions). As a matter of practice, the EU is represented by the institution alleged, directly or vicariously, to have caused the damage, and not always by the Commission, even though the latter institution does have a number of important representative functions.

14.2 The Conditions of Liability

The judicial evolution of the EC law on non-contractual liability has revealed the following as the necessary conditions of a successful action:

- a wrongful act or omission;
- damage to the plaintiff;
- a causal link between the two.

These conditions will be examined in turn.

14.3 The Requirement of a Wrongful Act

It is implicit in much of the Court's case law that some form of 'fault' is a necessary element of liability. The Court was given the opportunity in Cases 9, 11/71 *Compagnie d'Approvisionnement* v. *Commission* ([1972] ECR 391) to adopt the French doctrine of '*légalité devant les charges publiques*' (equal apportionment of public burdens) whereby the state may in certain circumstances be liable even in the absence of fault as a result of the simple fact that policy measures which it adopts may weigh more heavily on some citizens than on others. Since the Court concluded that the measures under challenge in Cases 9, 11/71, which were intended to offset the effects of the devaluation of the French franc in 1969, and in particular its disruptive effects on the Common Agricultural Policy (CAP), did not in fact impose a burden on the applicants, it was not required to consider this question.

A similar requirement of 'wrongfulness' or 'fault' is an essential element of the non-contractual liability of the EU institutions under the ECSC Treaty regime (see Case T-120/89 *Stahlwerke Peine-Salzgitter* v. *Commission* [1991] ECR II-279; Case C-220/91P *Stahlwerke Peine-Salzgitter* v. *Commission* [1993] ECR I-2393).

14.4 Wrongful Acts: Vicarious Liability and the Responsibility of the Institutions

In the one case in which it has been required to consider the nature of the EU's responsibility for a fault on the part of one of its servants (*faute personnelle*), the Court has given a restrictive interpretation of the extent of EU vicarious liability. Interpreting the equivalent Article 188(2) Euratom in Case 9/69 *Sayag* v. *Leduc* ([1969] ECR 329) the Court held (at p. 335):

> 'By referring at one and the same time to damage caused by the institutions and to that caused by the servants of the Community, Article 188 indicates that the Community is only liable for those acts of its servants which, by virtue of an internal and direct relationship, are the necessary extension of the tasks entrusted to the institutions.'

In *Sayag*, a reference for a preliminary ruling from a Belgian court, the question concerned whether a person injured in a traffic accident caused by an engineer employed by Euratom who had been travelling on official business in Belgium in his private car should be suing the engineer personally in the Belgian courts or the EU as vicariously liable in the Court of Justice. The restrictive interpretation given by the Court resulted in the conclusion that the driving of a private car on official business would not fall within the concept of *faute personnelle* except in the exceptional circumstances where the EU would not have been able to undertake the tasks entrusted to it without the official using private means of transport.

Clearly, also, the institutions will be liable for forms of employers' and occupiers' liability. For example, in Case C-308/87 *Grifoni* v. *Euratom* ([1990] ECR I-1203), the plaintiff was the proprietor of an Italian construction company who was injured in the course of carrying out maintenance work at the Commission's Ispra Research Centre in Italy. He had not been supplied with a safety harness, and the place where he was working was not fitted with a safety rail, contrary to the requirements of Italian health and safety law. The Court held that the EU was required to comply with Italian law on industrial safety, that this requirement applied also to an independent contractor, and that the EU was therefore liable in damages. The damages were reduced by 50 per cent, on account of contributory negligence on the part of Grifoni, who had agreed to go on the roof in the absence of the necessary protective devices.

14.5   Wrongful Acts: Carelessness within the Commission

One of the most infamous cases concerning the responsibility of the EU, and one of the relatively few which have resulted in a definitive award of damages, involved a clear case of carelessness within the Commission which was not imputable to any one official or to the organisation of the institution as an employer or a contractor, but to the administrative service as a whole (*faute de service*) (Case 145/83 *Adams* v. *Commission* [1985] ECR 3539). Stanley Adams, while working for the Swiss pharmaceutical company Hoffman-La-Roche (HLR), supplied the Commission with documents, on an assurance of confidentiality. The documents showed that HLR was violating EC competition law, and the Commission successfully took proceedings against the company. In the course of the proceedings, the Commission supplied HLR with documents which assisted them in identifying Adams as the informant. Although Adams had left HLR's employment by that time and was living in Italy, he was arrested under the Swiss industrial espionage laws when he returned for a visit. He was held in solitary confinement, unable to communicate with his family, and his wife, who was also interrogated, subsequently committed suicide. He was eventually convicted and given a one-year suspended sentence. When he claimed damages against the Commission, it was found by the Court to have violated its duty towards him, in particular when it failed to warn Adams when it discovered that HLR was planning to prosecute him. The damages payable were reduced by one-half in respect of Adams' own contributory fault in returning to Switzerland, which occasioned his arrest.

A less tragic case is Case 353/88 *Briantex* v. *Council and Commission* ([1989] ECR 3623) where the Commission was said to have misled the plaintiff into thinking that it could conclude contracts with Chinese companies in the context of an 'EEC–China Business Week', when in fact the Italian quota for the relevant good was already exhausted. The claim failed on the facts, as the applicants were unable to prove wrongful conduct on the part of the Commission. The same grounds were given by the Court for dismissing the application in Cases 326/86 and 66/88 *Francesconi* v. *Commission* ([1989] ECR 2087). This was an attempt to make the Commission liable for failure effectively to cooperate with a Member State and for bad management and supervision of the wine sector following the so-called glycol and methanol wine scandals in 1985–86. The claim, although unsuccessful, raises the possibility of an extension of Commission liability in the context of its cooperative and supervisory roles in relation to the implementation of EC law (see also 14.10).

14.6 Acts or Omissions?

For many years, there was little indication as to whether and to what extent the EU may be liable for omissions. In Cases 19, etc./69 *Richez-Parise* v. *Commission* ([1970] ECR 325) the Commission was held liable for the failure to correct the good faith, but incorrect, interpretation it had given to a number of officials regarding their pensions. However, in Case C-146/91 *KYDEP* v. *Council and Commission* ([1994] ECR I-4199) the Court held that the EU institutions could only be held liable for omissions in circumstances where they had breached a legal duty to act resulting from a provision of EC law. In circumstances where the institutions have a wide discretion as to the nature and form of their action (see 14.7 *et seq.*) it is exceedingly unlikely that an action to establish liability for an omission will succeed. In a recent example (Case T-572/93 *Odigitria AAE* v. *Council and Commission* [1995] ECR II-2025) the applicant failed in a contention that the Council and Commission had unlawfully failed to take into account the existence of a longstanding territorial dispute between Guinea-Buissau and Senegal before the International Court of Justice when they negotiated and concluded fishing agreements with these two countries. The applicant's contention was that this failure had caused it loss when one of its boats inadvertently became involved in this dispute with the result that it was seized and its cargo confiscated by the Guinea-Buissau authorities. The Court found no violation of a superior rule of law (cf. 14.9) by the institutions. On the other hand, the judgment of the Court does seem to indicate that the Commission might have been guilty of an unlawful omission in the conduct of its administrative duties in failing to warn the applicant about an escalation in the dispute which led to the incident in which the applicant's boat was seized (cf. 14.10). However, on the facts the Court found that it could not have been the failure to warn which caused the loss since it appeared that the applicant's captain in fact knew about the escalation (see 14.11).

14.7   Wrongful Acts: Acts having Legal Effects

In practice, the most important category of cases decided by the Court under Article 215 has concerned alleged liability for damage caused by acts which have legal effects such as an illegal refusal to grant an import or export licence, or measures of economic policy which impose more onerous financial burdens on one product than on a competing product, or which discriminate between producers of the same product. In these cases the wrongful act is quite different in nature to, for example, the breach of confidentiality which caused harm to Stanley Adams.

One of the most difficult questions in this context has been that of distinguishing between actions for annulment and actions for compensation; should recovery be governed by the same conditions which govern the annulment of acts with legal effects? If not, what conditions determine the circumstances in which the wrongful and damaging administrative or legislative actions of an EU institution give rise to an action for compensation?

14.8   The Relationship between Annulment and Compensation

The second paragraph of Article 176 EC states that the obligation on the institution whose act has been declared void to take the necessary measures to comply with the judgment of the Court of Justice 'shall not affect any obligation which may result from the application of the second paragraph of Article 215'. This appears to state clearly that annulment actions and actions for compensation are quite separate.

However, in Case 25/62 *Plaumann* v. *Commission* ([1963] ECR 95) the Court linked the two actions together. It will be recalled that in this case a German importer of clementines sought to challenge a Commission Decision addressed to Germany, refusing it the right to lower the duty on clementines from 13 to 10 per cent. Holding the Article 173 EC annulment action to be inadmissible on the grounds that the importer lacked *locus standi*, the Court went on to declare an Article 215 action for compensation admissible. However, the action failed on the merits (at p. 108):

'It must be declared that the damage allegedly suffered by the applicant issues from this Decision and that the action for compensation in fact seeks to set aside the legal effects on the applicant of the contested Decision.

In the present case the contested Decision has not been annulled. An administrative measure which has not been annulled cannot of itself constitute a wrongful act on the part of the administration inflicting damage upon those whom it affects. The latter cannot therefore claim damages by reason of that measure. The Court cannot by way of an action for compensation take steps which would nullify the legal effects of a Decision which, as stated, has not been annulled.'

This doctrine has since been reversed and there is now no need for an applicant under Article 215 to challenge directly or indirectly, via Articles 173, 177 or 184 EC, the legality of administrative or legislative measures in respect of which it claims compensation. In Case 4/69 *Lütticke* v. *Commission* ([1971] ECR 325), in the context of a claim for failure on the part of the Commission to address a directive or decision to Germany requiring it to modify certain taxes which the applicant had to pay, the Court stated (at p. 336):

'The action for damages provided for by Article 178 and the second paragraph of Article 215 was established by the Treaty as an independent form of action with a particular purpose to fulfil within the system of actions and subject to conditions for its use, conceived with a view to its specific purpose. It would be contrary to the independent nature of this action as well as to the efficacy of the general system of forms of action created by the Treaty to regard as a ground for inadmissibility the fact that, in certain circumstances, an action for damages might lead to a result similar to that of an action for failure to act under Article 175.'

The clearest statement of the separation of the actions for annulment and compensation came in Case 175/84 *Krohn* v. *Commission* ([1986] ECR 753) where the Court stated expressly that the existence of an individual decision which has become definitive because it had not been challenged under Article 173 was not a bar to the admissibility of a compensation action.

In practice, although annulment, or a declaration of invalidity under Article 177, is by no means a prerequisite of a successful action under Article 215, many actions for compensation are either linked to, or have been preceded by, successful annulment actions or declarations of invalidity (e.g. Case C-152/88 *Sofrimport* v. *Commission* [1990] ECR I-2477 – actions under Article 173 and 215 brought simultaneously; in the iso-glucose cases (see 14.9) Article 215 actions were brought at about the same time as actions in the national courts which resulted in references on the validity of the relevant measures under Article 177; in the milk quota cases discussed in the same paragraph the actions for compensation have followed findings of invalidity of a series of Council measures).

14.9   The Elaboration and Application of the *Schöppenstedt* Formula

The formula for determining whether there has been a breach of EC law in the context of a claim for compensation caused by an act having legal effects is quite different, and in many ways more restrictive, than the criteria which the Court uses to determine the legality of an act for the purposes of annulment or invalidity. It was elaborated by the Court in the first instance in Case 5/71 *Zuckerfabrik Schöppenstedt* v. *Council* ([1971] ECR 975) and it has consistently applied these principles since that time. The *Schöppenstedt* formula, as restated by the Court in Cases 83, etc./76 *Bayerische HNL et al.* v. *Council and Commission (Second Skimmed Milk Powder case)* ([1978] ECR 1209 at p. 1224) states that:

> 'The Community does not incur liability on account of a legislative measure which involves choices of economic policy unless a sufficiently serious breach of a superior rule of law for the protection of the individual has occurred.'

This formula applies only to legislative measures of the institutions, that is, to those which are of general application and involve an element of discretionary decision-making. Inevitably such measures will impact to varying degrees upon economic actors and, in order to avoid a flood of claims from aggrieved plaintiffs while at the same upholding the constitutional supremacy of the rule of law under the Treaties, the Court has chosen a restrictive definition of wrongfulness. This definition has in turn been applied in such a way as to exclude the majority of claims.

The first requirement is the breach of a superior rule of law for the protection of individuals. This is a reference to the range of general principles and fundamental rights evolved by the Court in its case law. For example, in Case 74/74 *CNTA* v. *Commission* ([1975] ECR 533) the Court held that the abolition with immediate effect and without warning of monetary compensatory amounts (MCA's), used to compensate agricultural traders for fluctuations in exchange rates which made the single pricing system under the CAP unreliable, could constitute a breach of the principle of legitimate expectations which is protected under EC law. In Case C-152/88 *Sofrimport* v. *Commission*, the Court found that importers of Chilean apples which were in transit to the EU had a legitimate expectation that they would be protected against the unfavourable consequences of protective measures against such apples which were introduced by the EU authorities. This was because the enabling Regulation specifically addressed the situation of those whose apples were actually already in transit to the EU, who could not therefore mitigate their loss by arranging for an alternative disposal of the products.

The prerequisite of a breach of a superior rule of law would normally be satisfied by a successful annulment action under Article 173, or a ruling of invalidity under Article 177, although it is arguable that a successful claim for invalidity on the grounds that the wrong legal basis had been used, or that Parliamentary prerogatives had not been observed would not satisfy the requirement that the rule of law which has been breached must be for the protection of individuals. The point was directly addressed by the Court in Case C-282/90 *Vreugdenhil* v. *Commission* ([1992] ECR I-1937).

The alleged breach was of a rule governing the exercise of delegated powers by the Commission, and involved the Commission exceeding the powers granted to it by the Council. The Court had already made a ruling of invalidity in respect of the same provision in Case 22/88 *Vreugdenhil* v. *Minister van Landbouw and Visserij* ([1989] ECR 2049) Faced with an action for damages, the Court held (at p. 1968):

'the aim of the system of the division of powers between the various Community institutions is to ensure that the balance between the institutions provided for in the Treaty is maintained, and not to protect individuals. Consequently, a failure to observe the balance between the institutions cannot be sufficient on its own to engage the Community's liability towards the traders concerned.'

In addition, the breach must be sufficiently serious. This is, in practice, the most stringent requirement, and in numerous cases the applicants' cases have failed at this hurdle. Cases 83, etc./76 *Second Skimmed Milk Powder* case concerned the attempt by the Community institutions to get rid of a skimmed milk powder mountain which stemmed from the overproduction of milk, by passing a Regulation obliging producers of animal feed to purchase skimmed milk powder from the intervention agencies. This had a damaging effect on soya, which was the alternative, and cheaper, source of protein in animal feeds. The result was also that farmers would have to pay more for their feed. The farmers succeeded in obtaining a declaration that the Regulation was invalid on the grounds that it infringed the principles of non-discrimination and proportionality (Case 114/76 *Bela-Mühle Josef Bergman* v. *Grows-Farm* [1977] ECR 1211), but failed in their tort actions because the institution concerned had not 'manifestly and gravely disregarded the limits on the exercise of its powers'.

Applying this formulation to the facts, the Court considered both the range of potential plaintiffs – which was a wide category of persons – and the effect of the infringement in terms of its impact on the price of the products in question, as compared to other factors such as fluctuations in world prices. It found this effect to be relatively small. It summed up the effect of the EU's measures as being within the normal range of risk inherent in activities in the economic sector concerned.

Soon after the *Second Skimmed Milk Powder* case, the Court made its first finding of tortious liability in respect of EU legislative acts. In Cases 64, etc./76 *Dumortier et al.* v. *Council and Commission (Quellmehl and Gritz)* ([1979] ECR 3091) the alleged tortious act was a Council Regulation withdrawing subsidies from the production of quellmehl and gritz, products used in baking which are in part in competition with starch, but leaving the subsidies in place for starch. The measure was declared invalid on a reference for a preliminary ruling (Cases 117, etc./76 *Ruckdeschel* v. *HZA Hamburg St-Annen* [1977] ECR 1753) on grounds of infringement of the principle of non-discrimination, and when the subsidies were restored for the future, but not retrospectively, the producers brought proceedings under Article 215 to claim the losses they had suffered during the period when there were no subsidies. In finding for the applicants, the Court pointed out that the producers were a small and ascertainable class, and that the loss they suffered went beyond the risks inherent in the economic activity in question. This was not the beginning of a radical change in approach, however, for shortly thereafter the Court rejected the tortious actions in the *Isoglucose* cases, reinforcing the perception that its judgments in this field are tempered by policy factors which it does not always make very clear.

In the *Isoglucose* cases, the Court ruled that a levy imposed on isoglucose was unlawful in so far as it amounted to discriminatory treatment of isoglucose producers in comparison to the treatment of sugar producers (Cases 103 and 145/77 Royal *Scholten-Honig (Holdings) Ltd* v. *Intervention Board for Agricultural Produce* [1978] ECR 2037). However, in Cases 116, 124/77 *Amylum and Tunnel Refineries* v. *Council and Commission* ([1979] ECR 3479) and Case 143/77 *KSH NV* v. *Council and Commission* ([1979] ECR 3583), it rejected the Article 215 actions. Neither the ruling of invalidity nor the special facts of the case, which showed that the victims were a very small group, that there was some evidence that the measure was aimed at driving isoglucose out of the market by making it uneconomical to produce and that the levy was so severe that it pushed at least one firm into liquidation, were sufficient for the Court to hold that the violation was sufficiently 'grave and manifest'. In that case, the Court appeared to push the definition of 'sufficiently serious' even further by requiring the actions of the institutions to be 'verging on the arbitrary'. It declared that the damage alleged must go beyond the bounds of the normal economic risks inherent in the sector concerned. Unsurprisingly, the *Isoglucose* cases were the subject of extensive criticism, and appear to mark a low point in the Court's unwillingness to interfere in the economic planning of the Council and Commission (Hartley, 1994: 492–94; Rudden, 1987: 183–215).

Although, as can be seen, the Court's case law in this area is uneven, it would appear that two factors are central to its evaluation of the nature of the breach: these are the conduct of the defendant and the effect of breach. If, as in Case C-152/88 *Sofrimport* v. *Commission*, the EU 'fails completely' to take into account the interests of a group of applicants which it was specifically mandated to consider 'without invoking any overriding public interest', and the effect of that breach upon a narrowly defined category of economic actors 'goes beyond the limits of the economic risks inherent in the business in issue inasmuch as the purpose of that provision [i.e. the one disregarded by the Commission] is precisely to limit those risks with regard to goods in transit', then the Court will be prepared to make a finding of liability. *Sofrimport* appears to have been the harbinger of a more liberal attitude on the part of the Court to actions for damages.

In Case C-220/91P *Stahlwerke Peine-Salzgitter* v. *Commission*, a case decided under the ECSC Treaty, the Court of First Instance stated specifically that the harmful conduct did not have to be verging on the arbitrary. The Court of Justice has also repeated both parts of the formula developed in *Sofrimport* (Case C-152/88) in what is, so far, its most 'generous' finding of tortious liability on the part of the EU (Cases C-104/89 and 37/90 *Mulder and Heinemann* v. *Commission and Council* ([1992] ECR I-3061). In that case, the loss stemmed from a Council Regulation fixing an exemption from levies on the production of dairy products by reference to the quantities which undertakings had marketed in a given earlier year. The applicants in the case had not marketed any dairy products in the reference year, since they had undertaken not to do so as part of the EU's attempts to reduce dairy overproduction. The applicants were not therefore allocated a 'reference quantity' excluded from production levies. The regulation was challenged, by means of actions in the Dutch courts and references on validity to the Court of Justice, which found a violation of the principle of legitimate expectations. Subsequent amendments to the Regulations giving a 60 per cent reference quantity were also successfully challenged. These cases are discussed in 12.13 (Case 120/86 *Mulder* v. *Minister van Landbouw en Visserij* [1988] ECR 2321; C-189/89 *Spagl* [1990] ECR I-4539).

In the action for damages which followed, the Court distinguished between the case where no reference quantity was given, and that where the reference quantity was set at 60 per cent. In the former case, it found the Council liable:

'In so far as it failed completely, without invoking any higher public interest, to take account of the specific situation of a clearly defined group of economic agents, that is to say, producers who, pursuant to an undertaking . . . delivered no milk during the reference year, the Community legislature manifestly and gravely disregarded the limits of its discretionary power, thereby committing a sufficiently serious breach of a superior rule of law' (at p. 3132).

However, the Court found no liability in respect of the 60 per cent rule, notwithstanding that it had found the same rule to violate the principle of legitimate expectations. It concluded that the breach was not sufficiently serious to merit liability. By adopting the amending regulation

'the Community legislature made an economic policy choice with regard to the manner in which it was necessary to implement the principles set out in those judgments. That was based, on the one hand, on the 'overriding necessity of not jeopardizing the fragile stability that currently obtains in the milk products sector' [a quote from the preamble to the Regulation] and, on the other, on the need to strike a balance between the interests of the producers concerned and the interests of the other producers subject to the scheme . . . Accordingly, the Council took account of a higher public interest, without gravely and manifestly disregarding the limits of its discretionary power in this area' (at pp. 3133-4).

One of the notable aspects of the case is that although the farmers represented a defined group of economic actors, they were nonetheless a very large group (up to 13,000 strong), and the financial consequences of paying compensation and reorganising the quota structure are considerable.

An attempt failed to use the *Schöppenstedt* formula in order to claim compensation for loss caused by an allegedly unlawful directive harmonising national rules affecting the creation of the internal market. In Case C-63/89 *Les Assurances de Credit SA* v. *Council and Commission* ([1991] ECR I-1799) the Court held that a Directive harmonising the conditions in which export credit insurance operations could be undertaken, but which did not apply to public sector insurance business, was not unlawful in the sense of giving rise to a claim for compensation. The Court did not accept the argument that the Directive discriminated against the private sector businesses. It held that the Council could validly pass a partial harmonisation measure and possessed complete discretion as to the timetable under which it adopted harmonisation measures.

14.10   Liability in Respect of Other Acts having Legal Effects

The *Schöppenstedt* formula is not used to assess whether individual acts having legal effects can give rise to the liability of the EU. For example, in Cases 5, etc./66 *Kampffmeyer* v. *Commission* ([1967] ECR 245) the Court found that the responsibility of the Commission was engaged by its wrongful and 'improper' application of a safeguard provision allowing protective measures to be taken to prohibit the import of certain agricultural products. The measure in question was a decision addressed to Germany, annulled by the Court in Cases 106, 107/63 *Toepfer* v. *Commission* ([1965] ECR 405).

In Case C-55/90 *Cato* v. *Commission* ([1992] ECR I-2533), the applicant sought to argue that the Commission was liable to compensate for loss caused by the approval, by means of a decision addressed to the UK, of what he considered to be an incorrect implementation of a Council Directive on the awarding of compensation to persons who decommissioned fishing boats. Cato argued that the UK implementing measures placed an excessive burden of proof on the party claiming compensation, and that the Commission should not have approved them. The Court simply referred, without either discussing or disapproving of it, to the applicant's contention that the Commission had committed a sufficiently serious breach of a superior rule of law for the protection of individuals, and was therefore liable to pay compensation, but dismissed the action on the facts for failure on the part of Cato to prove his contentions about the effect of the UK measures. In the event that the Court might hold the Commission liable for its failure adequately to supervise the implementation of EU obligations by Member States, it is arguable that the test to be used is one which should be different from that governing discretionary legislative activities. If the Commission is subject to a duty, in certain cases, to approve by Decision the correct implementation of particular Directives, a failure to fulfil such a duty does not involve a true exercise of discretion. It is in any event unlikely that the Court will encourage the development of a line of cases which seeks to make the Commission responsible for inadequate supervision. It has long been the tendency of the Court to encourage individuals to seek redress in respect of unimplemented or misimplemented Directives from Member States in national courts, and this line of case law was further strengthened by the decision on damages for failure to implement in Cases 6, 9/90 *Francovich* v. *Italian State* ([1991] ECR I-5357).

14.11 The Requirements of Causation and Damage

It is for the applicant to prove causation and damage; the Court does not draw an inference from the fact of unlawful conduct that the unlawful conduct caused the damage (Case 253/84 *GAEC* v. *Council and Commission* ([1987] ECR 123). The Court has not applied a 'but for' test in assessing whether there is a factual causal link between the unlawful act on the part of the EU and the alleged damage. Rather it has tended to focus on the fact that it will always be difficult to prove in a market situation that a legislative or other measure is 'the' cause of any damage due to a reduction of profits, and it has held (e.g. in Cases 64, etc./76 *Dumortier et al.* v. *Council and Commission (Quellmehl and Gritz)* that the damage must be a sufficiently direct consequence of the unlawful conduct of the institution concerned. This in practice has a tendency to restrict the ability of applicants to recover for losses of profit. For example, in Cases 5, etc./66 *Kampffmeyer* v. *Commission* the applicants had applied for permits to import maize from France into Germany at a time when large profits could be made because of a zero rate of levy. The German authorities wrongfully refused to grant the permit and the Commission upheld the refusal. Those applicants who had already concluded contracts and had to cancel them were held entitled to recover their cancellation fees and loss of profits, but with the latter discounted by 90 per cent, because of the speculative nature of the transactions. Those applicants who had not previously concluded contracts recovered nothing.

In a number of cases applicants have failed to recover damages despite establishing liability in principle, because they have been unable to prove damage. In Case 74/74 *CNTA* v. *Commission*, although they were able to establish that the sudden termination of MCAs engaged the tortious responsibility of the Community, the applicants were unable to establish that the currency fluctuations had in fact caused loss. Similarly, in Case 253/84 *GAEC* v. *Council and Commission*, the Court refused to consider the applicant's contention that a Council Decision authorising Germany to grant state subsidies to its farmers was unlawful because it was unable to prove that the effect of the subsidies had been to cause damage to French farmers through a lowering of prices on the French market because of competition from artificially cheaper German products. Statistics were produced by the defendants to demonstrate that prices in France had already begun to fall before the entry into force of the contested Decision.

The Court also applies the defence of contributory negligence (Case 145/83 *Adams* v. *Commission*; Case C-308/87 *Grifoni* v. *Euratom*) and the duty to mitigate losses (Cases C-104/89 and 37/90 *Mulder and Heinemann* v. *Commission and Council*) in order to restrict in practice the level of damages payable by the EU. In the latter case the Court deducted from the damages payable to the aggrieved dairy producers an amount representing what they would have earned if they had reasonably sought to undertake alternative commercial or agricultural activities during the period when they could not produce and sell dairy products. It held that damages had to be calculated on the basis of the

'general principle common to the legal systems of the Member States to the effect that the injured party must show reasonable diligence in limiting the extent of his loss or risk having to bear the damage himself' (at p. 3136–7).

Interest can be awarded on damages payable by the EU, since it is in general awarded under the rules common to the Member States (Case C-152/88 *Sofrimport* v. *Commission*).

In each case, the Court states the basis for calculating the damages (e.g. in Case C-152/88 *Sofrimport* v. *Commission* the difference between the price at which the apples were sold after the Court had suspended the protective measures in interim proceedings, and the price the applicants would have got for them had the measures not been imposed), and then sends the parties away to formulate, within a time limit, an agreed amount of damages which they must then communicate to the Court. In the event of a failure to agree, the parties must submit their views to the Court which will itself fix the amount.

14.12   The Problem of Concurrent Liability: National Court or Court of Justice?

Not all actions for loss ultimately attributable to unlawful conduct on the part of the EU can be brought in the Court of First Instance. Despite the fact that the EU operates a system of own resources, whereby the levies collected and sums paid by national administrations on behalf of the EU are in truth the EU's own money (see 5.12), the Court nonetheless refuses to consider certain applications for money damages. A distinction must be drawn to this end between what are essentially restitutionary claims, namely actions for restitution of a sum unlawfully levied and sums withheld in breach of an obligation, and actions for unliquidated damages such as loss of profit.

The case law on these questions was largely developed by the Court of Justice prior to the transfer of jurisdiction over those cases to the Court of First Instance and it is generally consistent with that Court's persistent encouragement to undertakings to begin their actions against unlawful conduct on the part of the EU by challenging the national implementing measures. For example, it requires actions for restitution of a sum unlawfully levied to be brought against the national authority which levied the sums in the national court, even though the sums in question may have been paid into the EU funds (Case 96/71 *Haegemann* v. *Commission* [1972] ECR 1005; Case C-282/90 *Vreugdenhil* v. *Commission*). Consequently, it would be wrong for a national court to deny the liability of the national authority, on account of its role as an 'agent' of the EU. In contrast, it would appear that an action for a sum withheld in breach of a lawful obligation can be brought in either the Court of First Instance or the national court. Since the case law on this point is mixed, however, prudence would seem to suggest that, unless damages at large in addition to the specified sum are claimed, the national court is a better place to start. Exceptionally, of course, there may, for some reason, be no national remedy; an example would be where there is no legal basis in national law for an action for compensation once the unlawful act has been removed from the field.

Similar considerations would appear to apply where the damage is alleged to have occurred as a result of the withholding of some other administrative act on the part of the national authority (e.g. the refusal of a licence as in Case 175/84 *Krohn* v. *Commission*). In its judgment in *Krohn*, the Court of Justice made clear that the Commission was the true author of the unlawful act, and that a national action would not have provided effective protection for the individual concerned against loss, and consequently held the action admissible.

Actions in respect of unliquidated loss, such as the additional loss suffered as a consequence of the unlawful levying of a sum by the national authority, must always be brought in the Court of First Instance in addition to the national action (Case 26/74 *Roquette* v. *Commission* [1976] ECR 677). Since the transfer of jurisdiction this raises difficulties, as any Article 177 preference will be heard by the Court of Justice.

The case law remains unsatisfactory, therefore, since it is wrong to impose an obligation upon an aggrieved undertaking to choose between the national court and the Court of Justice, or to take two actions where one should suffice. In reality, since the implementation of EU measures is frequently a result of a combination of EU and national action, it is difficult for the victim of the loss always to assess to whom in truth the wrongful conduct is attributable. Cases 89, 91/86 *L'Etoile Commerciale* v. *Commission* ([1987] ECR 3005) provide an example of the restrictive application of the rules on the admissibility of Article 215 claims where the alleged wrongful conduct was a decision adopted by the Commission which led a national authority to reclaim certain agricultural subsidies. The Court declared the action under Articles 178 and 215 inadmissible. There is a case for allowing an application of the principles of joint and several liability, widely recognised in the legal systems of the Member States, whereby the victim of a tort may sue one of several or joint tortfeasors in respect of the whole of the obligation, leaving the tortfeasors to recover contributions between themselves (see the analysis of AG Van Gerven in Case 201/86 *Spie-Batignolles* v. *Commission* [1990] ECR I-197 where he recognised the wide applicability of the rules on joint and several liability). However, the continuing organic separation of the Community judicative and the national courts, and the failure to recognise either that an EU institution may be a defendant in a national court, or that a Member State may be a defendant in the Court of First Instance in an action brought by an individual, represent conclusive obstacles to this more equitable solution of the problem (Wils, 1992). However, the decision of the Court of Justice to base the liability of Member States for breach of EC law on the same principles as the liability of the EU institutions (9.17, 10.6) might presage a convergence in relation to this question as well.

Summary

1   The non-contractual (i.e. tortious) liability of the EU is governed by Articles 178 and 215(2) EC.
2   The basic prerequisites of a successful action are:

  – a wrongful act (i.e. one involving some 'fault' or breach of EC law on the part of the EU institutions); exceptionally a wrongful omission;
  – damage to the plaintiff;
  – a causal link between the two.

3   The EU can be liable in respect of *fautes de service* (i.e. failures which are imputable to an institution) and *fautes personnelles* (i.e. unlawful acts of officials for which an institution is vicariously liable).
4   Much of the case law of the Court has been concentrated on attempted claims for damages for discretionary legislative acts. The Court applies the rules restrictively in such cases so as to limit access to compensation, although it does not require the applicant to have first successfully challenged the validity of the offending EU act either via an action under Article 173 or an action in the national court and a ruling on validity.
5   To be successful an applicant seeking damages for an allegedly wrongful legislative act involving choices of economic policy must prove a sufficiently serious breach of a superior rule of law intended for the protection of individuals (the *Schöppenstedt* formula).
6   The Court's interpretation of 'sufficiently serious breach' has been particularly restrictive, although there are some signs that the Court may be taking a more liberal view in recent cases.
7   Where the applicant's action consists of a restitutionary claim for money wrongfully paid to or withheld by a national authority acting on the basis

of an unlawful EU act, the Court will normally require the applicant to begin the action in the national court. Only actions for unliquidated damages against the EU institutions may be brought in the Court of Justice.

Questions

1 What are the basic elements of a successful damages claim against the EU?
2 What is the difference between a *faute de service* and a *faute personnelle*?
3 Should the Court require an applicant for compensation under Article 215 to challenge first the validity of the act in question?
4 What is the *Schöppenstedt* formula, and how and why has it been restrictively applied by the EU Courts?
5 Are there any policy factors which link together the successful actions for damages against the EU?
6 In what ways would the application of a doctrine of joint and several liability assist applicants who bring the claims in tort against the EU and the national authorities?

Workshop (for Chapters 12–14)

The State of Rubric is the sole source of imports of a rare desert orchid into the EU. The orchid is much in demand for its medicinal properties. Five firms in the EU, including a UK firm Orchids Alive plc, import the orchids from Rubric. The Commission adopts (fictitious) Regulation 6000 of 1996 imposing an additional import levy of 10 per cent *ad valorem* on imports of the orchids, following representations from the World Save the Orchid Campaign. The Campaign produced evidence of the activities of Orchids Alive plc, including allegations about the environmental damage caused to the eco-system in Rubric as a result of the harvesting of the orchids, and of bribery of public officials in Rubric to ensure that other firms based in the EU do not get access to the supplies there. The firm did not know of the Commission's intention to adopt the Regulation until it was published in the Official Journal. It is also known that a consortium of EU-based firms is planning to launch the farming under glass of the orchids within the EU, and that a group of officials within the Directorate-General of the Commission which was responsible for the Regulation has a financial interest in the venture.

Advise Orchids Alive plc as to which court or courts it should bring an action in, and assess its chances of obtaining the following forms of redress:

1 annulment of the Regulation, or a declaration of invalidity;
2 recovery of the additional import levy paid to the UK customs authorities;
3 compensation for the loss of profits on long-term supply contracts which it holds within the UK.

Further Reading

van Gerven (1994b), 'Non-contractual Liability of Member States, Community Institutions and Individuals for Breaches of Community Law with a View to a Common Law for Europe', 1 *MJ* 6.
Hartley (1994) Ch. 17, 'Community Obligations'.
Wils (1992), 'Concurrent Liability of the Community and a Member State', 17 *ELRev.* 191.

Part V

Conclusion

15 The Constitutional and Institutional Foundations of the European Union: Review and Conclusions

15.1 Introduction

The general objective of this book has been to explain and analyse the constitutional and institutional foundations of the European Union. Throughout the intention has been to identify the basic building blocks which are central to the understanding of the EU as a legal order. These building blocks take a number of different forms and are principally to be found in Chapters 3–14. After an initial introductory chapter reviewing the basic principles of European constitutionalism, we have considered the elements of the European legal order under three main headings: the work of the institutions; the relationship between national law and EC law; and the legal principles which govern the legality of the acts of the institutions. However, it is important to emphasise that these building blocks do not comprise simply dry and abstract legal principles and rules, but include a number of features and contexts which shape the impact which the legal aspect of the EU has upon the evolution of the integration process as a whole (15.2).

Obviously the types of rules and principles which we have examined in this book have an importance in themselves in that they show how the governmental power of the EU is exercised. But they do not address the question of what the EU is given that governmental power for. The answer to that question resides in the substantive principles of the EU Treaties: that is, in the provisions of the Treaties which determine that the objectives and tasks of the Union and the Communities are to create and maintain an internal market for commodities and factors of production, to have common policies in the fields of agriculture, transport and competition, etc., to harmonise national laws to the extent necessary to support the single market, to seek solidarity and economic and social cohesion between the Member States and their citizens, and now more recently, to create an economic and monetary union. These are the provisions which tell us for what purposes the European Union exists – beyond the general wish to ensure peace, security and stability in a particular geographical region which has historically been scarred by violent conflict.

Consequently, it must be emphasised that many of the rules and principles explained in this book can only be fully understood when they are examined in the context of fields of what is often termed the 'substantive' law of the EU. This is, however, often a difficult term to use because it leads to attempts to draw fine distinctions between what is 'substantive', what is 'procedural', and what is 'institutional'. It is perhaps better to refer to the 'economic and social law of the EU' – that is, the body of law concerned with structuring the economic and social relations of public authorities and private actors operating within, into and out of the European Union, where the activities of these bodies fall within the scope of the competence of the European Communities, or are included within the range of activities of the Union defined in the second and third pillars (CFSP and CJHA).

To provide an illustration of what it means to study the economic and social law of the EU, this chapter will offer a few examples of institutional and constitutional principles which reveal themselves best only when they are viewed in context (15.4). In other words, they become clearer when they are viewed in the light of the functions which they perform in particular fields of economic or social law of the EU. A simple example would be the horizontal direct effect of directives (9.11) where it helps to have a fuller understanding of the types of policy sectors in which the EU's primary regulatory intervention takes the form of directives. This is only the case in a restricted range of fields. However, before these examples can be developed, it is essential to describe in outline the scope of the economic and social law of the EU (15.3), in a discussion which builds directly upon 1.3 in which the mission of the European Union was set out.

15.2   Law and European Integration

The place of law in European integration – however important it has become – should never be taken for granted. There is a simple explanation for this: it was not for the purposes of establishing a 'European legal order' that the Treaties were concluded, that the institutions were established, or that the path towards some degree of 'union' amongst the nations of Europe has been followed. However, the legal order has become an important servant of these processes, offering an indispensable normative framework and providing the setting within which judicial actors (particularly the Court of Justice but also, to a lesser extent, certain national courts) have been able to play a significant and relatively autonomous role aimed at achieving the objectives of the Treaties.

One distinctive feature of the legal order is, of course, that it has been relatively overdeveloped in comparison to the political system of the European Communities and the European Union. In formal terms, the law of the EU constitutes the supreme source of law within the territory of the Member States (leaving aside such matters as international human rights instruments or other binding norms of international law). However, that is not the end of the story. This book has sought to show that other factors still need to be taken into consideration. These include:

- National constitutional systems and national constitutional values – although formally inferior to those of the EU – remain of vital importance, as was shown, for example, by the ratification processes surrounding the Treaty of Maastricht. In fact, in the context of amendments to the Treaties, national constitutional frameworks do not give second place to those of the EU. Moreover, it is the national constitutional systems which provide the basis or inspiration for the structures to be elaborated at EU level, and for the values which imbue such structures, as the example of Cases 46, 48/93 *Brasserie du Pêcheur and Factortame III* ([1996] 1 CMLR 889) on State liability (see Chapters 9 and 10) makes very clear. Here the Court simply claims to be applying a principle common to the laws of the Member States, namely that compensation should be payable in respect of loss inflicted by a wrongful act or omission.

- The authority and legitimacy of the Court of Justice itself should not be taken for granted. The position of the Court, the nature of the law and concepts of legal reasoning do not provide adequate explanations for the relative 'success' of the EU as a legal enterprise. It is not enough simply to state that the law is complied with because it is law, and because the Member States are law abiding states, or indeed that the Court of Justice has been rather successful because it is 'good' at its job. Consequently, it is necessary to keep constantly under review the role of the law and of the Court and to seek a better understanding of why exactly the Member States have – relatively speaking – accepted the authority of the Court and complied with (most of) its judgments over the last 40 years or so. Ironically, the Court might in the long run be strengthened by an enterprise which stressed the relevance to the Court and to EC law of approaches to the study of European integration which incorporated a cool and distant appraisal of legal institutions in the context of political institutions. The Court might be a more confident court if it were clearer about the links between political and legal institutions in the EU.

- The context of dynamic change and the depth offered by historical appraisals of the development of the EU legal order should also be stressed as essential components to an understanding of EC law. At the very beginning of this book we stressed the relatively instability of the EU legal order (1.1). It may be that constant change is now endemic to the EU legal order; it may be unable now to adjust to the slower more gradual and evolutionary change characteristic of most national legal orders at most points of history. However, the importance of change has been such that it is important always to remember that a con-temporaneous snapshot of the EU legal order gives an inadequate account of both its significance and its content. For example, focusing on the current status of the European Parliament – as a legislative and budgetary actor, as a body in which the *popular* legitimacy of the EU to a considerable extent resides, and as an actor in the legal/judicial processes – provides a misleading impression of how its role has developed. It deprives the emergence of the Parliament as a meaningful actor within the EU system of the depth which it can derive from the way in which it has exerted pressures and exploited opportunities to achieve strategic changes.

• One specific aspect of change concerns the relationship between the Court, EC law and the Intergovernmental Conference to review the Treaty of Maastricht which was convened in Turin in March 1996, due to run for between one and two years. The reaction of the Court to the IGC has been detailed in sections of this book, and reference has been made where appropriate to significant institutional or constitutional changes which might be expected. The very different political atmospheres which have surrounded the three major IGCs occurring within ten years (Single European Act, Treaty of Maastricht and now 'Maastricht II') have offered sharply contrasting contexts for the Court to go about its business as the guardian of the legal order. One point that this makes clear is that the legal order – however 'federal' it appears to be in formal terms – cannot operate entirely independently of the great history making changes within the framework and system of European integration which remain – so far – the prerogative of the Member States.

• Finally, it is important to cite the multinational, multilingual, and multicultural (including many legal cultures) facets of the work of the Court of Justice (and of the 'Community' – i.e. national – courts in the Member States), and of the legal order of the EU. These aspects of the culture within which the Court operates reinforce the diversity of influences which seek to impact upon it.

Despite all of these *caveats* it still seems legitimate to accept the Court's *dictum* that the Community has been a 'Community of law'. Law has been a dominant *leitmotiv* in the history of the first 40 years of the existence of the European Economic Community. In 1.1 we highlighted the strong sense of purpose exhibited by the Court of Justice, which has remained always a more or less fierce protagonist on behalf of integration. Although the clear sense of purpose has ebbed away somewhat in certain aspects of the Court's more recent case law where it has sometimes seemed to be appeasing the Member States rather than pursuing its own line, the integrationist strand has remained immensely strong – particularly in its work shaping the constitutional and institutional framework of the EU. Where the Court has on occasion plumped for a less 'integrationist' outcome – allowing Member State diversity – there has often been argument that greater national autonomy might in certain circumstances in fact lead to a paradoxical strengthening of the centre in the long run.

It is less clear that law will be such a dominant *leitmotiv* in the coming years of European history. It might legitimately be suggested that we are passing from a 'Community of law' to a 'Union of public debt management', as the particular – and highly contested – concerns of economic and monetary union (including the infamous 'convergence criteria') become more prominent. EMU raises profound and so far unresolved constitutional questions. It raises very different legal questions to those which arise from the constitution of an internal market through a combination of fundamental freedoms and legislative actions which seek to empower individuals and grant individual rights which they are encouraged to exercise (as consumer producers and service providers, etc). The role of law in the integration process will change if the core objectives of the EU shift more towards economic and monetary union, and indeed towards a political union incorporating common foreign policy and even common defence.

15.3   The Scope of the Economic and Social Law of the EU

As EMU remains so far a future possibility rather than a current reality, it is important to stress that the present focus of the economic and social law of the EU is on the internal market – its construction through primary norms of the Treaties, the case law of the Court and the legislative interventions of the institutions, and certain (common) policies which result from or 'flank' the internal market. It is not particularly helpful when studying EC law as a whole to draw a sharp distinction between 'economic' and 'social' law. Many fields of EC law have dual economic and social objectives. For example, internal market measures concerned with harmonisation of standards of protection for consumers (e.g. on the safety of products) shade imperceptibly into measures explicitly grounded in the autonomous consumer policy competence granted to the Community by Article 129A EC. Similarly, it is difficult to identify the precise objective of EU measures concerned with health and safety at work. Is it the creation of a level competitive playing field within a single internal market, or is it the pursuit of better working conditions for EU citizens proclaimed by Article 2 EC to be an objective of the Community? Even the flagship of social policy – the law on sex equality – is bedevilled by having a joint economic/social foundation. On the one hand, it is a fundamental right for all; on the other, it should be recalled that Article 119 EC guaranteeing equal pay for men and women was only included because France already had such a rule, and in order to avoid the distortion of competitive conditions.

It can plausibly be claimed that the relative levels of development reached by fields of law directly concerned with or contingent upon the internal market, in comparison to those fields of law which cannot be solely sustained by an appeal to the logic of the internal market, do distort the scope and shape of the economic and social law of the EU. The social objectives of the EU, and the activities in the social sphere, are described less fully and less precisely than those concerned with economic integration. The European *Economic* Community led the way with *economic* integration, and that remains the dominant theme. However, there are a number of rapidly developing fields of EC law – especially those concerned with consumer protection, with environmental protection and with the regulation of employment relationships or the position of workers in the enterprise – where broader social objectives cannot be ignored, and where there is a genuine demand for EU intervention from a number of different interested actors at EU and at national level (as well as opposition from others!). Overall, the approach that should be taken is not one which identifies areas of EC law as 'economic' or as 'social', but which begins with the internal market, examines the areas of the law necessarily directly linked to the internal market, and then moves to the fields of law which challenge as well as complement the objectives of the internal market. It would be wrong to search for a completed legal structure of social and economic law, or for a cohesive and coherent socio-economic vision in the law of the EU. The competence of the Community is restricted, by reference to the limited objectives and tasks set out on Articles 2 and 3 EC. Those competences which have been ascribed have not been fully exercised. Instead, the correct approach is one which looks directly to the continuing tension between negative and positive integration: between the pursuit of integration through the granting of 'freedoms', and the pursuit of integration through legislative or regulatory structures which facilitate or complement those freedoms. The freedoms secured in the context of negative integration are, moreover, 'constitutional' freedoms guaranteed directly within the framework of the Treaty. This suggests that the study of the economic and social law of the EU must begin with the examination of the Treaty-based freedoms, coupled with the legislative structures which are essential to the realisation of 'full' freedom.

First to be examined, therefore, are the four freedoms: goods, services, persons (including workers, establishments, professionals and enterprises), and capital. Since the completion of much of the legislative programme envisaged by the Commission's 1985 White Paper on the Completion of the Internal Market, these freedoms, and the case law which they have generated, must be examined in the light of the huge body of complementary legislation, supplementing or articulating Treaty guarantees, providing where necessary additional remedies (e.g. in the field of public procurement), restricting the ability of Member States to rely upon Treaty-based public policy or public health derogations, and providing EU level solutions (sometimes partial, sometimes complete) to cross-EU regulatory conundrums (e.g. on health and safety, consumer safety or environmental standards). A second focus of concern must be the control of interferences with the competitive structure of the market both by undertakings (the competition rules, control of mergers), and by the Member States themselves (liberalisation and regulation of regulated sectors such as utilities, control of state aids, restrictions on other state interferences with competition, etc.). Together these elements constitute the foundations of the internal dimension of the internal market; a separate concern is the external dimension, including the common customs tariff, external trade relations concerned with goods and services, the position of the EU in a global trading environment, and the controversial question of immigration into the EU and movement of third country nationals within the EU.

These points provide a basic, if incomplete, sketch of the main features of the law of the internal market. It is incomplete, for example, because some sectors of the European economy are not subject to the full rigours of the market economy, and are protected through the regulatory structures of common policies which themselves are more or less complete. Agriculture and fisheries provide one example, and transport is another. Also supplementing the law of the internal market are European level regulatory responses to common socio-economic problems. Sometimes these take the form of harmonisation legislation providing an underlying legislative substructure (e.g. health and safety at work, information and consultation of workers, the right to non-discrimination on grounds of sex, environmental standards). In other areas, the approach is less obtrusive and is restricted to complementary measures such as funding programmes (e.g. education and vocational training, public health, culture). Finally, there are policy areas which have a self-conscious relationship to the outcomes of the internal market policy, such as the policy on economic and social cohesion (regional development policy, support for social policy initiatives, 'trans-European networks', etc.). With the exception of agriculture and fisheries, which do look to provide an exhaustive EU-level regulatory structure which has almost entirely supplanted national competences, all of these EU interventions are inchoate. This is either because the focus is upon minimum standards to be instrumentalised through national law, or because the EU powers are limited to making a 'contribution' to national efforts, which concentrates solely on the 'European' dimension.

15.4   The Institutional and Constitutional Foundations of the EU Reviewed

The final part of this chapter offers just a few examples of how the institutional and constitutional foundations of the EU inevitably become clearer when they are reviewed and studied in the context of the economic and social law. It is not a complete restatement of the issues raised throughout the book, but simply suggests some areas where the reader might usefully want to cross-refer between the constitutional and institutional principles articulated in this book, and detailed discussions of fields of EC economic and social law.

The concept of competence, for example, seems abstract and impenetrable until it is re-examined in concrete terms when the EU institutions operate at the limits of their competence. Constant battles between the

Commission and the Member States over external trade powers, including the power to represent the EU and its Member States in international trading organisations, offer some of the best examples of the competence problem in action. Emphasising once more the importance of giving historical depth to the study of EC law, the development of new competences in relation, for example, to the environment, and their subsequent integration into the Treaty objectives and Treaty system through later Treaty amendments also illustrates the 'creeping' competence of the Community.

It is similarly difficult to appreciate the full subtleties of the systems of individual or decentralised enforcement of EC law constructed by the Court of Justice to secure the effectiveness and uniformity of EC law, and the protection of individual rights, in isolation from specific fields such as sex discrimination, labour law or environmental law. Where EU interventions take the form primarily of directives, which are intended to set minimum standards or bring about the harmonisation of national laws, national courts and the Court of Justice are frequently faced with vexed questions about the relationship between the EU measure and pre-existing or subsequent national legislation. They are faced with questions of interpretation and even, since Cases 6, 9/90 *Francovich* v. *Italian State (Francovich I)* ([1991] ECR I-5357), with the possibility that the Member State may be liable for failure to implement or misimplementation of the directive. In respect of the many Treaty obligations which fall on Member States, especially with regard to the internal market and the principle of non-discrimination on grounds of nationality, Cases 46, 48/93 *Brasserie du Pêcheur and Factortame III* suggest that closer attention in the future will be paid to national legislation which has continued to operate in violation of those principles, with the possibility for a party concerned of bringing a State liability action for compensation.

The final example to be explored concerns the rules of the Treaty on individual actions against the EU institutions, and the application of general principles of law such as proportionality to specific case situations. The twists and turns of the case law of the Court of Justice and, more recently, the Court of First Instance, on individual protection can only be fully appreciated with a knowledge of the specific areas of law at issue. Only then can the various rights and interests at issue be properly weighed up, to give a better sense of the policy factors which inevitably impact upon judicial discretion in such circumstances. So many of the rules on individual protection against EU action have emerged in the context of cases raising issues of agricultural or customs law which are not often studied in detail by students. That leads to a feeling that those rules of economic administrative law (standing, application of general principles of law to interferences with economic rights and interests, etc.), are somehow less vital to the construction of the EU legal order than, for example, the principles governing the relationship between EC law and national law. Nothing could be further from truth; the two areas will ultimately be seen, in a mature EU legal order, as being of equal importance.

To conclude, therefore, it should be emphasised that the ultimate test of the EU institutional and constitutional order is whether it provides an adequate and functional framework for the achievement of the mission of the EU. The constitutional order has little meaning on its own, beyond the sense of achievement which comes from constructing a higher order framework and the symbolic meaning for individual citizens, if it does not provide the correct tools for the attainment of concrete goals such as those laid down in the Treaties and identified at a political level by the Member States. Any conclusion as to whether the fine words of the Treaties and the hard graft of the institutions – especially but not only the Court of Justice – have passed that test must be reserved until after the study of the economic and social law of the EU has been undertaken.

378

Bibliography

Adams (ed.) (1992), *Singular Europe: Economy and Polity of the European Community after 1992*, University of Michigan Press, Ann Arbor.
Alter (1995), *Explaining National Court Acceptance of European Court Jurisprudence: A Critical Evaluation of Theories of Legal Integration*, EUI Working Paper RSC No. 95/27.
Alter (1996), 'The European Court's Political Power: The Emergence of an Authoritative International Court in the European Union', *W. Eur. Pols.* (forthcoming).
Andersen and Eliassen (1996b), 'EU-Lobbying: Between Representativity and Effectiveness', in Andersen and Eliassen (1996a).
Andersen and Eliassen (eds) (1996a), *The European Union: How Democratic Is It?*, Sage, London.
Anderson (1994), 'The Admissibility of Preliminary References' 14 *YEL* 179.
Arnull (1990a), 'Does the Court of Justice have inherent jurisdiction?', 27 *CMLRev.* 683.
Arnull (1990b), 'References to the European Court', 15 *ELRev.* 375.
Arnull (1993), 'Owning up to fallibility: precedent and the Court of Justice', 30 *CMLRev.* 247.
Arnull (1994), 'Judging the New Europe', 19 *ELRev.* 3.
Arnull (1995a), 'Private Applicants and the Action for Annulment under Article 173 of the EC Treaty', 32 *CMLRev.* 7.
Arnull (1995b), 'The Community Judicature and the 1996 IGC', 20 *ELRev.* 599.
Bankowski and Scott (1996), 'The European Union?', in Bellamy (1996).
Barav (1980), 'Preliminary Censorship? The Judgment of the European Court in *Foglia* v. *Novello*', 5 *ELRev.* 443.
Barav (1989), 'Enforcement of Community rights in the National Courts: the Case for a Jurisdiction to grant interim relief', 26 *CMLRev.* 369.
Barents (1994), 'The Quality of Community Legislation', 1 *MJ* 101.
Barnard (1995), 'A European Litigation Strategy: the Case of the Equal Opportunities Commission', in Shaw and More (1995).
Bebr (1982), 'The possible implications of *Foglia* v. *Novello II*', 9 *CMLRev.* 421.
Bebr (1988), 'The Reinforcement of the Constitutional Review of Community Acts under Article 177 EEC', 25 *CMLRev.* 684.
Bebr (1992), Case Note on *Francovich* v. *Italy*, 19 *CMLRev.* 559.
Bellamy (ed.) (1996), *Constitutionalism, Democracy and Sovereignty: American and European Perspectives*, Avebury, Aldershot.
Bellamy and Castiglione (1996), 'The communitarian ghost in the cosmopolitan machine: constitutionalism, democracy and the reconfiguration of politics in the New Europe', in Bellamy (1996).
Bellamy, Bufacchi and Castiglione (eds) (1995), *Democracy and Constitutional Culture in the Union of Europe*, Lothian Foundation Press, London.

Bermann (1989) 'The Single European Act: A New Constitution for the Community?', 27 *Columbia J. Transnational and International Law* 529.

Bermann (1994), 'Taking Subsidiarity Seriously: Federalism in the European Community and the United States', 94 *Col. L.Rev.* 331.

Bettlem (1995), 'The principle of indirect effect of Community law', 3 *ERPL* 1.

Bieber (1984), 'The Settlement of Institutional Conflicts on the Basis of Article 4 of the EEC Treaty', 21 *CMLRev.* 505.

Bieber (1990), 'Democratic Control of European Foreign Policy', 1 *EJIL* 148.

Bieber *et al.* (eds) (1988), *1992: One European Market? A Critical Analysis of the Commission's Single Market Policy*, Nomos, Baden-Baden.

Bradley (1988), 'The variable evolution of the standing of the European Parliament in proceedings before the Court of Justice', 8 *YEL* 27.

Bradley (1991), 'Sense and Sensibility: *Parliament* v. *Council* continued', 16 *ELRev.* 245.

Bradley (1992), 'Comitology and the Law: Through a Glass, Darkly', 29 *CMLRev.* 693.

Bradley (1995), 'Administrative Justice: A Developing Human Right?', 1 *Eur. Pub. L.* 347.

Brown and Kennedy (1994), *The Court of Justice of the European Communities*, Sweet & Maxwell (4th edn).

Buitendijk and van Schendelen (1995), 'Brussels Advisory Committees: A Channel for Influence', 20 *ELRev.* 37.

Bulmer and Scott (eds) (1994), *Economic and Political Integration in Europe. Internal Dynamics and Global Context*, Blackwell, Oxford.

de Búrca (1992), 'Giving Effect to European Community Directives', 55 *MLR* 215.

de Búrca (1993a), 'The Principle of Proportionality and its Application in EC Law', 13 *YEL* 105.

de Búrca (1993b), 'Fundamental Human Rights and the Reach of EC Law', 13 *OJLS* 283.

de Búrca (1995), 'The Language of Rights and European Integration', in Shaw and More (1995).

de Búrca (1996), 'The Quest for Legitimacy in the European Union', 59 *MLR* 349.

Burley and Mattli (1993), 'Europe Before the Court: A Political Theory of Legal Integration', 47 *IO* 41.

Cafruny and Rosenthal (eds) (1993), *The State of the European Community. Vol. 2. The Maastricht Debates and Beyond*, Lynne Rienner, Boulder, Col.

Cappelletti (1987), 'Is the European Court of Justice "Running Wild"?', 12 *ELRev.* 3.

Cappelletti *et al.* (1986), *Integration through Law: Part One, Vol. 1, Methods, Tools and Institutions*, Walter de Gruyter, Berlin.

Caranta (1995), 'Judicial Protection Against Member States: A new *Jus Commune* takes shape', 32 *CMLRev.* 703.

Carlin (1996), 'The Data Protection Directive: the introduction of common privacy standards' 21 *ELRev.* 65.

Cassese *et al.* (1991a), *Human Rights and the European Community: Methods of Protection*, Nomos, Baden-Baden.

Cassese *et al.* (1991b), *Human Rights and the European Community: The Substantive Law*, Nomos, Baden-Baden.

Cecchini (1988), *The European Challenge: 1992, the Benefits of a Single Market*, Wildwood House/Gower, Aldershot.

Chalmers (1995), 'The Single Market: From Prima Donna to Journeyman', in Shaw and More (1995).

Cheyne (1994), 'International Agreements and the European Community Legal System', 19 *ELRev.* 581.

Clapham (1990), 'A Human Rights Policy for the European Community', 10 *YEL* 309.

Clapham (1991), *Human Rights and the European Community: A Critical Overview*, Nomos, Baden-Baden.

Cockfield (1994), *The European Union: Creating the Single Market*, Wiley/Chancery Law, Chichester.

Collins (1990), *European Community Law in the United Kingdom*, Butterworths, London (4th edn).

Commission (1985), *Completing the Internal* Market, White Paper from the Commission to the European Council, COM(85) 310.

Commission (1995a), *Commission Report for the Reflection Group*, OOPEC, Luxembourg.

Commission (1995b), *European Union public finance. The Characteristics, Rules and Operation of the European Financial System*, OOPEC, Luxembourg.

Coppel and O'Neill (1992), 'The European Court of Justice: taking rights seriously?', 12 *LS* 227.

Craig (1993), '*Francovich*, Remedies and the Scope of Damages Liability', 109 *LQR* 595.

Craig (1994), 'Legality, Standing and Substantial Review in Community Law', 14 *OJLS* 507.

Craig and de Búrca (1995), *EC Law. Text, Cases and Materials*, Oxford University Press, Oxford.

Cremona (1994), 'The "Dynamic and Homogeneous" EEA: Byzantine Structures and Variable Geometry', 19 *ELRev.* 508.

Crouch and Marquand (eds) (1990), *The Politics of 1992. Beyond the Single European Market*, Blackwell/The Political Quarterly, London.

Crouch and Marquand (eds) (1992), *Towards Greater Europe? A Continent without an Iron Curtain*, Blackwell, Oxford.

Curtin (1990b), 'Directives: The Effectiveness of Judicial Protection of Individual Rights', 27 *CMLRev.* 709.

Curtin (1992), 'State Liability under Private Law: A New Remedy for Private Parties', 21 *ILJ* 74.

Curtin (1993), 'The Constitutional Structure of the Union: A Europe of Bits and Pieces', 30 *CMLRev.* 17.

Curtin (1995), 'Betwixt and between: Democracy and Transparency in the Governance of the European Union', in TMC Asser (1995).

Curtin and Heukels (eds) (1994), *Institutional Dynamics of European Integration*, Martinus Nijhoff, Dordrecht.

Cutler *et al.* (1989), *1992 – The Struggle for Europe*, Berg, London.

Dagtoglou (1981), 'The Legal Nature of the European Community' in Commission of the European Communities (ed.), *Thirty Years of Community Law*, OOPEC, Luxembourg, 33.

Daintith (1995a), 'European Community Law and the Redistribution of Regulatory Power in the United Kingdom', 1 *ELJ* 134.

Daintith (ed.) (1995b), *Implementing EC Law in the United Kingdom: Structures for Indirect Rule*, Wiley/Chancery Law, Chichester.

Dashwood (1994a), 'The role of the Council of the European Union', in Curtin and Heukels (1994).

Dashwood (1994b), 'Community Legislative Procedures in the Era of the Treaty on European Union', 19 *ELRev.* 343.

Dashwood (1996), 'The Limits of European Community Powers', 21 *ELRev.* 113.

Dashwood and White (1989), 'Enforcement Actions and Article 169 and 170', 14 *ELRev.* 388.

Dehousse (1994b), 'Community Competences: Are there Limits to Growth?', in Dehousse (1994a).

Dehousse (ed.) (1994a), *Europe after Maastricht. An Ever Closer Union?*, Law Books in Europe, Munich.

Demetriou (1995), 'When is the House of Lords not a judicial remedy?', 20 *ELRev.* 628.

Dinan (1994), *Ever Closer Union? An Introduction to the European Community*, Macmillan, London.

Docksey (1995), Case Note on *Johnson* v. *Chief Adjudication Officer*, 32 *CMLRev.* 1447.

Docksey and Fitzpatrick (1991), 'The Duty of National Courts to Interpret Provisions of National Law in Accordance with Community Law', 20 *ILJ* 113.

Docksey and Williams (1994), 'The Commission and the execution of Community policy', in Edwards and Spence (1994).

Duff (1994) 'Ratification', in Duff, Pinder and Pryce (1994).

Duff, Pinder and Pryce (eds) (1994), *Maastricht and Beyond. Building the European Union*, Routledge, London.

Dwyer (1994), 'When should a United Kingdom Court Refer Questions to Luxembourg?', *JBL* 528.

Earnshaw and Judge (1993), 'The European Parliament and the Sweeteners Directive: From Footnote to Inter-Institutional Conflict', 31 *JCMS* 103.

Earnshaw and Judge (1995), 'Early days: the European Parliament, co-decision and the European Union legislative procedure post-Maastricht', 2 *JEPP* 624.

Edward (1995), 'How the Court of Justice works', (1995) 20 *ELRev.* 539.

Edwards and Spence (eds) (1994), *The European Commission*, Longman, London.

El-Agraa (ed.) (1994), *The Economics of the European Community*, Harvester Wheatsheaf, London (4th edn).

Eleftheriadis (1996), 'Aspects of European Constitutionalism', 21 *ELRev.* 32.

Ellis and Tridimas (1995), *Public Law of the European Community: Text, Materials and Commentary*, Sweet & Maxwell, London.

Emiliou (1992), 'Subsidiarity: An Effective Barrier Against "the Enterprises of Ambition?"', 17 *ELRev.* 383.

Emiliou (1993), 'Treading a slippery slope: the Commission's original legislative powers', 18 *ELRev.* 305.

Emiliou (1994), 'Opening Pandora's Box: The Legal Basis of Community Measures before the Court of Justice', 19 *ELRev.* 488.

Everling (1984), 'The Member States of the European Community before their Court of Justice', 9 *ELRev.* 315.

Everling (1992), 'Reflections on the Structure of the European Union', 29 *CMLRev.* 1053.

Everling (1994), 'The *Maastricht* Judgment of the German Federal Constitutional Court and its significance for Development of European Union', 14 *YEL* 1.

Everson (1995), 'Independent Agencies: Hierarchy Beaters?', 1 *European Law Journal* 180.

Fischer and Neff (1995), 'Some American Thoughts about European "Federalism"', 44 *ICLQ* 904.

Fitzpatrick (1989), 'The Significance of EEC Directives in UK Sex Discrimination law', 9 *OJLS* 336.

Flynn (1995), 'Telecommunications and EU Integration', in Shaw and More (1995).

Foster (1995), *Blackstone's EC Legislation*, Blackstones, London (6th edn).

Gaja (1990), 'New Developments in a Continuing Story: The Relationship between EEC law and Italian law', 27 *CMLRev.* 83.

George (1990), *An Awkward Partner: Britain in the European Community*, Oxford University Press, Oxford.

George (1991), *Politics and Policy in the European Community*, Oxford University Press, Oxford (2nd edn).

Gerber (1994), 'Constitutionalizing the Economy: German Neo-liberalism, Competition Law and the "New" Europe', 42 *AJCL* 25.

van Gerven (1994a), 'The Horizontal Effect of Directive Provisions Revisited: The Reality of Catchwords', in Curtin and Heukels (1994).

van Gerven (1994b), 'Non-contractual Liability of Member States, Community Institutions and Individuals for Breaches of Community Law with a View to a Common Law for Europe', 1 *MJ* 6.

van Gerven (1995), 'Bridging the Gap Between Community and National Laws: Towards a Principle of Homogeneity in the field of Legal Remedies?', 32 *CMLRev.* 579.

van Gerven (1996), 'The Role and Structure of the European Judiciary now and in the future', 21 *ELRev.* 211.

Gormley and de Haan (1996), 'The democratic deficit of the European Central Bank', 21 *ELRev.* 95.

Grahl and Teague (1990), *1992: The Big Market*, Lawrence & Wishart, London.

Gravells (1989), 'Disapplying an Act of Parliament pending a Preliminary Ruling: Constitutional Enormity or Community Law Right?', *PL* 568.

Gravells (1991), 'Effective Protection of Community Law Rights: Temporary Disapplication of an Act of Parliament', *PL* 180.

Greaves (1986), 'Locus Standi under Article 173 EEC when seeking annulment of a Regulation', 11 *ELRev.* 119.

Greaves (1996), 'The Nature and Binding Effect of Decisions under Article 189 EC', 21 *ELRev.* 3.

Grief (1991), 'The Domestic Impact of the ECHR as Mediated through Community Law', *PL* 555.

Grimm (1995), 'Does Europe Need a Constitution?', 1 *ELJ* 282.

Gustavsson (1996), 'The European Union: 1996 and Beyond – a Personal View from the Side-line', in Andersen and Eliassen (1996).

Habermas (1994), 'Citizenship and National Identity', in van Steenbergen (1994).

Habermas (1995), 'Comment on the Paper by Dieter Grimm: 'Does Europe Need a Constitution?', 1 *ELJ* 303.
Hamson (1976), 'Methods of Judicial Interpretation', in *Proceedings of a Judicial and Academic Conference*, OOPEC, Luxembourg.
Harden (1994), 'The Constitution of the European Union', *PL* 609.
Harden, White and Donnelly (1995), 'The Court of Auditors and Financial Control and Accountability in the European Community', 1 *Eur. Pub. L* 599.
Harding (1980), 'The Private Interest in Challenging Community Action', 5 *ELRev.* 354.
Harlow (1992a), 'Towards a Theory of Access for the European Court of Justice', 12 *YEL* 213.
Harlow (1992b), 'A Community of Interests? Making the Most of European Law', 55 *MLR* 331.
Harlow and Rawlings (1992), *Pressure Through Law*, Routledge, London.
Harmsen (1994), 'A European Union of Variable Geometry: Problems and Perspectives', 45 *NILQ* 109.
Hartley (1994), *The Foundations of European Community Law*, Oxford University Press, Oxford (3rd edn).
Hartley (1996), 'The European Court, Judicial Objectivity and the Constitution of the European Union', 112 *LQR* 95.
Hayes Renshaw and Wallace (1995), 'Executive power in the European Union: the functions and limits of the Council of Ministers', 2 *JEPP* 559.
Hayes-Renshaw (1996), 'The Role of the Council', in Andersen and Eliassen (1996a).
Hayward (1995), 'Governing the New Europe', in Hayward and Page (1995).
Hayward and Page (eds) (1995), *Governing the New Europe*, Polity, Cambridge.
Herdegen (1994), 'Maastricht and the German Constitutional Court: Constitutional Restraints for an "Ever Closer Union"', 31 *CMLRev.* 235.
Hesse and Johnson (eds) (1995), *Constitutional Policy and Change in Europe*, Oxford University Press, Oxford.
Holland (1993), *European Community Integration*, Pinter, London.
Hurwitz and Lesquesne (eds) (1991), *The State of the European Community. Vol. 1. Policies, Institutions and Debate in the Transition Years*, Lynne Rienner, Boulder, Col.
Jackson (1992), 'Status of Treaties in Domestic Legal Systems: A Policy Analysis', 86 *AJIL* 311.
Jacobs, Corbett and Shackleton (1992), *The European Parliament*, Longman, London (2nd edn).
Jacqué and Weiler (1990), 'On the Road to European Union – A New Judicial Architecture: An Agenda for the Intergovernmental Conference', 27 *CMLRev.* 493.
Joerges (1994), 'European Economic Law, the Nation-State and the Maastricht Treaty', in Dehousse (1994a).
Kapteyn (1996), *The Stateless Market*, Routledge, London.
Kapteyn and VerLoren van Themaat (1989), *Introduction to the Law of the European Communities*, Kluwer, Dordrecht (2nd edn by Gormley).
Keohane and Hoffmann (eds) (1991), *The New European Community: Decisionmaking and Institutional Change*, Westview, Boulder.
van Kersbergen and Verbeek (1994), 'The Politics of Subsidiarity in the European Union', 32 *JCMS* 215.

Koopmans (1991a), 'European Public Law: Reality and Prospects', *PL* 53.
Koopmans (1991b), 'The Birth of European Law at the Crossroads of Legal Traditions', 39 *AJCL* 493.
Koopmans (1991c), 'The Future of the Court of Justice of the European Communities', 11 *YEL* 15.
Koopmans (1992), 'Federalism: The wrong debate', 29 *CMLRev.* 1047.
Koopmans (1994), 'The Quest for Subsidiarity', in Curtin and Heukels (1994).
Kronenberger (1996), 'Does the EFTA Court interpret the EEA Agreement as if it were the EC Treaty? Some questions raised by the *Restamark* judgment', 45 *ICLQ* 198.
Kutscher (1976), 'Methods of Interpretation as seen by a Judge at the Court of Justice', in *Proceedings of a Judicial and Academic Conference*, OOPEC, Luxembourg.
Laffan (1996), 'The Politics of Identity and Political Order in Europe', 34 *JCMS* 81.
Legrand (1996), 'European Legal Systems are not converging', 45 *ICLQ* 52.
Lenaerts (1990), 'Constitutionalism and the Many Faces of Federalism', 38 *Am. J. Comp. L.* 205.
Lenaerts (1991a), 'Some Reflections on the Separation of Powers in the European Community', 28 *CMLRev.* 11.
Lenaerts (1991b), 'Fundamental Rights to be included in a Community Catalogue', 16 *ELRev.* 367.
Lenaerts (1993), 'Regulating the regulatory process: "delegation of powers" in the European Community', (1993) 18 *ELRev.* 23.
Lenaerts (1994), 'Form and Substance of the Preliminary Rulings Procedure', in Curtin and Heukels (1994).
Lewis and Moore (1993), 'Duties, Directives and Damage in European Community Law', *PL* 151.
Lodge (1994), 'Transparency and Democratic Legitimacy', 32 *JCMS* 343.
Lodge (1996), 'The European Parliament', in Andersen and Eliassen (1996a).
Lodge (ed.) (1993), *The European Community and the Challenge of the Future*, Pinter, London (2nd edn).
Lyons (1996), 'Citizenship in the Constitution of the European Union: rhetoric or reality?', in Bellamy (1996).
MacCormick (1993), 'Beyond the Sovereign State', 56 *MLR* 1.
MacCormick (1995), 'The *Maastricht-Urteil*: Sovereignty Now', 1 *ELJ* 259.
MacKenzie Stuart (1977), *The European Communities and the Rule of Law*, Sweet & Maxwell, London.
MacLoed, Hendry and Hyett (1996), *The External Relations of the European Communities*, Oxford University Press, Oxford.
Magliveras (1995), 'Best intentions but empty words: The European Ombudsman', 20 *ELRev.* 401.
Maher (1994), 'National Courts as European Community Courts', 14 *LS* 226.
Maher (1995), 'A Question of Conflict: the Higher English Courts and the Implementation of European Community Law', in Daintith (1995b).
Maltby (1993), 'Marleasing: What is All the Fuss About?', 109 *LQR* 301.
Mancini (1989), 'The Making of a Constitution for Europe', 26 *CMLRev.* 595.
Mancini and Keeling (1991), 'From *CILFIT* to *ERT*: the Constitutional Challenge facing the European Court', 11 *YEL* 1.

Mancini and Keeling (1994), 'Democracy and the European Court of Justice', 57 *MLR* 175.

Marias (1994), 'The Right to Petition the European Parliament after Maastricht', 19 *ELRev.* 169.

Markesinis (1993), 'Judge, Jurist and the Study and Use of Foreign Law', 109 *LQR* 622.

Markesinis (ed.) (1994), *The Gradual Convergence*, Oxford University Press, Oxford.

Martin (1994), *The Construction of Europe. Essays in Honour of Emile Noël*, Kluwer, Dordrecht.

Mazey and Richardson (1994), 'The Commission and the Lobby', in Edwards and Spence (1994).

Mazey and Richardson (1995), 'Promiscuous Policymaking: the European Policy Style?', in Rhodes and Mazey (1995).

McLaughlin and Greenwood (1995), 'The Management of Interest Representation in the European Union', (1995) 33 *JCMS* 143.

Meads (1991), 'The obligation to apply European law: is *Duke* dead?', 16 *ELRev.* 490.

Mendrinou (1994), 'European Community fraud and the politics of institutional development', 26 *Eur. J. Pol. Res.* 81.

Mendrinou (1996), 'Non-compliance and the European Commission's role in integration', 3 *JEPP* 1.

Millett (1989), 'Rules of Interpretation of EEC Legislation', 10 *Statute L. Rev.*163.

Mitchell (1979), 'The Sovereignty of Parliament: the stumbling block that isn't there', *Intl. Aff.* 33.

Mitchell, Kuipers and Gall (1972), 'Constitutional Aspects of the Treaty and Legislation relating to British Membership', 9 *CMLRev.* 134.

Monar (1994), 'Interinstitutional Agreements: The Phenomenon and its New Dynamics After Maastricht', 31 *CMLRev.* 693.

Monar, Ungerer and Wessels (eds) (1993), *The Maastricht Treaty on European Union. Legal Complexity and Political Dynamic*, European Interuniversity Press, Brussels.

Mouffe (ed.) (1992), *Dimensions of Radical Democracy*, Verso, London.

Munro (1987), *Studies in Constitutional Law*, Butterworths, London.

Neill (1995), 'The European Court of Justice. A Case Study in Judicial Activism', in House of Lords Select Committee on the European Communities: *1996 Intergovernmental Conference*, Minutes of Evidence, HL Session 1994–95, 18th Report.

Nelsen and Stubb (1994), *The European Union. Readings on the Theory and Practice of European Integration*, Lynne Rienner, Boulder, Col/ London.

Nentwich and Faulkner (1996), 'Intergovernmental Conference 1996: Which Constitution for the Union?', 2 *ELJ* 83.

Neuwahl (1996), 'Article 173 Paragraph 4 EC: Past, Present and Possible Future', 21 *ELRev.* 17.

Nicoll (1993), '"Note the Hour – and File the Minute"', 31 *JCMS* 559.

Nicoll (1994), 'The European Parliament's Post-Maastricht Rules of Procedure', 32 *JCMS* 403.

Nugent (1994), *The Government and Politics of the European Union*, Macmillan, London (3rd edn).

Nugent (1995), 'The leadership capacity of the European Commission', 2 *JEPP* 603.

O'Keeffe and Twomey (eds), (1994), *Legal Issues of the Maastricht Treaty*, Chancery, London.

van Overbeek (1994), 'The Right to Remain Silent in Competition Investigations', 15 *ECLR* 127.

Partan (1995), 'The Justiciability of Subsidiarity', in Rhodes and Mazey (1995).

Passas and Nelken (1993), 'The fight against fraud in the European Community: Cacophony rather than harmony', 6 *Corruption and Reform* 237.

Pescatore (1983), 'The Doctrine of 'Direct Effect': An Infant Disease in Community Law', 8 *ELRev.* 155.

Pescatore (1987), 'Some Critical Remarks on the Single European Act', 24 *CMLRev.* 9.

Peters (1994), 'Agenda-setting in the European Community', 1 *JEPP* 9.

Petersmann (1995), 'Proposals for a New Constitution for the European Union: Building-Blocks for a Constitutional Theory and Constitutional Law of the EU', (1995) *CMLRev.* 1123.

Peterson (1994), 'Subsidiarity: A Definition to Suit Any Vision?', 47 *Parl. Aff.* 116.

Peterson (1995), 'Decision-making inthe European Union: towards a framework for analysis', 2 *JEPP* 69.

Phelan (1992), 'Right to Life of the Unborn v. Promotion of Trade in Services: The European Court of Justice and the Normative Shaping of the European Union', 55 *MLR* 670.

Pinder (1995), *European Community. The Building of a Union*, Oxford University Press, Oxford.

Plaza Martin (1994), 'Furthering the Effectiveness of EC directives and the Judicial Protection of Individual Rights Thereunder', 43 *ICLQ* 26.

Prechal (1995), *Directives in European Community Law*, Oxford University Press, Oxford.

Rasmussen (1980), 'Why is Article 173 interpreted against Private Plaintiffs?', 5 *ELRev.* 112.

Rasmussen (1986), *On Law and Policy in the European Court of Justice*, Martinus Nijhoff, Dordrecht.

Rasmussen (1992), 'Towards a Normative Theory of Interpretation of Community Law', *University of Chicago Legal Forum* 135.

Ress (1994), 'Democratic Decision-Making in the European Union and the Role of the European Parliament', in Curtin and Heukels (1994).

Rhodes and Mazey (eds) (1995), *The State of the European Union. Vol. 3. Building a European Polity?*, Lynne Rienner, Boulder, Col.

Ross (1990), 'Refining Effective Enjoyment', 15 *ELRev.* 476.

Ross (1993), 'Beyond *Francovich*', 56 *MLR* 55.

Ross (1994), 'Limits on using Article 177 EC', 19 *ELRev.* 640.

Ross (1995), *Jacques Delors and European Integration*, Polity Press.

Rudden (1987), *Basic Community Cases*, Oxford University Press, Oxford.

Rudden and Wyatt (1994), *Basic Community Laws*, Oxford University Press, Oxford (5th edn).

Sack (1995), 'The European Community's membership of international organizations', 32 *CMLRev.* 1227.

Sbragia (ed.) (1992), *Euro-Politics: Institutions and Policymaking in the 'New' European Community*, Brookings, Washington, DC.

Schermers (1990), 'The Scales in Balance: National Constitutional Court v. Court of Justice', 27 *CMLRev.* 97.

Schermers *et al.* (eds) (1987), *Article 177 EEC: Experiences and Problems*, North-Holland, Amsterdam.

Schmitter (1992), 'Representation and the Future Euro-polity', 3 *Staatswissenschaft under Staatspraxis* 379.

Schuppert (1995), 'On the Evolution of a European State: Reflections on the Conditions of and the Prospects for a European Constitution', in Hesse and Johnson (1995).

Schwarze (1991), 'Tendencies towards a Common Administrative Law in Europe', 16 *ELRev.* 3.

Schwarze (1995), 'Towards a Common European Public Law', 1 *Eur. Pub. L.* 227.

Scorey (1996), 'A new model for the Communities' judicial architecture in the new Union', 21 *ELRev.* 224.

Scott (1995a), *Development Dilemmas in the European Community. Rethinking Regional Development Policy*, Open University Press, Buckingham.

Scott (1995b), 'GATT and Community Law: rethinking the 'regulatory gap'', in Shaw and More (1995).

Shapiro (1992), 'The Giving Reasons Requirement', (1992) *UChic. Legal Forum* 179.

Shaw (1995), 'Decentralization and Law Enforcement in EC Competition Law', 15 *LS* 128.

Shaw (1996), 'European Union Legal Studies in Crisis? Towards a New Dynamic', 16 *OJLS* 231.

Shaw and More (1995), *New Legal Dynamics of European Union*, Oxford University Press, Oxford.

Slynn (1992), *Introducing a European Legal Order*, Sweet & Maxwell, London.

Smits (1994), 'A Single Currency for Europe and the Karlsruhe Court', *LIEI*, Issue 2, 115.

Snyder (1990), *New Directions in European Community Law*, Weidenfeld & Nicolson, London.

Snyder (ed.) (1993a), *European Community Law*, 2 vols, Dartmouth, Aldershot (International Library of Essays in Law and Legal Theory Series).

Snyder (1993b) 'The Effectiveness of European Community Law: Institutions, Processes, Tools and Techniques', 56 *MLR* 19.

Snyder (1994), 'Soft Law and Institutional Practice in the European Community', in Martin (1994).

van Steenbergen (ed.) (1994), *The Condition of Citizenship*, Sage, London.

Stein and Vining (1976), 'Citizen Access to Judicial Review of Administrative Action in a Transnational and Federal Context', 70 *AJIL* 219.

Steiner (1993), 'From direct effects to *Francovich*: shifting means of enforcement of Community Law', 18 *ELRev.* 3.

Steiner (1994), 'Subsidiarity under the Maastricht Treaty', in O'Keeffe and Twomey (1994).

Stone Sweet (1995), *Constitutional Dialogues in the European Community*, EUI Working Paper RSC No. 95/38.

388   *Bibliography*

Streit and Mussler (1995), 'The Economic Constitution of the European Community: From "Rome" to "Maastricht"', 1 *ELJ* 5.
Swann (ed.) (1992), *The Single European Market and Beyond. A Study of the Wider Implications of the Single European Act*, Routledge, London.
Szyszczak (1990), 'Sovereignty: Crisis, Compliance, Confusion, Complacency', 15 *ELRev.* 480.
Szyszczak (1992), 'European Community Law: New Remedies, New Directions?', 55 *MLR* 690.
Szyszczak (1996), 'Pregnancy and sex discrimination', 21 *ELRev.* 79.
Tassin (1992), 'Europe: A Political Community?', in Mouffe (1992).
Taylor (1995), *EMU 2000? Prospects for European Monetary Union*, Chatham House Papers/Royal Institute of International Affairs, Cassell, London.
Teasdale (1993), 'The Life and Death of the Luxembourg Compromise', 31 *JCMS* 567.
Temple Lang (1990), 'Community Constitutional Law: Article 5 EEC Treaty', 27 *CMLRev.* 645.
Tesauro (1993), 'The Effectiveness of Judicial Protection and Co-operation between the Court of Justice and the National Courts', 13 *YEL* 1.
TMC Asser Instituut (ed.) (1995), *Conference Reader. The Treaty on European Union: Suggestions for Revision*, TMC Asser Instituut, s' Gravenhage.
Toth (1994), 'A Legal Analysis of Subsidiarity', in O'Keeffe and Twomey (1994).
Toth (1995), Case Note on *Air France* v. *Commission*, 32 *CMLRev.* 271.
Tridimas (1994), 'Horizontal effect of directives: a missed opportunity?', 19 *ELRev.* 621.
Tridimas (1996), 'The Court of Justice and Judicial Activism', 21 *ELRev.* 199.
Twomey (1994), 'The European Union: three Pillars without a Human Rights Foundation', in O'Keeffe and Twomey (1994).
Uecker (1994), '*Francovich* and Beyond: A German Perspective', *EBLR* 286.
Ungerer (1993), 'Institutional Consequences of Broadening and Deepening the Community: the Consequences for the Decision-making process', 30 *CMLRev.* 71.
Urwin (1995), *The Community of Europe. A History of European Integration Since 1945*, Longman, London (2nd edn).
Usher (1976), 'The Influence of National Concepts on Decisions of the European Court', 1 *ELRev.* 359.
Usher (1981), *European Community Law and National Law: The Irreversible Transfer?*, Allen & Unwin, London.
Usher (1994), 'Individual concern in general legislation – 10 years on', 19 *ELRev.* 636.
Vesterdorp (1994), 'Complaints Concerning Infringements of Competition Law within the Context of European Community Law', 31 *CMLRev.* 77.
Vranken (1996), 'Role of the Advocate General in the Law-Making Process of the European Community', 25 *Anglo-American Law Review* 39.
Waelbroeck and Fosselard (1995), Case Note on *Codorniu* v. *Council*, 32 *CMLRev.* 257.
Wainwright (1994), 'The Future of European Community Legislation in the light of the Recommendations of the Sutherland Committee and the Principle of Subsidiarity', 15 *Statute L. Rev.*98.

Walker (1996), 'European Constitutionalism and European Integration', *PL* forthcoming.

Wallace (1994), *Regional Integration: The West European Experience*, Brookings Institution, Washington, DC.

Wallace (ed.) (1990), *The Dynamics of European Integration*, Pinter, London.

Wallace and Wallace (eds) (1996), *Policy-Making in the European Union*, Oxford University Press, Oxford (3rd edn).

Ward (1995), 'Effective Sanctions in EC Law: A Moving Boundary in the Division of Competence', 1 *ELJ* 1204.

Ward (1996), 'The European Constitution and the Nation State', 16 *OJLS* 161.

Watson (1986), 'Asser Institute Colloquium on European Law 1985: Experiences and Problems in Applying the Preliminary Proceedings of Article 177 EEC', 23 *CMLRev.* 207.

Weatherill (1992), 'Regulating the Internal Market: Result Orientation in the House of Lords', 17 *ELRev.* 299.

Weatherill (1994), 'Beyond Preemption? Shared Competence and Constitutional Change in the European Community', in O'Keeffe and Twomey (1994).

Weatherill (1995a), *Law and Integration in the European Union*, Oxford University Press, Oxford.

Weatherill (1995b), 'Implementation as a Constitutional Issue', in Daintith (1995b).

Weatherill and Beaumont (1995), *EC Law*, Penguin Harmondsworth (2nd edn).

Weigall and Stirk (1992), *The Origins and Development of the European Community*, Leicester University Press, Leicester/London.

Weiler (1981) 'The Community System: the dual character of supranationalism', 1 *YEL* 267.

Weiler (1989), 'Pride and Prejudice – *Parliament* v. *Council*', 14 *ELRev.* 334.

Weiler (1993), 'Journey to an Unknown Destination: A retrospective and prospective of the European Court of Justice in the Arena of Political Integration', 31 *JCMS* 417.

Weiler (1994a), 'Fin-de-Siècle Europe', in Dehousse (1994a).

Weiler (1994b), 'A Quiet Revolution: The European Court of Justice and its Interlocutors', 23 *Comp. Pol. Studs.* 510.

Weiler (1995a), 'Does European Need a Constitution? Reflections on Demos, Telos and the German Maastricht Decision', 1 *ELJ* 219.

Weiler (1995b), 'European Citizenship and Human Rights', in TMC Asser (1995).

Weiler and Lockhart (1995a), '"Taking Rights Seriously" Seriously: the European Court and its Fundamental Rights Jurisprudence – Part I', 32 *CMLRev.* 51.

Weiler and Lockhart (1995b), '"Taking Rights Seriously" Seriously: the European Court and its Fundamental Rights Jurisprudence – Part II', 32 *CMLRev.* 579.

Wellens and Borchardt (1989), 'Soft Law in European Community Law', 14 *ELRev.* 267.

Westlake (1994), *A Modern Guide to the European Parliament*, Pinter, London.

Westlake (1995), *The Council of the European Union*, Cartermill/Longman, London.

Wils (1992), 'Concurrent Liability of the Community and a Member State', 17 *ELRev.* 191.

Wincott (1995a), 'Political Theory, Law and European Union', in Shaw and More (1995).

Wincott (1995b), 'The role of law or the rule of the Court of Justice? An "institutional" account of judicial politics in the European Community', 2 *JEPP* 583.

Winter (1972), 'Direct Applicability and Direct Effect: Two Distinct and Different Concepts in Community Law', 9 *CMLRev.* 425.

Wistrich (1994), *The United States of Europe*, Routledge, London.

de Witte (1991), 'Community Law and National Constitutional Values', *LIEI* 1991/2, 4.

de Witte (1995), 'Sovereignty and European Integration: The Weight of Legal Tradition', 2 *MJ* 145.

Wyatt (1981), 'Following up *Foglia*: Why the Court is Right to Stick to its Guns', 6 *ELRev.* 447.

Wyatt (1982), 'New Legal Order or Old?', 7 *ELRev.* 147.

Wyatt and Dashwood (1993), *European Community Law*, Sweet & Maxwell, London (3rd edn).

Index